Lee Ehman

Howard Mehlinger

John Patrick

Indiana University

Toward Effective Instruction In Secondary Social Studies

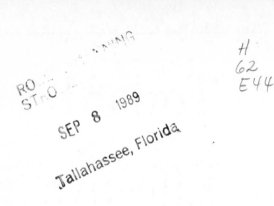
Printed in the U.S.A.

Library of Congress Catalog Card Number:
73–11769

ISBN: 0–395–17625–5

To Carolee, Jackie, and Pat

Contents

WHAT QUALITIES must a person have to be judged an outstanding social studies teacher in a secondary school? Certainly, such a teacher must know his subject well. Students are unlikely to experience high-quality history instruction from a teacher who knows little history, and they are unlikely to gain much help in analyzing current topics from an instructor who lacks interest in current, domestic, and foreign affairs or who lacks powerful ways of thinking about such events. A pleasing personality is helpful. Students are more likely to respond positively to instruction if they like the teacher and if the teacher is friendly, lively, and receptive to new ideas. An outstanding secondary school teacher understands teen-agers; he is a semiprofessional adolescent psychologist and sociologist.

And he knows *how* to teach. He communicates complex and significant ideas clearly, efficiently, effectively, and interestingly. He recognizes that the final test of good instruction is not what the teacher knows but what students learn via his instruction. He approaches each lesson as an important event, not as merely an exercise to consume time. He has a clear idea of what he wants students to learn, prepares for instruction carefully, and manages the class so that learning takes place.

The process of becoming an outstanding social studies teacher is not easy, but fortunately the role is open to nearly anyone with above-average verbal ability who is willing to make self-conscious efforts to improve. The satisfaction and ego enhancement an outstanding teacher achieves—rewards typically unavailable to those who are judged poor or mediocre—seem worth the effort.

This book is designed to help social studies teachers who want to be judged outstanding by students, their parents, colleagues, and school administrators. It cannot compensate for basic deficiencies in subject-matter competence or for unattractive personalities. Nor can it substitute for what each teacher must learn for himself by direct experience in the classroom. However, this book, which treats principles of successful social studies teaching, can provide a way of thinking about social studies instruction that will improve the chances for effective instruction by teachers who know their subject, who are eager to help youth, who are willing to work hard, and who have an experimental spirit toward their work.

Toward Effective Instruction in Secondary Social Studies, therefore, is about *how to teach* social studies, especially about *how to think about the instructional process* in order to maximize the teacher's efforts. It has a point of view that is shared by many, but not all, social studies educators. In our opinion it is a point of view that is growing in significance. Some will be disappointed because we have ignored topics they believe to be important—for example, how to manage a classroom in such a way as to minimize problems of discipline and how to design a teaching unit. We recognize these and other topics, which we have approached indirectly rather than directly, as important and deserving discussion in "methods" classes. Certainly, classroom discipline is a paramount concern to beginning teachers. We have, however, observed that the development of confidence and judgment derived primarily from classroom experience plus well-planned instruction resolve most of a novice teacher's disciplinary problems. We cannot provide for the former; the book focuses on the latter.

Other social studies educators may wish that we had advocated a particular approach to the selection of course content for social studies in secondary schools. Some would prefer an emphasis on academic disciplines, such as history, political science, and geography. Others believe that social studies should become more multidisciplinary or interdisciplinary in its approach, drawing not only from history and the social sciences but from science and the humanities as well. Still others argue that social studies should focus primarily on the fundamental problems in our society. Individually, we have personal preferences regarding where emphasis should be placed in regard to the subject content of the social studies curriculum, but we have elected to write a book that we believe is useful and appropriate for all teachers regardless of subject preferences; and we have attempted to illustrate our ideas by drawing content illustrations that are exemplars of various approaches.

This book differs from other social studies "methods" books we have examined in its commitment to a basic teaching model that rests on a competency-based approach to instruction. Thus, we have drawn heavily from Benjamin S. Bloom's theories relating to mastery learning. Probably more attention has been given to the topic of developing clear, measurable statements of instructional objectives than the authors of other books have deemed important. More space is allocated to the evaluation of instruction than is usually the case, because without valid and reliable systems of evaluation, it is difficult for the teacher to know whether instruction is successful.

As former high school teachers, as teachers of teachers, and as developers of social studies instructional materials for high schools, we have tried to be reasonable in our expectations of social studies teachers. Some will believe that we are expecting too much when we demand teaching competencies that too few teachers presently possess, but these competencies, in our opinion, are an absolutely essential core for outstanding instruction. Others will charge us with demanding too little of teachers. Clearly, the emphasis throughout the book is on how to make teachers better selectors, consumers, and adapters of instructional materials developed by others, rather than on the teacher as the designer and developer of his own instructional materials.

Although a tiny fraction of teachers do become skilled authors, the vast majority of social studies teachers lack the time, the money, and the access to libraries and consultants necessary to prepare books that can compete with the best products on the market. Certainly, we applaud those instances in which teachers can and do prepare high-quality materials, but instances of this are too rare to make this role a requirement of all social studies teachers. In short, a teacher can be outstanding without creating all of his own instructional materials.

With this in mind, we have used many examples of instructional materials drawn from the special social studies projects that developed materials in the 1960s and 1970s. Not only do these illustrate instructional principles that we wish to foster, but they introduce the reader to materials he might adopt and adapt for use in his classroom.

Finally, the structure of the book itself is organized around our approach to instruction. We have tried to link theories of knowledge to practice by liberal use of illustrative examples. We have provided opportunities for the student reader to interact with us and to test his understanding at different points throughout the book.

There are no short cuts to successful teaching. The outstanding professional teacher has the same responsibilities to work hard and to stay abreast of his field that professionals in other fields do. We believe, however, that this book can help one who is serious about becoming a good social studies teacher. For the teacher-in-training it can provide a way of thinking about instruction that will make it easier to profit from later classroom teaching experience. For the experienced teacher, we hope it will provide an opportunity to reflect on his experience and to correct weaknesses when they exist.

L. E.
H. M.
J. P.

Acknowledgments

FREQUENTLY THE most original aspect of a textbook is the unusual way the authors have used the ideas of other people. We believe that the approach taken here toward social studies instruction is unique for "methods" books. In the process of developing this book, we have relied typically on our own experience and our interpretation of the ideas of many other people, only a fraction of whom can be identified here.

Some of the people we admire are specialists in the psychology of learning. Along with others in social studies, we have profited from Jerome Bruner's writings. But we have found equally useful the writings of others who are not well known to some social studies educators, such people as Robert Gagné, David Ausubel, Benjamin S. Bloom, John DeCecco, Barak Rosenshine, and B. F. Skinner. We have mixed and matched their ideas in ways they might never have thought of doing. We hope that we did not injure their views seriously.

We have obviously been influenced by the "new social studies" projects of the 1960s and 1970s. Many of the developers are close personal friends and have, through private conversations as well as through their writings, influenced our perspectives. Not all will rejoice with each aspect of our formulations, but we hope that each can discern his marks on our thinking. We are particularly grateful to those developers, professional associations, and publishers who have permitted us to use examples from their work to illustrate major points throughout the book.

We believe ourselves fortunate to teach at Indiana University because of the stimulation we receive from faculty, colleagues, and students. As one would expect of a faculty in an intellectually rich university setting, we are not all of one mind. Some of our colleagues will be happy with this book; others will be disappointed that they failed to dissuade us from one or more of our ideas. Among our colleagues who have had a special interest in the book and who have criticized early drafts, we are particularly indebted to James Becker, Judith Gillespie, Robert Hanvey, Gerald Marker, Frederick Smith, and Philip Smith. In addition, Beverly Armento, Thomas Brown, and Michael Stentz offered useful suggestions. Tom Castellano and David Horst helped assemble the

data appearing in Appendix A: An Annotated List of
Organizations Providing Publications and Services for
Social Studies Teachers in Secondary Schools.

Various chapters were used many times in undergraduate
and in-service courses by us and by colleagues. Our students
have also helped to shape this book; much prose that appeared
in early drafts was later rejected when they found ideas
uninteresting, unreasonable, or unimportant.

The typing of the manuscript was shared by several
competent people. We are especially indebted to Connie
Ducker, Susan Garafolo, Carolee Mehlinger, Diane Nelson,
Patricia Patrick, Eve Russell, and Karen Waterford. Finally,
we acknowledge our appreciation for patient and understanding families, including young children who must
have thought at times that "the methods book" was some
kind of social disease that quarantined adult males for
long periods in their offices.

L. E.
H. M.
J. P.

Toward Effective Instruction In Secondary Social Studies

1

Curriculum Planner

PART ONE provides the background knowledge a social studies teacher requires. Chapter 1 is an introduction to social studies instruction and treats two major issues: What is the social studies? And what is the role of a social studies teacher? Chapter 2 sets forth our point of view regarding the overarching purpose of social studies. It also introduces the reader to terms that will be used throughout the book. In Chapter 3 the reader will come to grips with social studies goals and objectives—what they are, their origins, and how they are developed.

The principal objectives of Part One are to prepare teachers to:

1. Explain what the social studies is and what a social studies teacher does.
2. Identify some of the pressures that shape the role of a social studies teacher.
3. Recognize the differences in opinion among authorities about the nature and purposes of the social studies.
4. Understand what is meant by the statement: "The overall purpose of formal instruction in the social studies is to help students increase the number of meanings they derive from their social environment and to equip them to judge the validity of their meanings according to widely accepted canons of a scientific culture."
5. Identify five factors that should be considered in judging the "best" approach to instruction.
6. Define the terms *technique*, *mode*, *strategy*, and *method*.
7. Discriminate between the terms *educational goals* and *instructional objectives*.
8. Identify sources of educational goals.
9. Write instructional objectives and classify them according to whether they are primarily cognitive, primarily psychomotor, or primarily affective.
10. Classify cognitive objectives according to whether they are objectives of "higher" or "lower" order according to the Bloom taxonomy.
11. Defend the use of instructional objectives for social studies.
12. Link broadly stated educational goals to precisely stated instructional objectives.
13. Understand the basic teaching model recommended by us and the role of instructional objectives within that model.

THE SCENE IS a conference room in one of the buildings on the campus of a large state university. Present for a meeting are representatives of the state department of public instruction, a half dozen chairmen of high school social studies departments, two professors of social studies methods from the school of education, and five professors representing the departments of history, political science, geography, sociology, and economics. The meeting was called by the state department of public instruction to consider the implications of new certification requirements that high school social studies teachers will have to meet in the future in order to receive teaching licenses from the state. The discussion has been under way for approximately one hour. The economics professor has been visibly uncomfortable for much of this time. Finally, with a gesture of authority and some disdain, he pulls off his glasses, leans back in his chair, and in a voice expressing exasperation and annoyance asks, "What in the hell is social studies anyway?"

While the scene described above is fictional, similar situations have occurred many times and in many places. Although the public has a clear idea of what it means to teach algebra, physics, physical education, music, English, German, and even home economics, many remain puzzled about social studies. What is (or are) social studies? What do students learn in a social studies course? What does a social studies teacher do?

This first chapter is an effort to help you begin to think about these questions. It will not provide final answers; rather its purpose is to have you reflect on the profession of social studies teaching and what may be entailed by that role. The chapters that follow are designed to assist you in increasing your capacity to play the teacher role successfully.

The first section of this chapter presents some evidence regarding social studies instruction. Certainly, only a small fraction of social studies is revealed by the data, but it is sufficient to provide an impression of what social studies has been in American high schools. The second section is an essay about some of the forces that determine how teachers conceive their role. The final section provides information about changes currently under way in social studies instruction and the effects they are having on the teachers' role.

Data on the Image and Content of Social Studies

A good way to form impressions about social studies instruction is to visit high schools, to observe social studies classes, to talk to students, and to interview social studies teachers. Also helpful is talking with social studies specialists, those who write books on social studies and train social studies teachers. While it would be more useful and interesting for you to gather such data for yourself, we have gathered representative pieces of the kind of evidence you might collect. These data should help you to begin thinking about what it means to be a high school social studies teacher.

WHAT STUDENTS THINK

One group that can provide data about social studies in secondary schools is the students who take the courses. As evidence of student opinions about social studies instruction, we have assembled two kinds of data. The first con-

TABLE 1.1.

What students think of their courses.

| | MOST USEFUL | LEAST USEFUL | MOST DIFFICULT | MOST IMPORTANT | MOST BORING | MOST IRRELEVANT | CHANGES NEEDED TO IMPROVE | |
							Quality	*Relevance*
English (grammar, composition)	33%	14%	21%	52%	25%	14%	6%	4%
Mathematics	28	17	35	30	19	14	6	4
Science	20	16	22	13	14	13	11	8
Business and secretarial	18	5	6	9	7	6	10	8
History (including black)	15	18	12	12	19	18	8	7
Current affairs, politics	9	7	4	7	8	5	11	11
Foreign languages	8	13	13	5	10	10	15	6
Shop, technical	8	3	1	3	2	3	13	16
Home economics	6	2	*	2	2	2	2	3
Art	5	3	1	2	1	2	4	5
Physical education	3	10	*	2	1	9	3	5
Music	2	4	*	1	1	4	2	4
Drama, public speaking	2	*	*	1	1	1	2	2
Agriculture	1	1	*	*	*	1	2	2
Driver education	1	*	*	*	1	*	2	1
Personal hygiene	1	2	*	1	1	2	2	4
Humanities, ethics	1	2	*	2	3	3	3	4
Psychology	*	1	*	1	*	1	5	5
Literature	*	2	1	2	2	2	2	*
Geography	*	2	1	*	1	1	1	*
Family planning	*	*	*	1	1	1	5	6

SOURCE: *Life* 66, no. 19 (May 16, 1969) : 31.

*Less than 0.5%.

sists of the results of a national poll conducted in 100 schools by Louis Harris and Associates and published in *Life* magazine in May, 1969.[1] The second type of data is an interview by one of us of four tenth-grade students in Bloomington, Indiana, on August 7, 1971. We do not assume the interview data to be representative of all students, all tenth-grade students, or even all tenth-grade students in Bloomington. Indeed, the views of these students may deviate sharply from the views of others. Nevertheless, they all attend the same school and sit in the classroom of a social studies teacher. What they think would surely be important to that teacher. Moreover, the ways they react to social studies instruction may be instructive to other teachers.

A national poll. How do students judge their social studies courses in comparison with other courses? See Table 1.1. (See page 4.)

An interview with four tenth-grade students. As you read the following interview, try to analyze the students' understanding and expectations of social studies.

INTERVIEWER: *What grade will you be in when school starts?*

BRAD: *Tenth.*

CHRISTINE: *We will all be sophomores.*

INTERVIEWER: *Will you take a social studies course this year?*

JIM: *No, not this year.*

DIANE: *We could; it's offered but not required.*

INTERVIEWER: *Did you take a social studies course last year?*

JIM: *Yes—World Studies.*

INTERVIEWER: *And the year before that—did you have a social studies course?*

DIANE: *Yes.*

JIM: *Yes.*

INTERVIEWER: *What was that course?*

BRAD: *American Studies.*

JIM: *Social Studies.*

CHRISTINE: *It was Social Studies, it was about everything.*

INTERVIEWER: *Social Studies? Is that what the course was called?*

CHRISTINE: *Yes.*

INTERVIEWER: *Of all the courses you take, what are your favorites?*

CHRISTINE: *Gym.*

JIM: *English.*

BRAD: *Phys. Ed.*

INTERVIEWER: *What is your second-favorite course?*

DIANE: *English.*

BRAD: *English.*

JIM: *I'll pass. I don't know.*

INTERVIEWER: *What is your worst course?*

CHRISTINE: *Spanish.*

DIANE: *French.*

BRAD: *Algebra.*

INTERVIEWER: *What do you think about the social studies course that you took last year? I don't really care who the teacher was, but compared with all the courses you took, did you think social studies was fun, not fun, the worst course? Well, was it more like Spanish or more like Gym?*

CHRISTINE: *More like Spanish.*

JIM: *It was quite fun.*

INTERVIEWER: *Fun?*

JIM: *Yes.*

DIANE: *It was like French.*

BRAD: *I didn't like it.*

INTERVIEWER: *Why do you prefer Gym to Spanish, Christine?*

CHRISTINE: *I don't know, you get out and do something; in Spanish you just sit there.*

BRAD: *Lectures.*

INTERVIEWER: *Lectures? You said Algebra was your worst course?*

BRAD: *That's right.*

INTERVIEWER: *Was that because of lectures?*

BRAD: *Yes, lectures and stuff.*

INTERVIEWER: *So, the courses that you like the best are those in which you can do things?*

JIM: *Yes.*

INTERVIEWER: *Why didn't you like World Studies?*

CHRISTINE: *I thought there was too much paper work, and I just don't enjoy writing papers.*

BRAD: *I thought the subjects were dull.*

DIANE: *Well, we had to write papers that were too long for freshmen to write, and it wasn't really World Studies; it was everything the teacher wanted to know about.*

INTERVIEWER: *But you liked it, Jim. Why did you think it was fun?*

JIM: *I had a different teacher than the others. We didn't have to write all that junk. We were divided into groups, and she assigned us stuff that we could do in our groups. So, we didn't have to work alone.*

INTERVIEWER: *Can any of you tell me about one topic or one subject from World Studies that you enjoyed?*

BRAD: *Games!*

INTERVIEWER: *What kind of games were these?*

BRAD: *One was called "Revolution," and there was—*

CHRISTINE: *One about poverty.*

BRAD: *Yes, we had to figure out a budget.*

INTERVIEWER: *Diane, can you remember anything that was particularly interesting?*

DIANE: *Well, we had a game. It was about Puerto Rico and Cuba, and there were merchants and things like that, and we studied the economy of those countries.*

INTERVIEWER: *Did you learn anything in World Studies last year that seemed useful in helping you understand something that you are doing every day? In other words, was there anything in World Studies that was useful? Do you understand some things better because of the course than you did before?*

CHRISTINE: *Nothing!*

BRAD: *Nothing for me.*

INTERVIEWER: *You didn't learn anything useful? Well, what did you learn that was new? And can you remember it now?*

CHRISTINE: *We learned about some tribes.*

BRAD: *There were a lot of things we didn't know—most of the stuff we didn't know, but we can't remember it.*

INTERVIEWER: *Can you recall any of the things that you read about for the first time? For example, do you remember any of the tribes that you studied about?*

DIANE: *No, we didn't study any.*

INTERVIEWER: *You didn't study about tribes in your class?*

DIANE: *I had the same teacher as Christine, but we had a choice.*

INTERVIEWER: *What period of time did most of the course cover?*

BRAD: *We studied Egypt, the Middle East. We studied pretty much current affairs, and Russia. . . . We went from the Revolution almost up to the present. So it was all around the scale.*

INTERVIEWER: *Did all of you study Russia?*

JIM: *No!*

INTERVIEWER: *Two studied Russia and two did not? Let's take Russia as an example. Can you tell me anything that you remember from the study of Russia that you didn't know before?*

BRAD: *It has a lot of different ethnic groups, I guess.*

INTERVIEWER: *What does that mean?*

BRAD: *I don't know.*

INTERVIEWER: *World Studies was your ninth-grade program. What about the eighth grade? You had social studies then. Can you remember anything from eighth-grade social studies that has been useful to you?*

DIANE: *We learned about the Depression.*

CHRISTINE: *I really liked eighth-grade social studies. We had a good teacher, and what I learned really sank in.*

INTERVIEWER: *And what did you learn that you found useful?*

CHRISTINE: *Well, nothing was really useful. It was just stuff I didn't know that I found interesting.*

INTERVIEWER: *Okay, so social studies topics were interesting to know about, but I think you are telling me that social studies hasn't been useful thus far. At least you can't think of any way it has been useful. Do you expect that it will be useful some day?*

DIANE: *Not unless I go into another World Studies program this year.*

INTERVIEWER: *Why do you think people require students to take courses in social studies if none of it is useful?*

CHRISTINE: *Probably to learn the history of the world. So, like if you go some place, you will know something about the world.*

INTERVIEWER: *I see; so you study about Russia in case you ever go there.*

JIM: *Yes.*

BRAD: *When you are young, they teach you everything they can because you don't know what you are going to do. They teach social studies in case you decide to become a social studies teacher or something, and you won't have to start all over with history.*

INTERVIEWER: *So you think they are teaching you about those things to get you ready for an occupation?*

BRAD: *You need a little bit of everything so you know something when you decide what you want to major in.*

INTERVIEWER: *If you were to be a carpenter, Brad, or a fireman, or a painter, do you think social studies courses would be of any use to you?*

BRAD: *No.*

CHRISTINE: *Yes. If you are reading in the paper, and like if they talk about a date in history, we would at least know what was going on then.*

INTERVIEWER: *If you had to list the topics that are most likely to be taught in social studies, what would they be?*

DIANE: *Wars, definitely.*

BRAD: *Revolutions.*

JIM: *The Depression, all over.*

BRAD: *Industrialization.*

INTERVIEWER: *Okay, industrialization, wars, depressions, revolutions. Let me try out five terms to see if you recognize any of them; and if you know any of them, stop me and say, "I know that one and I can tell you a bit about that." Okay? The terms are:* social class, culture, role, status, socialization. *Do any of those words ring a bell?*

DIANE: Culture.

INTERVIEWER: Culture? *Okay,* role *and* social class? *You learned about* social class *in your social studies course?*

CHRISTINE: *We learned about all of them in the eighth grade, but I can't remember any of them.*

INTERVIEWER: *Can anyone give me a working definition of* culture? *How might it be used?*

DIANE: *This is really awful because we had to write a definition for it, and I can't remember any definition.*

INTERVIEWER: *You remember the term but not how it might be used?* Social class?

BRAD: *I didn't get that one.*

INTERVIEWER: *And* role? *You said you remember studying the word* role.

DIANE: *Yes, but I don't remember.*

INTERVIEWER: *Let me ask you a different kind of question. So far we have been talking about social studies. But, if I were to give you a math problem, do you think it would be easier to work a math problem from what you have studied in the past than to remember the specific kinds of questions I've been asking you about social studies? Suppose I asked you to multiply or divide or figure an algebra problem, for instance, do you think you would remember that better?*

DIANE: *I think I would because each year, when we have math, it is usually the same thing then, going into more detail; but when we have social studies, it's always new things.*

INTERVIEWER: *Have you ever had a social studies teacher who has tried to build upon what was learned the year before? In other words, has any social studies teacher said, "Well, last year you learned these things, so now we are going to add to that"? Have you ever had a social studies teacher do that?*

ALL FOUR: *No!*

INTERVIEWER: *If you could plan the social studies curriculum and decide what you would study, is there anything you would like to learn about?*

DIANE: *I think the drug problem. I mean you could put that in health or social studies because it's all around us. But you usually can't get a teacher who knows what he's talking about, because usually the students know more.*

INTERVIEWER: *Can you think of any other topics? Have you studied anything about politics or American government?*

DIANE: *We started it last year, but it just didn't interest anybody so we kind of dropped it.*

INTERVIEWER: *It was in your World Studies class that you began studying politics?*

DIANE: *We talked about pollution and then we'd go to drugs and then we'd go to the war. It was all back and forth.*

INTERVIEWER: *But on a particular topic like drugs, the students often know more than the teacher?*

DIANE: *Yes.*

INTERVIEWER: *Suppose I were to ask you, "What is social studies?" Could any of you tell me, briefly?*

CHRISTINE: *No.*

BRAD: *No.*

---

1. On the basis of this interview, what impact do you think the social studies has had on these four students?
2. What do they remember most from social studies courses?

3. What seems to hold the greatest interest for these students?
4. If you were their teacher and had this interview data, would you change your instruction? If so, how would you change it?
5. Do you think these students are typical of tenth-grade students? Would you have responded to the questions in the same way at their age?

WHAT A HIGH SCHOOL SOCIAL STUDIES TEACHER THINKS

The student data provided a rather dismal view of high school social studies. But we should not depend solely on the opinions of students, particularly the small sample represented by the interview. Because teachers may see the social studies quite differently, we asked one experienced teacher for his opinions about the status of social studies instruction.

Mr. Lee Smith teaches in a high school near Minneapolis, Minnesota. In 1972, at the time of the interview, he had been a teacher for 14 years. While he has taught most of the typical high school social studies courses at one time or another, he is primarily a teacher of World Studies. On the basis of the interview, what does Mr. Smith say are the major problems teachers of social studies face? In what ways does he believe social studies is changing?

INTERVIEWER: *What kind of attitudes do students, colleagues, parents, and administrators have toward social studies, and do these attitudes affect your instruction in any way?*

SMITH: *The attitudes are about as varied as people. It is difficult to generalize, but I might mention three attitudes that seem important to me. One attitude on the part of many people, both students and adults, is that teachers should provide final answers. Even some teachers feel this way. There is a fear of ambiguity, a desire to make things tidy. Let me give you an illustration. A few years ago we had a course called World History. The title of the course actually blocked what teachers wanted to do with it because most people knew what world history entailed—you start with the Egyptians and work all the way up to the present in the last chapter of the book. Any deviation from that organization was difficult because of this mental set that people had toward a course with the title World History. By changing the title to World Studies, which really wasn't much of a change, a number of interesting things began to happen. First of all, it gave us some freedom to experiment, to try new materials, new ideas. What we have now is a series of electives within a world studies area*

*that looks little like a typical world history course, although history is still
very much represented in the course.*

*A second attitude that presents problems for social studies is the belief that
anybody can teach social studies because they live in a social world. Even
some school administrators—although this is not a problem in our school—
believe that special training is unnecessary to teach social studies well.*

*And a third attitude that we have to overcome is one held by students. They
begin a high school social studies course with the belief that it will be boring
and useless. And when they begin with that kind of an attitude, it is difficult
to overcome it. Somehow that attitude must be changed as it makes the task
of the social studies teacher very difficult.*

INTERVIEWER: *Do you find that the administrators have a different degree of professional
expectation for social studies teachers than they do for math teachers, physics
teachers, or foreign language teachers, for example?*

SMITH: *I don't think that is true in our system. We have been particularly fortunate
in this way. Our administrators expect our social studies teachers to be as
competent as other teachers. We expect our teachers to have a strong background in course work, in travel, and in real-life experiences.*

INTERVIEWER: *But on the basis of your earlier statements, I assume you find still existent
in other school systems the attitude that nearly anyone with a college education who has taken courses in history and social science should be able to
teach social studies successfully.*

SMITH: *I think that attitude is still present and is difficult to alter.*

INTERVIEWER: *Do you think that social studies is very different today from what it was five
years ago? And, if so, how is it different?*

SMITH: *Well, I think it can be different. One difference is a consequence of the special
curriculum development projects of the sixties. Today, as compared with
ten years ago, teachers have many alternative programs from which to choose.
And these alternatives are quite different from what we had before. For example, in world history there might have been a half dozen or a dozen textbooks, produced by different companies, that were essentially the same. Maybe
the color of the pictures varied a little, perhaps the style of writing was different, but in essential ways they were identical. Today, we have a rich variety
of instructional materials: multimedia packs which provide audio-visual
components built into the program, case studies, readings, and many other*

items that expand the resources we have for teaching. Now, while all of this is true, in some places teachers remain bound to system adoptions, city adoptions, even state adoptions, of textbooks. Often the criteria for selection are pretty inflexible: the adoption criteria may require a hardback textbook to be used for five years that must fit closely a prescribed course of study. This means that in terms of the curriculum the publisher still has much influence over what happens in the classroom. You asked whether social studies is different than it was five years ago. Yes, it is; it can be; but it can also be slow to change, too. I think this depends a great deal on whether teachers are willing to fight for better programs.

INTERVIEWER: *Do you think students are any different?*

SMITH: *Sure.*

INTERVIEWER: *Do students today make demands different from those of five or six years ago?*

SMITH: *Well, we've gone through the Sputnik era. During that period we increased the demands on ourselves and our students beyond the point of usefulness. And we are now having a reaction to the great stress on academic excellence. I think we are experiencing a kind of apathetic reaction. At the same time that kids are apathetic, however, they are also, in part, an overstimulated generation.*

INTERVIEWER: *What do you mean?*

SMITH: *They are bombarded today by the media which stimulate them. Television provides information that students of prior generations did not have, both in quantity and quality. Today, students raise some fairly significant questions, better questions than students did a decade ago. This may be a function of their training, also.*

INTERVIEWER: *Does this make it easier or more difficult to teach social studies today than five years ago?*

SMITH: *It makes it different.*

INTERVIEWER: *Different?*

SMITH: *Yes, it forces us to deal with some topics that we should have been treating anyway. Teachers must become very conscious of the changes taking place in society and plan their instructional program in terms of social change.*

INTERVIEWER: *I wish to ask another question. Would you compare social studies with other courses in the school curriculum? I'm particularly interested in any special problems or advantages social studies has, as compared with other courses. Can you think of any?*

SMITH: *I think one of the problems social studies faces is that it is such a diverse field. No branch of history and no branch of social science has a handle on truth. Hence, any problem that might be treated in a social studies class can be viewed from a number of perspectives. What I'm trying to say is that each of the social studies disciplines, including history, provides insights and ways of knowing that help to make the world intelligible. To what extent physics, for example, or a foreign language is dependent on other disciplines, I am unable to say. However, in the social studies there is this enormous breadth and diversity which offers advantages, once you learn to live with it. However, the problem of keeping informed, of knowing what kinds of questions a sociologist or a political scientist or an anthropologist might bring to a set of data or to a problem, makes social studies extraordinarily complicated. Therefore, it's a rich and exciting field in which to teach but a tough one because it is so vague.*

INTERVIEWER: *Your comment suggests at least one major point to me, Lee. As compared to the opinion that anyone can teach social studies, it appears that a truly outstanding social studies teacher cannot afford to stop learning.*

SMITH: *Exactly! Once you stop being a student, you have quit as a teacher. If teachers would see themselves in that perspective, they could continue to improve.*

INTERVIEWER: *You referred to the academic disciplines. I wonder whether you could comment on the relationship that exists between the academic disciplines as they appear in colleges and universities and the social studies program in high schools.*

SMITH: *This is a complicated issue. We are concerned about knowledge, not only what we know from the past but ways of knowing as well—the processes by which new information, new insights, are acquired. But the crucial question is deciding on what knowledge for what purposes. The idea of sitting in a graduate course in history, taking copious notes on the professor's thinking, and then of attempting to pass the professor's ideas on to students in a form comparable with the way it was first received is quite inadequate; this is not what social studies is about. I do not mean, however, that a teacher can do without a good academic background. We need teachers who have a fundamental knowledge of the social studies. A superficial understanding is not enough. If the social studies courses are to be powerful, teachers must know the disciplines well. But this is far different from just passing on what a teacher learned in a college course.*

INTERVIEWER: *Finally, what do you think is the greatest single problem a new social studies teacher faces when he begins to teach?*

SMITH: *I don't think there is a greatest single problem. There are many problems, and we've touched on some of them in our discussion. I guess one thing a beginning teacher must learn is how to understand what students are thinking and experiencing. This involves a set of communication skills; in part it involves a special kind of listening. It does not mean that a teacher must become like the students, because he can't. The students believe it is fundamentally dishonest for a 35-year-old or a 25-year-old or a 22-year-old adult to attempt to be 16. The task for the teacher is to be sufficiently in tune with the students to truly understand them without talking down to them or trying to be like them. It is a very delicate balance. But a good social studies teacher needs to perceive the world, at times, as it is seen by his students.*

WHAT COLLEGE SPECIALISTS THINK

One of the issues that appeared in the interviews with the students and with Mr. Smith is the matter of deciding what social studies is or should be. For example, should social studies be the study of "wars, revolutions, and depressions" as the students described it, or should it focus on issues that they would like to study—for example, drugs? Is high school social studies merely a way of disguising the study of history, political science, economics, geography, sociology, anthropology, and psychology? Or is social studies something else, perhaps a separate discipline that draws on the social sciences as well as on other disciplines?

A number of people in colleges and universities specialize in social studies education. They teach social studies teachers, write textbooks, and publish articles regarding what social studies is and should be. Let's ask them what social studies is.

From a few of the leading authorities in social studies education, we have assembled brief statements and have grouped them in two categories. We do not imply that these statements represent the opinions of all social studies authorities; however, major positions in the field are represented. The statements provide answers to the following questions:

1. What view of the social studies do the people in Group A share? Are there differences within the group?
2. What view of the social studies do the people in Group B share? Are there differences within the group?
3. Are there points on which the people in Group A agree with the people in Group B? What are these points, if any?
4. Skim through the table of contents of this book and decide whether the authors would be more likely to agree with Group A or Group B. What indicators did you find to support your speculation?
5. Which group of authorities do you most agree with? Why?

Group A.

1. Social studies [is] that part of the school's general education program which is concerned with the preparation of citizens for participation in a democratic society. Social studies is not, then, simply an offshoot of the social sciences, with content to be dictated by the interests and desires of academicians in the social studies and history.—James P. Shaver, "Social Studies: The Need for Redefinition," *Social Education*, vol. 31, no. 8 (November, 1967), p. 589.
2. The most important aim of social-studies education in a democracy is to help students acquire a store of tested social theory, or body of principles, relevant to contemporary social issues and beliefs.—Maurice P. Hunt and Lawrence E. Metcalf, *Teaching High School Social Studies: Problems in Reflective Thinking and Social Understanding*, New York: Harper & Row, 1968, p. 53.
3. A . . . shortcoming of the notion that the social studies are merely the social sciences simplified for pedagogical purposes is the inadequacy of the social sciences, when taken alone, to fulfill the need of citizenship education. This is not to say that the social sciences are not an important part of the education of citizens. It is merely to say that they are not a sufficient basis for such education. To make the social sciences the sole basis of the social education of citizens is to ignore the increasingly recognized fact that children and youth learn more of their social behaviors from the informal theatres of education outside the regular course structure than they learn within organized education. These theatres include the life of the school itself. To make the social sciences the sole basis of citizenship is to place values and the valuing process outside the pale of social education, since the social sciences are value free; they are not concerned with how people make social judgments. . . . To make the teaching of different social sciences, and only some of them at that, the only source of citizenship education is to treat our problems piecemeal, for no social science taken alone describes more than a fraction of human behavior. . . . To make the teaching of the social sciences the sole basis of citizenship education denies the student the experience, under tutelage, of working with information provided by the social sciences as well as other important sources in the necessarily topical manner in which social problems arise in life. Citizenship education

should place its focus on the utilization of knowledge from whatever source in meeting the practical problems which confront a citizen. . . . Conceived thus, the social education of citizens, called social studies or not, is an applied field—not a scientific one *per se*. It involves applying information to social problems and using responsible, intellectual processes to the resolution of these problems.—Shirley H. Engle, "The Future of Social Studies Education and NCSS," *Social Education*, vol. 34, no. 8 (November, 1970), pp. 778, 780.

Group B.

1. The social studies in the secondary school curriculum are distinguishable from the social science disciplines in the following four basic respects: (1) scope, (2) size, (3) purpose, and (4) level of difficulty. In both scope and size the social sciences are much more extensive than the social studies. Scholars representing the various social science disciplines research a greater diversity of social and human relationships and gather considerably more data and information than it is conceivably possible to include in the secondary social studies program. The purpose of the social scientist is to search and contribute new knowledge to his discipline. The objective of the secondary social studies teacher is to direct students in their learning of selected segments of what the social scientists have discovered. Social studies material draws upon the literature of the social sciences, but its purpose is not to report the discovery of new research. In their research social scientists deal frequently with abstract theories and sophisticated modes of inquiry that, in most instances, are beyond the comprehension of many secondary students. The social studies instructor, therefore, selects content based upon the research of social scientists and develops innovative techniques for translating it into comprehensible materials for the secondary student. Thus, there exists no absolute delimitation between the social sciences and the social studies. Rather, there is a difference in methodology and application.—Randall C. Anderson, *Current Trends in Secondary School Social Studies*, Lincoln, Nebr.: Professional Educators Publications, 1972, pp. 11–12.

2. The social studies are a group of elementary and secondary school courses which are designated by a common label to distinguish them from other parts of the school curriculum, but which, practically speaking, are not based on any single philosophy of education nor aimed at achieving any unified set of educational goals. They tend in varying degrees to be organized around content—data, concepts, and general propositions—drawn from the social sciences and to foster thought patterns practiced in these disciplines, but in many cases they must be considered much broader in scope. This is especially true of social studies courses which focus on helping students make value judgments and choices and/or develop behavior consistent with a democratic belief system.—Morris R. Lewenstein, in correspondence with Howard Mehlinger, November 1, 1972.

3. The social sciences are foundations of the social studies in three distinctive ways. First, the social sciences are primary sources of the content of the social

studies: the concepts, generalizations, and methods of inquiry. Second, the social foundations of curriculum planning in the social studies draw data from the social sciences related to societal values, problems, changing conditions, and our democratic heritage. Third, the psychological foundations of curriculum planning in the social studies draw data from the social sciences related to social processes, learning, child development, and other psychological-methodological aspects of instruction.—John U. Michaelis and A. Montgomery Johnston, "The Social Sciences: Foundations of the Social Sciences," in *The Social Sciences Foundations of the Social Studies*, ed. by John U. Michaelis and A. Montgomery Johnston, Boston: Allyn and Bacon, 1965.

SOCIAL STUDIES COURSES

In general, when teachers say they "teach" social studies and students assert they are "taking" social studies, they are referring to structured courses in the curriculum. For all practical purposes social studies is treated by school administrators, teachers, parents, and students as formal courses, usually one or two semesters in length, in which students learn a body of content suggested by the course label. Thus, one way to examine secondary school social studies is to see what courses students are most likely to encounter.

*The national pattern.** As you study Tables 1.2,[2] 1.3,[3] and 1.4[4] the answers to the following questions will be apparent. (For tables, see pages 21, 22, 24.)

1. What does social studies mean to the typical American secondary school student? What subjects or topics will he learn most about? What subjects or topics is he least likely to study?
2. What is the most typical pattern of course offerings in grades 9 through 12?
3. What courses tend to be taken by a large number of students as full-year courses and which as half-year courses?
4. What are the major trends in social studies offerings since 1890? Which courses are growing in importance and which are declining in significance?

State requirements and recommendations. The pattern of social studies instruction is remarkably similar throughout the United States. Although we have no federally imposed curriculum, the social studies courses offered in a high school in Scottsdale, Arizona, for instance, are likely to be very similar to those in Vergennes, Vermont. Textbook publishers produce books for a

---

*Although these figures are based on the 1960–61 national school census—the latest figures of this kind available—the course titles continue to be more or less representative of social studies offerings nationally.

Subject Field and Subject	Total	Pupils Enrolled In Half-year Courses	In Full-year Courses
SOCIAL STUDIES	11,802,499		
Social studies, grade 7	267,553	12,667	254,886
Social studies, grade 8	233,156	9,584	223,572
History, grades 7–8			
United States	1,695,956	118,497	1,577,459
State	651,790	183,200	468,590
World	324,947	33,598	291,349
Civics, grades 7–8	54,498	32,555	21,943
Geography, grades 7–8	1,045,069	206,335	838,734
Social studies, grade 9	54,004	4,889	49,115
Social studies, grade 10	8,653	1,217	7,436
Occupations	82,216	50,275	31,941
Orientation	87,124	44,475	42,649
Civics, grades 9–10	732,609	163,314	569,295
History, grades 9–12			
United States	1,994,068	36,978	1,957,090
State	374,517	182,688	191,829
World	1,471,531	41,192	1,430,339
Ancient and medieval	103,960	26,666	77,294
Modern	75,108	14,542	60,566
Miscellaneous	11,908	6,438	5,470
World geography, grades 9–12	585,541	111,111	474,430
Geography, misc., grades 9–12	9,609	2,183	7,426
Civics or government, grades 11–12	780,123	343,423	436,700
Problems of democracy	380,453	95,056	285,397
Economics	293,175	217,401	75,774
Psychology	140,377	88,041	52,336
Sociology or social problems	289,408	177,799	111,609
Consumer education	30,245	14,489	15,756
International relations	17,006	12,073	4,933
Honors or advanced placement	3,223	842	2,381
Miscellaneous, grades 7–12	4,672	2,712	1,960

TABLE 1.2. *Offerings and enrollments in grades 7 through 12 of public secondary schools, by subject: United States, 1960–61.*

SOURCE: Grace S. Wright, *Summary of Offerings and Enrollments in High School Subjects, 1960–61* (Washington, D.C.: Department of Health, Education, and Welfare, 1964), p. 5.

national market on the assumption that most schools will continue to offer world history at grades 9 or 10, American history at grade 11, and American government at grade 12.

TABLE 1.3.

Number of pupils enrolled in selected subjects in grades 9 through 12, and the percent this number is of the total enrollment in the grade in which the subject is usually offered: United States, 1960–61 and 1948–49.

SUBJECT FIELD AND COURSE	Usual Grade of Course Offering	1960–61 Number of Pupils	1960–61 Percent of Total Grade Enrollment[a]	1948–49 Number of pupils	1948–49 Percent of Total Grade Enrollment[b]
ENGLISH					
Grade 9	9	2,397,708	98.2	1,564,358	95.3
Grade 10	10	2,072,940	97.8	1,397,897	93.8
Grade 11	11	1,838,189	96.1	1,198,018	96.4
Grade 12	12	1,469,897	84.2	955,617	93.1
College-level English	12	9,220	0.5		
Honors courses	12	2,381	0.1		
World literature	12	66,701	3.8	5,438	0.5
Speech and public speaking	11	454,347	23.8	246,213	19.8
Creative writing	12	38,097	2.2	4,626	0.5
Journalism	12	136,671	7.8	100,147	9.8
SOCIAL STUDIES					
U.S. history	11	1,994,068	104.3	1,231,694	99.2
World history	10	1,471,531	69.4	876,432	58.9
Civics (elementary)	9	732,609	30.0	c	
Civics (advanced)	12	780,123	44.7	431,916	42.1
Problems of democracy	12	380,453	21.8	282,971	27.6
Economics	12	293,175	16.8	254,770	24.8
Psychology	12	140,377	8.0	46,547	4.5
Sociology and social problems	12	289,408	16.6	185,901	18.1

Nevertheless, each of the fifty states is legally responsible for the operation of schools within its borders, and state departments of public instruction can, and often do, influence social studies instruction in powerful ways. In some states a certain number of hours must be spent on a study of the state constitution, or students may have to pass a test on it in order to graduate. During the late 1950s and early 1960s, public concern over the "Communist threat" led several states to require special instruction about Communism in schools. The following excerpt from a concurrent resolution (54, 1960) of the Louisiana legislature is typical both of manifestations of public concern over the challenge posed by Communism and of ways that states can influence social studies instruction.

Whereas, it is the belief of the Louisiana Legislature that every high school and college student in the State of Louisiana should be required to take a separate course

TABLE 1.3. (*Continued*)

SUBJECT FIELD AND COURSE	1960–61			1948–49	
	Usual Grade of Course Offering	Number of Pupils	Percent of Total Grade Enrollment[a]	Number of Pupils	Percent of Total Grade Enrollment[b]
MATHEMATICS					
General mathematics (elementary)	9	1,027,205	42.1	649,810	39.6
General mathematics (advanced)	12	400,107	22.9	42,600	4.2
Advanced high school or college mathematics	12	40,031	2.3		
Elementary algebra	9	1,607,356	65.8	1,042,451	63.5
Intermediate and advanced algebra	11	741,661	38.8	406,515	32.7
Plane geometry	10	959,825	45.3	599,336	40.2
Solid geometry	12	173,196	10.0	93,944	9.2
Trigonometry	12	246,225	14.1	108,551	10.6
Trigonometry-algebra, integrated	11	22,995	1.2		
SCIENCE					
General science	9	1,549,271	63.5	1,073,934	65.4
First-year biology	10	1,686,318	79.6	989,756	63.4
First-year chemistry	11	708,143	37.0	406,662	32.8
First-year physics	12	385,148	22.1	278,834	27.2
Advanced general and physical science	12	276,816	15.9	56,291	5.5

SOURCE: Grace S. Wright, *Subject Offerings and Enrollments in Public Secondary Schools* (Washington, D.C.: Department of Health, Education, and Welfare, 1965), p. 100.

[a]Total enrollment: grade 9, 2,441,668; grade 10, 2,119,393; grade 11, 1,912,465; grade 12, 1,745,750.

[b]Total enrollment: grade 9, 1,641,406; grade 10, 1,490,628; grade 11, 1,241,505; grade 12, 1,025,913.

[c]Not available.

or unit of study as a part of the regular and mandatory curricula at some time during the latter portion of his period of high school or college studies respectively, which would not only give to each student a clear understanding of and a deep loyalty to the ideals, principles, traditions, advantages and institutions of representative democracy and free capitalism in a federation of sovereign states as established by the drafters of the Constitution of the United States; but, which would at the same time, by comparison, teach every student why Communism and Socialism are evil and vicious, why they destroy the freedom, well being, dignity

TABLE 1.4.

Number of pupils enrolled in certain subjects in grades 9 through 12
of public secondary schools: United States, selected years from
1890 to 1961

SUBJECT	1890	1900	1910	1915	1922	1928	1934	1949	1961
Total enrollment[a]	202,963	519,251	739,143	1,165,495	2,155,460	2,896,630	4,496,514	5,399,452	8,219,276
English (regular 9–12)		199,803	422,051	680,871	1,652,232	[b]2,696,633	4,071,094	5,015,890	7,778,734
Journalism					2,224	6,639	31,246	100,147	136,671
Speech and public speaking							103,183	246,213	454,347
U.S. history					329,565	517,331	779,489	1,231,694	1,994,068
English history					61,766	25,203	21,913	1,043	1,011
Ancient history	55,427	198,125	406,784	589,067	371,392	301,794	304,025		
Medieval and modern history					330,836	327,313	278,236	192,847	179,068
World history						175,628	536,178	876,432	1,471,531
Civics and government						192,497	268,338	431,916	780,123
Community civics, grade 9		112,465	114,965	183,294	416,329	387,910	465,954	[c]	732,609
Geography						8,790	94,071	301,652	565,150
Problems of democracy						30,200	156,707	282,971	380,453
Economics					103,540	147,035	221,874	254,770	293,175
Sociology					51,288	77,117	111,718	185,901	289,408
Psychology		12,368	7,109	13,626	18,786	29,669	15,025	46,547	140,377
Algebra	92,150	292,287	420,207	569,215	865,515	1,020,323	1,367,210	1,448,966	2,349,017
General mathematics					266,918	228,231	333,348	704,742	1,427,312
Geometry	43,294	142,235	228,170	309,383	488,825	573,668	767,171	893,280	1,133,021
Trigonometry		9,915	13,812	17,220	32,930	36,855	59,858	108,551	246,225
General science					393,885	507,038	798,227	1,121,980	1,826,087
Biology			7,883	80,403	189,288	393,391	656,693	995,930	1,776,306
Botany			116,497	106,520	82,241	46,062	41,075	7,670	4,996
Zoology			51,370	37,456	32,956	22,165	27,275	5,051	5,924
Physiology		142,401	113,252	110,541	109,519	77,650	81,632	53,592	65,953
Earth science		154,513	155,401	178,693	97,140	81,017	78,559	20,575	76,564
Chemistry	20,503	40,084	50,923	86,031	159,413	204,694	339,769	412,401	744,820
Physics	46,184	98,846	107,988	165,854	192,380	198,402	282,896	291,473	402,317
French	11,858	40,395	73,161	102,516	333,162	406,012	488,710	255,375	661,190

Subject	1890	1900	1910	1915	1922	1928	1934	1949	1961
German	21,338	74,408	175,083	284,294	13,918	53,250	106,672	43,025	141,517
Italian					359	2,552	10,434	15,552	15,733
Latin	70,411	262,767	362,548	434,925	593,086	636,952	721,320	422,304	637,475
Russian								14	9,342
Spanish			4,920	31,743	242,715	273,564	280,329	443,995	806,827
Physical education					123,568	435,383	2,277,775	d3,747,220	6,061,376
Music				367,188	544,770	754,245	1,148,732	d1,625,235	d2,302,900
Art				266,492	317,825	339,485	391,754	d486,232	d1,589,140
Industrial arts				130,155	295,905	391,529	946,128	d1,064,508	1,960,000
Vocational-industrial								369,794	344,704
General business training						86,629	276,672	279,577	461,794
Bookkeeping				39,816	270,517	310,232	446,463	472,163	630,714
Typewriting					281,524	439,379	749,315	1,216,142	1,902,592
Shorthand					191,901	251,631	404,237	421,635	550,321
Business law					19,611	76,434	144,342	130,585	167,101
Office practice					7,721	44,364	80,104	108,201	189,935
Home economics			27,933	150,276	307,553	477,503	751,807	1,304,846	1,901,128
Agriculture			34,418	83,573	110,242	106,086	159,763	364,185	507,992

SOURCE: Grace S. Wright, *Subject Offerings and Enrollments in Public Secondary Schools* (Washington, D.C.: Department of Health, Education, and Welfare, 1965), p. 99.

NOTE: When necessary, the subjects reported in previous surveys were analyzed, and appropriate components were either recombined, separately listed, or eliminated (with corresponding changes in the number enrolled) in a manner to yield as close comparability as possible with the data of the current (1960–61) survey.

aFor the years 1910 to 1934 the figures represent the number of pupils enrolled in the last 4 years of public secondary day schools that returned usable questionnaires. For 1890, 1949, and 1961 the figures represent the total number of pupils enrolled in the last 4 years of all public secondary day schools.

bIncludes enrollment in composition and in literature.

cComparable data for 1948–49 are not available.

dEnrollment in grades 9 to 12 estimated from the total. This estimation was necessary because the data for the subject did not fully identify grades 9 to 12 enrollment apart from grades 7 and 8.

and happiness of the individual, and why they are our implacable enemy, to the end that these students will understand the propaganda and dishonesty of Soviet Russia, Red China, and the other apparatus and affiliates of organized communism and national socialism. . . .[5]

Although such statements as the one above are not unique to Louisiana, they do not represent the most typical kind of influence that state departments of public instruction have on the social studies. Table 1.5[6] establishing offerings of social studies courses in the state of Indiana is more characteristic of the type of influence a state exerts. (See page 27.)

Courses in two Indiana high schools. In Table 1.5 you noted the recommendations and requirements for social studies as established by the Department of Public Instruction in the state of Indiana. Although states establish the general parameters for instruction (nearly one-half of the states decide which textbooks can be used) and set standards for teachers, individual school systems have considerable freedom to maneuver. The program of one high school in a state may vary to some degree at least from that of other high schools in the same state.

Figures 1.1 and 1.2 are class schedules for the social studies faculty in two Indiana high schools whose enrollments are between 500 and 750 students each. The schedules are similar but not identical. They indicate the courses taught by the faculty. Coaching responsibilities and sponsorship of extra-curricular activities are not shown here. The following questions will guide your analysis of the schedules.

1. Which school follows most closely the recommendations of the Indiana State Department of Public Instruction?
2. What course is taught most frequently?
3. How many different courses is a teacher likely to teach?
4. How many hours each day does a typical teacher spend in the classroom?

If you were a social studies teacher in an Indiana high school, what might you teach? Which courses are most likely offered in every Indiana high school?

Influences on the Role of Social Studies Teachers

By this time you should have discovered that there is little agreement about what social studies is or should become. Compared with the fields of foreign language, mathematics, science, and business education, social studies is in disarray. A person preparing to be a teacher of German or algebra has a rather clear conception of what is expected of him. The beginning American

TABLE 1.5.
Social studies established
for grades 9 through 12:
Indiana, 1961.

SUBJECTS	YEAR	PERIODS PER WEEK	SEMESTER	UNIT VALUE
Citizenship	9	2–5	1 or 2	.5 or 1
Vocational Information	9	5	1 or 2	.5 or 1
Current Problems in Our Democracy[a]	9 or 10	5	1	.5
World History[b]	10 or 11	5	2	1
Early World History[b]	10 to 12	5	2	1
Modern World History[b]	10 to 12	5	2	1
United States History[c]	10 to 12	5	2	1
United States Government[c]	12	5	1 or 2	.5 or 1
Economics	11 or 12	5	1	.5
Social Problems (Sociology)	11 or 12	5	1	.5
High School Geography (Physical, Economic, Social)	11 or 12	5	1 or 2	.5 or 1
Our American Neighbors	11 or 12	5	1 or 2	.5 or 1
Governments of the World[d]	12	5	1	.5
Pacific Relations	11 or 12	5	1	.5
Latin American Civilization	10 to 12	5	1	.5

SOURCE: William E. Wilson, *The Administrative Handbook for Indiana Schools* (Indianapolis: Indiana Department of Public Instruction, 1961), Bulletin no. 225, p. 229.

[a]This course is preferably placed in the tenth year to give most pupils, before leaving school, a better understanding of everyday problems confronting the people of our democracy. Such a course is necessarily more elementary than, and does not take the place of, the established course in United States Government. Basic principles and problems of government and of society should be studied so that the pupils gain a greater appreciation for the United States government and the American way of life.

[b]Large schools having sufficient demand for extra courses may offer Early World History and Modern World History instead of/or partially parallel with the one-year course in World History. However, credit cannot be given for courses whose content overlaps.

[c]For graduation, all students are required to earn 1 unit of credit in United States History and 1 additional unit of credit in citizenship courses, always including the first semester of *United States Government.*

Studies in such subjects as Current Problems in Our Democracy, Our American Neighbors, Social Problems, Governments of the World, and Pacific Relations are also regarded as citizenship courses. The Social Studies course for the ninth grade shall not be construed as meeting the requirements of a full year in advanced Citizenship, which comprises courses in United States History and Government and in the study of the Constitution of the United States and of the State of Indiana.

[d]This course is designed for advanced pupils with a strong basic foundation, who are interested in understanding by means of comparative study how other governments operate. It is so organized as to deepen the pupil's appreciation of our democratic ways of life. Schools desiring to offer this course should get the approval of the State Department of Public Instruction and obtain a course of study outline for it.

Grades 9-12 Teacher's Name	8:30-9:30 Period 1	9:35-10:30 Period 2	10:35-11:00 Period 3	11:35-12:30 Period 4	LUNCH 12:30-1:05 1:05-2:00 Period 5	2:05-3:00 Period 6
Mr. Pettijohn	Amer. St. II S103	Sociology S103	US History S103	Sociology S103	Preparation	Department Chairman
Mr. Grier	US History J124	World St. II J124	Preparation	World St. II IG J124	World St. II IG J124	World St. II J124
Mr. Perkins	Government S102	Study Hall S130	Government S102	Psychology S102	Inter. Rel. S102	Preparation
Mr. Tuck	Preparation	US History S101	Values & Issues S101	US History S101	US History S101	US History S101
Dr. Matriano (Part-time)					Economics S103	World St. II J144
Mrs. Williamson	Preparation	World St. II J120	World St. II J120	World St. II J120	World St. II J120	World St. II J120

FIGURE 1.1.

Second semester schedule for social studies classes, grades 9 through 12. University Junior-Senior High School, Bloomington, Indiana, 1970–71.

FIGURE 1.2.

First semester schedule for social studies classes. Mount Vernon Senior High School, Mount Vernon, Indiana, 1969–70.

Teacher's Name	Period 1 8:15-9:10 Course	Rm. No.	Period 2 9:14-10:09 Course	Rm. No.	Period 3 10:13-11:08 Course	Rm. No.	ECA* 11:20-11:57 Rm. No.	Period 4** 12:01-1:31 Course	Rm. No.	Period 5 1:35-2:30 Course	Rm. No.	Period 6 2:34-3:29 Course	Rm. No.
Mr. Martin	Government	53	Preparation		Government	53		Amer. Pol.	53	Government	53	Amer. Pol.	53
Mr. Herron	Economics	45	Economics	45	Economics	45	45	Economics	45	Preparation		Geogr.	45
Mr. Horning	U.S. Hist.	51	Government	51	Psychology	51	51	U.S. Hist.	51	Preparation		U.S. Hist.	51
Mrs. Kuhlen-schmidt	Sociology	52	U.S. Hist. B	52	U.S. Hist.	52	52	U.S. Hist.	52	U.S. Hist. B	52	Preparation	
Mr. Wilhoit	Audio-visual	40	U.S. Hist.	50	Preparation		50	World Aff.	50	U.S. Hist.	50	World Hist.	50

*ECA stands for extracurricular activities. This period is a time when school activities and clubs can meet. Students not attending an activity go to a homeroom for study hall.

**Thirty minutes of period 4 are used for lunch. Each teacher has lunch with his own class.

history teacher—to the extent that he is aware—will be faced with competing beliefs regarding what appropriate instruction in American history is. A critic would say that the field of social studies is a shambles; an advocate might argue that these disputes make the field richer, livelier, and more exciting.

To a great extent the social studies teacher has considerable freedom to decide for himself what social studies will become in his own classroom. Nevertheless, he is not a completely free agent. Whether he is conscious of them or not, a number of forces operate upon him to guide his views. The teacher who is aware of these forces is better able to cope with them while retaining a sense of direction.

Although the three forces to be discussed in this section are not the only ones that determine how the role of social studies teacher will be played, they are important. Furthermore, they are especially significant in shaping the attitudes of beginning teachers. These three forces are: the examples and advice of college professors, the institutional demands placed upon social studies teachers, and the impact of the student culture. The pressures they exert do not operate with equal strength or in the same direction. Usually the teacher finds himself in a cross-pressure situation requiring accommodation of conflicting forces. Being able to cope successfully with these strains may be important to finding satisfaction as a teacher.

COLLEGE PROFESSORS

One of the first important sources of influence that affect a teacher's perception of his role as social studies teacher is college professors. The influence is primarily exerted in two ways: *by example* when teachers-in-training admire and seek to emulate particular college instructors and *by instruction* when they take courses in history and the social sciences or in professional education that are expected to provide them with important knowledge and skills for teaching.

Two groups of college professors seem particularly relevant to social studies teachers: those who teach "content" courses and those who teach "methods" courses. The former consists primarily of historians and social scientists; the latter consists primarily of faculty in schools of education.* Of course, to distinguish between methods and content is to distort reality. It implies that teaching content and instructing methods are distinctively different processes,

---

*It should be noted, however, that this distinction makes little sense in many colleges that lack separate schools of education. In such cases members of the various disciplines also provide the methods courses.

whereas they tend to merge. The college historian projects an instructional model—good or bad—when he teaches history, and no methods instructor can survive a half-hour without using content examples to support his instructional ideas. Nevertheless, despite the obvious defect in presenting these as distinct processes, many college professors act as if the categories were empirically accurate. Their belief in and commitment to the separation of content and methods have a number of consequences for social studies instruction. A typical negative result is a debilitating rivalry between some faculty members in the academic disciplines and others in the school of education which may enhance the vanity of individual professors but does little to help a prospective social studies teacher.

While preparing in college to teach, prospective teachers encounter contending claims about what social studies is, what is wrong with current social studies instruction, and what a good social studies teacher needs to know. One way to account for these claims is to identify the position of the spokesman. When a professor says that "social studies is based upon the structure of the social science disciplines" or that "social studies consists of history and the social sciences" or that "what social studies needs most are teachers who know more about history," often the listener is confronted by a member of a history or a social science department. Those who argue that social studies is primarily "education for citizenship" or an "inquiry into problematical areas of society" or insist that "teachers should pay more attention to interaction patterns in class" are most often professors in schools of education. It is pointless to debate which group is "right." What is significant for a prospective social studies teacher to recognize is that he is not being exposed to the gospel but to contending positions about appropriate courses of action. Furthermore, it is undoubtedly true that both "knowing more history" and being aware of "interaction patterns" are useful.

The teacher-in-training need not be frustrated or misled by competing advice. Rather, if he understands the setting in which the advice is given, he can be challenged by it and can profit from it. What is important to remember is that if the college or university is a good one, the teacher-in-training has highly professional instructors. As professionals, they are influenced strongly by the norms within their own disciplines. Moreover, often they were employed by the college or university on the basis of the recognition they had received within their respective fields of study, their research and writing, and perhaps their capacity to direct graduate research. A professor is likely to appreciate, to teach about, and to encourage others to pursue those topics he knows most about. Thus, one should expect historians to teach history and try to inculcate a respect for the study of history. A person should expect similar behavior from professors in schools of education toward topics of special importance to them. What a teacher-in-training must remember is that a high school is not a college. Merely transferring what was learned in a senior political science seminar to a high school civics class is rarely—if ever—sufficient. The teacher-in-training must learn as much as he can from all his professors and then act intelligently on what he learned in order to plan appropriate instruction for young adolescents. Few college courses can or should be taught as though they were exact models of high school instruction. The teacher-in-training who understands this fact will avoid disillusionment later.

Following is a hypothetical illustration of what too frequently occurs during the college preparation of social studies teachers. A college senior named John wants to become a high school teacher. To become certified to teach in his state, John must have 20 professional hours in education, including 3 hours in "methods" of social studies instruction, a total of 40 hours in the general area of history and the social sciences, and at least 12 hours in the specific subject field he wishes to teach. By the time John completes his B.A. degree, he will have 16 hours of credit scattered over geography, political science, sociology, and economics, and he will have earned a major in history with 12 hours in American history and 12 hours in other history courses. The courses relating to world history that John has taken are Greek history (3 hours), modern European history (3 hours), Renaissance (3 hours), and the Russian Revolution (3 hours).

John wanted to take a survey course on world history, but the history department does not offer one. Indeed, most of the history instructors think the idea of teaching a history of the world is ridiculous. Therefore, John anticipates being expected to teach a course to high school students that few college historians would attempt. While John has studied hard in the history courses he has taken and has detailed notes from readings and lectures, he has concluded after looking at a high school world history textbook that he is adequately prepared to teach about one-sixth of the course content. Moreover, John has received little or no help from his history teachers regarding the best ways to teach history. In the history courses he has taken, the instructor either lectured all the time, or in the one seminar he took, the class spent the entire semester discussing bibliography and the papers written by students. John thinks that neither teaching technique will be appropriate for high school students.

John's methods instructor is sympathetic to his problem but is not able to provide the world history support John requests. In the same methods class are people preparing to be teachers of civics, geography, sociology, and American history. The instructor encourages John to consider the world history course as an opportunity to study man's persistent problems on the

Few communities are willing to abdicate to social studies teachers a responsibility for deciding what the essentials of the "free society" are and what changes "modern conditions demand." Therefore, social studies teachers are frequently subject to the kinds of community pressures that do not beset mathematics, science, language, and shop teachers. Many parents want to know what values and public policies are being "advocated" in social studies classes; a number of interest groups wish to have their positions represented. Thus, the teacher is caught in a splendid dilemma: Few credit him with any special knowledge or capacity to deal with social issues; if he treats them in class, he may encounter community and parental pressure; if he ducks all the interesting topics and issues, he does not satisfy the purposes of social education as defined by the leaders in his own professional field.

Autonomous professional or bureaucratic worker? A social studies teacher encounters another kind of tension. He occupies a kind of twilight zone between a professional and a bureaucrat. He is trained in college to think of himself as a professional, skilled in his subject matter, and as an artist in instructional technique. His "professional associations" preach a professional ideology. Nevertheless, his pay is not equal to that of other professionals, for example, doctors and lawyers; he cannot choose his clients; he has little control over his time. Beginning teachers often have little choice about the courses they will teach or even the textbooks they will use.

The school administration determines how a teacher will spend his day. The schedule in Figure 1.3, typical of a majority of schools, is from a Nebraska high school. It conveys some feeling for the way a school day is structured.

The typical social studies teacher in this Nebraska high school teaches 150 students scattered over five periods. Assuming that he does not teach Period 1, he arrives at school around 8:00 A.M. and does not leave until 4:00 P.M. During that eight-hour stretch, he spends all but one hour with students. One hour is used for preparation and recuperation. Even the lunch hour is likely to involve some monitoring of students in the lunchroom.

The typical teacher has two preparations, perhaps American history and world history. As a conscientious teacher he wants to prepare well for his classes. He assigns papers for students to write and devotes time to carefully evaluating their work. But as a husband and parent, he is likely to decide that he cannot use evenings and weekends for schoolwork and begins to look for shortcuts. Either he devotes less time to lesson preparation and grading of student papers, or he begins to do his work at school, setting aside class time for "supervised study" while he prepares for the next day.

A typical social studies teacher works very hard at exhausting tasks. He has little time to plan, to attend meetings, to reflect on his work. Consequently,

FIGURE 1.3.
Daily schedule for a typical senior high school in Nebraska.

SENIOR HIGH BELL SCHEDULE 1973-74
(Subject to possible revision)

7:30	Lights on and building opens
7:45- 8:40	Period 1
8:45- 9:40	Period 2
9:45-10:40	Period 3
10:45-11:40	Period 4
11:45- 1:05	Period 5 and lunch (see details below)

        11:45-Period 5 begins for students on B
           and C lunch. A lunch begins
        12:10-A lunch ends; A classes begin.
           B lunch begins
        12:40-B lunch ends; B classes reassemble.
           C lunch begins
       1:05-Period 5 classes and C lunch end

1:10- 2:05	Period 6
2:10- 3:05	Period 7
3:10- 4:05	Activity meetings and make-up period
4:30	Building closes except for supervised activities

NOTE: Corridor lights will go off one minute after the beginning of each period and go back on one minute before the end of each period.

Tentative School Lunch Schedule

The following is the tentative lunch schedule for 1973-1974. Notify your <u>fifth</u> period class so that they will know when to go to lunch each day.

A lunch   11:45-12:10   B101, B102, B103, B104, B201, B202, B204, B206, B208, B210, B214, B216, B219, B221, B222, B227

B lunch   12:10-12:40   B4, B42, B109, B110, B111, B112, B113
                           (looks light)

C lunch   12:40- 1:05   B1, B5, B30, B31, B33, B34, B105, B106, B107, C3, C4, C18, D5, D12, D20

NOTE: Additions and transfers will be necessary.

school systems employ specialists who perform these tasks for him. Supervisors and administrators often decide what the social studies program will be, what training teachers will require, and so on. Teachers are ambivalent about these constraints. Few challenge the rights of administrators to make decisions that affect their instruction. Their typical response is to engage in passive resistance to administrative policies and practices they dislike.

From the perspective of the administration—regardless of how sensitive individual administrators may be—the social studies teacher is a functioning component of the overall operation to "educate" students. Students enter at one end of the "factory" (around age 6) and emerge at the other end (around age 17). In between, teachers have "educated" them, in a way somewhat analogous to workers applying parts to a machine on an assembly line. If the state or community wants students to study American history, the administrator must employ American history teachers who can teach "the American history course." Efficiency requires, for example, mass purchase of textbooks and everybody's using rented films on the same day. All students must be assigned; all workers must be at their posts. If a social studies teacher wants to take one class on an all-day field trip, someone has to cover his other classes, and since the students who went on the field trip miss other teachers' classes, this requires extra effort from the other teachers. It is much easier to maintain the regular schedule and avoid such interruptions.

The United States has a commitment to mass education which leads to demands for organizational efficiency which reduces opportunity for idiosyncracy. In short, the drive to make the school an efficient bureaucracy is strong.

Teaching is private work. It is hard to imagine how teaching can be viewed as a private, even lonely, occupation when it involves being with 150 students each day. But unlike workers in many other occupations, teachers have few opportunities to talk to colleagues. Except during their free period, when their colleagues are teaching, they are with students. Many principals want teachers in their rooms all day and will not permit them to be called to the telephone except in an emergency.

Teachers not only lack opportunity to talk to colleagues, they rarely visit each other's classrooms. Indeed, very few outsiders ever visit a secondary school classroom. Primary grade teachers are used to having parents in the room, but parents rarely, if ever, visit a social studies classroom in a secondary school without a special invitation. The principal or supervisor may visit a teacher's classroom once or twice during the year for purposes of evaluation. But it is almost unknown for teachers to visit each other's classrooms during their free periods. An unspoken agreement seems to exist: I won't visit your class, if you won't come to mine.

Moreover, teachers do not customarily discuss their instruction with colleagues. They do not talk about such as lesson plans, tips for good instruction, special activities, and particular problems they are having. When teachers meet in the cafeteria or lounge, they discuss disciplinary problems, extracurricular activities of the school, teacher-welfare concerns, the weather, and current events. Only rarely does talk turn to lesson content or pedagogical practices that teachers are using. It violates the norms of most schools for a teacher to ask another for a favorite lesson, and he does not offer suggestions to colleagues on how they might teach better. Teaching is a private affair. And from all appearances teachers like it that way.

Don't smile until Christmas. The last thing that most social studies teachers in secondary schools talk about is the essence of social studies. Questions about whether the "structure of the disciplines" or "inquiry into persistent problems of mankind" should form the core of social studies seem pale in comparison with very real problems such as: How do I interest 150 students a day in a course in American history that they are required to take and most hate? How do I breathe life into a textbook that is dry as dust? How do I make a class interesting and lively without losing control of it? How do I teach the same lesson five straight hours without losing my voice or going insane? How do I organize my class so that I don't bore the best students or pitch the course at such a level that the lower third is completely lost? How do I make the course useful for those who are planning to attend college and relevant to those who will quit school when they reach age 16?

These are the questions that plague most young teachers. It is interesting that the first advice a beginning teacher receives from his principal and colleagues usually has little to do with the content of his subject or with pedagogy. Apparently they assume that his college professors have handled these issues. The advice the new teacher receives is directed toward classroom control, and it frequently consists of such slogans as: (1) "You have a choice. You can have the students' friendship or respect. Choose respect, and you can make friends later." (2) "Start tough and relax the controls later." (3) "Let them know at the beginning that you're the boss." (4) "Don't smile until Christmas."

Thus, our hypothetical world history teacher, John, who was concerned about whether he knew enough world history, finds upon arrival at his first job that his substantive background is not the primary concern of his principal and colleagues. They worry more about whether he can "control" the class. Subtly John will be made to realize that his tenure in that school depends more on his ability to discipline the students than on his capacity as an historian.

Yes, "anyone can teach social studies—*poorly*." But to teach social studies well requires sensitivity, a capacity for hard work, a keen mind, and maturity. This book can contribute very little to the development of these qualities. But those who have them also require certain knowledge and skills to become outstanding social studies teachers. That knowledge and those skills are what this book is all about.

STUDENT CULTURE

Teen-agers constitute a remarkable subgroup in American society, one perhaps unique in human history. It is a group with its own symbols, language, values, status system, interests, and activities. Children must move through this adolescent society before they emerge to accept roles as adults. The culture of American teen-agers is not only influenced by the total American society but in turn influences the total society as witnessed, for example, by teen styles in dress, music, and movies.

American teen-agers are unique in other ways. As a group they are remarkably affluent and incredibly sophisticated. They are more worldly-wise than were their parents at the same age. Yet, as a group, they have little responsibility for the major decisions that affect them. They are subject to the demands of adults—parents, teachers, policemen. They are people who are being "prepared" by adults for something other than what they are now. And the institution that has the primary responsibility for their preparation is the school.

Those who have studied the American high school have given us a vivid description of its peer culture. While there are differences among schools, it is clear that the things students value are not the same objects officially sanctioned by the schools. For example, a decade ago Coleman found that the most admired boys tended to be the best athletes and that the most admired girls tended to be those most active in extracurricular activities and those most sought after for dates, rather than the best students. Nevertheless, Coleman found some differences among the high schools he studied regarding the bases of status in the peer culture.[9]

Some new factors have probably appeared since Coleman's study. There seem to be regional differences in adolescent peer culture; politicization of the peer culture seems to be more advanced in far western and northeastern high schools than in midwestern and southern high schools. Moreover, changes seem to have occurred within schools. Today, black youths frequently acquire status as leaders of black militant causes, and many intellectual white boys clearly are admired by girls who share their political beliefs. It appears also that the role of girls in the peer culture of some high schools is changing. No longer are some content to stand on the sidelines and cheer for male athletes. Increasingly, they have become coleaders of political movements, along with boys. Whether the leading group of a given high school gains status through athletics, dating, automobiles, or political activity, the fact remains that the sources of prestige among adolescents bear little relationship to the official norms and values of the school. The "teacher's pet" rarely is the most influential among his peers.

While they are at school, students are subject to a network of rules and regulations over which, in the past, they have had little control. Students are not permitted to choose the school they wish to attend; they are required to attend school by law. They have little control over how they will spend their six- to seven-hour day and a limited choice in deciding who will teach them and what they will study.

Students are regimented through a school day with little or no free time of their own. At many schools the outer doors are not unlocked until a few minutes before classes begin each morning; they are locked again shortly after school closes in the afternoon and students have left the building. Once they are admitted to the building, they are kept under close surveillance.

Throughout the day students move from one class to another according to a schedule planned by the administration. Little time is allowed for passing between classes. During such times teachers are expected to be in the hallways to make certain the flow of students is continuous. A bell rings, signaling the start of a new period, and each student must be in his seat. Those who are late to school are sent to the principal's office to secure written permission to enter or are punished by being made to remain after school.

When lunch time arrives, students are sent to the cafeteria according to their class schedule. They cannot eat lunch when they wish. They seldom have any control over the menu but must stand in line, pay their money, and eat whatever the school has decided to prepare. If they do not like the food, they may bring their own lunch. The lunch hour is short, often only thirty minutes. By intention this is just enough time to allow students to stand in the cafeteria line, eat, and return to their classrooms.

Throughout the day the movement of students is carefully controlled. If a student leaves a class, he must have the permission of his teacher and a signed pass providing details about where he originates, where he is going, what time he left, and the reason for his trip—even if it is only to the drinking fountain. A student apprehended without a pass is treated much as a citizen in an alien country without a passport. To check on passes, to prevent vandalism, and to enforce school rules, some schools have established squads of senior boys and girls to act as agents for the administration. In return for special privileges they sit at the ends of corridors, acting as checkpoints, or they roam the corridors, rest rooms, and parking lots, searching for student offenders.

Violations of rules can result in various forms of punishment: a lecture by a teacher or an administrator, forced confinement of from fifteen minutes to an hour after school, deprivation of something a student values such as his right to drive a car to school, or paddling.*

But it is not the system of punishment that is the principal mechanism of control in the school; it is mainly the system of bribes and rewards. While every society depends on such a system, it is worth examining that used by the school. One of the bribes involves the program of extracurricular activities, planned and supervised by adults. As noted earlier, student values toward school are much more oriented to extracurricular activities than to the school's central purpose. The school subtly uses these activities as a device to control the student body. For example, athletics not only serve as a harmless outlet for releasing tensions but also contribute a constructive influence for the entire school program. The student government is encouraged to develop codes on student conduct, dress, and hair style. Administrators know that they facilitate control, and it is easier to legitimate the punishment of students if the code has been written by them.

But the system of grades is the principal control device. In order to gain permission to participate in varsity athletics, to be a cheerleader, or to run for class office, students must maintain "eligibility." Some are bribed into doing assignments in which they have no interest because the teacher has the authority to deprive them of something they want. Moreover, grades rarely depend upon objective measures of knowledge and skill alone. Students are also evaluated on such criteria as "participation in class discussion," "attitudes toward work," "citizenship," and attendance and punctuality. In this manner students are subject to subtle but powerful pressure to behave in a manner acceptable to teachers.

To whom can a student complain if his teacher is incompetent, unfair, lazy, or a racist? There is no ombudsman to intervene on his behalf with the bureaucracy. Counselors are really agents for administrators, despite the professional ideology of counseling.

A student must either accommodate himself to the situation, or he can rebel—silently, by dropping out of school or by turning in poor work, or overtly, by setting fire to trash cans and triggering fire alarms. Nor is "due process" available to students. When they are accused by teachers of violations of school rules, they already stand convicted. There is no presumption of

---

*It is interesting to compare each of these punishments with the kinds of treatment an adult citizen might expect from a court of law: a lecture by a judge to a motorist charged with speeding, a sentence of thirty days in jail, a $100 fine, or flogging—a punishment rarely used today as it is viewed as being unusually cruel and inhuman.

FIGURE 1.4.

A student accommodates himself to the situation.

innocence until evidence is heard. No witnesses are called; little opportunity
is afforded the student to defend himself. The administration and the teaching
faculty of a school form a united front to maintain control, and a principal,
even when he suspects the teacher is wrong, is more likely to take the side
of the teacher than the student in order to maintain "teacher morale."

In short, the official structure of the school is primarily an authoritarian
bureaucracy that attempts to shape students according to adult expectations.
Whether the system influences the behavior of the teachers or whether the
system attracts certain types of individuals to teaching is unclear, but one
study after another has shown that high school teachers as a group have a

great need for respect and authority.[10] Thus, the first official social institution, after his own family, that an adolescent must cope with on an extended basis is one that is structured along authoritarian, bureaucratic lines.

Schools Can't Be Democracies*

A writer in Saturday Review *laments that high schools are undemocratic and observes that they deprive students of such constitutional rights as free speech and due process of law.*

Of course they do. And how can it be otherwise if the schools are to maintain order and carry out their assigned mission?

Given full constitutional protection at school, a student could stand up and interrupt the class with impunity, publish the school paper without adult interference, carry weapons, and demand a trial in a court of law if deprived of 15 minutes of his liberty after school from making a nuisance of himself.

Thus, upon a minute's reflection, one realizes that it's absurd to talk about full constitutional protection at high school. High school is not and cannot be a miniature democracy.

When school administrators clearly stray beyond their proper domain in applying discipline, they obviously should be brought up short—and usually are. But the hard fact remains that the public school is, by public consent and necessity, a benign dictatorship.

But it does not follow that all students are miserable at school. Quite the opposite! In fact, for most students it is a pleasant place to be, especially for a member of the leading clique in school. In exchange for accommodating himself to the school ritual and accepting authority without complaint, an adolescent is free to pursue the extracurricular activities through which he wins prestige and status with his peers. The school on the other hand gains order, reasonable, if sometimes minimal, academic performance, and a successful extracurricular program.

Moreover, students have ways to keep teachers' expectations at a tolerable level. What occurs in a typical classroom is similar to what occurs on a prison farm or on the assembly line of a factory.

"Don't you know we don't have to learn anything from you unless we want to?"—Comment to a high school administrator as reported by Ronald Lippitt

---

Guest editorial, Bloomington Herald-Telephone, June 29, 1971. Reprinted from Detroit News.

Just as prisoners sent out to clear roadside ditches frequently do as little as possible and industrial workers sometimes use group pressure to make certain that ambitious workers do not exceed quotas, so students often struggle with teachers to secure a reduced workload. Sometimes the conspiracy is raised to the conscious level and is planned; more often it is unspoken but understood.

Most experienced teachers silently participate in the conspiracy by adjusting the workload to the kinds of students enrolled in a course. Often, at the beginning of the year, a teacher seeks to influence the contest by announcing that his course is very difficult and that he expects students to work hard. Neither the teacher nor the students take such rhetoric seriously. As teachers cannot fail all the students, they strive to find a point at which most students can pass, and in the process the teachers lower their standards. This practice is most apparent in the ghetto schools where conflicts between students and teachers have been the greatest and where teachers expect very little and pass students to the next grade although they have failed to achieve the minimum standards of the grade they are in.

What does all this have to do with teaching social studies and with the role of the social studies teacher? There are many implications. First, it is unlikely that a majority of students, given complete freedom of choice, would choose to take the typical social studies course at all. Most students arrive at the class under partial duress. The teacher must either attract their interest or look forward to an uncomfortable year. Second, many students believe social studies lack "relevance." Not only do many courses fail to speak to social issues that students deem important, but few students see any relationship between what they are doing and what they are studying. Nevertheless, all sorts of linkages are possible for a good teacher. He can take advantage of the students' society and culture to teach concepts, such as role, culture, status, and leadership, and theories of decision-making and conflict resolution. In doing so he not only is teaching adolescents ideas that might prove useful when they become adults but may also help to explain their present behavior. Third, a social studies teacher should know that the school system itself acts as a "social studies teacher" and that there may be a gap between what is being taught in the classroom, for example, about the rights and responsibilities of citizens, and what the student experiences in school. Thus, the wise teacher takes into account the social instruction students are gaining from the school as a social system and adjusts his classroom instruction accordingly. Fourth, students are not only preparing *to become* something, they *are* something. They are involved actively in a society and culture that impinges on and is part of, but not identical with, adult society and culture. A wise social studies teacher must understand and respect adolescent culture, avoid threatening it, and when possible take advantage of it for instructional purposes, while simultaneously maintaining the respect of his colleagues and school administrators.

The "New Social Studies"

At this point in the chapter, you might be excused if you ask: "Why should anyone want to become a social studies teacher? The leaders in the field seem confused about the purposes of social studies, the institutional demands on the teacher's role seem designed to sap energy and discourage creativity, and the pressures to satisfy contending groups lead to inevitable tension and frustration. And the salary and community status anyone can expect to achieve as a teacher seem less than is deserved following four or more years of college education. Why should anyone bother to teach?"

Our purpose in providing a realistic glimpse of the status of traditional social studies instruction and the role of the social studies teacher in a traditional school has not been aimed at discouraging people from becoming social studies teachers. Rather, we had two purposes in mind. First of all, it is unfair and essentially dishonest to treat the social studies as anything other than what it is, or at least has been until recently. Many teachers will continue to teach social studies under less than optimum conditions. They should know what they may be in for. But second, and more important, social studies is changing. To appreciate the changes, it is necessary to understand what it has been. Probably, there has never been a more exciting time to be a social studies teacher. The legitimacy of traditional ways of thinking about social studies has been successfully undermined by pressures from society and by leadership from within the profession.

Today, social studies is in a state of flux, and teachers who enter the profession now have greater opportunities to determine its future than any prior groups. The inflexible, lazy, and insensitive should be discouraged from entering the profession because the times require those with energy, intelligence, sensitivity, and a commitment to scholarship. Those who possess these latter qualities will find the challenges and excitement of teaching social studies in the future sufficient to satisfy many, if not most, of their professional needs.

The social studies began to experience fundamental change more than a decade ago, but the reform has only recently begun to affect a majority of high schools. This reform, often referred to as the "new social studies," began in the late 1950s as an effort to strengthen the academic content of social studies courses. The effort was parallel to similar efforts in science, mathematics, foreign languages, and English. At first, emphasis was given to providing college-level courses in history and the social sciences for academically talented high school students. As a result various kinds of "advanced placement" courses were launched which enabled students to earn college credit while in high school.

In the early stages of the new social studies, effort focused on making the traditional courses, such as American history and European history, more "respectable," that is, more like their college-level counterparts. Later the emphasis shifted toward efforts to undermine the traditional social studies curriculum by creating attractive alternatives to the traditional courses and by developing materials that could be included within the traditional courses while altering their purposes and perspectives.

The effort to undermine the existing social studies curriculum was led by curriculum-development projects, usually sponsored by professional associations or universities, with generous support from private foundations and the federal government. The projects shared similar characteristics. First, they tried to weld "content" and "pedagogy" together in ways that had not been attempted before. Leaders in the various disciplines were recruited to write curriculum materials so that the lessons for students would reflect modern scholarship. The authorities on content were joined on the projects by experts in pedagogy as well as by practicing high school teachers in order to ensure that the materials could be taught successfully and in an exciting way to adolescents.

A second characteristic of the projects was a deliberate effort to deviate from the past. Unlike textbook publishers who in order to make a profit must seek out the largest possible markets and strike at the center of what currently exists, the projects did not depend upon profits for their existence. They saw their role to be one of *changing* what schools were doing rather than of supporting present practices.

Third, the projects tested their materials in schools. The result was not only the development of superior materials but also the wide-scale dissemination of new instructional materials and procedures. Soon teachers not associated with the projects began to design individual lessons based on project ideas.

The special curriculum-development projects also helped stimulate changes in the pre-service and in-service training of teachers. While many teacher trainers had been advocating ideas similar to those represented by the special projects before they were established, the projects heightened the demand for teachers who were prepared to teach new course content using the latest techniques. To further accelerate reforms in teacher education, first the foundations and later the federal government supported a large number of teacher-training programs designed to acquaint teachers with new methods, content, and instructional materials.

During the last fifteen years the new social studies has continued to evolve. It began as an effort to strengthen traditional high school courses for academic elites. Its emphasis shifted to include subject matter not previously incorporated in traditional courses, and it moved to widen its impact so that all students would be served by the new instruction. It has changed from a primary emphasis on single disciplines to an increasing tendency to become multidisciplinary in its approach. The new social studies has shifted from an almost total reliance on efforts to strengthen the cognitive aspects of instruction to an increasing recognition of the affective components of the social studies. It has moved from an emphasis on year-long or semester-long sequential courses to a greater dependence on shorter, more flexible modules of instruction which teachers can string together according to their own goals or student demands. And the new social studies is changing from programs that operate with boundaries set by classroom walls to programs that extend beyond the school to include the entire community.

Some educators describe the new social studies as if it were a *thing*, a course, a project, or a new method. But it is a reform movement whose ultimate destination is unclear. What seems certain is that the traditional social studies curriculum has been effectively undermined—not everywhere because the new social studies has not yet affected all teachers and all schools. But relentlessly the reform continues, with new programs leading to mutations and to additional new programs. No longer is it completely hierarchical. While special projects and centers continue to test ideas, an increasing fraction of the leadership for new instructional ideas has shifted to teachers in the schools. The result has been an expansion of alternatives and an acceleration of change.

Summary

We began this chapter with the questions "what is the social studies?" and "what is the role of the social studies teacher?" Most of this chapter treated the social studies and the role of the teacher as they have been. The last section dealt briefly with what social studies is becoming.

This book is designed for teachers who are members of the "new social studies" generation. Throughout the book sample lessons from projects in the new social studies are used as examples of good lessons. Pedagogical skills that are necessary to be a successful teacher of the new social studies are emphasized throughout.

This book is not a substitute for courses in history and social science. Nor can it substitute for formal instruction in professional education and for internship experience in high school. It can help teachers to think about the instruction they have received, to use their training creatively, and to develop effective and interesting ways to instruct high school youth in social studies.

APPLICATION 1.1: THE HOT LINE

Following is a newspaper item relating to a particular school issue. Suppose you were a world history teacher at a nearby high school. One of your students gave you the clipping and asked whether it could be discussed in class. Would you set aside time to discuss the clipping? If so, why? If not, why not? Refer to the positions taken by the four students, Lee Smith, and the college specialists in social studies in defending your response.

HOT LINE[11]

QUESTION: My daughter attends Edgewood High School where she is on the gymnastic team. Last Monday the principal of the school announced a change in the dress code, and girls can now wear slacks to school.

But my daughter has been told that because she is in an extracurricular activity, she could not wear slacks; that none of the girls on the gymnastic team could nor could the cheerleaders.

I have called the school and the superintendent, and talked to everyone I could to see why this is, but they just say these girls can't wear them because they want them to set an example for the school.

It seems to me the girls involved in sporting activities should be the ones able to wear the slacks most of all. Can HOT LINE help? My daughter wants to wear slacks to school.
Mrs. R. R., Ellettsville

ANSWER: HOT LINE contacted the principal of the school, Thomas McConnell. He said the girls would not be able to wear slacks because coaches had set down the rule at the beginning of the season and the original rule applied to the entire season.

McConnell said while other students operate on a semester basis and the new dress code will start at the beginning of the second semester, Jan. 25, those students involved in extracurricular events must see out their season before the rule can apply to them.

He said they would be able to wear slacks next year. But the original rule still holds as set down at the beginning of this year. McConnell said, "It's my decision, and I'll stand behind it."

The athletic director at the school, Willard Cazell, said he had nothing to add to the principal's statement since it was his decision.

However, he did say, "They are representing the school. We like for them to present the best image possible at all times."

APPLICATION 1.2: METRO UNIVERSITY PLACEMENT SERVICE

Suppose the placement office of your college gave you the following information about an available position.

1. *Job Description*: Secondary school social studies teacher
2. *School Location*: Slavsky School Corporation, Slavsky High School (1,800 students), Slavsky, North Dakota
3. *Salary*: $6,800.00
4. *Educational Requirements*: Minimum requirement, B.S. or B.A. degree from accredited university. Experience and master's degree desired, but not necessary.
5. *Position Available*: A secondary school social studies teacher is needed to fill a vacancy at Slavsky High School. The applicant must be prepared to teach three courses in eleventh-grade American history and two courses in twelfth-grade government. The average class size is 35 students. In addition, the candidate must be able to coach debate or to sponsor the yearbook.
6. *Course Description*:
    a. Eleventh-grade American history course: The textbook for this course is *Land of the Free*. The teacher will be expected to cover the period from the founding of the Republic through World War II.
    b. Twelfth-grade American government course: The textbook for this course is *Structure and Institutions of American Government*. The course treats local, state, and national government. Particular attention is given to a study of the U.S. Constitution.

7. *Social Studies Curriculum Organization*:
   Grade
     7 Geography*
     8 American history*
     9 Civics
   10 World history*
   11 American history*
   12 American government (one semester)*
        Economics (one semester)
        Sociology (one semester)

You have applied for the job and have been invited for an interview. Whom would you want to talk to in the Slavsky School Corporation and what kind of questions would you want to ask?

Notes

1. *Life* 66, no. 19 (May 16, 1969) :31.
2. Grace S. Wright, *Summary of Offerings and Enrollments in High School Subjects, 1960–61*, Washington, D.C.: Department of Health, Education, and Welfare, 1964, p. 5.
3. Grace S. Wright, *Subject Offerings and Enrollments in Public Secondary Schools*, Washington, D.C.: Department of Health, Education, and Welfare, 1965, p. 100.
4. Ibid., p. 99.
5. Richard S. Miller, *Teaching about Communism*, New York: McGraw-Hill Book Company, 1966, p. 268.
6. William E. Wilson, *The Administrative Handbook for Indiana Schools*, Indiana Department of Public Instruction Bulletin no. 225, Indianapolis, 1961, p. 229.
7. In 1971 Richard Remy conducted a study of 1,369 high school seniors. One question was: "Courses seem to vary in terms of how much new knowledge students learn from them. Listed below are some courses commonly taught in high school. For each course you have taken (or are now taking) indicate how much new knowledge you learned. (New knowledge means knowledge you had not learned before in other courses or from other sources such as parents, TV, or books and articles you had read on your own.)

---

*These are required courses.

The results were as follows, stated in terms of percent of students who claimed course provided "almost everything I learned new."

Science courses	77%
Mathematics courses	72%
Literature courses	50%
World history courses	30%
Civics and government courses	27%
U.S. history courses	16%

Richard C. Remy, "High School Seniors' Attitudes toward Their Civics and Government Instruction," *Social Education*, vol. 36, no. 6 (October, 1972), p. 594.

8. National Council for the Social Studies, "A Guide to Content in the Social Studies," in *Crucial Issues in the Teaching of Social Studies*, ed. by Byron G. Massialas and Andreas M. Kazamias, Englewood Cliffs, N.J.: Prentice-Hall, 1964, p. 20.

9. James Coleman, *The Adolescent Society: The Social Life of the Teenager and Its Impact on Education*, New York: The Free Press, 1961.

10. See, for example, Harmon Zeigler, *The Political Life of American Teachers*, Englewood Cliffs, N.J.: Prentice-Hall, 1967.

11. *Herald-Telephone* (Bloomington, Ind.), January 19, 1971.

Suggested Reading

Danforth Foundation. *The School and the Democratic Environment.* New York: Columbia University Press, 1970. This book is a collection of papers prepared for a 1969 conference, held in Washington, D.C., under the same title as the book. The conference, convened under the auspices of the Ford and Danforth foundations, considered such issues as how schools were governed and the effects present patterns of school governance had on the social education of youth.

Engle, Shirley, and Wilma S. Longstreet. *A Design for Social Education in the Open Curriculum.* New York: Harper & Row, 1972. In this book the authors argue that changes under way in American society require that social studies education concentrate on helping students interpret changing situations and complex social data. They do not believe that basing the social studies curriculum on the disciplines is sufficient. Rather, they favor a topical approach for organizing instruction.

Hunt, Maurice P., and Lawrence E. Metcalf. *Teaching High School Social Studies: Problems in Reflective Thinking and Social Understanding*, 2d ed. New York: Harper & Row, 1968. This book, first published in 1955, has influenced the beliefs of many educators regarding the purposes of social studies education. The authors argue that social studies should be a reflective study of major cultural problems facing the society. The book presents the authors' philosophy toward the teaching of social studies and suggests how this philosophy might be practiced in the classroom.

Shaver, James P., and Harold Berlak. *Democracy, Pluralism, and the Social Studies: Readings and Commentary.* Boston: Houghton Mifflin, 1968. This book contains articles by authors representing a variety of perspectives. Taken together they contribute to the understanding of many of the issues that plague social studies instruction today.

Smith, Frederick R., and C. Benjamin Cox. *New Strategies and Curriculum in Social Studies.* Chicago: Rand McNally, 1969. This book summarizes many of the developments of the 1960s that fall under the label "new social studies." The authors probe many of the assumptions of the reform movement and treat briefly a number of the projects that produced new kinds of social studies instructional materials.

2

Thinking about Teaching

ON THE BASIS of information presented in Chapter 1, it should be clear that there is no consensus regarding the content and central purposes of the social studies. As compared with teachers in other subject fields, social studies teachers can choose among a variety of paths and can find one or more authorities to approve their decisions. Whether the variety of legitimate choices has weakened or strengthened the social studies field overall is debatable. What is not debatable is that the choices are significant.

Often teachers wish to postpone thinking about the assumptions that underlie their behavior as social studies teachers. They tend to be occupied by more practical problems such as: How do I maintain control of the class? How can I teach in an interesting way? How will I decide on grades for students? The more philosophical issues that surround teaching seem too abstract to be useful.

Failing to come to grips with underlying assumptions, however, has important implications for the teacher and for his students. There is no way to avoid adopting a particular philosophical view toward teaching; those who deliberately and consciously do not consider underlying assumptions will find that they are unconsciously acting upon assimilated beliefs. Once the teacher begins to feel comfortable with a particular posture or attitude toward teaching, it is very difficult for him to examine his views critically and to change his approach to instruction. This suggests that a teacher should devote some attention during his training to a consideration of the alternative roles available to him in order that important decisions about the kind of teacher he will be are made consciously and not by default.

This book has a point of view about social studies and about the role of the social studies teacher. It will not treat equally the range of options available to teachers. Rather, in a systematic way, it attempts to contribute to the preparation of teachers who can be successful according to our criteria. The intent of Chapter 2 is to establish for you what we believe to be the major purposes of social studies instruction and the most appropriate role for a social studies teacher. Subsequent chapters provide detailed information regarding how these purposes can be met and the role satisfied.

Five Assumptions about Teaching Social Studies

USEFUL KNOWLEDGE
Schools are structured social settings, designed to facilitate learning. They are supported by the public through taxes or tuition because the public believes that schools enable youth to acquire useful knowledge.[1]

It is true that schools also serve other functions for the community. They may act as cheap day-care centers, enabling parents to escape parental responsibilities for a few hours while the school keeps their children off the street and out of court. Schools, especially those in small communities, can become entertainment centers, providing choruses, bands, plays, and sports spectaculars. Schools may serve as mental health centers as teachers are thrust into therapy roles, attempting to provide some children with the love, affection, and attention that most children receive from other adults and peers. Although these functions are important, such extra responsibilities can distract teachers from their primary duties. A few relish the custodial role and behave as if they were guards in a reform school; others like the therapist role; and some teacher-coaches prefer the visibility acquired through coaching varsity sports to the less acclaimed responsibilities of successful classroom teaching. But all these functions are secondary to the primary mission of the schools: instruction for useful knowledge.

What is "useful knowledge"? Certainly, knowledge means more than information. Teachers can dispense information to students without making any assumptions about the acquisition of knowledge, useful or otherwise. Information is necessary but not sufficient for knowledge—knowledge depends on the capacity of the learner to organize and take advantage of information. It implies a cognitive structure that enables the learner to process and mobilize information efficiently.

Knowledge is "useful" if it satisfies personal and social goals for the learner. A major responsibility for the social studies teacher is to make judgments about useful knowledge, to plan instruction that is likely to have value for the learner.

PART OF THE GENERAL EDUCATION PROGRAM

Social studies is part of the general education program of schools. Social studies is neither professional education, such as a graduate school seminar in history, nor vocational education, such as a course in automobile mechanics. As one or more social studies courses are required of all students in secondary schools, social studies presumably has appropriate content for everyone, regardless of career goals.

Typically, social studies teachers have difficulty with this issue because their most recent models—college historians and social scientists—frequently see their roles as providing either for the general education of elites or for the professional education of those engaged in career training. Thus, a first task of teachers is to consider thoughtfully how what they have learned can be made useful to the purposes of general education.

That social studies is primarily general education is made clear by the fact that educators in the field typically define social studies and defend it in terms of "education for citizenship," a role available to all Americans. Thus a common way of stating its overall purpose is: Social studies should prepare youth to live responsible, productive lives as adult citizens.

Few social studies teachers bother to argue with the above statement. The problem is that it is so broad in scope and so elastic in meaning that it can accommodate a wide variety of instructional theories and practices, some of which are contradictory and incompatible. For example, one teacher may instruct in a supernationalistic and chauvinistic way while defending his instruction on the basis that all Americans should be informed about "the traditions that made this country what it is." Another teacher systematically requires students to test statements of American purpose and ideals against actual performances by the government. He argues that his instruction prepares students to be critical thinkers and that democracy cannot survive unless it has adults who are so equipped. Despite the inherent possibilities for disparate interpretations, the concept of citizenship education carries with it the argument that social studies is for everyone.

MORE THAN THE COURSES

The opportunities for social learning are not limited to formal courses in the social studies. One problem with the formulation of citizenship education is that it provides little guidance for the social studies teacher regarding his unique contribution to the education of citizens because he clearly has no monopoly on it. Within the school many subjects and extracurricular activities contribute to helping prepare youth "to live responsible, productive lives as adult citizens." Outside the school, parents, churches, mass media, Boy Scouts, teen-age gangs, and many others help shape attitudes, values, and beliefs of high school youth. Students do not appear in a social studies teacher's class as blank slates on which a teacher can chalk the fundamentals of citizenship education. A more appropriate image is to conceive students to be dynamic human organisms, possessing many beliefs based on prior experience and on formal or informal instruction. These beliefs may be scattered across continuums ranging from simple to complex, from valid to invalid, and from barely understood to deeply held. And students are not alike. In a class of thirty students, a teacher is faced with thirty similar but nonetheless different belief systems.

In some ways teachers are less powerful and less convincing agents of social learning than are others in society. Both parents and peers are more likely to shape attitudes than are high school teachers, and the mass media are viewed as more accurate, comprehensive, and up-to-date sources of information than are social studies teachers. Thus, the social studies teacher must carefully decide how he will spend his energies so that they are most likely to count.

Lest the teacher appear too weak and destined for frustration and a sense of futility, we hasten to add that he can function powerfully in ways that will affect youth, ways that are not available to any other agency in the society. The social studies classroom can be a setting where ideas are tested without fear of sanction, where prejudices can be explored without fear of ridicule, and where students can try on new roles, new beliefs, new concepts of reality, without having to become totally committed to them and without having to defend them before they are accepted. A social studies classroom can be a "cool" setting for social learning as compared to the "hot" environments outside the classroom where commitments are demanded. Parents rarely expect sons and daughters to reflect on the values they, the parents, wish to impose; they want compliance. So do peer groups and churches, among others. The mass media features headlines and the latest data. Rarely do they afford an opportunity to reflect on what the events mean, what the trends in society are, whether the trends are good or bad for society as a whole. Equally important, most socializing agents must assume the lowest common denominator of comprehension. The mass media must be understandable to the literate mass. Even public officials must inform at the level that ordinary citizens can grasp.

Unfortunately, one of the reasons that social studies is respected less than it deserves is that teachers often fail to understand the unique contribution they can make to the social education of youth. When they become "reporters," they are pale in comparison with the mass media. When they are preachers of values, they are less convincing than those who have greater authority over students' lives. When their capacity to interpret events is no more sophisticated or powerful than any educated layman, they confirm the oft-quoted administrative axiom: Anyone can teach social studies. The fact that anyone could teach social studies as well as it is frequently taught should challenge all social studies teachers to think hard about what they can do in their classrooms that requires professional skill and that would make them irreplaceable.

IMPROVEMENT THROUGH LIMITED GOALS
Social studies instruction can be improved if limited goals are pursued consciously in a systematic manner. A criticism that could be made of many social studies teachers is that they seem adrift, lacking sail, rudder, anchor,

even a sense of direction. Even an oarsman can make progress, if he knows where he is rowing. But too many teachers seem unsure of what they are about. They drift through textbooks without being certain about what is most important for students to remember or why they should know it. They arrive at class, eager to be distracted from the lesson by students who suggest more interesting topics for discussion. Such teachers view each class hour as something "to get through" rather than as a period in which they have the opportunity to provide students with important knowledge and intellectual skills.

Social studies is rarely criticized because the courses are too demanding. Students believe they learn more in the sciences, mathematics, and in English. A particular social studies course may be judged "hard" because the teacher requires his students to recall great detail for examinations without providing them with any structure for linking and utilizing the data which would facilitate recall. But social studies courses are more typically judged "easy" because those who are verbally facile find little to challenge them.

Chapter 3 treats in detail the topic of goals and objectives. At this point it is necessary only to stress that until social studies teachers begin to identify some important goals they wish to achieve with their students—goals the students are unlikely to achieve in other ways—and begin to pursue these goals in a systematic way, social studies is likely to remain a much-maligned part of the high school curriculum.

OVERALL PURPOSE

The overall purpose of formal instruction in the social studies is to help students increase the number of meanings they derive from their social environment and to equip them to judge the validity of their meanings according to widely accepted canons of a scientific culture.[2] A person who has taken part in a good social studies program should perceive more in what is happening about him, and his explanations of why things are happening as they are should be more closely linked to modern scholarly views than those of others who have not had the advantage of excellent social studies instruction.

Two of us have developed an alternative approach to high school courses in civics and government. The title of this year-long program is "American Political Behavior." Throughout the program we teach students a number of the basic concepts that social scientists have found useful in studying how and why Americans behave politically as they do.

Political socialization is one concept that receives treatment in the program. It represents the process by which people learn their political attitudes, values, and beliefs. We assumed that if students acquired this concept, among others, they would begin to interpret common experiences in new ways; they would see new meaning in everyday situations.

A parent of a ninth-grade youngster enrolled in American Political Behavior reported the following incident to us which suggested that the program was working as intended. The father had taken his daughter to a junior high basketball game. Before the game the band played the national anthem. Everyone stood at attention until the band finished. While the band was playing, the daughter poked a friend standing next to her and asked, "Do you know why we are standing?" Her friend said, "No." The daughter replied, "Political socialization!"

The point of the story is that for the first time the girl had noticed that everyone was behaving in the same manner to the same musical notes. The concept political socialization learned in class seemed to fit the situation, and from the experience she derived meaning unnoticed by the rest of the people in the gym. Not only did she "see" something that others had not noticed, but she interpreted the experience in a way that would seem reasonable to a large number of social scientists.

High school students gain a social education whether or not they enroll in social studies courses. The major task for social studies teachers is to provide instruction that makes apparent the difference between those who have taken the courses and those who have not. The essential difference between an "educated" and an "uneducated" person in any society is that the former sees more meanings and is able to ground them in the accepted standards for belief in his society. In the context of social studies this means that students must learn social science concepts that have proved useful in teasing great meaning from human events and that they should acquire systematic ways of testing their ideas according to principles of modern social science.

It is important to note that there are many ways of "knowing" and many kinds of "truth." Folk tales, religion, aesthetics, all make contributions to our capacity to understand the human condition. And we do not claim that social science has the truth, while all other systems of thought are reduced to providing myths and falsehoods. We do insist that the social sciences have developed some special ways of knowing which are unlikely to reach students without formal instruction in social studies. Many other ways of knowing are provided informally by different groups in the society or by teachers of other subjects.

Saying that students need help to measure the "validity" of their knowing according to canons of modern social science is simply recognition that our society has become increasingly dominated by a scientific culture. American students who are unable to operate within the tenets of a scientific culture are deprived in the same sense that a child growing up in a traditional society and uninformed about its folklore is disadvantaged.

A persistent problem in public education is to provide equal opportunities for learning useful knowledge. If only those students who attend colleges or universities have opportunities to acquire the tools for social scientific ways of thinking, they gain advantages over those whose formal education ended with a high school diploma. Or if social science courses are limited to affluent suburban high schools or "academic tracks" in comprehensive schools, many youths will be deprived of the advantages the social sciences offer. Not only may this affect an individual's opportunity to pursue an intellectually satisfying life, it may also contribute to divisions within the society itself, as one group of people will possess perceptions that give it greater insight into and control over events than is available to others.

In a democracy schools are obligated to share knowledge as equitably as possible. This is necessary to ensure equality of opportunity; it is also basic if citizens are to be able to accept and promote enlightened public policies. Obviously an instructional program that challenges deeply held beliefs or that enables children to derive greater meaning from events than their parents can appear—in fact, *is*—threatening. Teachers should expect to encounter opposition as well as praise for their effort to provide useful instruction about society. But good teachers can do no less than this.

What Is the Best Way to Teach?

Probably more educational research has been devoted to discovering the "best" way to teach than to any other purpose. The results of all this research are disappointing; there is no unequivocally best approach for all purposes. Some approaches may be preferred for learning skills while others may be best for acquiring concepts. The fact that there is no simple teaching formula that will resolve all a teacher's problems does not mean, however, that devoting attention to how to teach is useless. Much of the remainder of this book provides suggestions for ways to make your teaching more effective. But, first of all, it is important to have some criteria in mind for judging what good teaching is. Following are five criteria that a teacher ought to consider in judging approaches to instruction.

TO ENABLE THE LEARNER

The approach ought to enable the learner to achieve the instructional objective. Occasionally educators become ideological about teaching procedures. For instance, some would oppose the use of lectures because lecturing to students does not fit their notion of good instruction. Nevertheless, a teacher can defend his approach provided it enables students to meet the instructional objectives. (Chapter 3 will treat the development and evaluation of instructional objectives.)

TO CONTRIBUTE TO THINKING

The approach should contribute to thinking. Perhaps the most telling criticism of typical social studies instruction is that frequently teaching is at the read-recite level. Teachers assign pages from a textbook, ask students to answer questions based on the reading, and then drill them in the correct answers. Cramming for a test is primarily putting to memory for short-term recall specific facts the teacher is expected to ask on the examination. Not only does this lead to boring instruction, but it is inefficient because most of what was "learned" is soon forgotten.

The effort to create a "new social studies" in the 1960s was primarily to re-emphasize *thinking*. "New" kinds of instructional materials and arguments for "new" teaching approaches were directed at overturning mindless rote learning and replacing such practices with instruction that would depend on more sophisticated thought processes.

What does thinking mean? One way to explain thinking is to provide an illustration of a person thinking. The illustration appears in a book by H. Gordon Hullfish and Philip G. Smith entitled *Reflective Thinking: The Method of Education* (Dodd, Mead, 1965). The authors of the book refer to an incident reported in an Arthur Conan Doyle story about Sherlock Holmes. According to this account, Watson in an attempt to test Sherlock Holmes's powers of reasoning said to him:

I have heard you say that it is difficult for a man to have any object in his daily use without leaving the impress of his individuality upon it in such a way that a trained observer might read it. Now, I have here a watch which has recently come into my possession. Would you . . . let me have an opinion upon the character or habits of the late owner?

At this point Watson handed Holmes the watch, and Holmes looked it over very carefully, opened the back of the watch, studied it with a magnifying glass, and otherwise observed it very closely. He then returned the watch to Watson and told him the following:

The watch has been recently cleaned which robs me of my most suggestive facts. . . . I should judge [however] that the watch belonged to your elder brother, who inherited it from your father. . . . [Your brother] was a man of untidy habits—very untidy and careless. He was left with good prospects, but he threw away his chances, lived for some time in poverty, with occasional short intervals of prosperity, and finally, taking to drink, he died.

Watson acknowledged that Holmes was right in all his details, but he was certain that Holmes could not possibly have gathered all this evidence from just looking at the watch. Therefore, Holmes explained his reasoning process as follows:

What seems strange to you is only so because you do not follow my train of thought or observe the small facts upon which large inferences may depend. . . . [The initials H. W. were on the back of the watch.] The W suggests your own name. The date of the watch is nearly fifty years back, and the initials are as old as the watch; so it was made for the last generation. Jewelry usually descends to the eldest son, and he is most likely to have the same name as his father. Your father has, if I remember rightly, been dead many years. It has, therefore, been in the hands of your eldest brother.

Holmes explained his reasoning further by interpreting out loud the dents and marks on the watch case: the habit of keeping his expensive watch in the same pocket with other hard objects like coins or keys indicated a careless man. From the inherited and expensive watch itself Holmes said it was fair to infer that the man must have been well provided for in other ways. Then Holmes pointed out the four pawnbrokers' numbers scratched with a pin point on the inside of the case and visible to a lens; he inferred that Watson's brother was often down and out. His secondary inference from the numbers was that occasionally the man had been prosperous—able to redeem the watch. Finally Holmes explained the hundreds of tiny scratches all around the keyhole on the inner plate, an indication to Holmes that it was a drunkard's watch, wound at night by an unsteady hand.

Few teachers expect to train detectives in their social studies classrooms. Nevertheless, the attention to data, the ability to put forward plausible hypotheses, and the ability to build explanations are characteristic of thoughtful people regardless of career. One important basis for judging teaching procedure is: Does it contribute to students' abilities to think reflectively?

TO SUSTAIN INTEREST

A good teaching approach ought to sustain student interest. Any procedure that satisfies the short-run instructional objective but effectively destroys student interest in the subject cannot be admired. Programmed learning has had to cope with this problem. Acting upon principles of reinforcement learning, it has been demonstrated to be an efficient way to acquire certain kinds of knowledge. Nevertheless, sustained use of programmed booklets over a long period of time may lead to a decline in student interest in the topic, which in turn could lead to a decline in performance.

Some teachers defend their use of lectures on the basis that they prepare students for college. They claim that students will soon be forced to sit in lecture halls and take notes on boring lectures. The students might as well become accustomed to this technique in high school. This is not to argue that lectures should never be used or that they cannot be powerful and interesting ways to learn. But, if lectures are destroying student interest, they cannot be defended as a good teaching technique any more than another instructional practice can be defended on the basis that students like it, but they are learning nothing useful.

TO SUIT THE CIRCUMSTANCES

A good teaching approach should be economical, that is, reasonable—given the teacher's time, energy, and resources. It may be that a tutorial system, featuring one teacher with one student, is the best way to teach, but it is unrealistic. The "best approach" must be evaluated not in terms of some ideal but against the real-life experience of typical teachers: 30 students per hour $\times$ 5 hours a day. Perhaps students should conduct their own investigations in the community and call on the teacher only when they need help, but few teachers will find themselves in school settings that will tolerate such practices except on a short-term basis. Most school libraries are poorly equipped for social science research; teachers have constraints on the time, money, and manpower to create their own instructional materials. Thus, one criterion must be: Is the approach economically viable?

TO SUIT THE INDIVIDUAL TEACHER

A good teaching approach should fit the personality and capacity of the teacher. This is a slippery criterion and difficult to apply. On the one hand it can serve as an excuse for poor instruction. We know one teacher who had the following routine for every week of the year:

Monday: The teacher put the chapter questions on the board; the students read the chapter in class and answered the questions.

Tuesday: The students used the entire period to write answers to the chapter questions.

Wednesday: Class time was used for students to recite and correct answers to the chapter questions.

Thursday: The students took a test on the chapter, and the test was graded in class.

Friday: This was always "current events" day. Students used one-half of the period to read from a student newspaper; during the last half of the period, they discussed the key articles. Sometimes the teacher gave a test on the newspaper to make certain that students read the paper carefully.

What we are faced with is a lazy teacher. He should be fired. There is no reason why students should be forced to accommodate themselves to this kind of instruction.

When instruction is as poor as that described above, it is easy to recognize. Unfortunately, most instruction is not so easily categorized. Some teachers are able to conduct an exciting, open classroom in which ideas are being challenged and tested each day—while he retains a strong leadership role. In other cases, and with similar results, the teacher is nearly indistinguishable from the students. Students are divided into small groups for discussion and investigation purposes and seem to turn to the teacher for advice only when necessary. One teacher is comfortable with the latter approach for organizing instruction. Another is not. Both can be judged successful by the preceding criteria.

Categories for Thinking about Teaching

Thus far we have used the terms *teaching approach* or *teaching procedures* when referring to ways of teaching. It is necessary now to become more specific. Four terms will be used throughout this book in discussions of ways of teaching. These terms are *technique*, *mode*, *strategy*, and *method*.

TECHNIQUE

Technique will be used to describe specific instructional devices employed to teach lessons. Social studies teachers have available a wide variety of techniques. These include 16 mm. films, simulations, classroom games, oral discussion, project activities, textbooks, library study, lectures, role-play exercises, and field trips. Reliance on only one or two techniques usually leads to boring instruction. Good teachers depend on a wide variety of these and other techniques to enhance interest and to facilitate learning.

Two teachers who wish to achieve the same instructional objective may use different techniques. One may assign a topic for written reports by students and provide time in the library for them to prepare their reports. Another teacher may choose to meet the objective by presenting the information himself or by showing a movie. None of these techniques by themselves are clearly superior to the other. Which technique is best depends largely on what the teacher hopes to accomplish, the time and resources available, and the degree to which the technique provides variety in instruction.

MODE

Mode refers to a particular style of instruction adopted by the teacher. An instructional mode uses instructional techniques. A teacher operating in a "discovery mode" will sequence lessons differently than does a teacher who is working in an "expository mode." (Discovery and expository modes are treated at length on pages 125 to 149 in Chapter 4.) In one case the teacher, seeking to start a classroom investigation, organizes the presentation of data so as to provoke student questions and to encourage interest in the problem. Another teacher might present the problem and provide data to show how it can be resolved. The purposes of the teachers are quite different; therefore, the ways in which the lessons are presented are likely to be different. Nevertheless, they may use the same techniques. For example, both teachers might use a slide-tape on the same topic. However, the way the tape is used in class could be very different: one uses the slide-tape to pose problems leading to fruitful inquiry; the second uses the same slide-tape to provide reinforcement for the generalizations presented by the teacher.

It is common for a teacher to operate in various modes at different times, depending on his purposes. As with technique, which mode is best is determined by the teacher's purpose, his resources, and the degree of variety the mode contains.

STRATEGY

Strategy refers to an overall plan developed by a teacher to satisfy his instructional objectives. In planning an instructional strategy, the teacher will use both techniques and modes. A variety of techniques and modes can be orchestrated so as to produce a variety of outcomes and to satisfy student interest.

As an illustration, imagine a teacher who has decided to organize his course in units of content, each approximately three weeks in length. Following some experimentation, he arrives at an instructional strategy that consists of four stages: confrontation, rule-example, application, and value judgment. Each of the units in the course will be developed according to these stages. Each lesson within a unit will be an example of one of the stages and will be linked to preceding and succeeding lessons according to the purposes it serves.

The confrontation stage consists of one or more lessons at the beginning of each unit that are designed to focus attention, to motivate the students, and to cause them to speculate about the topic or problem to be explored in the unit. The rule-example stage provides systematic instruction relating to the unit topic or problem. Students acquire new concepts and skills, and test hypotheses. The application stage is one in which students apply the knowledge acquired in the second stage to fresh situations. And the value-judgment stage enables teachers and students to explore many of the value and ethical issues that surround the unit topic. (See Chapter 8 for a more complete discussion of instructional strategy.)

Throughout each unit the teacher uses many instructional techniques, including games, simulations, programmed lessons, case studies, films, and transparencies for the overhead projector. He also works in different instructional modes, including discovery and expository modes. Both mode and technique are altered frequently to satisfy instructional purposes and to hold student interest. The important issue to note is that a conscious strategy of instruction is built into his course design, a strategy that deliberately manipulates technique and mode for course purposes.

METHOD

Method will be used throughout this book to refer to a particular philosophical position that a teacher adopts toward himself, his subject, and his students. Thus, teaching method is not identical with *technique, mode, or strategy*. It subsumes all of these. A method does not dictate to the teacher which technique he should use (show a film, hold a discussion, give a lecture); nor does it prescribe a particular mode of instruction. Rather, it sets guidelines for the patterns of behavior the teacher expects in his classroom.

We believe that teaching method can be divided into two "ideal" types: *method of authority* and *method of inquiry*. Probably no single social studies teacher consistently practices either method. Rather, these two methods should be viewed as a continuum, and teachers can be found at different points along the continuum as in Figure 2.1. We believe that it is better for a teacher to be like teacher D than like teacher A. Indeed, we believe that the more a teacher practices the method of inquiry, the better social studies teacher he will be.

FIGURE 2.1.
Teachers along the continuum between the method of authority and the method of inquiry.

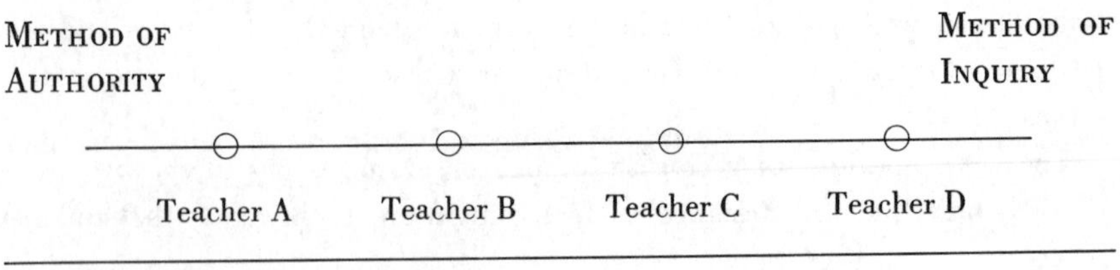

METHOD OF AUTHORITY			METHOD OF INQUIRY
Teacher A	Teacher B	Teacher C	Teacher D

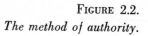
FIGURE 2.2.
The method of authority.

"Of course, boys and girls, this is only a suggestion, but let's not forget for a moment who's making it!"

Method of authority. Authority is used here in a special way. In the classroom all teachers practice authority in at least one sense. They are given the authority by school officials to keep class records, to assign grades to students, to determine what shall be taught each day, and—perhaps most important of all—to set the tone or "climate" of the classroom. We see no way that a teacher can avoid this type of authority; even if he shares portions of it with his students, it is always his prerogative to offer it, withhold it, or even to take it back once it was shared.

Authority is often linked to the term *authoritarian.* An extreme authoritarian teacher is one who tramples upon the rights and feelings of others. Such a person enjoys the exercise of power, fears debate, prefers an "orderly" class-room to one in which there is much activity, tends to use punishment more than reward, views students as undisciplined individuals who require control, and is uncomfortable in learning situations in which he is not acknowledged as the intellectual leader. Certainly such an individual is unlikely to practice the method of inquiry. However, the method of authority is more than that of an authoritarian personality, although those who have such personalities are likely to be examples of teacher A in Figure 2.1.

However, one need not be a fascist to practice the method of authority. Rather, one can be like teacher B. Some teachers have a limited view of their function and of what knowledge is. A teacher who believes his primary function is to teach commitment to "the American way" will organize his instruction so as to impose one set of attitudes, values, and beliefs on his students. Even though he does not view himself as a propagandist, his techniques and purposes resemble those of propaganda. Clearly, no social studies teacher will hold a position very long if he behaves as an iconoclast or devotes all his energies to challenging student belief, and such an individual can be just as authoritarian as one who seeks to impose community norms. Moreover, the classroom cannot function as a setting for trying out new ideas if the teacher conceives his primary function to be imposing one set of beliefs.

Some teachers have a limited sense of what social studies knowledge is. Drilling students in the facts of history as if the facts had some life of their own without organizing purpose, requiring students to accept one interpretation of events as the only "true" interpretation, while ignoring processes which give rise to new interpretations—these are some of the attitudes toward knowledge that characterize the teacher who practices the method of authority.

Method of inquiry.[3] A teacher who wishes to establish a climate for learning in which all ideas can be expressed safely and without fear of sanction is practicing the method of inquiry. The inquiry teacher wishes to teach students attitudes, values, skills, and knowledge that will enable them to become more thoughtful inquirers of their social environment. This does not mean that the classroom lacks direction, that the teacher lacks purpose. Indeed, the *techniques, modes,* and *strategies* may at times resemble those used by teachers practicing the method of authority. For example, the teacher may impose an operational definition to overcome obstacles in discussion. The fundamental difference is in the attitude the teacher takes toward students and the nature of knowledge.

The inquiry teacher in preparing students for adult roles as independent inquirers may devise strategies that will successfully impose skills and concepts needed to support successful inquiry. Moreover, the inquiry teacher is imposing an attitude: a desire for evidence to support empirical claims and a commitment to seek out contending points of view. He believes that knowledge is tentative and subject to new interpretations.

The inquiry teacher seeks to expand the number of meanings the learner can derive from any situation; the teacher of authority tends to worry more about students' learning the "right" meaning. A proficient learner under the method of inquiry is able and willing to challenge his teacher's and his classmates' beliefs. The successful learner in the method of authority does not challenge the teacher; he accepts what the teacher believes. The teacher of authority is likely to greet a student answer with such questions as: "What did I tell you?" or "What does your book say?" The inquiry teacher asks students: "What is your evidence?" or "What criteria are you using to support that value judgment?" In a classroom based on the method of authority, one typically finds students busily taking notes or engaged in recitation; one does not expect vigorous debate among students or between students and teacher. In a classroom dominated by the method of inquiry, students are encouraged to challenge each other to provide evidence to support claims. In the classroom dominated by the method of authority, the subject matter of the course is often limited to that contained in the course syllabus or the textbook. In a classroom dominated by the method of inquiry, students may seek data from many sources to support their positions.

How an inquiry teacher behaves in class may be more important than what he says. If the teacher encourages debate, is fair, is willing to take a stand and defend his beliefs, is attentive to current issues, and uses evidence rather than depending on his status in arguments, he can project a model of what the inquiring learner should be.

In our opinion the method of inquiry is more appropriate for the goals of social studies instruction than the method of authority. The method of authority aims at fixing certain beliefs, attitudes, and knowledge that, it is presumed, will remain useful throughout the learner's lifetime. The method of inquiry aims at preparing an independent learner who can adjust his attitudes and beliefs, and can easily absorb new knowledge throughout his lifetime. Whether a person is a consumer about to make a purchase or a citizen about to choose among alternative policies or political leaders, he will make better choices if he has been taught to think reflectively about the questions that confront him.

The method of authority is not designed to prepare the reflective citizen. Primarily it is designed to help people accept the opinions of others without questions, to accept advice without challenge, and to behave as others direct. The method of inquiry is more appropriate for a society in which the political system is based on choices by an informed electorate, in which the economic system forces choices upon consumers, and in which the social system tolerates competing lifestyles.

Technique, mode, strategy, and method can be conceptualized as having a hierarchical relationship to each other. Thus, a teacher who practices the method of inquiry needs an instructional strategy which depends on instructional modes which in turn employ teaching techniques. The same relationships are true for a teacher who practices the method of authority.

By our definition, a successful social studies teacher is one who practices the method of inquiry; who deliberately plans, paces, and sequences instruction according to a carefully designed strategy; who is able to move easily and efficiently from one mode of instruction to another, according to his purposes; and who uses a wide range of teaching techniques to hold student interest and to make his instruction more powerful.

Summary

No social studies teacher has a monopoly on the social education of youth. Children acquire their social learning from a variety of sources. Some of what a teacher might wish to teach will run counter to what a child has learned from other sources. Even within the school, the social studies faculty has no exclusive authority over the child's social learning. The child is acquiring attitudes, values, beliefs, and knowledge from peers, from other teachers, and from the operation of the school system as a whole.

Nevertheless, the social studies classroom can provide a setting that is unavailable to students elsewhere in the society. The social studies classroom can be a neutral place where students can adopt roles without commitment, test ideas without fear of sanction. The primary role of the social studies teacher is planning ways to expand the number of meanings a student derives from his experience and teaching him ways to validate these meanings according to canons of modern social science.

The method of inquiry is an appropriate teaching method regardless of the age level of students, their intellectual capacities, or the setting in which instruction occurs. This method can be defended philosophically in terms of the contribution it makes toward the preparation of responsible citizens for a democratic society. Moreover, the method of inquiry is likely to establish a setting in which learning can most efficiently occur.

APPLICATION 2.1: BLACK STUDIES CONTROVERSY

You are an eleventh-grade American history teacher at Central High School in Metro City. This is your first teaching position. You teach five classes in American history. Three of the classes are for "low track" students; these students are primarily those who have performed poorly in the past, who have a high absentee and dropout rate, and who have indicated no interest in attending college. You have one "middle track" class and one "high track" class. It is assumed—often incorrectly—that most of the high track students and many of the middle track students will attend college.

At one time Central High School had a reputation for being the best academic high school in the city. It once served a largely upper middle-class population. In the last few years the neighborhood around the school has changed. The school no longer draws children from upper middle-class homes, and its academic reputation has suffered, much to the distress of older members of the faculty.

Today, Central High School is racially mixed. Most of the students in the low track are black students and Chicanos, while most of the students in the high track are white. The school has had much tension and a few outbreaks of violence among the several racial and ethnic groups. The principal, who is concerned above all with the safety of his students and faculty, has established strict rules about when students may arrive and leave the school and pass between classes; in addition he has posted nonuniformed guards in the hallways to enforce school rules. On your first day in the school, the principal told you that your most important task was to keep your students busy and under control. "Don't give them an opportunity to get into mischief," he said.

While you have found interesting features in all your classes, you like your first-hour class best. Despite the fact that it is one of your low track classes, that absenteeism is high, that some students often arrive late, and that the boys sometimes sleep through part of the class, you have found a number of interesting students whom you like and who seem to like you. Most of the students understand that you want to make the class interesting and helpful, and cooperate with you.

Recently, you decided to add a unit on black studies in your American history course, believing that such a unit might capture the interests of your students. Frustrated by the lack of information in the textbook and in the school library, you asked for help from the director of a local Community Action Program who was able to collect enough used paperback books about black people in American society to enable you to assemble a classroom library. Much class time has been given to reading the paperbacks and to various classroom activities relating to the black experience that you thought would hold the students' interest. These include role-play exercises, debates, brief student reports, and games.

Student interest has been higher during this unit than at any other time during the year. Nevertheless, it has brought some unexpected problems as you have begun to receive complaints about your instruction from a number of people.

Your task is to write brief paragraphs in which you try to respond to each of the following complaints. Your answers should reflect your understanding of the role of social studies instruction and how social studies should be taught.

High School Principal: The principal tells you that he has received a number of complaints from parents objecting to words used by some of the authors of books in the black studies library. He wants to know how you justify the use of books containing four-letter words.

White Parent: A parent of one of the few white students in your first-hour class complains bitterly about the attention given blacks. He believes that his child is demeaned by this study and wonders sarcastically when you expect to have a unit on whites.

Department Chairman: The chairman of the social studies department asks why you are teaching a unit on black studies. He notes that other American history teachers are not offering such a unit and that it is not included in the approved study guide for the eleventh-grade American history course. He asks what American history goals you expect to achieve through this unit.

Teacher in Adjoining Classroom: This teacher has objected on several occasions to the noise that occurs during the first-hour class when students are engaged in role-playing, simulation, and debate. He wonders whether any learning can be taking place when your classroom is so noisy and disorganized.

_____

_____

_____

_____

Counselor: The counselor reports that your unit on black studies must be having some impact. He says that he hears it discussed by both students and faculty. He expresses a fear, however, that the unit may tend to increase rather than decrease racial tensions in the school. He asks what you are doing to teach students how to get along with one another.

_____

_____

_____

_____

Student: One of the students stops you after class and wonders when you will get back to more serious work. He fears that the unit on black studies is doing little to prepare him for college.

_____

_____

_____

_____

_____

Notes·

1. For one elaboration on this argument, see Robert L. Ebel, "What Are Schools For?" *Phi Delta Kappan,* vol. 54, no. 1 (September, 1972), pp. 3–7.

2. As was revealed in Chapter 1 through the quotations of various social studies specialists, various people assert somewhat different purposes for the social studies. This section highlights our beliefs about the primary purpose of the social studies.

   The belief that the purpose of education is to increase the meaning one derives from his experience is hardly an original idea. It is so commonly stated that it is pointless to cite all the authorities who have expanded on it. On the other hand, we owe a special debt to Robert Hanvey, who has written and spoken often during the past decade about the need for social studies teachers to focus instruction on increasing the *number* of meanings students derive from their experience and on helping students to test the *validity* of their meanings by social science procedures. (See especially his unpublished paper, "A Proposal for a 'Radical Alternative' in the Social Studies," and "Raising the Standard of Learning in the Social Studies," *Social Education,* vol. 27, no. 3 (March, 1963), pp. 137–141.) We do not know whether Mr. Hanvey would agree with some of the ways in which we have expanded on his ideas, but we are indebted for the inspiration they have provided. Most of this book is directed at helping teachers become adept at providing high school students with some of the tools of modern social science in order that they might further the purposes of social studies instruction that we embrace.

3. The term *inquiry* is a popular term among social studies educators. However, people use the term to mean different things. We recognize that our use of it differs from the way it is used by many others.

   Some use *inquiry* as a synonym for the term *scientific method.* Thus, Edwin Fenton, for example, discusses the "steps in a mode of inquiry." (See Edwin Fenton, "Inquiry and Structure," in *Inquiry in the Social Studies: Theory and Examples for Classroom Teachers,* edited by Rodney F. Allen, John V. Fleckenstein, and Peter M. Lyon, Washington, D.C.: National Council for the Social Studies, 1968, pp. 90–91.) Certainly, we do not object to helping students understand procedures used by scientists to test hypotheses. However, this use of the term *inquiry* is too limited for our purposes.

Some authors use *inquiry* in a way that is analogous to *discovery learning*. We treat discovery learning as an instructional mode. While we support the views of these authors toward one type of learning, we believe the use of inquiry to describe an instructional mode is too limited also. (See especially J. Richard Suchman, "Learning Through Inquiry," *Inquiry in the Social Studies,* pp. 56–57.)

Recently, the effort to give greater attention to affective goals has stimulated an interest in value inquiry. We do not deny the importance of value inquiry; indeed, it is treated at length in Chapter 7. However, investigation of values is only one responsibility of an inquiry teacher.

Suggested Reading

Broudy, Harry S. *The Real World of the Public School.* New York: Harcourt Brace Jovanovich, 1972. Broudy provides a highly personal, candid interpretation of what schools are like and the issues they face, and what the public has a right to expect of schools. You will find this to be a refreshingly common-sense analysis of current school controversies.

Bruner, Jerome. *The Relevance of Education.* New York: W. W. Norton, 1971. Perhaps more than any other individual, Bruner influenced the curriculum reform movement of the 1960s. This book is a collection of essays that he prepared for various purposes between 1964 and 1970. They reveal a person who is seeking to find a formula for education that will cherish intellectual excellence, without producing smugness, and will be socially responsible, without becoming anti-intellectual.

Fair, Jean, and Fannie R. Shaftel. *Effective Thinking in the Social Studies.* Washington, D.C.: National Council for the Social Studies, 1967. This book contains a number of essays, focusing on how to promote effective thinking in social studies instruction. Of particular interest is Chapter 2 by Hilda Taba, who was one of the social studies curriculum reformers in the 1950s and 1960s.

Morrissett, Irving, and W. William Stevens, Jr. (eds.). *Social Science in the*

Schools: A Search for a Rationale. New York: Holt, Rinehart and Winston, 1971. This book contains the papers and round-table discussions of a conference held at Purdue University in 1967. Overall, the book is an argument for the contributions the social sciences can make to the social education of youth.

I MAGINE YOURSELF AS the travel agent in the following dialogue. The travel agent's intention is not to sell a particular "package" trip but to be helpful to the customer and provide him with the information he needs to travel where he wants.

AGENT: *May I help you?*

CUSTOMER: *I think so. I may want to take a trip.*

AGENT: *You have come to the right place. We specialize in helping people plan vacations, and I personally have helped hundreds of people like yourself. How long a trip are you planning?*

CUSTOMER: *I have a total of nine months available, but I don't know whether I want to travel all of that time.*

AGENT: *Where do you want to go?*

CUSTOMER: *I'm not sure.*

AGENT: *What kind of places do you like?*

CUSTOMER: *I like to visit new places, to have fun, relax, and gain new experiences.*

AGENT: *How do you like to travel?*

CUSTOMER: *I have my own car and enjoy driving, but I think I might like to fly or go by boat or train.*

AGENT: *Which direction do you wish to go?*

CUSTOMER: *I don't care.*

AGENT: *How much money do you have to spend?*

CUSTOMER: *I am not sure.*

It is difficult to see how any travel agent could help such a customer. The customer lacks goals and objectives, and until these are determined, the agent is powerless to help. The agent could supply the goals—for example, tell the customer he should fly to Europe—but is unlikely to do so. Ordinarily a customer is expected to have goals in mind when he visits a travel agent, and the agent's job is to help the customer satisfy his goals.

Successful instruction requires that teachers and students have goals and objectives. Unless teachers and students understand what is to be accomplished, it is doubtful that instruction can proceed efficiently. Obviously, a person can and does learn incidentally through unplanned and unexpected experiences, but schools are established to sponsor planned educational opportunities. A teacher who fails to plan—who lacks goals and objectives—is shirking his responsibility.

Thus far, we have used the terms *goals* and *objectives* without discriminating between them. Although they are related, we shall attach different meanings to them. Statements of educational goals are statements of long-range purposes and intentions. Frequently goal statements are vague and open to various interpretations. Educational goals represent results a teacher values, strives for, and will be happy if they are reached. The statement "social studies has the responsibility for preparing youth for roles as active participants in their communities" is an example of an educational goal. In Chapter 2, we stated our belief that the overriding purpose of the social studies is "to help students increase the number of meanings they derive from their social environment and to equip them to judge the validity of their meanings according to widely accepted canons of a scientific culture."

By the term *objectives* we mean *instructional objectives*, sometimes referred to as "behavioral objectives" or "performance objectives." An instructional objective is a measurable statement describing what the student can do or will produce following instruction. Good instructional objectives are precise, unambiguous, measurable, and achievable. An example of an instructional objective is: As a result of instruction students can state hypotheses relating ethnic group identity to political efficacy and describe a procedure for testing their hypotheses.

Educational goals and instructional objectives might be placed on a continuum of purposive statements (Fig. 3.1), ranging from those that are general, abstract, and long range (goals) to those that are precise, measurable, and capable of satisfactory achievement (objectives).

Educational Goals

All teachers have goals. They may not write them down or articulate them clearly, but it is difficult to imagine a person managing his professional life

EDUCATIONAL GOALS	INSTRUCTIONAL OBJECTIVES

Vague, long-range, lofty, inspirational	Precise, measurable, unambiguous, achievable, short-range

without some purpose. Teachers' goals may range from "survive the year" and "cover the book" through "prepare my students for college" to "help students become active inquirers."

Goals serve teachers in important ways. Although often vague and subject to various interpretations, they provide an overall orientation. For example, suppose that the "customer" in the dialogue above had told the travel agent: "I wish to get away from here. I wish to go where no one knows me, where it is peaceful and quiet, where I can rest and reflect on what I want to do with my life. It should be some place that is comfortable while being inexpensive and that provides a new experience without forcing me to become intimately involved with people." With this kind of information the travel agent could begin to be helpful. While there are many places in the world that might satisfy these criteria, a large number of popular vacation spots—New York City, Los Angeles, and Paris, for example—have been excluded. Perhaps the customer will spend nine months in Greece or Mexico.

Some goal statements are merely platitudes and nearly worthless. Thus, a statement that "social studies should prepare youth to live happy, productive lives" is what a propaganda analyst would call a "glittering generality." It is so vague that it is difficult to see how it could help a teacher orient his instruction. The better that teachers can arrive at goals that suggest clear directions, the more useful goal statements become. And the better that a school system as a whole can reach agreement on its educational goals, the better a teacher can locate his contribution to the overall instructional effort.

CATEGORIES OF GOALS

In 1969 Lee Anderson and James M. Becker completed a study for the United States Office of Education that provides an extensive list of educational goals for a K–12 social studies curriculum.[1] It is not possible to reproduce the entire list here, but some excerpts will indicate how a comprehensive, integrated list of educational goals can help teachers orient their instruction. Seven major categories of goals were cited by Anderson and Becker. They are:

I. The K–12 curriculum should develop students' knowledge and cognitive understanding of the world system.

II. The K–12 curriculum should develop the capacity of students to view the world system as a whole and particular phenomena within it, conceptually, comparatively, and globally.

III. The K–12 curriculum should develop the capacity of students to make logically valid and empirically grounded analytical judgments.

IV. The K–12 curriculum should develop the capacity of students to make rational, analytical, explicit and humane normative judgments or evaluations.

V. The K–12 curriculum should develop the capacity of students to understand and to critically analyze and judge foreign policy decisions.

VI. The K–12 curriculum should develop students' capacity to intelligently and critically observe current history of the world system.

VII. The K–12 curriculum should develop the capacity of students to constructively adapt to the "realities of the human condition."

Admittedly these categories are vague and very general. However, under each category, or general goal, Anderson and Becker specified various subgoals which provide more specific guidance for teachers. Thus, one subset of goals under category III appeared as follows:

III. *The K–12 curriculum should develop the capacity of students to make logically valid and empirically grounded analytical judgments.*

A. The curriculum should develop within students an understanding of and some skill in the process of social scientific inquiry.

1. Developing students' inquiry skills. Included are:

a. An ability to distinguish statements expressing descriptive beliefs, explanatory beliefs, predictive beliefs, and normative beliefs.

b. An ability to identify and formulate in question form analytical problems inherent in a set of data or in an argument about a given phenomena and to critically appraise these formulations.

c. An ability to identify alternative beliefs about a given phenomena and to state these beliefs in the form of explicit propositions or hypotheses.

d. An ability to recognize and to explicate the logical implication of hypotheses.

e. An ability to identify the concepts that must be defined and the variables that must be "measured" in order to empirically test propositions or hypotheses.

f. An ability to conceptually define these concepts and to think of or "invent" ways in which variables might be measured.

g. An ability to critically examine conceptual definitions and operational measures.

h. An ability to identify the kind and form of information or data that a test of propositions calls for; that is, the kind and form of data implied by proposed operational measures of variables.

    i. An ability to identify and to evaluate possible sources of data.

    j. An ability to collect, organize and to evaluate data in terms of their apparent validity and reliability.

    k. An ability to evaluate hypotheses or propositions in light of data and then to accordingly reject them, accept them, or modify them.

    l. An ability to relate two or more propositions together to form a "theory."

    m. An ability to recognize or identify the logical implications of a theory.

    n. An ability to judge or evaluate the merits of alternative theories.

Although it is unlikely that any single teacher would expect to achieve all these goals in a single year, if an entire school system, or even the social studies teachers in a single high school, could agree that these goals are important, it could decide how the goals would be advanced in each class; and each teacher would have a better idea than before of the expectations others had for his course. While such goals do not inform teachers or students regarding what is to be accomplished within a single class period—instructional objectives have this burden—educational goals can act as a compass to keep teachers on course.

SOURCES OF GOALS

Some teachers self-consciously and deliberately develop educational goals to guide their instruction; others rarely think about their goals and would be pressed to articulate their purposes clearly if asked to do so. Nevertheless, both groups of teachers are guided by goals: the former consciously, the latter unconsciously. It seems useful for teachers to reflect on where their goals, stated or unstated, originate.

The process of goal-setting is as much a political process as it is an intellectual one. Teachers are not entirely free to select goals. Even when teachers think they are acting independently, their thoughts are influenced by the social forces operating on them. Thus, one source of educational goals is society at large.

Society. Obviously the influence of society on a given teacher is a selective and unpredictable pressure. Throughout the period of the Vietnam War, many teachers altered instructional goals to take into account public attitudes about it. Some teachers began to include units of instruction about war, its origins, and effects. Undoubtedly the specific purpose of these units varied from teacher to teacher and from community to community. In some schools teachers defended American policies and cited the war as an illustration of national resolve and willingness to defend freedom at whatever cost. In other schools teachers treated the tragedy of the war and critically appraised American responsibility for prolonging it. In either case, the educational goals were prompted by pressures from ongoing societal events.

During the last five years there has been an increase in interest in "value education" and "affective education." Some teachers have adopted new educational goals aimed at humanizing the curriculum. Their interest was probably prompted by developments in society at large, illustrated by public interest in such as "T-groups" and "encounter groups."

During the 1950's teachers were expected to avoid discussions of communism for fear that students might be attracted to it. Later, in the 1960s, public opinion was reversed, and schools in many parts of the country were required to include units on the "evils of communism," presumably as a kind of inoculation against the dread "social disease." Perhaps, current interest in sex education and drug education is based on similar assumptions.

Many more illustrations might be cited, but it should be clear that teachers are not free agents, even when they believe they are acting freely. The society in which the teacher lives subtly or forcefully applies pressure on the selection of educational goals.

Legal agencies. To some extent government agencies influence educational goals. Such influence may take the form of regents examinations prepared under state auspices and administered to most students in a state. Some states prescribe courses, such as American history, or units within courses; for example, all students in Illinois must study and take an examination on the state constitution prior to high school graduation. Many states publish elaborate curriculum guides that teachers are expected to consult. These establish the goals for instruction and suggest resources teachers can use. Teachers who closely follow such guides find that a large number of their educational goals have been selected for them. In those states that choose the textbooks to be used by teachers, textbook adoption committees can influence educational goals by the kinds of instructional materials selected.

Professional organizations. Teacher organizations such as the American Federation of Teachers and the National Education Association with their state affiliates offer advice on educational goals. Probably the most helpful organization for social studies teachers is the National Council for the Social Studies. Through its programs and publications it attempts to provide national leadership for teachers at all levels of schooling. In 1971 the NCSS published a position statement entitled "Social Studies Curriculum Guidelines." This statement sets forth NCSS-recommended educational goals for the social studies.[2]

Educational experts. Certain individuals have unusual influence on the thinking of many social studies teachers. Earlier in this chapter goals devised by Lee Anderson and James M. Becker were cited. These goals are being adopted or modified for use by some school systems. In the 1950s Arthur Bestor and Hyman Rickover had important influence on educational goals; in the 1960s such people as Jerome Bruner, Edwin Fenton, and Donald Oliver were significant spokesmen; and in the 1970s new leaders are certain to emerge. Such people articulate prevailing views in education, and their formulations tend to be admired and adopted by others.

School. A number of forces operate within schools to affect the choice of educational goals made by teachers. Through teacher committees or administrative fiat many schools develop system-wide educational goals. Often, at least in large-city school systems, curriculum guides are developed to help teachers carry out these goals.

A school or system-wide committee of teachers, administrators, or both may be empowered to select and purchase the textbooks teachers will use. A social studies department or the chairman of the department may make decisions regarding the courses to be offered in a single school. And the principal may give special attention to what students are studying in their social studies classrooms. Thus, social studies teachers will likely feel peer and administrative pressures on their selection of goals.

Nor can one ignore the influence of students. In some schools students are invited to participate, along with faculty, on official committees to plan the curriculum. Even where such official sanction is withheld, most teachers find it necessary and important to respond to student interests and concerns. Black studies are in the curriculum of many schools as a result of student pressure; environmental studies may also grow due in part to student interest in such problems as pollution and population.

Student interest is not the only way in which students are considered when educational goals are established. Studies of cognitive growth and development of children suggest that certain topics and certain ways of teaching are more appropriate at particular ages of development than at others. Thus, curriculum planners attempt to sequence instruction in ways that take advantage of the natural maturation of youth.

The teacher's choices. We began this section by indicating that establishing goals was more a political process than an intellectual one. We intended to stress that teachers do not select educational goals in a vacuum; educational goals are decided by teachers, consciously or unconsciously, through balancing and accommodating a variety of pressures.

Nevertheless, the final decision remains the teacher's to make. Although someone has prepared a curriculum guide for his use, he can lean on it, ignore it, or use it selectively. He can teach how he wishes and ignore the regents examinations, drill students on past regents examinations during the week prior to the test, or plan his entire course according to what he believes the examination will cover. He can base his course on the textbook, on what students say they wish to study, or on his favorite topics. Whatever choices he makes will be a personal response to similar pressures faced by other teachers in the school, filtered through his own personality and value system. No two American history teachers in the same school will teach identical courses, although they are responding to similar pressures. On the other hand, their courses will tend to be more alike than those of teachers in the same school who are teaching other social studies courses or those of other American history teachers in different cities and states.

A good social studies teacher consciously identifies the forces operating on him, consciously accommodates these forces in a manner most acceptable to him, and selects and publishes his educational goals in order that all can observe what he hopes to accomplish with his instruction.

APPLICATION 3.1: EVALUATING EDUCATIONAL GOALS

1. Following are five statements of educational goals for eleventh-grade American history. Rank the goals in the order of their importance.

————Students will be proud of their American heritage.

————Students will acquire a skeptical attitude toward popular accounts of American history and become better critics of unsupported assertions about American traditions.

————Students will acquire knowledge of American history that will ensure them success in college history courses.

————Students will learn that all Americans should be treated equally.

————Students will become familiar with the historical background of many current American problems.

2. Write a paragraph justifying why you ranked the goals as you did.

_____

_____

_____

_____

_____

3. Identify one or more sources of pressure that may influence the acceptance
   or denial of each of the five goals and tell how you would respond to the
   presumed pressure.

_____

_____

_____

Instructional Objectives

An instructional objective is a measurable statement describing what a student
can do or will produce following instruction. Note that the emphasis is on
what the *student* can do or will produce. Statements that do not have this
emphasis are not instructional objectives by our definition. Following is a
series of statements; place a check mark by those that are instructional objectives.

1. From a list of people important in American history, students can identify
   those who served as president of the United States.
2. The teacher will explain to students the four main reasons for the spread
   of Christianity.
3. The course will cover the following regions of the world: Asia, Western
   Europe, Africa, and Latin America.

4. The teacher will organize students in teams of four to debate the question: *Resolved,* That the Nuremberg trials established a valuable historical precedent.
5. Given demographic tables of two nations, students can identify correctly which nation has a modern, highly industrialized economy and which has not.
6. This semester students will study the following concepts: social class, socialization, culture, and value systems.
7. Students will demonstrate their understanding of the concepts political efficacy and social class by writing a provable hypothesis that links these concepts.

Statements 1, 5, and 7 satisfy the definition of instructional objectives. In statement 1, students are expected "to identify"; presumably this would be done orally, by pointing, or by placing a check mark before the correct names. Statement 5 demands a higher order of thinking, but the performance of the task is similar to that of statement 1. Statement 7 requires a "product" from the student. He must write a hypothesis that demonstrates his ability to work with the concepts political efficacy and social class.

Statements 2 and 4 are statements of what the *teacher* will do. What the students will be expected to do as a result of such instruction is unclear. Statements 3 and 6 identify topics to be treated in the course. Such statements are useful for preparing course syllabi, but they are far too general to guide lesson development and daily instruction.

To be useful, statements of instructional objectives should be *measurable.* Statements 1 and 5 contain the verb *identify* which can be measured easily. The student can either identify something or he cannot. Statement 7 contains the word *writing.* A student can either write a hypothesis or he cannot. Other verbs less easy to measure are *know, understand,* and *appreciate.* How can you properly measure the objective "The student will *know* American history" or "He will *understand* the significance of the French Revolution" or "He will *appreciate* classical music"? In order to be useful instructional objectives, statements must be written in a way that makes it easy to determine whether or not instruction was successful; that is, the objective must be measurable.

Check those statements in the following list that satisfy the criteria of "measurable statement."

1. Students will demonstrate their understanding of the concept totalitarianism by classifying ten nations according to two general categories, "high tendency toward totalitarianism" and "low tendency toward totalitarianism," using the categories for evaluating totalitarian systems acquired through instruction.
2. Students will really understand the meaning of the concept feudalism.

3. As a result of a study of Galileo, students will appreciate what it means to be caught in a conflict between one's beliefs and one's loyalty to authority.
4. As a result of a study of Nazi Germany, students will be more sympathetic to Israel's preoccupation with problems of national security.
5. Students can compare the Bay of Pigs decision with the Cuban Missile Crisis decision on the basis of seven important factors that influence presidential decision-making.

Statements 1 and 5 are the only useful statements of instructional objectives. While a purist might wish to know specifically how students will "classify" in statement 1 or "compare" in statement 5, it is relatively easy to see how this could be successfully done orally or in writing. On the other hand statements 2, 3, and 4 are much vaguer. What does "really understand . . . feudalism" mean?

The important point is that teachers should try to write instructional objectives that are precise, unambiguous, and easy to measure. Certain verbs contribute more to such statements than other verbs. Following is a list of verbs that frequently appear in good statements of instructional objectives:

identify	synthesize	extrapolate
distinguish	evaluate	state
write	name	construct
recite	order	transfer
solve	rank	differentiate
list	describe	reject
contrast	design	choose
compare	apply	select
analyze	interpret	

By this time you should begin to understand what an instructional objective is. See if you can demonstrate your understanding by meeting the following instructional objective: Readers can rewrite statements that do not satisfy the criteria for an instructional objective so that they are transformed into proper instructional objectives. The statements must satisfy two criteria: they must show what the student will do or will produce following instruction, and the statements must be precise, unambiguous, and measurable.

1. The teacher will teach students about the Crusades.

1a. (Your statement) _____

2. The course will devote one week to the study of the Russian Revolution of 1917.

2a. _____

3. The teacher will assign students to read about the causes of World War I.

3a. _____

4. The next chapter is on the Industrial Revolution.

4a. _____

CHARACTERISTICS OF INSTRUCTIONAL OBJECTIVES

Proponents of instructional objectives usually indicate that good instructional objectives have four elements: (1) the objective is stated in terms of what the student will do or will produce following instruction, (2) the objective is stated in measurable terms, (3) the objective statement indicates how the objective will be tested, and (4) the objective statement contains qualifying terms that indicate the minimum standard of performance that the instructor will accept. We have treated the first two elements; let's now examine the two remaining features of instructional objectives.

The objective statement indicates how the objective will be tested. Some examples of instructional objectives that satisfy this requirement follow.

1. *Given a list of ten American presidents,* a student *will select the names of Lincoln, Garfield, McKinley, and Kennedy*—the four presidents on the list who were assassinated while in office—*and in writing describe the occasion of each assassination, the names of the assassins, and the presumed cause of each assassination.*

2. The student will demonstrate his ability to analyze propaganda *by finding advertisements in newspapers and magazines that employ each of the seven categories of propaganda studied in class, by displaying these advertisements on a sheet of construction paper, and by correctly labeling each of the advertisements by category.*

3. The student will demonstrate his interest in the forthcoming political campaign *by reading newspaper accounts, by watching TV news reports of the campaign, and by reporting voluntarily and orally his opinions and reactions to the class.*

The italicized phrases in the above statements indicate the testing circumstances for each instructional objective. By specifying the test (sometimes referred to as the *criterion measure*) the teacher knows exactly how the objective will be used to measure student accomplishment and can, if he wishes, build into his instruction appropriate practice that is identical with or analogous to the planned testing situation. Specifying the test in advance should make the instruction more efficient because both the teacher and student are aware of the anticipated outcome; it also enables instruction to be easily replicated by other teachers.

The objective statement contains qualifying terms that indicate the minimum standard of performance that the instructor will accept. Let us re-examine the three instructional objectives above and add this final element of minimum standard.

1. Given a list of ten American presidents, a student will select the names of Lincoln, Garfield, McKinley, and Kennedy—the four presidents on the list who were assassinated while in office—and in writing describe the occasion of each assassination, the names of the assassins, and the presumed cause of each assassination. *To achieve an acceptable level of performance, a student must choose correctly all four of the presidents who were assassinated while not selecting others, write the names of at least three of the assassins, and list at least one cause for each assassination from among the several causes listed in the textbook. At least 90 percent of the class will achieve a minimal level of performance.*

2. The student will demonstrate his ability to analyze propaganda by finding advertisements in newspapers and magazines that employ each of the seven categories of propaganda studied in class, by displaying these advertisements on a sheet of construction paper, and by correctly labeling each of the advertisements by category. *Each student will give an example of each of the seven categories on the list while making no more than one mistake in classification. All members of the class will satisfy the minimum standards of performance.*

3. The student will demonstrate his interest in the forthcoming political campaign by reading newspaper accounts, by watching TV news reports of the campaign, and by reporting voluntarily and orally his opinions and reactions to the class. *A student should comment on the campaign at least once during the campaign, referring specifically to a news article or TV report. A minimum of 75 percent of the students in the class will meet minimum individual performance.*

By including the terms that describe a minimal level of performance, a teacher has clear guidelines for evaluating successful achievement of the objective, he can communicate clearly to students why further work is required when they fail to achieve the minimum performance standard, and the teacher can communicate his grading standards clearly to other teachers. Additional advantages are that the teacher has a clear way to compare students across classes and from one year to the next, providing he uses the same objective statement in the other settings. Moreover, students are likely to perform better if they are informed about the standards to be used for the evaluation and know that their grades are based not on some kind of "normal curve" but on their capacity to achieve the objective.*

COMPARATIVE ADVANTAGES OF THE CHARACTERISTICS

Each of the four elements of instructional objectives illustrated above are important. In our opinion, however, the two elements reported first—stating the objective in terms of what the learner will do or produce and stating the objective in measurable terms—are more important than the two described last. The first two elements are crucial; without them the statement does not satisfy the essential definition and purpose of an instructional objective. The latter two elements are useful and can contribute in important ways, but without them the objective can serve the teacher. This opinion of ours would not be accepted by many proponents of instructional objectives and therefore requires some explanation.

First of all, the criterion measure is frequently an arbitrary measure in any case. For instance, in the third objective statement the purpose is primarily affective, to arouse student interest in the political campaign. The teacher will be satisfied if this new interest takes a number of routes. One student might discuss politics more frequently with his friends and parents; another might contribute money to support a candidate; while another might actually work on behalf of a candidate. Any of these three indicators of interest is as appropriate as the one cited in the objective. Indeed, it is possible that a particular student could be devoting many after-school hours to the political campaign but failing *to report voluntarily and orally* on any newspaper account or TV report. He would be judged by the teacher as having little or no interest in the campaign, while in reality his interest could be greater than that of any other student in the class.

The minimal level of performance is equally arbitrary. On what basis can a teacher logically defend one voluntary report as a minimal standard for an individual student and the performance by 75 percent of the members of the class as the minimal performance for the class as a whole? What if those students who give reports average 3.5 reports per individual, but only 50 percent of the class volunteers to give reports? What does the teacher conclude, particularly when he knows that 50 percent of the class ordinarily assumes responsibility for class discussion while the remaining 50 percent seldom participates?

---

*Terms such as *normal curve* and *criterion measure* are treated in detail in Chapter 9, "Premises for Evaluating Student Performance."

But the principal reason for avoiding emphasis on the latter two elements is the practical consequences. Instructional objectives can contribute to better instruction. However, if the task of writing them is viewed by teachers to be an undue hardship, to be worth less than the time needed to write them, it is unlikely that teachers will make the effort to use instructional objectives. Currently, although interest in instructional objectives is growing, many teachers resist their use. They continue to work with vague goal statements and avoid the use of clear instructional objectives. Often neither the teacher nor the students are clear about what is to be learned until the teacher writes the test at the end of the unit.

If teachers can be encouraged to clarify their instructional purposes *prior* to instruction—to develop one or more instructional objectives for each day's lesson—teachers will be more efficient and students will become more successful learners. If possible, teachers should consider also, prior to instruction, how they plan to measure each objective and should include a statement about the future measurement of the objective. Teachers who can "teach for the test," because they and the students know how learning will be measured, add to their efficiency. Nevertheless, teachers should not avoid the use of instructional objectives because they lack the time necessary to develop tests of the objectives prior to instruction. If instructional objectives include the first two elements treated above, measures of the objective will be sufficiently implied for students to acquire a clear picture of what the teacher will expect of them.

Figure 3.2 plots the directions that teachers' instructional objectives might take. It assumes that teachers A, B, and C all have educational goals but unequal commitment to clearly stated objectives. A teacher should regularly strive to move his instructional objectives toward the right of the continuum as best he can. If he must choose between having objectives that are "perfect" in terms of satisfying the elements of the definition for instructional objectives, and having no objectives at all (that is, he continues to depend upon vague goal statements only), it would be better to be teacher B or even A.

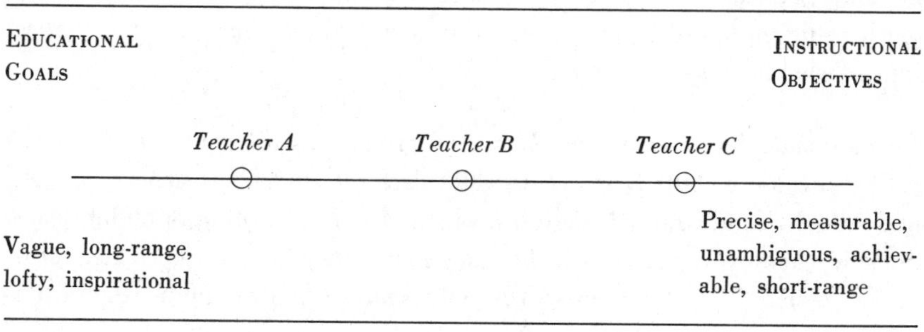

EDUCATIONAL GOALS

INSTRUCTIONAL OBJECTIVES

Teacher A   Teacher B   Teacher C

Vague, long-range, lofty, inspirational

Precise, measurable, unambiguous, achievable, short-range

FIGURE 3.2.
The continuum of Figure 3.1 showing the relative positions of three teachers in regard to instructional objectives.

An Instructional Model Based on Instructional Objectives

ADVANTAGES

In the preceding discussion references have been made to the advantages that clear instructional objectives afford the teacher. The most important of these advantages are the following.

Instructional objectives guide the teacher in planning instruction. Vague statements of goals do not offer an advantage in planning instruction. Goal statements are useful in helping to orient the teacher and to delimit the content domain he will treat, but they are largely inefficient helpers in the design of specific lessons. For example, a goal statement might be: Students will learn concepts that will enable them to understand better the environment in which they live. Few would quibble with the goal; but what does it mean? Which concepts? What environment? How are the concepts to be taught? And so on.

How can this goal be linked to the statement of an instructional objective? Assume that one concept to be taught is the concept *political efficacy*. This concept can be used to compare people's sense of political influence. A person with a low sense of political efficacy believes that he has little opportunity to affect political events; a person with a high sense of political efficacy believes that he can wield influence.

Logically, you might assume that you cannot teach the concept political efficacy until students know the meaning of the terms *politics, political,* and *efficacy.* Thus, in designing instruction you will have to decide whether students already know the base concepts, affording an opportunity to move forward to the compound term, or whether you will have to teach the base terms.

Second, you will have to decide what operational definition to accept for the term *political efficacy* and how to ask students to use the term. These decisions will lead you to plan lessons that enable the students to acquire the definition of the concept and to apply it accurately. You will want some exercises that provide students with appropriate practice in the use of the concept; you will need one or more test items that enable students and teacher to evaluate the learning that has taken place. A teacher who has instructional objectives is much better equipped to plan instruction than one who has only the fuzziest idea of what he is to do each day.

Instructional objectives aid teachers in devising appropriate tests. The overriding purpose of tests is to secure valid data for students, teachers, parents, and school administrators regarding whether or not learning is taking place. Some teachers worry about whether they have "easy items," "hard items," or "average items" on their tests. The only sound criterion for a test item is whether it is an appropriate measure of the instructional objective. Students should be tested on what was taught. When teachers are unclear about what they are teaching, they cannot devise appropriate tests.

On a typical evening before a test, students are occupied in trying to "psych" out the teacher, by trying to guess what the teacher will ask on the test. Meanwhile the teacher is devising questions, often aimed at outwitting the students. More appropriately, students should be engaged in a review of the instructional objectives for the unit, confident that if they can meet the objectives, they will perform well on the test. At the same time the teacher should be devising the best test measures for the instructional objectives that he can.

Instructional objectives facilitate learning because students know what is expected of them. Some teachers behave as though teaching were a contest among students or between students and teachers, a contest in which there are winners and losers. This is a poor image of what teaching should be. Every teacher should do his best to help every student learn what is expected of him. Every potential obstacle to clear instruction should be eliminated. A good teacher tries to be absolutely clear about what he wants students to learn. Far too frequently students fail to achieve because they are not certain of what the outcome of instruction should be. This is hardly surprising if the teacher is unsure of his objectives.

Having clear statements of instructional objectives contributes to student understanding of the learning tasks set before him. Knowing what he must do contributes to motivation; success in achieving objectives builds confidence and interest in the subject and adds to student success and teacher satisfaction. It is difficult to understand why teachers would resist developing instructional objectives, given their obvious advantages.

ELEMENTS OF THE BASIC TEACHING MODEL

Five major questions a social studies teacher should ask about his teaching are: (1) What should I teach? (2) Do my students already know what I wish to teach or are they prepared to take full advantage of what I wish to teach them? (3) How do I conduct the instruction in order to ensure successful learning? (4) How do I find out if the instruction was successful? (5) If instruction was unsuccessful, how should I change in order that students learn successfully in the future? These questions are represented in Figure 3.3.

The teaching model (Figure 3.3) suggests that successful instruction requires that teachers give careful attention to three phases of instruction. Poor planning in the preinstructional stage will lead to inefficient instruction. De-

FIGURE 3.3.
Basic teaching model.

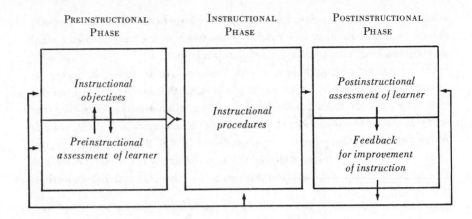

<table>
<tr><td>PREINSTRUCTIONAL PHASE</td><td>INSTRUCTIONAL PHASE</td><td>POSTINSTRUCTIONAL PHASE</td></tr>
<tr><td>*Instructional objectives*

Preinstructional assessment of learner</td><td>*Instructional procedures*</td><td>*Postinstructional assessment of learner*

Feedback for improvement of instruction</td></tr>
</table>

cisions about objectives and what students know or are capable of learning must be linked tightly to the instruction itself. Furthermore, what students are asked to do in the postinstructional stage to demonstrate that they have learned successfully must be tied to the instructional procedures and, through them, to the objectives and prior estimates of student capabilities.

The basic teaching model serves as a convenient and useful way to conceptualize instruction. Since a majority of the chapters in this book can be conceived as detailed elaborations of the model, it is useful to provide a brief explanation about each of the model's five subcomponents.

The importance of instructional objectives for well-planned instruction has been emphasized throughout this chapter. Unless teachers have clear statements of their intentions, they cannot expect learning to occur.

Preinstructional assessment of the learner. In an earlier discussion relating to teaching the concept political efficacy, the need to make judgments about what the student brings with him to instruction was stressed. The good teacher does not undertake instruction until he has determined whether or not students are able to take full advantage of it.

While stress has been placed on discovering whether the student has the prerequisite knowledge and skills to profit from instruction, it is equally important to find out what he knows in order to avoid redundancy. It is obviously pointless to devote time to teaching students knowledge, attitudes, and skills they already possess to a satisfactory degree.

One of the important problems for social studies teachers is how to avoid redundancy in instruction. For example, students typically study American history in grades 5, 8, and 11. Eleventh-grade students are not surprised to learn that George Washington was the first president, that the North won the Civil War, and that Franklin D. Roosevelt was elected president for four terms.

All this is ground that most students have covered *ad nauseam*. Social studies teachers can save time and provide a more interesting and challenging course if they avoid devoting most of their time to reteaching what students already know.

A number of ways may be used to carry out a preinstructional assessment of the student. Teachers may wish to develop inventory tests of knowledge, attitude, and skills. They can interview students. They can talk to teachers who have taught the students in earlier grades. And they can administer standardized tests. (These and other evaluation suggestions will be discussed in Chapter 9.) The important point is that formally or informally teachers should make judgments about what students know in order to tailor instruction properly.

It is important to notice that the basic teaching model indicates that the relationship between instructional objectives and preinstructional assessment of the student is a dynamic one. Each process contributes to the other. It is difficult to know what to assess until instructional objectives are stated; on the other hand, a final statement of achievable objectives rests on a careful assessment of learner competence prior to instruction.

Instructional procedures. As has been indicated in Chapter 2, instruction includes a variety of modes and techniques that are selected by a teacher to meet particular objectives. Obviously the instructional procedures selected will vary according to the preferences of the teacher, the age and ability of the students, available resources, and the nature of the objectives. Chapters 4 through 8 will deal with the development of successful instructional procedures.

Postinstructional assessment of the learner. In order to determine whether or not his instruction was successful, the teacher must assess student outcomes. The overarching purpose of such assessment is to acquire valid data on whether the objectives were met. Designing test items deliberately to scatter students along some type of "normal curve" is not consistent with the spirit of this teaching model. If the preinstructional assessment was accurate, most students would score poorly on the evaluation instrument prior to instruction. If the instructional strategy was successful, most—perhaps all—students should be able to meet the objectives. Thus, all or a large majority should score very high on the evaluation instrument following instruction. When this does not occur, at least one of four major factors may be at fault: (1) The evaluation instrument was weak and inappropriate. (2) The instruction was poor. (3) The student was not prepared to take advantage of instruction. Or (4) the instructional objectives were inappropriate.

Feedback for the improvement of instruction. When instruction fails, the teacher has a responsibility to locate the cause of the failure. If it is in his test, he should improve it. If it lies in the instructional strategy, he must identify the deficiencies and strive to avoid those in future units of instruction. The cause is in the preinstructional assessment, he should ask whether he is striving for competence that exceeds the capacity of his students. Perhaps he is asking them to read materials that are too difficult. Perhaps the range of background experience and ability is too great in his class, and this factor is presenting instructional problems to the class as a whole. Maybe certain requisite skills were overlooked in the preinstructional assessment. Sometimes the instructional objectives themselves are inappropriate. They could be too vague or poorly sequenced. The teacher may learn that in order to secure success in the unit the objectives themselves must be changed.

The teaching model outlined here is simple and easy for a teacher to put into practice. Teachers who apply this model to teaching social studies will have a convenient and efficient tool for designing classroom instruction. But without clear statements of instructional objectives, the model is seriously crippled.

Arguments against the Use of Instructional Objectives

While we believe firmly in the utility of instructional objectives and believe clear statements of objectives to be a basic ingredient of successful instruction, we recognize that all social studies educators do not share our enthusiasm for instructional objectives. Therefore, we have provided the following hypothetical discussion that might take place if we and some of our critics were to arrange a meeting on the importance of instructional objectives.

CRITIC: *It is difficult to predict all that a student is learning in class. Much learning occurs incidentally, not as a result of planned instruction.*

AUTHOR: *True, but what is the point? The implication is that one cannot learn by planning, that we should leave all learning to accident. Having clear instructional objectives merely ensures that some things the teacher believes are important are taught. Much more than the objective specifies is likely to be learned also.*

CRITIC: *But instructional objectives are always trivial. How can one write an instructional objective for the important outcomes of instruction, for example, helping students to become independent learners?*

AUTHOR: *Unfortunately, it is easier to write instructional objectives aimed at factual recall than objectives that seek more complex learning outcomes. Nevertheless, the fact that the task is difficult does not mean it should be avoided, because the alternative is to do nothing. The problem with a phrase such as "helping students to become independent learners" is that satisfactory performance of the role implies a host of skills, attitudes, and knowledge that must be taught. Independent learners are made, not born. Unless someone decides what is needed to become an independent learner and instructs students in those attributes, independent learners will not be developed.*

CRITIC: *Instructional objectives overlook the most important aspects of education— attitudes and intellectual skills.*

AUTHOR: *It is true that teachers tend to select knowledge objectives more often than attitude or skill objectives. These latter objectives are more difficult to state defensibly and to achieve. Nevertheless, it is not instructional objectives that put this emphasis on knowledge objectives. Studies of teacher performance in classrooms reveal that this is how teachers believe they should invest their time. By requiring teachers to state their objectives, it may be possible for the first time to demonstrate to teachers the apparent overemphasis on knowledge objectives and to encourage them to devote more time to skill and attitude objectives.*

CRITIC: *But it is dehumanizing for a teacher to describe how he plans to change the student. Students should not be manipulated in this way.*

AUTHOR: *If by manipulation you mean structuring the learning experience in such a way that students acquire more powerful ways to think reflectively about their environment, we plead guilty. The purpose of formal education is to increase the student's capacities through instruction. Those who use instructional objectives intend to make this process work more efficiently. On the other hand, if you use manipulation to mean an effort to control what students think and to keep them under the influence of adults in schools, we do not see how instructional objectives are relevant. Indeed, the best way to manipulate a person is to control his thoughts without letting him in on what is happening. The purpose of using instructional objectives is to inform the student candidly of the teacher's purposes.*

CRITIC: *If instructional objectives were to win widespread support, it might further the movement to hold teachers accountable. And I fear that the accountability movement will force on the schools some rather trivial objectives which will appear attractive because they are easily measured.*

AUTHOR: *I suspect you are right, at least about the first part of your statement. However, most states that have adopted accountability laws leave the specification of objectives to teachers.*

CRITIC: *If social studies teachers were to describe what they are teaching in terms of instructional objectives, it would reveal how vacuous much current instruction is.*

AUTHOR: *I agree. But we must not be satisfied with present instruction in social studies. One way to launch a reform is to state instructional objectives clearly, work for increasingly better objectives, and teach them successfully.*

CRITIC: *Who should judge the objectives?*

AUTHOR: *Objectives are normative statements about what should be learned. Instructional objectives ought to be linked to educational goals. And decisions about the goals of education should be a concern of the entire community. Thus, objectives should be operational statements by teachers of how they will advance the general, agreed-upon goals of education.*

CRITIC: *But it is very difficult to write good instructional objectives; it requires both time and skill. Teachers lack both.*

AUTHOR: *Unfortunately, you are right again. But teachers can learn to write instructional objectives, and as they gain practice, they will find that objectives become increasingly easy to develop. Teachers have far less time than they need, but time—whatever is available—devoted to specifying objectives can have enormous payoffs for instruction. Teachers cannot afford to avoid spending some time in the preparation of good instructional objectives. Perhaps they can write only one or two each day; perhaps their objectives will not be very sophisticated in the beginning; surely teachers will fail to find time to develop objectives on occasion. But it is important to begin and to do the best possible. Moreover, acquiring an ability to write instructional objectives will help teachers become better evaluators of instructional materials and better adapters of objectives contained in published materials. Social studies instruction is not likely to show marked improvement until teachers become clearer about what they are doing.*

Classifying Instructional Objectives

The principal advantage afforded by instructional objectives is that clearly stated objectives inform the teacher and student regarding what instruction is to accomplish and thereby facilitate efficient instruction. The principal advantage in classifying objectives is that teachers are better able to analyze their instructional objectives and to judge their worth. Writing instructional objectives helps teachers evaluate whether learning has taken place. Classifying instructional objectives helps teachers decide whether they are accomplishing all that they want. These decisions contribute to better instructional planning as teachers may delete some objectives and add new ones.

Teachers tend to emphasize knowledge objectives over all other kinds. Although they are concerned for objectives aimed at teaching intellectual skills and at promoting positive attitudes, values, and beliefs, research on classroom instruction reveals that most teachers spend most of their time teaching for factual recall.

Following are three instructional objectives. Rank the statements in the order of their importance for American history instruction.

—————As a result of instruction, students will be able to write at least one paragraph describing the nature of the conflict between Thomas Jefferson and Alexander Hamilton.

—————As a result of instruction, students will acquire new interest in American history that will be demonstrated by their voluntarily reading books on American history that have been checked out of the school and public libraries.

—————As a result of instruction, students will be better critics of historical evidence as shown by their ability to apply standards of internal and external criticism.

Most teachers probably would prefer to have students develop more interest in the study of history as a result of their course and become more critical readers of history books than remember the details of the debate between Jefferson and Hamilton. Nevertheless, the tendency for American history teachers, and that of other social studies teachers as well, is to emphasize the kind of objective given in the first statement above and to ignore the latter two in their daily instruction. When teachers begin to classify their objectives, they acquire evidence that may convince them that certain types of objectives are being sacrificed.

Instructional objectives can be classified according to three domains: *cognitive*, *affective*, and *psychomotor*. Most instructional objectives fall into the *cognitive domain*. Learning the "content"—the factual data, concepts, principles, and theories—of any particular subject field involves instruction in the cognitive domain. Objectives in the *affective domain* are concerned with attitudes, values, and feelings. Encouraging students to become more sensitive to the feelings of other people implies an affective purpose. Objectives in the *psychomotor domain* are concerned primarily with helping students develop motor skills. Teaching first-grade children how to tie their shoes is an example of a psychomotor objective. Although psychomotor objectives are very important in certain subject areas of the high school—for example, physical education, industrial arts, home economics, music, and arts courses—they are of relative insignificance to high school social studies teachers. In the sections that follow we shall focus primary attention on objectives drawn from the cognitive and affective domains.

It should be noted that most instruction overlaps all three domains. A student who has an interest in history (affective domain) is likely to acquire more knowledge of history (cognitive domain) than one who dislikes the subject. Thus, the successful teacher searches for means to make instruction appealing as one way to facilitate the acquisition of cognitive outcomes. The student making a map or creating a graph to display statistical data must use psychomotor skills as well as cognitive ones. Nevertheless, for purposes of analysis, it is possible to classify objectives as being *primarily* cognitive, *primarily* affective, or *primarily* psychomotor.

Following is a list of statements of instructional objectives. Mark those that are primarily cognitive, primarily affective, or primarily psychomotor with C, A, or P, respectively.

_____1. Students can list the presidents of the United States and the periods they served in office.

_____2. Students can make a concrete model of a typical feudal castle, showing its major features.

_____3. Students will demonstrate their respect for public property by returning in good condition all school-owned textbooks at the end of the year and by reporting acts of vandalism to school officials.

_____4. Each student will demonstrate his willingness to take a stand for his beliefs by publicly and voluntarily stating his opinion on a controversial topic.

_____5. Students can apply Rostow's theory of "takeoff" in economic growth to the economy of a nation not previously studied in class.

_____6. Students can evaluate the arguments used to defend American foreign policy in Southeast Asia by testing the claims with the formal rules for logical argument.

A system for classifying cognitive objectives was developed by Benjamin S. Bloom and his associates.[3] The system is hierarchical because it is believed that the mental states required to operate at different levels of the taxonomy become increasingly complex and that a capacity to operate at the highest levels of the hierarchy requires mastery of "lower" and simpler mental processes. The lowest level of the hierarchy is termed "knowledge"; the next above it is "comprehension," and together they represent the process of acquiring knowledge. The remaining four levels describe various intellectual abilities and skills relating to the use of knowledge. The cognitive domain is outlined briefly in Figure 3.4.

LEVEL OF MENTAL STATE	GENERAL TYPE	TAXONOMIC CATEGORIES
Complex	Using knowledge	6. Evaluation
		5. Synthesis
		4. Analysis
		3. Application
Simple	Acquiring knowledge	2. Comprehension
		1. Knowledge

FIGURE 3.4.
Outline of the cognitive domain.

Knowledge. The first level of the cognitive domain is knowledge. Knowledge refers to the recall of specific data, generalizations, concepts, principles, and theories of any area of investigation. It involves little more than remembering something that was learned in the past. A very large proportion of instruction is aimed at this level of cognition. Examples of instructional objectives are:

1. Students can list the twelve steps by which a bill becomes law.
2. Students can describe orally the function of the electoral college.
3. Students can match specific events with the following dates: 1492, 1776, 1914, and 1945.

Comprehension. Comprehension is also a part of the process of acquiring knowledge. The student can interpret what a particular event means. For example, he not only recalls the date of the signing of the Declaration of Independence but can explain the significance of the event. Examples of instructional objectives are:

1. Given a list of five characteristics of the Judeo-Christian tradition, a student can explain orally how each of these might have affected contemporary American social institutions.
2. Given the name of Thomas Carlyle and a quotation from his writings, students will classify Carlyle as representing the "great man" interpretation of history.
3. Students will be able to describe how the following agents influence political attitudes: family, peer group, schools, churches, mass media.

Application. Application involves the use of abstractions in particular and concrete situations. The student is asked to recall the concept, principle, procedure, or method and then to apply it to a fresh situation. Thus, he is asked to "use" knowledge that was "acquired" earlier. Examples of instructional objectives are:

1. Students can apply their understanding of sampling techniques by describing a procedure for drawing a representative sample of the student body for the purpose of conducting an attitude survey.
2. Students can apply the principle of "comparative advantage" in a discussion of whether a certified public accountant should employ a painter to paint his house or whether he should paint the house himself.
3. Students can apply knowledge of decision-making strategies to a case study of President Truman's decision to drop an atomic bomb on Hiroshima.

Analysis. The breakdown of a communication into parts and an examination of the relationships among the parts and of the way they are organized involves analysis. Examples of instructional objectives are:

1. Students will be able to analyze the campaign strategies employed by President Nixon in 1968, especially as they related to the use of television.
2. Students can prepare a formal debate on the topic: *Resolved,* That the solution to pollution and current environmental decay rests on the willingness to increase our investment in science and technology.
3. Students can analyze any particular school policy decision and decide whether the major consequence of the decision was to further political change, political maintenance, political development, or political conflict.

Synthesis. Synthesis involves putting together pieces or parts to form a whole that was not obvious before. While the act of synthesis may not be "new" in the sense that it has never been accomplished before, it should be new to the learner and represent the result of his own intellectual effort. Examples of instructional objectives are:

1. Students can demonstrate their knowledge of political campaign techniques by devising a campaign strategy for a hypothetical candidate running for the office of mayor.
2. Students can propose a policy position that seeks to accommodate the interests of civil rights advocates and of those who oppose busing children to schools away from the neighborhoods in which they live.
3. A student can write a letter recommending to a Congressman what his vote should be on a specific piece of legislation. His recommendations should be supported by a statement that assesses long-range tendencies in the society, making a particular position on the intended legislation necessary.

Evaluation. The process of making judgments about a particular policy, product, or practice is evaluation. The student must apply criteria learned previously and evaluate the quality or quantity of the phenomenon according to the given criteria. Examples of instructional objectives are:

1. Students can write an opinion on whether or not the policies of the Democratic party tend to favor "big business" or organized labor.
2. Students can judge the merits of arguments by those who favor a progressive income tax, a state sales tax, or a property tax as the best way to increase revenues for improving the services of state and local governments.
3. Students can evaluate and state an opinion in response to the claim that public morality is declining in the United States.

It should be clear that as the student moves up the hierarchy, progressing from simple to complex levels of intellectual skills, he must take advantage of capacities required of lower levels of thought in order to perform successfully at higher levels. For example, evaluation requires ability to analyze, synthesize, and apply. It may also be apparent that it is sometimes difficult to make clear distinctions among the various levels of intellectual skills because the skills tend to overlap.

Although it is useful to be aware of the distinctions among the various levels of intellectual skills, it is unrealistic to expect teachers to use the six levels of the cognitive domain in their regular analysis of instructional objectives. Rather teachers might best be served by classifying cognitive objectives into two gross levels as shown in Figure 3.5 (page 102).

Even though social studies teachers will seldom worry about whether their

FIGURE 3.5.
*Gross categorization of
cognitive domain.*

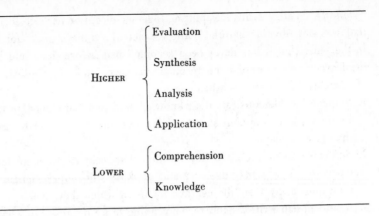

instructional objective is an example of an application or an analysis objective, they should decide regularly whether their objectives are primarily those of the higher or lower order. As teachers tend to write objectives almost exclusively at the knowledge level, the taxonomy can remind them of their obligation to develop objectives aimed at increasing students' capacities to use knowledge in ways involving higher levels of thought.

AFFECTIVE DOMAIN

When teachers list educational goals for social studies, affective goals occupy a prominent place. Some examples of typical affective goals in the social studies are:

1. Social studies should teach students to respect and admire the American form of government.
2. Social studies should teach students to become loyal and law-abiding citizens.
3. Social studies should teach commitment to fundamental principles of democratic government, including a belief in majority rule and respect for minority rights.
4. Social studies should help students to appreciate cultures different from their own.
5. Social studies should teach respect for all men, regardless of race, creed, or nationality.

Affective goals present special problems for social studies teachers. On the one hand, the problem is identical with that faced in the use of educational goals in the cognitive domain. Unless goals are translated into precise instructional objectives, they are often little more than slogans—statements to include in a course syllabus or to tack on the bulletin board, but not to be taken seriously through systematic instruction. But the problem goes beyond this familiar situation. It is more difficult for a high school teacher to affect a change in attitudes than in cognition; it is more difficult to construct acceptable instructional objectives in the affective domain, and teachers are ambivalent about the responsibility for teaching values.

Issues relating to value education will be treated extensively in Chapter 7. Therefore only a few comments, as these relate to the problem of instructional objectives, will be cited here. There is a tendency for teachers to avoid teaching *substantive values* (but not entirely) yet to accept a responsibility for teaching *procedural values*. Thus, a teacher who hopes his students will prefer peace to war, and has this as an educational goal, may avoid the opportunity to make this an instructional objective by teaching opposition to a specific war. Or a teacher who is committed to the abstract right of minority groups to engage in practices that deviate from the norm may ignore specific circumstances in class that would provide an opportunity to advance that right as a goal. Teachers fear that such instruction would bring down the charge of indoctrination. Thus, rather than teach deliberately the attitude expressed in the goal, they are more likely to raise such issues as an opportunity to study value conflicts.

Teachers are less timid about imposing procedural values. They require students to be honest in the preparation of their work, to prefer evidence to unsupported opinion in judging arguments, to use reason rather than force in debate, and to be respectful but critical in classroom debate. Teachers may even punish those who do not respect these values.

Although teachers will vary in their opinions about the proper role of affective objectives in the social studies and what proportion of time should be devoted to instruction in the affective domain, all teachers can profit by the ability to classify objectives as being primarily affective or primarily cognitive and by knowing how to analyze affective objectives in order to facilitate instruction.

Like objectives in the cognitive domain, affective objectives also can be categorized in terms of a hierarchy of competencies. Figure 3.6 is an ab-

INTERNALIZATION	CATEGORIES
High ↑ Low	5. Characterization by a value or value complex
	4. Organization
	3. Valuing
	2. Responding
	1. Receiving or attending

FIGURE 3.6.
Outline of the affective domain.

breviated version of a taxonomy of the affective domain by one group of authorities.[4]

Receiving. Receiving implies that the learner is aware of certain phenomena and is willing to attend to them. It may range from a single awareness that a situation exists to selective attention to it. Currently many Americans are becoming aware for the first time of a sexist bias in American society. It is not possible, however, to change a person's attitude regarding female and male roles until he becomes aware of the presence of a value problem. Thus, a major instructional effort of female "libs" must be to focus the attention of Americans on sexism in American life.

Responding. Complying in some way with a new attitude involves responding. To continue with the example used in the paragraph above, a person is responding when he not only has become aware of sexist bias in society but is making an effort to eliminate elements of the bias from his own speech and practices. When he is responding to the new attitude, he often derives a sense of satisfaction from his new behavior.

Valuing. Valuing means that the student believes that a new attitude or belief has worth. He holds the belief consistently and begins to seek ways to influence others to believe as he does. Our man or woman liberated from sexist bias discusses his beliefs with others and tries to convince them to accept his point of view.

Organization. At the level of organization, the individual begins to relate values in such a way as to form a system of values. Thus, a new attitude toward women's roles in society begins to form part of a complex of values that represent an acceptance of various social roles for a variety of people regardless of sex, age, race, and so on. Thus, new attitudes toward women become linked with attitudes toward blacks, Chicanos, and other groups that may have been the objects of special and discriminatory treatment.

Characterization. Characterization by a value or value complex represents the most advanced step in the internalization of values. At this level the individual may no longer be conscious that he is practicing a particular value; the value has become a part of his lifestyle, and it is difficult for him or others to imagine his not practicing the value. Such a person has so eliminated sexist bias from his thoughts and actions that he is no longer conscious that he is behaving in a new way. People who become wholly committed to a particular ideology or theology represent this level of acceptance. To be a complete Christian or a devoted Communist is to make a commitment to a particular kind of life that represents a set of values.

The importance of this hierarchy for teachers is that successful teaching in the affective domain requires more than simply making people aware of value conflicts. To truly affect the way people act, it is necessary to move to more advanced stages in the affective domain.

Summary

This chapter has treated the use of educational goals and instructional objectives for improving social studies instruction. You have learned that educational goals can serve an important purpose in delimiting content and providing an orientation for the teacher. However, successful instruction requires clear statements of instructional objectives.

Not only should teachers learn to specify clear instructional objectives for each lesson, but they should classify their objectives according to lower and higher levels of cognitive objectives and affective objectives. In so doing, teachers will remain conscious of the need to stress higher-level cognitive objectives rather than to depend solely or primarily on knowledge objectives, and they will begin to include affective objectives in their daily instruction.

APPLICATION 3.2: GOALS AND OBJECTIVES IN TANDEM

This lesson will afford the opportunity for you to demonstrate your ability to state educational goals and instructional objectives, to link instructional objectives with an educational goal, and to classify instructional objectives according to whether the objective is primarily cognitive (higher or lower level) or affective.

You are to write two educational goals and five instructional objectives for a high school American history course. The five objectives should be linked closely with at least one of the goals. Classify each objective by noting whether it is primarily cognitive (*CH* to indicate cognitive higher level or *CL* to indicate cognitive lower level) or affective (*A*).

To explain further what is expected, an example from world history is given below.

Educational goal: A study of world history informs students about ideas from the past that influence American ideas and institutions today.

Instructional objective: Following a study of Sparta and Athens in the fifth century A.D., students can apply at least one idea derived from each of the two city-states and specify how these ideas are practiced in the United States today. (CH)

Notes

1. James M. Becker, "An Examination of Objectives, Needs and Priorities in International Education in U.S. Secondary and Elementary Schools," Final Report, U.S. Office of Education, Washington, D.C. July, 1969, pp. 264–273. Mimeographed.
2. National Council for the Social Studies, *Social Studies Curriculum Guidelines: Position Statement,* Washington, D.C.: National Council for the Social Studies, 1971.
3. Benjamin S. Bloom et al., *Taxonomy of Educational Objectives, Handbook I: Cognitive Domain,* New York: David McKay, 1956.
4. David R. Krathwohl et al., *Taxonomy of Educational Objectives, Handbook II: Affective Domain,* New York: David McKay, 1964.

Suggested Reading

Flanagan, John C., Robert F. Mager, and William M. Shanner. *Social Studies Behavioral Objectives: A Guide to Individualizing Learning.* Palo Alto, Calif.: Westinghouse Learning Press, 1971. A major obstacle for teachers who wish to use instructional objectives is to find time to write them. This book contains a list of behavioral objectives, organized first around level of schooling, next around subject discipline, and finally around topic or skill. While teachers may not wish to use the objectives exactly as they are stated, the book presents many excellent illustrations to help teachers develop their own objectives.

Kapfer, Miriam B. *Behavioral Objectives in Curriculum Development: Selected Readings and Bibliography.* Englewood Cliffs, N.J.: Educational Technology Publications, 1971. This book contains articles by leading advocates of the use of behavioral objectives for instruction. It might be consulted by those who wish to learn about many of the technical arguments surrounding the use of behavioral objectives, arguments that were not treated in Chapter 3.

Kibler, Robert J., Larry T. Barker, and David T. Miles. *Behavioral Objectives and Instruction.* Boston: Allyn and Bacon, 1970. Teachers who wish further information relating to the task of developing instructional objectives might wish to consult this book. Using a semiprogrammed instruction format, the book instructs the reader in stating instructional objectives. A useful appendix includes samples of behavioral objectives and helpful elaboration on the Bloom and Krathwohl hierarchies of cognitive and affective objectives, respectively.

National Council for the Social Studies, *Social Studies Curriculum Guidelines: Position Statement.* Washington, D.C.: National Council for the Social Studies, 1971. The major professional association representing social studies teachers has prepared this pamphlet to help teachers make judgments about the social studies curricula in their schools. The document can serve also as a guide for those teachers and administrators who are seeking ways to improve their instructional programs.

Popham, W. James, and Eva T. Baker. *Establishing Instructional Goals.* Englewood Cliffs, N.J.: Prentice-Hall, 1970. This simple, easy-to-read book is an efficient introduction to the use and development of instructional objectives. Available also is a filmstrip-tape instructional program that is coordinated with the book. The filmstrip-tape can be purchased from Vimcet Associates, Inc., P.O. Box 24714, Los Angeles, Calif. 90024.

2

Instructor

PART TWO has five chapters which are about various aspects of instruction and learning in the social studies. The main purpose of these chapters is to help you to master ideas and skills that can enable you to become a more competent appraiser, selector, and user of instructional method, modes, techniques, and strategies in the social studies.

Chapter 4, "Competency-based Instruction," introduces a particular view of instruction and learning in the social studies which provides a frame of reference for the remaining chapters of Part Two. Chapter 5, "Teaching the Use of Concepts," presents discussion of the meaning and uses of concepts in the social studies and of how to design instruction for concept learning. Chapter 6, "Teaching the Use of Hypotheses," is about teaching students to use social science as a way of stating and verifying beliefs about reality. Chapter 7, "Teaching the Analysis of Values," consists of commentary about how to find warrants for value judgments in the social studies. Chapter 8, "A Strategy for Integrating Lessons," discusses lesson sequencing and the fit between instructional objectives and procedures.

The main instructional objectives of Chapters 4 through 8 are to prepare teachers to:

1. Describe instruction in terms of the following teacher moves: (a) gaining and maintaining attention, (b) providing for recall and reinforcement of pertinent prior learning, (c) providing appropriate practice to assist the student to develop desired competencies, (d) providing for application to demonstrate achievement, and (e) providing for remediation, if necessary
2. Describe instruction as the arrangement of means that are likely to lead to the achievement of particular objectives, or learning
3. Describe higher-level learning in terms of intellectual skills such as using concepts to organize and interpret information, formulating and testing hypotheses in order to describe and explain social phenomena, and evaluating factual and value claims
4. Identify examples of instruction aimed at eliciting lower and higher levels of cognition and learning
5. Identify and judge expository and discovery lessons
6. Distinguish more useful from less useful concepts in the social studies
7. Determine instances of concept learning
8. Judge instruction for concept learning
9. Judge statements about the value and purposes of concept learning
10. Identify hypotheses that can be tested empirically
11. Describe the major ways of gathering and using data to test hypotheses in the social sciences
12. Identify warranted descriptive and explanatory statements as products of hypothesis testing in the social sciences
13. Describe the main limitations or weaknesses of the products of hypothesis testing in the social sciences
14. Judge instruction designed to develop skills of hypothesis formulation and testing
15. Understand the nature and importance of value analysis
16. Distinguish between factual and value statements
17. Understand and identify, in classroom dialogue, eight components of value analysis
18. Understand and identify tests to challenge value conclusions of students
19. Create a set of lesson plans that are integrated in terms of an instructional strategy
20. Make judgments about the best fit between instructional objectives and procedures
21. Judge a set of lesson plans.

PRECISELY STATED OBJECTIVES are necessary to the design of effective instruction. Objectives indicate desired outcomes: where you want to be as a result of some experience. If you are vague about your objectives, then you are unsure of where you are going, and "if you are not sure where you are going, you are liable to end up someplace else—and not even know it."[1] This is the message of Chapter 3.

The message of this chapter is that you may know exactly where you want to go, but you can only contemplate your destination when you know how to get there and can implement this knowledge. Thus, mastery of an appropriate concept of instruction, and capability to implement this concept in the social studies classroom, is as necessary as the precise statement of objectives is to the achievement of desired educational outcomes. To perform the role of teacher successfully, you must know what instruction is and the relationship between instruction and learning.

4

Competency-based Instruction

What Is Instruction?

There are various ways to think about instruction and learning. Following are three very different viewpoints that might be expressed by a group of social studies teachers who are called on to justify their practices. As you read these statements, identify the main differences in beliefs about instruction and learning toward deciding which, if any, of the beliefs you agree with and why you agree or disagree with them.

MS. GREEN: *I believe that the best approach to instruction is to generate lessons from the classroom interactions of students and teachers. Instructional decisions should flow from the teacher's day-to-day perceptions of the interests and needs of students. Students learn best when they are free to pursue answers to questions that have meaning for them, that are connected to their experiences and concerns. Thus, teachers should never impose their concerns, their questions, and their instructional objectives on students. It follows that teachers should not impose reading materials or other instructional devices on students. Rather, they should be allowed the freedom to explore, to inquire, and to discover knowledge on their own within an environment that contains numerous and varied resources suited to the different interests and needs of the students. The teacher should serve mainly as a resource person, a provider of information and ideas to students who ask for help when they feel the need for it.*

MR. BROWN: *I believe that the main goal of social studies instruction should be to teach students facts that they need to know in order to live successfully as adults. Teachers should know what facts all students ought to learn, and they should know the academically respectable, time-honored ways to transmit these facts. Students must be adjusted to the content and techniques of instruction prescribed by the teacher rather than having the substance and style of instruction adjusted to meet the needs of different students. The most effective teaching technique is to transmit facts through lectures and readings. Through this approach the student's mind is strengthened, and he becomes a better thinker.*

MR. BLUE: *I believe the teacher has the responsibility to be a manager of learning, a designer of conditions that facilitate learner achievement of instructional objectives. To turn students loose to inquire, to seek knowledge on their own without teaching them the skills that are necessary for fruitful inquiry, is to abdicate responsibility for teaching. However, teaching all students the same thing in the same way is to court failure in the classroom. To use only one teaching style, whether it is a lecture or a class discussion, is to teach inefficiently, to ignore the facts that there is no one best teaching technique for all learning situations and that good teaching depends on fitting instructional techniques to differences in students and to desired outcomes of instruction. Requiring all students to learn only the same basic facts is to stunt intellectual growth and to blunt development of the ability to gather and interpret facts and to think and learn independently, which should be the ultimate goal of education.*

I believe that all students should have the opportunity to learn, as fully as their potential allows, the skills necessary for independent thought and action. Teachers should help them to learn these intellectual skills as efficiently as possibly. Thus, the primary responsibility of the teacher is artfully and systematically to select whatever instructional means are necessary to help students acquire the ability to think and learn independently about mankind and society.

You probably observed several basic differences in the approaches to instruction of these three teachers. The most important difference concerns teacher direction and control of learning experiences. Ms. Green would completely adjust the substance and style of instruction to student concerns. In contrast, both Mr. Brown and Mr. Blue would assume responsibility for specifying the substance and style of instruction. Mr. Blue is much more flexible than Mr. Brown is. He believes in varying instructional techniques and materials to accommodate differences in students and objectives. And Mr. Blue, unlike Mr. Brown, believes that it is important to help students acquire higher-level thinking ability which enables them to use facts to make independent judgments about social phenomena.

Each of the teacher's ideas about instruction and learning is practiced in many social studies classrooms. However, only Mr. Blue's ideas are entirely consistent with our belief that the basic purpose of the social studies should be to develop knowledge and intellectual skills that can help students more fully understand their social world so that they think and move most effectively within this world. Mr. Blue's ideas are most compatible with our competency-based concept of social studies instruction: a way of thinking about instruction and learning that focuses on what students can do before and after experiences designed to yield particular changes in their abilities, or competencies, to think and act.

A competency-based concept of instruction fits the instructional phase of the basic teaching model (Fig. 3.3), described in Chapter 3 (pages 91 to 94). The instructional objectives of this model are descriptions of competencies, that is, measurable changes in students to be achieved through instruction. The instructional procedures of the basic teaching model are the modes, techniques, and strategies used to achieve precisely stated instructional objectives. (See Chapter 2 for a discussion of instructional modes, techniques, and strategies.) These procedures are systematic efforts to alter the student's environment in order to change his competence as efficiently as possible. For example, techniques such as lecturing, discussion, role-playing, educational games, and filmed documentaries are examples of instructional procedures if they are used to change student behaviors, or competencies, in terms of precisely stated objectives. Thus, to *instruct* is to engage in "the process whereby the environment of an individual is deliberately manipulated to enable him to learn to emit or engage in specified behaviors under specified conditions or as responses to specified situations."[2]

Instruction is a means to *learning*, a relatively permanent and measurable change in competence which results from experience and which is not attributable to physical maturation or disability. To determine that learning has occurred, it must be shown that an individual can do something as a result of interaction with the environment that he could not do previously. Robert M. Gagné has defined learning as follows:

Learning is a change in human disposition or capability, which can be retained, and which is not simply ascribable to the process of growth. The kind of change called learning exhibits itself as a change in behavior, and the inference of learning is made by comparing what behavior was possible before the individual was placed in a "learning situation" and what behavior can be exhibited after such treatment. The change may be, and often is, an increased capability for some type of performance. It may also be an altered disposition of the sort called "attitude" or "interest" or "value." The change must have more than momentary permanence, it must be capable of being retained over some period of time. Finally, it must be distinguishable from the kind of change that is attributable to growth, such as change in height or the development of muscles through exercise.[3]

Learning often occurs without instruction. Some people learn to swim by jumping into a swimming pool; they literally "sink or swim." Much of our learning is derived from direct, unadulterated experience, through trial-and-error efforts. However, trial-and-error learning is often inefficient and ineffective. Some who jump into eight feet of water sink rather than learn how to swim. Others may swim, but not as skillfully as would be possible following good instruction.

The point of competency-based instruction is to reduce the elements of chance in a learning situation and to help students move as efficiently and extensively as possible toward the achievement of specified outcomes, or competencies. Thus, the primary purpose of the social studies teacher is to select and implement instructional modes, techniques, and strategies with which the student interacts and which are likely to bring about particular changes in his ability to think and act with reference to the social world. Those who would "turn students loose" to learn mainly through trial and error or through relatively unguided discovery abdicate their main responsibilities as teachers.

Designing and Implementing Competency-based Instruction

Competency-based instruction stresses the relationship between instructional procedures, or means, and instructional objectives, or ends. The teacher is most concerned with helping the student to achieve desired changes in competence. Thus, teaching effectiveness is determined by assessing the relationship between the means used to achieve desired changes in competence and the actual changes in student competence that are demonstrated. Remedial instruction is provided for slower learners, those who at first fail to achieve the instructional objectives. A main assumption of competency-based instruction is that continued failure on a massive scale reflects serious inadequacy of either the design or the implementation of instruction.

REQUIREMENTS

The design and implementation of competency-based instruction requires at least these moves:[4]

1. Gaining and maintaining the student's attention
2. Providing for recall and reinforcement of pertinent prior learning
3. Providing appropriate practice to assist the student to develop desired competencies
4. Providing for application to demonstrate achievement
5. Providing for remediation, if necessary.

Gaining and maintaining attention. An instructional sequence, or set of lessons, should begin with a "mind-grabbing experience," an activity that fixes students' attention, arouses their curiosity, motivates them, and provides them with a sense of purpose to guide subsequent study. For example, a set of lessons about the effects of the Industrial Revolution on the English working class in the eighteenth and nineteenth centuries might be initiated by showing several slides depicting working conditions and lifestyles before and during industrialization. After viewing the pictures, the class can be asked to speculate about the effects of the Industrial Revolution on the working class. This introductory lesson should raise questions and controversies among students because they are likely to make various inferences from the vivid, but somewhat limited and impressionistic, evidence shown via the slides. Students might be motivated by this set of lessons to investigate ideas and facts pertinent to their discussion of the slides in order to check out their speculative answers. Finally, this initiating activity can help students to perceive the purpose of the entire set of lessons. This sense of purpose can enable them to stay on the right track and to move systematically and efficiently toward attainment of objectives as they experience subsequent lessons.

Providing for recall and reinforcement. To facilitate learning, the teacher should link prior learning to current instruction, with the result that the student is prompted to remember and to relate relevant knowledge gained from earlier instruction to the new learning situation. Providing for the recall of prior learning not only facilitates new learning but reinforces the prior learning and enhances its retention. For example, prior learning about social class structures in preindustrial Europe and in other societies is most relevant to instruction about the impact of industrialization on English society. The teacher can prompt student recall of this prior learning to help them connect it to their lessons about industrialization.

Providing appropriate practice. Students must have the opportunity to practice what they will be required to do if they are to demonstrate their achievement of instructional objectives. Thus, the teacher must arrange conditions of learning, or instruction, that help students to develop desired competencies. For example, in order to learn about the effects of the Industrial Revolution on the English working class, they need to be exposed to evidence presented in various sources such as statistical tables, letters, diaries, travelogues, newspaper articles, and textbooks. Those who are unable to interpret evidence skillfully from one or more of these sources must be provided with instruction that helps them to develop the necessary skill. Instruction designed to develop desired competencies should require active learning: the use of data, ideas, and skills as they are presented. Feedback information about the worth of responses is necessary to the success of active learning. The indication of correct responses helps to guide students in the direction specified by instructional objectives. The indication of incorrect responses is a guide to deficiencies which must be corrected before objectives can be achieved.

Providing for application. To demonstrate that learning has resulted from instruction, students must be able to perform as specified by instructional objectives. Lessons that require students to apply knowledge and skills acquired during previous activities to the successful completion of new, but related, exercises or problems are tests of mastery learning, the achievement of objectives after appropriate practice. For example, to demonstrate knowledge of the effects of industrialization on the English working class, students can be required to examine critically a brief, one-sided interpretation of the impact of industrialization on English life. Students who note the biases in the one-sided interpretation demonstrate mastery learning, the ability to apply successfully knowledge learned in one context to a fresh, related context.

Providing for remediation. Students who fail to achieve mastery should have an opportunity for remedial instruction designed to eliminate deficiencies that prevent attainment of objectives. For example, some might fail to master the application lesson described above due to lack of knowledge about the impact of industrialization on workers' income and living standards. The teacher finds that the lack stems from an inability to read statistical tables which present evidence about income and living standards. Thus, the teacher knows that additional instruction to develop table-reading skills is necessary to help the failing students to succeed. After having remedial instruction, the students should achieve mastery learning.

Implementors of competency-based instruction should be aware of both the main strengths and the weaknesses of this approach to teaching and learning the social studies. Competency-based instruction is a very useful way to think about helping students to gain knowledge and intellectual skills systematically and efficiently. Each lesson is planned to move students as efficiently as possible toward the achievement of specific objectives, or competencies. Thus, undirected, random, trial-and-error learning is minimized.

However, two major assumptions related to the competency-based approach are sometimes difficult to implement. The assumptions are that measurable objectives can be specified for every desired outcome of instruction and that the impact of instruction on learning can be measured in every learning situation. These assumptions are practicable to a considerable extent; if they were not, competency-based instruction would not be viable. Yet it must be acknowledged that some higher-level intellectual skills that involve divergent thinking or very complex evaluational or analytical moves may be difficult to specify and measure as exactly as one would prefer. The appropriate response to these difficulties in instructional planning and design is to state all objectives as clearly and pointedly as possible and to accept the fact that some desired learning outcome may not be as amenable to precise statement and measurement as others.

Another important difficulty associated with competency-based instruction is that the empirical ground which can support decisions about how to manipulate conditions of learning to achieve particular objectives is not as large and stable as it could be. Some instructional decisions can be supported on solid empirical ground. For example, programmed instruction can be used effectively to develop simple skills such as map reading and table reading. However, many decisions about how best to arrange conditions of learning must be based on artful hunches or common sense rather than on scientific research. Despite the difficulty of always making an exact fit between instructional procedures and particular objectives, it is most useful to think as carefully as possible about how most fruitfully to tie instructional means to ends.

The competency-based approach is a potentially powerful way of thinking about instruction and learning in the social studies. It can be used for various purposes. It can serve the achievement of shallow or profound instructional goals. It can help to teach mindless conformity to authority or to develop the intellectual skills necessary to critical thinking and inquiry. It can aid social studies teachers to achieve predominantly lower- or predominantly higher-level competencies. Every social studies educator must think long and hard about what is worth achieving through the implementation of competency-based instruction. Chapters 2 and 3 offered some guidelines for thinking about the ends of social studies education. The following section builds upon these directives.

INSTRUCTING FOR LOWER- AND HIGHER-LEVEL LEARNING

Two very different approaches to instruction and learning are illustrated in the following classroom discussions. As you read the discussions, you will be able to identify the main differences in the two instructional approaches and can speculate about which of the two is the better example of instruction.

CLASSROOM DISCUSSION 1

TEACHER: *I believe everyone in the class has finished the reading assignment about the Industrial Revolution. Let's find out what you have learned. What was the most important invention of the Industrial Revolution?*

MARY: *The spinning jenny.*

TEACHER: *No! George, tell Mary what was the most important invention of the Industrial Revolution.*

GEORGE: *It said in the book that the steam engine was the most important invention.*

TEACHER: *Very good, George. When was the steam engine invented?*

GEORGE: *In 1769.*

TEACHER: *Right! Now, let's move to the second discussion question on our list. Why did the Industrial Revolution happen in England?*

MIKE: *England has lots of coal and iron.*

JIMMY: *And England had a lot of inventors.*

MARTHA: *And the book said that there was a lot of capital in England.*

TEACHER: *Let's stop at this point and examine what's been said. You've said that the Industrial Revolution happened in England because natural resources like coal and iron were available. I'll write "available natural resources" on the board as the first reason why the Industrial Revolution happened in England. The second reason that you mentioned was inventions which I'll write on the board. The third reason was availability of capital. What does that mean, Martha?*

MARTHA: *Well, ah, I'm not sure, but it said in the book that it was important.*

BOBBY: *I know what it means. Capital is wealth used to produce more wealth.*

TEACHER: *Very good, Bobby. What else can we add to our list on the board?*

CLASSROOM DISCUSSION 2

TEACHER: *You have examined several tables and graphs about population changes and industrial development in England during the period 1750 to 1900. What generalizations can you make from these data?*

JOHN: *There was a lot of population growth at the same time there was a lot of industrial growth.*

TEACHER: *Do you agree or disagree with John?*

HAROLD: *I agree with him.*

TEACHER: *Why? What evidence do you have to support John's generalization?*

HAROLD: *Well, Table 1 shows that the population of England and Wales doubled between 1800 and 1850. And by 1900 there were four times as many people in England as in 1800.*

TEACHER: *What was the industrial growth rate during this period of time?*

HAROLD: *According to Graph 1, industrial production was nine times greater in 1900 than in 1800.*

TEACHER: *All right. You've backed up John's generalization with evidence from the table and graph. Who can make another generalization from these data?*

As you undoubtedly noticed, the primary difference between the two classroom discussions is that the teacher in the first example stressed the *recall* of facts presented in a prior reading assignment, and that the teacher in the second example stressed the *use* of more specific facts to support or reject general propositions. In the first example the students were learning at the very lowest level of cognition, and in the second example they were performing higher-level intellectual moves. What are the differences between lower- and higher-level learning? Why should teachers stress higher-level learning in the social studies?

What is higher-level learning? Thinking can be conceived in terms of various levels, ranging from the mere recall of facts through higher-level cognitive operations which involve the use of both facts and ideas to answer questions and solve problems. For example, Benjamin S. Bloom and associates specified six distinct levels of cognition which range from the recall of knowledge, the lowest level, to evaluation, the highest level in the cognitive domain.[5] (See pages 97 to 102 in Chapter 3.) Robert M. Gagné specified eight conditions of learning which range from the mindless responding associated with "signal learning" to the higher-level cognitive operations of concept learning, principle learning, and problem solving.[6]

Schemes for categorizing cognition are not cited with the objective that teachers should become highly skilled classifiers of levels of learning. Rather the objective is to alert them to the possibilities for planning lessons that require students to function at the higher levels of the cognitive domain. Too many teachers behave as if they believe that the recall approach is the most, or even the only, appropriate way to teach. Studies of classroom behavior indicate that social studies teachers tend to stress recall in their planning and execution of lessons.[7]

Teachers can profitably use questions or learning activities aimed at the recall of important ideas and facts without stressing recall, or rote learning, to the minimization or exclusion of higher-level cognition. For example, teachers should prompt student recall of facts and ideas, presented in previous lessons, that pertain to a current lesson. And students should be helped to remember facts and ideas relevant to thinking about important questions and issues. It is important to realize that lower-level learning of specific material is often necessary to set the stage for higher-level activities, such as problem solving.[8] However, the key to the retention of learning is meaningful use; those who continually apply related facts and ideas to the study of significant questions and issues are more likely to remember the facts and ideas than are those who do not.[9]

Higher-level learning involves the development of intellectual skills that make possible the meaningful use of facts and ideas. These skills, shown in Figure 4.1, enable determination of the grounds for supporting or rejecting statements about the way the world is or ought to be.

Basic Intellectual Tools	Basic Intellectual Skills
A. CONCEPTS	Critical thinking skills
B. DESCRIPTIONS	1. Devising standards to judge basic intellectual tools
C. EXPLANATIONS	2. Applying standards to judge basic intellectual tools
D. EVALUATIONS	
	Inquiry skills
	3. Constructing and applying conceptual frameworks
	4. Formulating hypotheses to describe and explain
	5. Devising ways to support or reject hypotheses
	6. Applying ways to support or reject hypotheses

FIGURE 4.1.
*Basic intellectual tools
and skills.*

Figure 4.1 describes intellectual skills and their relationships to the basic intellectual tools: concepts, descriptions, explanations, and evaluations. Intellectual tools are instruments for thinking about the world. They help thinkers to construct images of reality which enable them to comprehend and cope with their surroundings.

Concepts help us to organize and interpret perceptions and information, and to sort systematically the vast array of stimuli which surround us. Thus, they are the foundations for our descriptions and explanations of reality. (Concept learning is the subject of Chapter 5.)

Descriptions are statements about the way things are. They range from simple, concrete facts (Nixon became president in 1969) to complex hypotheses with general applicability (rapid social change is associated with open social class systems). Descriptions are built with concepts. For example, you must know the concepts social change and social class systems in order to build or to understand the above descriptive statement.

Explanations are statements about why things are a particular way. Explanatory statements indicate causal relationships: how changing one factor leads to changes in other factors. For example, this is an explanatory statement: An increase in a sense of political efficacy leads to an increase in the likelihood of participation in public elections. Our explanations and descriptions are intellectual tools which help us to make decisions and to solve problems. (Learning to formulate, test, and use descriptive and explanatory hypotheses is the subject of Chapter 6.)

Evaluations are intellectual tools that help us to make judgments about what is good or bad, better or worse. Evaluations are statements about the way things ought to be. (Learning to make evaluative judgments is the subject of Chapter 7.)

Intellectual skills are those necessary to critical thinking and inquiry. Critical thinking skills, as shown in Figure 4.1, enable one to make judgments about the worth of basic intellectual tools. Critical thinkers can appraise concepts, descriptions, explanations, and evaluations. They can criticize their own intellectual tools and those of others (such as authors, journalists, television commentators, friends, and teachers). Inquiry skills, as shown in the figure, enable one to use basic intellectual tools to make more or less accurate factual statements, propositions about the way it is. They are necessary to the construction and justification of hypotheses, to the marshaling of evidence to support or reject descriptive and explanatory statements.

Numerous studies of cognitive development have demonstrated that most adolescents have the cognitive capacity to acquire and use intellectual skills.[10] During the age period 11 through 13, youngsters are at the threshold of ability to deal effectively with abstractions, to reason from premises, to theorize, and to perform high-level intellectual moves. Fifteen-year-olds manifest the potential to use high-level intellectual skills consistently and competently. Thus, it is reasonable to believe that normal adolescents can achieve high-level learning in the social studies. Should adolescents strive to acquire intellectual skills? What is the value of higher-level learning?

The value of higher-level learning. Higher-level learning is potentially very transferable to new situations and problems.[11] Intellectual skills learned in the process of solving a particular problem can be applied, or transferred, to the solution of new, related problems. In contrast, rote learning has very limited transferability.

Transfer of learning may be either positive or negative. Positive transfer aids subsequent learning, while negative transfer impedes new learning. For example, positive transfer is demonstrated when the mastery of graph-reading skills in the classroom helps in reading graphs in news magazines. In contrast, negative transfer might occur when a group of students, after learning about public policy-making processes from a highly idealistic and misleading textbook, tries to influence public policy making in their community. Unless instruction is designed systematically and pointedly to yield particular kinds of positive transfer, negative consequences may occur often. (See pages 214 and 216 in Chapter 6 for a discussion of the instructional procedures that enhance the likelihood of the positive transfer of learning.)

Learning that facilitates positive transfer is fundamentally relevant, since it prepares one to deal with change. Much attention has been focused recently on the importance of a relevant education, and much nonsense has been written about what is or is not relevant. Those who recognize the importance

Wee Pals

WEE PALS © KING FEATURES SYNDICATE

FIGURE 4.2.
What is relevant education?

of preparing youth to cope with change use the idea of transferable learning to judge the relevance of educational experiences. Their criterion is: learning is relevant to the extent that it transfers positively to new situations or problems.

According to Jerome Bruner, relevant learning is "what you know that permits you to move toward goals you care about."[12] This definition draws attention to the link between relevance and variation and change. Goals and knowledge vary not only among individuals at a given time but from one time to another. What many would consider relevant today is likely not to be considered relevant in the future. Change is a most obvious constant of our social life. Much of this change is unforeseen and even unnoticed at the time it is occurring. To teach for relevance strictly in terms of "essential" facts and values—yesterday's wisdom—is to risk creating severe future problems or failures. For example, France's Maginot Line was a magnificent and relevant response to a past problem but was irrelevant to future needs. When the "future" arrived in the form of Hitler's blitzkrieg, France paid dearly for her ill-considered view of what military tactics were most relevant.

Too many students are expected to learn too many facts, most of which they will forget and many of which are very likely to become obsolete. Most of this factual learning is probably irrelevant, in the fundamental sense, but may be transmitted to students in the cause of relevancy and supposed applicability to present and future concerns. For example, some educators claim that to teach facts about current issues and problems is to teach for relevance.

FIGURE 4.3.
*Relevance is more than
facts or fashionable terms.*

"I passed factual recall, but flunked inferential thinking."

REPRINTED FROM THE PHI DELTA KAPPAN

However, by overemphasizing what is current or fashionable, we may circum-scribe our students with banality and impede the development of the capability to cope with change, with the unforeseen, and with the necessary interplay between constancy and variation. Teachers should not require the study of current issues and problems mainly to teach facts about the present; social studies instruction does not immediately become highly relevant and useful simply by becoming infused with contemporary materials. Rather the exciting and important concerns of the present can be used as the raw material of a basically relevant educational experience—the development of skills and knowledge that enable one to cope with the future.

Social science as a way of thinking and doing is more likely to remain basically unchanged, and thus relevant, than is social science knowledge and common sense, which may indeed change radically from one time to the next. Margaret Mead has illustrated this point very well by her account of the public health nurse in Philadelphia who complained that she had spent her youth telling immigrant women *not* to breast-feed their children and to cook their dirty vegetables to kill the germs and protect their families' health. This same nurse spent her old age telling the daughters of these immigrant women to breast-feed their children and to eat fresh food to get vitamins which would enhance their families' health.[13]

A most relevant social studies curriculum yields a continually applicable social education. Such an education consists of learning the intellectual skills associated with history and the social sciences. Mastery of these skills enables one to formulate problems and hypotheses; to gather, to organize, and to interpret information; to use evidence to confirm or reject hypotheses; and to extrapolate from the known to highly reasonable speculations about the unknown. The facts of a highly relevant social studies curriculum are those that pertain to hypotheses, questions, and problems about man. These relevant facts are learned not as ends in themselves but as means to the development of intellectual skills that enable a learner to obtain and use unknown facts to cope with unforeseen problems. If students learn to identify issues and problems exactly, to inquire about these problems and issues systematically, and to communicate the results of their inquiries precisely and interestingly, then they have acquired a relevant education, an education that is likely to be continually applicable to their concerns regardless of changing knowledge and goals.

A primary goal of social studies instruction should be to develop intellectual skills, high-level competencies of thinking and learning. Instruction for higher-level learning is relevant and facilitates retention and positive transfer of knowledge and skills. What instructional procedures can be used to help students achieve higher-level learning?

Two Modes of Instruction

Discovery and exposition are two very different modes of instruction which require contrasting teaching styles and techniques. These two instructional modes are derived from different theories of learning and are supported by distinct assumptions and bodies of research. However, both discovery and exposition are necessary to the successful implementation of our competency-based concept of instruction. Each mode is most appropriate to different types of learning situations and to the development of different competencies. Thus, good instruction includes both discovery and exposition. An important teaching skill is making the right fit between the learning situation and the instructional mode. The following discussion is designed to help you determine when and how to use discovery and exposition in order to develop competencies in the social studies.

DISCOVERY

Instruction for discovery is designed to challenge students to derive their own answers from incomplete information. Discovery lessons confront students with an intriguing and perplexing problem or exercise and challenge them to formulate questions and tentative answers to the problem. Often these lessons consist of fragments of information from which students must construct generalizations.[14]

To fit our competency-based concept of instruction, discovery lessons must be designed in terms of specific instructional objectives and must involve the arrangement of learning conditions that facilitate "discovery." In our view, discovery lessons that involve student meandering at random, that is, lessons not structured in terms of objectives, are little better than trial-and-error learning experiences and are to be avoided. Hilda Taba, a leader in designing discovery lessons for the social studies, strongly urged structured discovery learning:

Learning by discovery requires a teaching-learning strategy that amounts to setting conditions to make discovery possible. All descriptions of discovery learning imply a specific teaching strategy, even though the existence of this strategy is not always so recognized.

Central in this strategy is the confrontation of learners with problem situations that create a feeling of bafflement and start the process of inquiry. Withholding certain kinds of information and certain kinds of crucial generalizations to challenge the search behavior and to preserve the opportunity for autonomous exploration and experimentation is also usually practiced. The teaching strategy is usually aimed at placing on the individual the responsibility of transforming information and reassembling it to get new insights. . . .

The act of discovery occurs at the point in the learner's effort at which he grasps the organizing principle imbedded in a concrete instance or in a series of instances and can therefore transform this information: the learner can see the relationship of the facts before him, he can understand the causes of the phenomenon and he can relate what he sees to his prior knowledge. This point in the learner's efforts is also referred to as the moment of insight.

These acts of discovery are the product of the individual's intellectual effort; the nature of these acts, however, is dictated by the structure of the subject matter with which the learner deals. If the discovery is not related to the logic or the structure of the subject matter, we have what Wertheimer calls "dirty," "ugly," or "insensible" procedure.[15]

The teaching style appropriate to discovery lessons is guiding and prompting student thinking and discussing rather than giving answers and thereby foreclosing student inquiry. The teacher's role is to conduct open-ended discussion and to provoke student responses to cues present in the lesson. The teacher should not evaluate responses, since the point of discovery lessons is to generate motivation to investigate relevant concepts and facts. During a discovery lesson, the flow of discussion should be mainly from student to student rather than from teacher to student to teacher. Students should be encouraged to criticize one another and to air disagreements. The teacher should play the role of discussion manager and facilitator rather than answer giver or judger of student responses.

Confronting a class with a packet of primary sources is one means to spark questioning and speculating by students and to prompt the examination of relevant concepts and facts. For example, a teacher might initiate a study of the causes of the American Revolution by confronting students with a packet of documents which includes excerpts from several primary sources: British laws, colonial petitions in response to British laws, private letters, newspaper articles, and tables and graphs which present data about British and colonial manufacturing and trade. On the basis of this information, which is a small representative sample of primary sources about conditions leading to the American Revolution, students can be challenged to speculate about why the colonists rebelled. To complete this lesson, which may consume two or three class periods, students must practice skills of organization and interpretation. They must seek relationships between pieces of information in order to construct propositions about why the colonists rebelled. This immersion in interesting evidence is likely to prompt insightful questions as well as insightful speculative answers. Both questions and speculations can guide subsequent investigation.

After generating questions and speculations about why the colonists rebelled, students can be permitted to consult secondary sources to confirm, reject, or modify their speculations and to find answers to their questions. They can attempt to check their "discoveries" against the work of experts after attempting to think through a puzzling situation independently. After these efforts to approximate the historian's way of thinking, students can use the products of historical scholarship.

The preceding example illustrates the use of instruction for discovery as an introduction to a set of lessons. The discovery mode also can be used at the end of a set of lessons to assess the extent to which students have learned knowledge and skills presented in preceding lessons. If students can apply, or transfer, prior learning to a discovery lesson, they provide evidence of competence. For example, the last of a set of lessons about the causes of the American Revolution can involve a fresh packet of data about why the revolution occurred, and students are challenged to organize and interpret it. This exercise requires them to apply knowledge and skills learned previously to the solution of a historical problem. To show competence, students should be able to discriminate less reliable from more reliable evidence, and they should be able to interpret these data in terms of concepts and facts acquired in previous lessons. Through this discovery exercise, students have the opportunity to demonstrate their previous learning about the causes of the American Revolution and to extend this learning as they contemplate and use fresh information.

Proponents of discovery learning claim some important advantages for this approach to instruction.[16] First, they claim that discovery lessons are powerful means to the development of problem-solving skills. Mastering discovery lessons is supposed to develop a learning set that is transferable to the solution of almost any problem or task that one might encounter. According to this view, students who learn to formulate significant questions and to extrapolate speculative answers from limited data are acquiring skills necessary to independent learning and thinking and to the gathering and use of relevant knowledge. Artfully formulated questions and speculations are prods to inquiry and guides to relevant concepts and facts.

Second, discovery learning is presumed to contribute powerfully to retention of what is learned. Students who seek and use information for the purpose of mastering discovery lessons have organized their own information in terms of their cognitive structures and presumably know how to recall the information when it is needed.

Third, discovery learning is supposed to increase intrinsic motivation. It is presumed that discovery lessons perplex, challenge, and interest the student to pursue inquiry. The rewards of discovery provide reinforcement and inducement for him.

The discovery mode fits particular instructional purposes very well, purposes such as introducing a set of lessons or developing problem-solving skills. The discovery mode, however, is not superior to any other way of teaching for all instructional purposes. Thus, discovery lessons should be used in combination with expository instruction. To rely entirely, or even extensively, on the discovery mode would be an inefficient and ineffective way to teach.

Following is a summary of the main ideas about the design and use of the discovery mode of instruction. These ideas can serve as rules or criteria to guide the design and use of discovery lessons.

1. Discovery lessons should be carefully designed in terms of clearly indicated instructional objectives.
2. The conditions of learning surrounding discovery lessons should be arranged so as to facilitate the achievement of clearly indicated instructional objectives.
3. Teachers should help students to understand what their task is and to perceive the purpose of the assignment.

4. Teachers should help students to stay on the track—to avoid digressions and meandering from the point of the lesson.

5. Teachers should avoid asking questions and providing answers that foreclose thought and student inquiry.

6. Teachers should provide prompts and cues, if necessary, to facilitate the successful completion of discovery lessons.

7. Discovery lessons should be used in combination with expository instruction rather than as *the* single teaching method.

8. Discovery lessons can function as "mind grabbers" and motivators to inquiry. Thus, they are appropriately used to initiate a set of lessons.

9. Discovery lessons can also function as tests of comprehension—as devices to determine the extent to which students understand what was presented in preceding lessons. If they can apply what was presented earlier to the successful completion of a discovery exercise, then they provide evidence of competence.

APPLICATION 4.1: THE SITE MAP LESSON[17]

Following is an example of a discovery lesson designed by the Anthropology Curriculum Study Project of one of the early versions of their experimental course. After reading the description of the lesson, prepare answers to these questions:

1. Is it a "good" example of a discovery lesson? Why?

_____

_____

_____

2. How would you use the lesson in your class? What objectives would you try to achieve through it? How would you attempt to achieve them?

_____

_____

_____

3. What type of instruction, if any, would you use in combination with the lesson in order to achieve your instructional objectives?

This lesson depends on the site map (Figure 4.4). This map represents the remains, as noted by an archeologist, of a group of Bushmen, a nonliterate group which lives in the Kalahari Desert of southwest Africa. The site map presents every feature of a Bushman's campsite which was studied by the archeologist. On the basis of the clues in the map, students are expected to formulate questions and to make inferences about the way of life of the Bushmen.

The site map lesson has been used as the introductory lesson of a unit about early man and his way of life. Following is an excerpt from the teacher's guide to the lesson.[18]

In the course of the first few days [of this unit] the students are given a map of an abandoned Bushman campsite along with illustrations of the artifacts found there. . . . They are not to be told, however, that the site is a Bushman site. They are asked to interpret the information provided them as an archeological problem and to reconstruct as much of the way of life of these "unknown" people as they can on the bases of the "archeological" evidence at hand.

Students then discuss their reconstructions to find the extent of their agreement. What kind of statements can they make as certainties? as probabilities? as possibilities?

The teacher then plays a slide tape exposition of Bushmen culture and ecology which "incidentally" provides a context for all the archeological evidence previously examined. It describes, in fact, the same site with people in it.

Following is a dialogue between a teacher and his eleventh-grade students who are using the site map lesson.[19] (It is quoted from *Day One* by Robert Hanvey et al.) In terms of the preceding discussion of discovery learning, criticize the teacher's use of this lesson. How would you have handled this lesson differently?

The place: a midwestern high school in an older middle-class suburban community; the school is ten years old. Mr. A has been teaching in the school for nine years. The students are eleventh graders. On Day 1 of the unit they have been back in school after summer vacation for only eleven days. The group is homogeneously grouped and is considered low–average in ability. The teacher begins, as suggested in the teaching plan, with definitions of archeology and anthropology. This occupies about twenty minutes of a period that is sixty minutes long. The tape transcript below begins after that initial discussion, at the point where consideration of the site map begins.

TEACHER: *You've got to keep this in mind. Now basically, what we want to do for the next five to ten minutes is look at this map very carefully, and I want you to see what kinds of questions we can ask of the data on this map.*

Now, keep in mind what you're trying to do. Remember that people lived at this site on the map. Remember that these people had a style or a way of life—like you have. They were real human beings; you see, they had a way of life. Now, from these data, from this map, we want to get some notion of what these people were like; what kind or style of life they must have had socially.

Now, what I want you to do—I want you to think about what kinds of questions—remember when we were talking about how the historian works, we said: "One thing that the historian does, he asks questions." Now, we went through a number of exercises by asking questions and so forth. Now, that's pretty much the same kind of thing that I want you to do here. I want you, first of all, to identify them: what kinds of questions would you ask? So, if you want to jot this down in your notebooks—because this is what I want you to do in the next few minutes.

Now, let me point out a couple of things: I'm not going to tell you very much about this, because I want you to figure it out yourself. Down here on the map you've got a key, and I assume that your geography experience tells

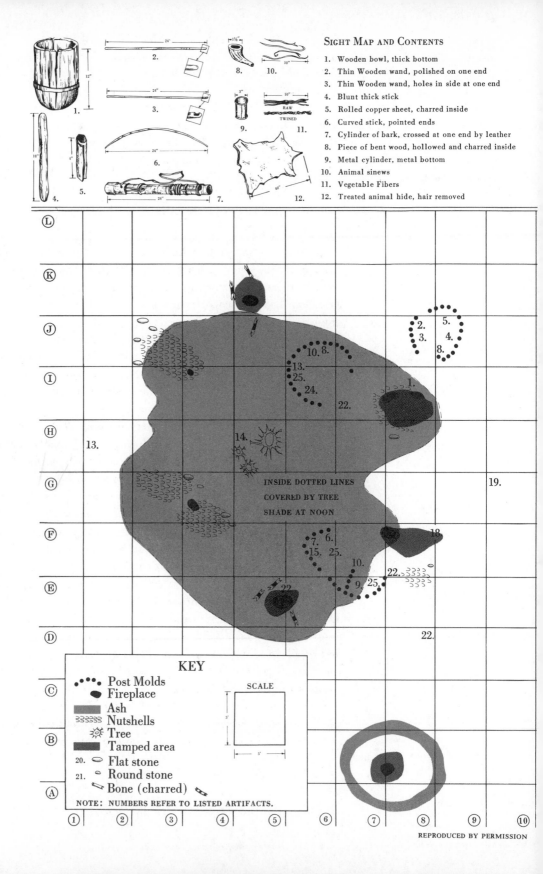

FIGURE 4.4.
Site map.

SIGHT MAP AND CONTENTS

1. Wooden bowl, thick bottom
2. Thin Wooden wand, polished on one end
3. Thin Wooden wand, holes in side at one end
4. Blunt thick stick
5. Rolled copper sheet, charred inside
6. Curved stick, pointed ends
7. Cylinder of bark, crossed at one end by leather
8. Piece of bent wood, hollowed and charred inside
9. Metal cylinder, metal bottom
10. Animal sinews
11. Vegetable Fibers
12. Treated animal hide, hair removed

INSIDE DOTTED LINES
COVERED BY TREE
SHADE AT NOON

KEY

•••• Post Molds
⬤ Fireplace
▬ Ash
ⁿⁿⁿⁿⁿ Nutshells
☀ Tree
▬ Tamped area
20. ⬭ Flat stone
21. ◖ Round stone
⟋ Bone (charred)

SCALE

5'

5'

NOTE: NUMBERS REFER TO LISTED ARTIFACTS.

2'

RAW
TWINED

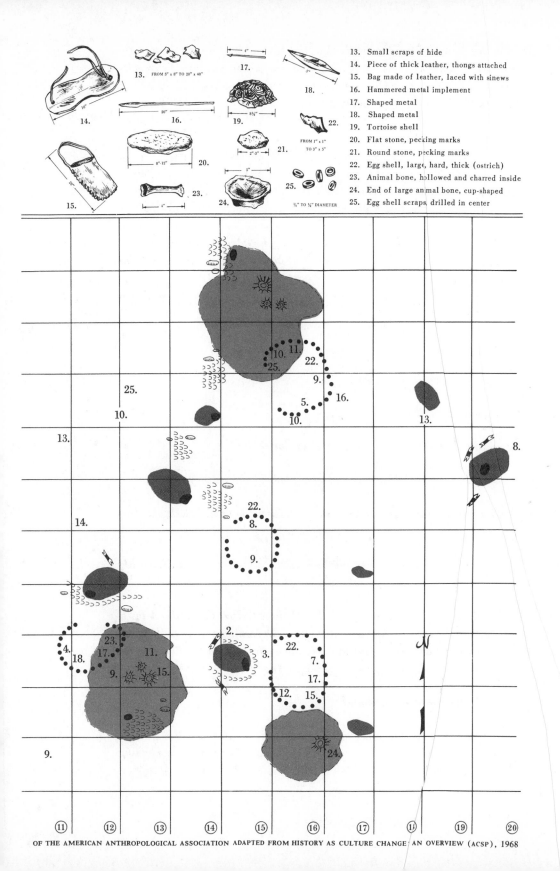

13. Small scraps of hide
14. Piece of thick leather, thongs attached
15. Bag made of leather, laced with sinews
16. Hammered metal implement
17. Shaped metal
18. Shaped metal
19. Tortoise shell
20. Flat stone, pecking marks
21. Round stone, pecking marks
22. Egg shell, large, hard, thick (ostrich)
23. Animal bone, hollowed and charred inside
24. End of large animal bone, cup-shaped
25. Egg shell scraps, drilled in center

you that this is something important that you have to pay some attention to. See the scale? Each of these blocks is 5 × 5 feet. Now, you can figure this out for yourself. The average lot size in this community is 50 × 128 feet. Now, that means that your lot is probably 50 feet wide and runs back toward the alley about 128 feet. That gives you roughly some idea of what you are dealing with.

Also, I want you to pay some attention to the contents that you have up here at the top, and, of course, the numbers regarding each one of these things would be worth paying attention to because it will give you a description of what the article is and you can refer down here to where the article was found. I want you to play around with this for a while, and see what kinds of questions you could possibly ask of this map; of the data on the map, to find out what is going on and to find out the life of these people. So jot down your questions, if you will.

(After a few minutes for student perusal.) What's the question that you want to ask of the data?

GIRL: *Where is the site?*

TEACHER: *Why might you want to know that?*

BOY: *What is the climate like?*

TEACHER: *Why would you want to know what the climate was like?*

BOY: *You'd want to know about housing and what kinds of clothes they wore.*

TEACHER: *O.K. This raises certain questions, I suppose, about housing, clothing. Anything else?*

BOY: *Did they use fire just to cook—or did they use it to keep warm, and stuff like that?*

TEACHER: *All right. What about the use of fire? And, I should think that too, relates to the climate, as you might want to put it. O.K., Debbie, can you think of another reason why you might want to know about the climate for this reason? (Pause) We'll come back to you, then, O.K.? Anyone else about the climate?*

BOY: *What about the flora and the fauna?*

TEACHER: *If you know where the site was located, you might be able to tell a little bit more about it. What do you people think? You're pointing to something, you're pointing to something that you want; that you don't have. What is it? Well, let's pursue this a little further, then. Anyone else have any notion why you might want to know where the site is? Paul?*

PAUL: *If it was in one of the seven cradles of civilization, you know, they had differ- ent techniques of farming and stuff, and you could, maybe, draw that up by the type of implements found, you know, in some places they raise their food, and stuff.*

TEACHER: *What kind of a question is Paul asking? What's the nature of his question, really?*

PAUL: *What age was this in? What time . . .*

TEACHER: *No, no, I don't think that's what you're really asking. How did they make their living, really? Isn't that what you're asking?*

PAUL: *And it also depends on how far advanced their brain was, you know, what they . . .*

TEACHER: *The kind of crops they had? All right, I think that's a relevant question to be asking at this time: What kind of crops did they have? But before you can begin to think about what kinds of crops they had, it seems to me that there's a lot of questions we have hinted at already. What am I talking about? Would the climate have anything to do with what kind of crops they would have? So, it might be useful to know something about their climate, right? Are there any other questions that you might begin to ask about this? Bill?*

BILL: *There appears to be some metal.*

TEACHER: *All right, you say that there appears to be some metal. What do you call those things that are left over?*

BILL: *Artifacts.*

TEACHER: *Artifacts. All right, they are metal artifacts. All right, what's your question?*

BILL: *Did they have a working knowledge of it?*

TEACHER: *Did they have a working knowledge of metal? All right, that's a legitimate question. All right, what other kinds of questions might we begin to pose here? Debbie?*

DEBBIE: *I'd like to know how they got the ostriches.*

TEACHER: *You would like to know how they got the ostriches, huh? With the ostrich egg shells. Why are you interested in that particular question, Debbie? Something there apparently intrigues you. Do you think they spent the afternoon at the zoo, is that what? . . .*

DEBBIE: *I was wondering what they did, and how they did it.*

TEACHER: *All right: How did they get these things? How did they get the ostriches? All right, are there any other questions we might profitably ask here?*

BOY: *Well, I don't know—we would like to know if this was a permanent site, or if they were just nomads, sort of, passing through.*

TEACHER: *Is this something that's just temporary? That's a very good question. Why is the answer to that question really important to us: whether this is a temporary site, or whether this is a permanent one, where they may have lived a long time? Let's pursue that a little bit. Paul?*

PAUL: *Well, if it was a temporary one, they might have picked up some of these articles from other places and dragged them here; but if it's a permanent one, the articles must have come from the general vicinity.*

TEACHER: *All right, anything else that's relevant to this question? Debbie?*

DEBBIE: *How would you be able to find out?*

TEACHER: *How would you be able to detect? I don't know. How would you think they would be able to detect; whether they lived there a long time, or, you know, just came and camped for a couple of days and shoved off?*

DEBBIE: *I don't know.*

ALLEN: *Take a look at their shelter or housing, whether it's temporary or more complex.*

TEACHER: *All right, you think, maybe, if we could take a look at some of the artifacts, and somehow reconstruct the kind of housing that these people might have had, that this might somehow tell us a little something about their style of life; whether they moved around a lot; that makes sense. If they were con-*

stantly on the move, it would be pretty foolish to invest a great deal of time and energy, effort and material in rather permanent housing. It just doesn't make sense, does it? Nevertheless, they might.

GIRL: *If they were moving around a lot, they wouldn't raise so many crops.*

TEACHER: *All right, you conclude that if they were moving around a lot, they wouldn't raise too many crops. All right, it seems to me that we're doing certain things here; we're doing two things, really: we're drawing conclusions already, and I don't want you to do that. But you're also, at the same time that you're doing that, you're raising some good questions, and I hope you keep this in your minds that it's all very tentative. Really we're asking, it seems to me, a couple of kinds of questions. What kinds of questions have we been asking? Relative to these questions that you've been asking, now, you can break them into two categories: what kinds of questions have you been asking? One is the question about what? What's one kind of question that you've been asking? All right, we've been asking questions about what, really?*

BOY: *The people themselves?*

TEACHER: *The people themselves. You've been asking, and I suppose this is what we really . . . you know, we talked about objectives here. We wanted to find out about something from the site: about how the people lived. So we're asking questions about that. What's the other question we're asking; the other type of question?*

BOY: *About the environment?*

TEACHER: *Well, about the environment, and even more specifically—Allen?*

ALLEN: *Survival?*

TEACHER: *Well, maybe.*

GIRL: *Well, how they lived.*

TEACHER: *Well, that's about people, too, I think; how they lived and how they survived. This is about people, isn't it? But, we're asking another type of question. Anybody catch it? Come on, you're right on it. Billy?*

BILLY: *Environment.*

TEACHER: *Well, yes, we're asking about their environment; but, we're not only asking about their environment . . .*

PAUL: *We're asking about articles—the things that they had?*

TEACHER: *We're asking questions about these data, aren't we? Aren't we asking questions about this: the artifacts, the materials they left behind. O.K., by asking questions about the data, this raises questions about the people and the environment and so on. Now, one thing becomes glaringly obvious to me: What's your problem, in part? In other words, you're saying what? You need more data; you need more information, don't you? Now, one kind of data which you have identified, that might be useful, is data or information about the natural environment; the flora, the fauna, the climate and so forth.*

(End of transcript. The teacher at this point shows slides of the Kalahari environment. As homework, students are asked to read a pamphlet titled "Kalahari–1: A Site Report," which gives information about flora, fauna, climate, and geology.)

Appraisal of the lesson's format. The site map is in many ways an excellent model of a discovery lesson. The map contains pieces of information that pertain to the way of life of an unspecified group of people. Students are challenged to probe the meaning of the map and to generate questions and speculative answers about the way of life of the people whose remains are depicted by means of the map. To complete the lesson, the students must make inferences from limited evidence in order to reconstruct the main features of the group's way of life. Obviously this lesson is designed to be a mind grabber, an arouser of curiosity, and a motivator to inquiry.

The main weaknesses of the lesson format are that objectives of instruction are not exactly stated and questioning strategies are not specified to help the teacher to manage classroom discussion of the site map. The objectives of the lesson are suggested by the teacher's guide in *Day One.* However, the lack of specific guidance in the teacher's guide may be related to the rather artless implementation of this lesson by the teacher in the preceding classroom example.

Appraisal of the discussion. A number of criticisms can be made of this teacher's use of the site map discovery lesson. First, the teacher talked too much. The point of a discovery lesson is to involve the students as actively and fully as possible. However, this teacher dominated the discussion so extensively as to limit student involvement.

Second, the flow of discussion was entirely from teacher to individual students. Students did not interact with one another to accomplish the assigned task.

Third, the discussion was poorly focused. The teacher's introduction of the discussion was too long and rambling. And he used a "scatter shot" approach to question asking throughout the discussion rather than systematically developing a pointed question-asking strategy. Thus, student attention was not always held to the objective of the lesson. Students did not always seem to know what to do or why they should be responding.

Fourth, the teacher's choice of questions was very poor and was perhaps a major reason for the inferior quality of the discussion. The teacher's guide suggests that the main point of the lesson is to prompt student reconstruction of the way of life of the group whose remains are symbolized on the map. Thus, the teacher might have asked students to respond to one basic question throughout the discussion: From the evidence in the site map, what inferences can you make about the way of life of this group of people? By persistently requiring students to respond to this one basic question, the teacher could have kept the attention of students pointedly focused.

Fifth, the teacher at times became impatient and provided answers, instead of artfully cuing student responses. The point of a discovery lesson is blunted when the teacher rather than the students makes the discoveries.

Sixth, the teacher often failed to follow up student responses. Many were seemingly ignored or left hanging. Some responses were followed up very superficially or meaninglessly. When a teacher fails to react meaningfully to the responses of students, they may get the impression that he does not value their participation and may refuse to participate in future classroom discussions.

Finally, the teacher at times interacted clumsily with students. For example, he crudely cut off Paul's responses; he rather unfeelingly put down Debbie's comments with sarcasm. Moves such as these can trigger student dissatisfaction and can inhibit participation in classroom discussions.

EXPOSITION

Expository instruction is presenting to students the entire content of what is to be learned.[20] Students are required only to master the material presented to them rather than to reason beyond the material in order to make independent discoveries. Expository instruction may be presented through various media: lectures, films, tapes, teaching machines, or standard textbooks.

Most high school teachers rely primarily on some form of expository instruction. In recent years these procedures have been attacked severely on the grounds that they lead to meaningless rote learning by students and authoritarian practices by teachers. Critics have claimed that expository instruction encourages passive and formalistic acquisition of meaningless discrete facts which are painfully learned and quickly forgotten. Much criticism of exposition is valid; many instances of rote learning and authoritarian teaching can doubtlessly be found. However, the expository mode of instruction does not necessarily produce bad results. The fault is not with it per se but with poorly designed and executed expository instruction.

Expository instruction may lead to meaningful verbal learning, rather than to rote learning, if instruction is designed and used properly. Meaningful verbal learning occurs when the student is actively engaged in acquiring and using ideas and facts so that the ideas and facts are integrated into his cognitive structure, the framework of previously learned concepts and principles that the student brings to the instructional situation. The ultimate test of meaningful verbal learning is demonstrated capability to apply facts and ideas acquired from expository instruction to an exercise or problem that has not been encountered before.[21]

David P. Ausubel has provided strong arguments for the value of properly designed expository instruction. He maintains that "verbal exposition is actually the most efficient way of teaching subject matter and leads to sounder and less trivial knowledge than when pupils serve as their own pedagogues." Ausubel argues that "beginning in the junior high school period, students can acquire most new concepts and learn most new propositions by directly grasping higher order relationships between abstractions." As students mature and acquire increasing capability for verbalization and higher-level cognition, discovery learning becomes very inefficient, and properly designed expository instruction becomes feasible. Most youngsters in the age group 12 and 13 have developed sufficient cognitive capability to learn effectively from properly arranged expository instruction. "Hence, it is unnecessary routinely to introduce concrete-empirical props or time consuming discovery techniques in order to make possible or to enhance intuitive understanding of abstract propositions."[22]

Ausubel and others have argued very effectively against the claim that expository instruction is necessarily authoritarian and that it inevitably produces passive, uncritical learners.[23] Expository instruction is authoritarian when teachers present their ideas or those of a particular textbook as dogma to be learned without criticism or question. However, expository instruction is not necessarily autocratic or mind deadening. Expository lessons can develop skills of critical thinking which can be applied to the appraisal of subsequent expository lessons. Alan and Samuel Guskin say that "what makes an exposition by a teacher or a text autocratic is that implicit orientation of the writer that 'you must think the way I tell you because I say so.' In contrast, the writer or teacher who provides objective evidence for his position seems to be saying, 'My word is not enough. You be the judge of the current position. You participate in deciding on the truth.' "[24] A basic way of determining if expository instruction is autocratic is to find out whether the student has an opportunity critically to appraise the presentation and to accept or reject it. Properly designed expository instruction can be highly stimulating and produces higher-level cognition and learning.

The proper design and execution of expository instruction is based at least on the following rules.[25] First, students should be told clearly at the beginning of a lesson what they are expected to learn. Numerous studies have indicated that students who are informed about what they are expected to achieve are more likely to learn and remember what they learn than are those who do not have a clear sense of direction.

Second, unfamiliar ideas and facts should be explained in familiar terms. Well-designed expository instruction connects new meanings to old meanings.

Third, the expository instruction must be relatively free of qualities that could interfere with smooth and easy learning. For example, the facts and ideas to be learned should be clearly related. The lesson should be clearly ordered in terms of distinct parts, and these parts should be clearly connected. Instruction should be straightforward; excess verbiage as well as decorative frills and embellishments should be avoided.

Fourth, the instruction should be designed to require active learning. Throughout the lesson students should read a brief expository discussion and then use the materials presented in the discussion to answer a question or to complete an exercise.

Fifth, knowledge of correct responses to questions and exercises should be provided immediately by either the teacher or the instructional material. Confirmation of correct answers provides reinforcement to learning, and the indication of incorrect answers alerts the student and the teacher to learning problems.

Sixth, redundancy should be artfully built into the instructional materials. Students should encounter the same basic facts and ideas over and over as they move through a social studies course. This contrived redundancy provides them with ample opportunity to practice using fundamental facts and ideas. To reduce boredom and to maximize comprehension, students should encounter the same facts and ideas in different combinations and contexts.

APPLICATION 4.2: THE VOTING BEHAVIOR LESSON

Following is an example of expository instruction about voter behavior and elections. Read the lesson* carefully to answer these questions.

1. Is it a "good" example of expository instruction? Why?

_____

_____

_____

2. What is your appraisal of the teacher's use of the lesson? Would you in any way use it differently? If so, how and why?

_____

_____

_____

_____

3. What type of instruction, if any, would you use in combination with the lesson in order to achieve your instructional objectives?

_____

_____

_____

*Adapted from *American Political Behavior* by Howard D. Mehlinger and John J. Patrick.

© Copyright 1972 by Indiana University. Published by Ginn and Company. Used with permission.

The lesson, part of a unit of instruction, follows one about the relationship between election laws and voting. It is designed to lead students, in a step-by-step fashion, to learn generalizations about nonlegal factors related to participation in public elections.

The objective of instruction presented in the *Teachers' Guide*[26] is:

Students can state [these] relationships between voter turnout and personal factors:
(a) Individuals who see a connection between voting and some personal gain or loss are more likely to vote than individuals who are not similarly motivated.
(b) Individuals who are interested in politics are more likely to vote than are individuals who are not interested.
(c) Individuals with a higher sense of political efficacy are more likely to vote than individuals with a lower sense of political efficacy.
(d) Tendency to vote decreases with an increase in social detachment.
(e) Individuals who have a higher sense of civic duty are more likely to vote than are individuals with a lower sense of civic duty.
(f) Tendency to vote is likely to increase with an increase in sense of personal involvement in politics.
(g) Individuals with a strong attachment to one of the major political parties are more likely than individuals without this attachment to vote.
(h) Tendency to vote is likely to increase with an increase in socio-economic status.

The sample lesson about variations in participation in public elections is presented below.[27] To what extent does it and the accompanying description of subsequent instruction conform to the rules for designing expository instruction presented in this chapter?

Failure to satisfy legal requirements explains why some people do not vote in public elections. However, the legal factor does not explain why several million American citizens, who meet the legal qualifications for voting, choose not to register or often fail to vote if registered. . . .

Political scientists have speculated that personal factors can contribute to an explanation of non-voting in public elections. Personal factors are such variables as sense of political efficacy, political interest, sense of citizen duty, and concern with election outcome.

Political scientists who have studied the relationship of these personal factors to non-voting have defined these variables as follows: Sense of political efficacy is a person's beliefs about how much power people like him have over what public officials do. For example, people with a high sense of political efficacy believe that they can and should influence governmental decisions. People with a low sense of political efficacy believe that they can do little or nothing about what government does.

Political interest refers to the amount of interest a person has in the election campaign. People with a high degree of political interest are very concerned about campaign issues and the characteristics of the candidates.

Concern about the election outcome means caring about who wins an election and about the results that might stem from the election outcome. A person with a low degree of concern about the election outcome cares little or nothing about which candidates win or what these candidates might do once they assume public office.

Sense of civic duty is the responsibility a person feels to participate in a public election. A person with a high sense of civic duty believes that he should take part in public elections and that those who fail to participate are not very good citizens.

Political scientists have constructed questionnaires to measure these personal factors, or variables, and administered these questionnaires to randomly selected samples that are representative of the population of the United States. Some of their findings are revealed in Diagrams 1–4.

What is the relationship of each of four personal factors to tendency to vote as indicated in these diagrams?

Political scientists sometimes combine the four personal factors just studied under the concept *personal involvement in politics*. Hence, *a high sense of personal involvement in politics* is indicated by a high sense of political efficacy, a high degree of political interest, a high sense of citizen duty, and a high degree of concern about the election outcome. *A low sense of personal involvement in politics* is

DIAGRAM 1.

TENDENCY TO VOTE	SENSE OF POLITICAL EFFICACY	
	Lower	*Higher*
Lower	X	
Higher		X

DIAGRAM 2.

TENDENCY TO VOTE	SENSE OF CIVIC DUTY	
	Lower	*Higher*
Lower	X	
Higher		X

DIAGRAM 3.

TENDENCY TO VOTE	DEGREE OF POLITICAL INTEREST	
	Lower	*Higher*
Lower	X	
Higher		X

DIAGRAM 4.

TENDENCY TO VOTE	DEGREE OF CONCERN WITH THE ELECTION OUTCOME	
	Lower	*Higher*
Lower	X	
Higher		X

indicated by a low ranking in each of the four personal factors. On the basis of Diagrams 1–4, and the discussion in the preceding paragraph, indicate the correct relationships between personal involvement in politics and tendency to vote in Diagram 5. For example, should a mark be placed in Box A, B, C, or D to indicate this relationship?

DIAGRAM 5.

TENDENCY TO VOTE	PERSONAL INVOLVEMENT IN POLITICS	
	Lower	*Higher*
Lower	A	B
Higher	C	D

Findings about the relationship of personal involvement in politics to several other variables are indicated in Diagrams 6–8. Use evidence provided in the diagrams to answer the questions that follow the diagrams.

What is the relationship of the political party identification to sense of personal involvement in politics? From evidence presented in Diagrams 1–6, what inferences can you make about the relationship of political party identification to tendency

DIAGRAM 6.

	PERSONAL INVOLVEMENT IN POLITICS	IDENTIFICATION WITH DEMOCRATIC OR REPUBLICAN PARTY	
		None or weak	*Strong*
	Low	X	
	High		X

DIAGRAM 7.

	PERSONAL INVOLVEMENT IN POLITICS	SOCIOECONOMIC STATUS	
		Lower	*Higher*
	Lower	X	
	Higher		X

DIAGRAM 8.

	TENDENCY TO VOTE	SOCIAL DETACHMENT	
		Lower	*Higher*
	Lower	A	B
	Higher	C	D

to vote? From the evidence presented in Diagrams 1–6, how would you attempt to explain the relationship that you inferred between political party identification and tendency to vote?

What is the relationship of socioeconomic status to personal involvement in politics? From evidence presented in Diagrams 1–7, what inferences can you make about the relationship of socioeconomic status to tendency to vote? From the evidence presented in Diagrams 1–7, how would you attempt to explain the relationship that you inferred between socioeconomic status and tendency to vote?

Social detachment is a variable that political scientists have applied to studies of political participation. A high degree of social detachment means that an individual is a marginal member of society, a fringe person who is not involved in activities that are basic to the functioning of a society. A person with a high degree of social detachment has little or no stake in the success of the society and shows little interest in trying to support the groups that comprise the society. A low degree of social detachment means that an individual is involved extensively in the affairs of his society. A person with a low degree of social detachment has a great concern for the success of his society and works hard to support the groups that comprise the society. Based on this definitional discussion of social detachment, what is your hypothesis about the relationship of social detachment to tendency to vote? State your hypothesis in terms of Diagram 8 . . . For example, would you place a mark in Box A, B, C, or D to indicate your hypothesis? How would you attempt to explain your hypothesis about social detachment and tendency to vote?

Following is an excerpt from a classroom dialogue between a teacher and a group of twelfth-grade students who used the voter behavior lesson. What is your appraisal of the teacher's use of the lesson?

TEACHER: *Your homework assignment was to do the text exercise "Nonlegal Factors That Influence Voter Turnout in Public Elections." I assume that all of you completed the assignment. Am I right about that? How about you, Billy—did you finish the exercise? Did you have any trouble with it?*

BILLY: *Yeah, I finished it. I think I did it right, too.*

TEACHER: *We'll see about that right now. I'm going to ask you, Billy, and some others to tell me your answers to each part of the exercise. I'll provide feedback about whether your answers are right or wrong. Those who don't understand why a certain answer is right or wrong ought to raise their hands, and we'll stop and talk about the problem. Billy, what is your answer to the first question, about the relationships between each of four personal factors to tendency to vote that is shown by Diagrams 1 to 4?*

BILLY: *Well, Diagram 1 shows that people with a high sense of political efficacy are more likely to vote than people with a low sense of political efficacy. Diagram 2 says that people with a high sense of civic duty are more likely to vote than those with a low sense of civic duty. Diagram 3 tells that tendency to vote increases or decreases with political interest. And Diagram 4 says the same kind of thing about degree of concern with the election outcome and tendency to vote. Those with a higher degree of concern are more likely to participate.*

TEACHER: *Okay, Billy, that was just fine. But then that was the easiest part of the lesson.*

BILLY: *Yeah, but I did the other parts right, too.*

TEACHER: *I'm sure you did, Billy. But let's ask Susie how she answered the next question, the one about the relationship between personal involvement in politics and tendency to vote. Susie, which box did you mark in Diagram 5 to show the correct relationship between the variables?*

SUSIE: *I put a mark in Boxes A and D.*

TEACHER: *That's correct. Any questions about that or about what it means? Morton, what's the answer to the next group of questions, the ones under Diagram 6?*

The remainder of the discussion continued according to the pattern illustrated in the classroom dialogue. The students were able to move through the lesson without serious difficulty. Indeed, the lesson was designed to help students learn some generalizations about voter behavior as efficiently as possible.

The lesson does conform to a considerable extent to the criteria for judging expository instruction presented on pages 139 to 141. At the outset of instruction, students are told the point of the lesson. The instructional material is presented in a step-by-step fashion which builds students' knowledge systematically as they move through the lesson. The presentation is straightforward and contains no decorative trappings, verbal or pictorial, that could interfer with learning. This lesson requires students to be active learners, continually to use information to complete exercises; they must regularly make precise intellectual moves in order to complete the lesson. For example, students must reason deductively to answer this question which appears in the middle of the lesson: "From the evidence presented in Diagrams 1–7, what inferences can you make about the relationship of socioeconomic status to tendency to vote?" The deductive line of reasoning is as follows:

If individuals with higher socioeconomic status are more likely than those with lower socioeconomic status to have a higher personal involvement in politics, and,
 if individuals with a higher personal involvement in politics are more likely than those with a low personal involvement to vote in public elections,
 then individuals with a higher socioeconomic status are more likely than those with a lower socioeconomic status to vote in public elections.

The responsibility of the teacher, as shown by the classroom dialogue, is to assign the lesson, to be certain that students perceive the purpose of the lesson, and to provide feedback, knowledge of the correct responses to the questions and exercises that permeate the lesson.

This lesson is basically self-instructional. Most students should be able to move through the set of exercises without help from the teacher other than confirmation of correct responses. However, the teacher should be ready to assist students who have difficulty in completing it.

The propositions about voter behavior, which are developed in this lesson, are applicable to several subsequent lessons in the course from which this prototype was taken. Students are required to demonstrate that they have learned these propositions about voter behavior by applying them to the analyses of case studies and the completion of exercises which constitute subsequent lessons.

The preceding discussion of the merits of the discovery and expository modes of instruction demonstrates that both approaches can contribute to successful competency-based instruction for higher-level learning. Learning by discovery is most appropriate when correct responses are less clear or obvious, when students bring little or no relevant experience to the instructional situation, or both. For example, open-ended questions and problem-solving activities that permit divergent responses are most appropriately presented via the discovery approach. In contrast, expository instruction designed to achieve meaningful verbal learning is most appropriate when the correct responses are clear and concrete, when students bring ample relevant experience to the learning task, or both.

At their best, discovery lessons can facilitate the development of basic intellectual skills and the ability to transfer learning from one situation to another. At their worst, these lessons result in inefficient trial-and-error learning which represents an abdication by the teacher of responsibility for instruction. At their best, expository lessons prompt direct, efficient, active, and meaningful learning which can develop high-level learning ability. At their worst, expository lessons yield rote learning and passive learners. A well-designed curriculum for high school social studies includes an artful blend of both modes of instruction.

Summary

This chapter is an introduction to a particular view of instruction and learning which places a heavy responsibility on teachers to be systematic selectors and implementors of instruction. *Learning is defined as a relatively permanent change in capability that results from practice and that is not attributable to physical maturation or physical disability.* This definition indicates that learning results from experience and from interaction between an organism and its environment. To enhance learning, you must artfully and systematically manipulate the student's environment so that there is a high probability that a particular experience will yield a particular outcome or change in the student's capability. This view of learning implies that *instruction is the creation of conditions that facilitate learning; it involves the manipulation of the student's environment to induce changes in capability efficiently and extensively.*

Our definitions of learning and instruction constitute a *competency-based concept* of education in the social studies. This concept emphasizes a tight connection between instructional means and instructional objectives and focuses on the learner. The key instructional question for every teacher who holds a competency-based concept of instruction is: What do I want the student to be able to do as a result of instruction? The teacher then tries to design or implement instruction that can lead to attainment of desired outcomes.

Competency-based instruction in the social studies can range from attempts to develop low-level competencies, such as the ability to recall facts, to attempts to develop high-level capabilities, such as skill in formulating and testing hypotheses. Teachers who stress memorization and recall of facts influence the development of passive and recalcitrant students, ritualistic acquirers, and regurgitators of discrete information. In contrast, teachers who stress the application of facts to relevant purposes influence the development of active learners, the avid acquirers or users of evidence in the pursuit of meaningful educational objectives. Teachers who stress higher-level learning enhance the development of the capability to think and learn independently. They should strive to design instruction that encourages the development of intellectual skills pertinent to higher-level learning. Students practice higher-level learning when they are required to apply concepts to the organization and interpretation of facts, to apply facts to the confirmation of hypotheses, and to apply facts and hypotheses to the solution of problems.

Both discovery lessons and expository instruction may be designed to elicit higher-level learning and the development of intellectual skills. Discovery lessons are designed to require students to use facts and ideas to make reasonable speculations and hypotheses about the unknown. Discovery lessons deeply involve students in the development and application of intellectual skills. Expository lessons can also be designed to require active learning, the purposeful acquisition and application of facts to the completion of exercises, the analysis of cases, or the solution of puzzles or problems. Unfortunately, expository instruction has been associated only with rote, passive learning. This association all too often has been an apt description of expository instruction in social studies classrooms. However, appropriately designed expository lessons can facilitate the development of the ability to inquire and to think critically.

Instruction that requires students to practice higher-level learning is most relevant. The capability to think critically, to conduct inquiry, and to determine the basis for the confirmation or rejection of propositions will remain relevant to a variety of concerns, regardless of changing purposes or knowledge which mark the development of our culture.

APPLICATION 4.3: EVALUATION OF A LESSON PLAN

Following is a description of a bad lesson plan aimed at teaching facts. After you examine this instructional plan, apply what you have learned from this chapter to the appraisal of the lesson.

LESSON PLAN — FEBRUARY 28, 1974

Instructional Objectives

1. Students can list the causes of World War I which are stated in the textbook.
2. Students can tell the dates of each of the following events which are associated with the outbreak of World War I:
   a. The Moroccan Crisis
   b. The Bosnian Crisis
   c. The Agadir Crisis
   d. The First Balkan War
   e. The Second Balkan War
   (27 similar events were included in this list.)
3. Students can debate about which European statesmen contributed the most to the outbreak of World War I.

Classroom Procedures: Day 1

Assign pages xxx to xxx in the required textbook. Tell students to answer these questions.
1. What were the causes of World War I? List them.

2. On what date did the following key events associated with the outbreak of World War I occur? (List the key events for students.)

3. Which individuals contributed most to the outbreak of World War I?

Classroom Procedures: Day 2

Conduct a discussion of the three questions assigned on the previous day. Be certain to determine which students did not do the assignment. Require students to answer questions 1 and 2 exactly as indicated in the book. Tell the students that question 3 is a "thought question" and that they are to give their opinions as answers to this question. Encourage students to freely exchange their opinions, and stress that in a discussion such as this, every opinion is likely to be equally good.

1. What is your evaluation of this lesson?

_____

_____

_____

_____

_____

_____

2. How would you design instruction about the conditions associated with the outbreak of World War I? Why?

_____

_____

_____

_____

_____

_____

Notes

1. Robert Mager, *Preparing Instructional Objectives*, Palo Alto, Calif.: Fearon, 1962, p. vii.
2. Stephen M. Corey, "The Nature of Instruction," in *Programmed Instruction*, 66th National Society for the Study of Education Yearbook, Part II, Chicago: University of Chicago Press, 1967, p. 6.
3. Robert M. Gagné, *The Conditions of Learning*, New York: Holt, Rinehart and Winston, 1965, p. 5.
4. W. James Popham and Eva L. Baker, *Systematic Instruction*, Englewood Cliffs, N.J.: Prentice-Hall, 1970, pp. 77–88.
5. Benjamin S. Bloom et al., *Taxonomy of Educational Objectives, Handbook I: Cognitive Domain*, New York: David McKay, 1956.
6. Gagné, op. cit., pp. 31–61.
7. G. Weber, "Do Teachers Understand Learning Theory?" *Phi Delta Kappan*, vol. 46, no. 9 (May, 1965), pp. 433–435. Norris Sanders, *Classroom Questions: What Kinds?* New York: Harper & Row, 1966, p. 2.
8. Gagné, op. cit., p. 167.
9. Robert F. Biehler, *Psychology Applied to Teaching*, Boston: Houghton Mifflin, 1971, pp. 254–257.
10. Jean Piaget, *Six Psychological Studies*, New York: Random House, Vintage Books, 1968. Joseph Adelson and Robert P. O'Neil, "Growth of Political Ideas in Adolescence: The Sense of Community," *Journal of Personality and Social Psychology*, vol. 4, no. 3 (1966), pp. 295–306.
11. Henry Ellis, *The Transfer of Learning*, New York: Macmillan, 1965.
12. Jerome Bruner, *The Relevance of Education*, New York: W. W. Norton, 1971, p. 114.
13. Lewis A. Dexter, "The Relevance of Political Science to the Social Studies Curriculum," Paper presented at the annual meeting of the National Council for the Social Studies, Houston, Tex., November, 1969, p. 9.
14. Jerome Bruner, *The Process of Education*, Cambridge, Mass.: Harvard University Press, The Belknap Press, 1960. *Toward a Theory of Instruction*, Cambridge, Mass.: Harvard University Press, The Belknap Press, 1966.
15. Hilda Taba, "Learning by Discovery," *The Elementary School Journal*, vol. 63, no. 6 (March, 1963), pp. 310–315.

16. John P. DeCecco, *The Psychology of Learning and Instruction,* Englewood Cliffs, N.J.: Prentice-Hall, 1968, pp. 469–471.

17. Robert Hanvey et al., *Day One,* Chicago: Anthropology Curriculum Study Project, 1967.

18. Ibid., p. 7.

19. Ibid., pp. 15–20.

20. DeCecco, op. cit., p. 468.

21. David P. Ausubel, *Educational Psychology: A Cognitive View,* New York: Holt, Rinehart and Winston, 1968, pp. 83–88.

22. Ibid, pp. 86–87.

23. Ibid, pp. 490–491.

24. Alan Edward Guskin and Samuel Louis Guskin, *A Social Psychology of Education,* Reading, Mass.: Addison-Wesley, 1970, pp. 36–49.

25. DeCecco, op. cit., pp. 322–384.

26. Howard D. Mehlinger and John J. Patrick, *Teachers' Guide for American Political Behavior,* Lexington, Mass.: Ginn, 1972, p. 68.

27. Howard D. Mehlinger and John J. Patrick, *American Political Behavior,* Lexington, Mass.: Ginn, 1972, pp. 204–207.

Suggested Reading

Bruner, Jerome. *Toward a Theory of Instruction.* Cambridge, Mass.: Harvard University Press, The Belknap Press, 1966. Bruner has been a chief advocate of discovery learning. In this book he discusses research and assumptions relevant to the discovery approach and develops guidelines for instructional procedure. The book contains may examples of instruction from *Man: A Course of Study,* an innovative social studies curriculum. The book is highly readable.

Craig, Robert C. *The Psychology of Learning in the Classroom.* New York: Macmillan, 1966. This book is a brief review of alternative learning theories and their implications for instruction. Stimulus-response or associationist theories are contrasted with cognitive or field theories. Guidelines to instructional practice are offered throughout the book.

Popham, W. James, and Eva L. Baker. *Systematic Instruction.* Englewood Cliffs, N.J.: Prentice-Hall, 1970. This book advocates a competency-based approach to instruction. It is written in a light, easy-to-read style and includes chapters on instructional objectives, curriculum planning, instructional design, and evaluation of instruction.

Skinner, B. F. *The Technology of Teaching.* New York: Appleton-Century-Crofts, 1968. This book is a concise presentation of the assumptions underlying stimulus-response learning theory and of the implications for instruction of this theory. Skinner argues persuasively for systematic expository instruction designed to maximize opportunities for students to achieve instruction objectives. Suggestions for lesson planning and implementation are offered.

5

Teaching
the Use of
Concepts

IMAGINE YOURSELF AS the host of two foreign guests who are visiting North America for the first time. One visitor is from New Zealand and the other from Afghanistan. Both speak English. You are introducing an American custom to your guests: watching a televised professional football game on Sunday afternoon. You and your visitors intently follow the organized mayhem on the TV screen and listen carefully as the sportscasters describe the action.

(As you read the following dialogue, try to "listen" with the ears of your foreign guests. What do the words mean literally? What do you imagine is happening when you understand the words literally—without the context of football? Is it possible for your foreign guests to learn the meaning of the words from their context?)

SPORTSCASTER A: *The Vikings are lined up in a pro-set formation. The flanker is going in motion as the quarterback, Fran Tarkenton, barks a long count. He seems to be calling an audible. Now he drops back to pass. He's facing enormous pressure from the Chicago front four. Tarkenton scrambles out of the pocket. . . . Oh! he's sacked back on his own thirty-yard line for a fifteen-yard loss!*

SPORTSCASTER B: *The Bears called a safety blitz that time. Butkus and Buffone red-dogged, and Smith, the strong safety, came barreling in to make the big play.*

SPORTSCASTER A: *Now its third down and long-yardage. Will Tarkenton call the draw, as he did the last time he faced this situation, or will he go for the bomb?*

Your guests look at you in dumbfounded amazement. Although each visitor speaks English very fluently, neither of them understands the sportscasters' language. And although each visitor is a sports enthusiast, neither has ever seen anything quite like an American professional football game. Your foreign guests are witnessing the same events and hearing the same commentary, but they literally do not "see" and "hear" what you do.

As you continue to watch the game, you try to explain to your guests what is happening but with little success. Most of your words and the words of the sportscasters are familiar enough to them since the visitors do speak English well. However, they attach different meanings to such terms as *man in motion, strong safety, red-dog, pocket, blitz,* and *bomb;* and special ones such as *pro-set formation, flanker,* and *quarterback* probably have little or no meaning for them.

As the game unfolds, you watch the players with pleasure and appreciation. They perform well, and the contest is close and exciting. Your guests watch politely but with little comprehension and enthusiasm. To them the scene is almost unintelligible, a massive whirl of confusing movement.

The fundamental barrier to communication and understanding is conceptual; the foreign guests do not share your frame of reference, your way of viewing the action of the football game. Although they perceive what you do, they do not apply the same *concepts* to these perceptions. Thus, they interpret these perceptions much differently than you do.

What are concepts? How do concepts serve learning and thinking about football games or anything else? Why is knowledge about concept learning important to social studies teachers? These are questions for you to think about as you read and study this chapter about concept learning in the social studies.

The Meaning and Uses of Concepts

During recent years social studies educators with very different points of view about instruction and learning have been able to agree that concept learning is important. However, there appears to be considerable disagreement and confusion in social studies circles about what concepts and concept learning are all about. Peter H. Martorella notes this ambiguity in *Concept Learning in the Social Studies:*

This apparent consensus on the importance of concept learning is deceptive, however, as a careful analysis of the literature will reveal. Terminology is, at best, fuzzy, and definitions usually are absent or lack precision. In many respects, the term "concept" has become a catch-all category for cognitive operations and frequently is often used synonymously with "idea," "generalization," "structure," "topic," or "labels."[1]

Reducing confusion about the meaning and use of concepts in the social studies can contribute significantly to improved instruction for concept learning. What is your level of understanding of the meaning and uses of concepts? Test your knowledge by making your response to each of the following six statements to indicate: A, agree; B, disagree; and C, uncertain.

————1. A concept is a good idea.

————2. A concept is a category.

————3. A concept is a word.

————4. A concept is a general statement such as this: Labor union members tend to vote for the Democratic party.

_____5. A concept is a fact.

_____6. A concept is a definition.

Explain your answers.

What *is* a concept? Statements 2 and 6 are different, but complementary, ways to think about what a concept is. Statement 2 indicates that to have a concept is to be able to group things with common characteristics into a category. Statement 6 indicates that a definition is the means one uses in deciding how to group things with common characteristics: how to place objects or events that conform to a definition within a category and to place other objects or events outside the category. In other words, a concept is a definition, a criterion, or a set of criteria for categorizing—that is, for grouping objects or events having something in common.[2]

Another way to think about the meaning of concept is to imagine that the box below is a category that includes everything that is part of the hypothetical concept X.

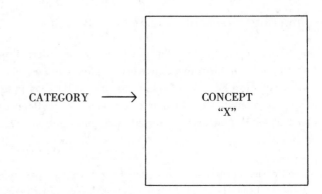

Everything that is not concept X, the noninstances of the concept, belongs outside the box; everything that is concept X, the instances of the concept, belongs inside the box. Thus, the content of this box, this category, is what concept X is all about.

Your definition of X is your means, or rule, for deciding what goes in or stays out of the box category. To know this definition is to be able to look at objects or events and to discriminate the instances from the noninstances of concept X.

Monogamy and ethnocentrism are names for concepts used by social scientists. Each of these words is a symbol for phenomena with common characteristics that can be grouped (as a category) according to a criterion (a definition). For example, monogamy is marriage to only one person at a time. Individuals who share this characteristic of marriage to only one person at a time are grouped and labeled monogamous. Ethnocentrism is the belief that your own culture, national group, or ethnic group is inherently superior to other cultures or groups. Individuals with the common characteristic of belief in the inherent superiority of their culture or group are categorized and named ethnocentric.

The words *monogamy* and *ethnocentrism* are not to be confused with the concepts that the words symbolize. Words are names or labels for concepts that facilitate communication, but words are neither concepts nor characteristics of concepts. It is possible to have a concept of something without knowing the conventional name or word associated with it. And it is possible to have a concept while using an unconventional word to talk or write about it, although this flouting of custom may impede communication with others. The conventional names of concepts sometimes change with time; as a language grows and develops, new conventions emerge and old usages decline. However, despite changing labels, the categories of objects or events which the words stand for may remain the same. As Shakespeare said, "A rose by any other name would smell as sweet."

Definition of X: the criterion for what goes in this box

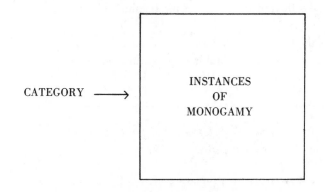

The definitions of *monogamy* and *ethnocentrism* or of other concepts are not to be confused with the facts, the instances of the concepts, which are grouped in terms of definitions. For example, these are hypothetical facts that fit the definition of monogamy: George is married to Barbara; Mike is married to Mary; Stanislaus is married to Katya. These three facts about marriage are instances of monogamy, as specified by the definition of monogamy. Thus, these are instances of the category, or concept, labeled monogamy. The following hypothetical fact does not fit the definition of monogamy: Abdullah is married to Fatima and Ria. This fact is a noninstance of the concept labeled monogamy.

Note the relationship between the definition of monogamy and the above statements of fact which either do or do not fit the definition. The definition is a device for organizing and interpreting the facts; it is a way of giving particular meaning to the facts. However, the definition is not a factual statement. (See Chapter 6 for a discussion of descriptive and explanatory factual statements.)

The previous discussion has stressed that our concepts are definitions that enable us to put phenomena in categories in order to organize the objects and events in our world. Concepts pertain to sensory experience, to perceptions that may be established as facts. As the means to organize and interpret perceptions and facts, our concepts are more or less useful aids to thinking and learning. What makes a concept more or less useful?

USES OF CONCEPTS IN THE SOCIAL STUDIES

Following is an example of a classroom dialogue that can help you to think about the uses of concepts in the social studies. The teacher had previously assigned the reading of five examples of political behavior. The students are required to discriminate the examples of democratic political behavior and those of nondemocratic political behavior and to specify the criteria they used to make their distinctions. After reading this dialogue, try to answer these questions:
1. What is the *use* of concept-learning activity?
2. How can concepts serve thinking and learning in the social studies?

TEACHER: *You have had the opportunity to read five brief cases of political behavior. Which of these cases describes democratic political behavior?*

CARL: *I think cases 1, 3, and 4 are descriptions of democratic political behavior.*

TEACHER: *Why do you say that, Carl?*

CARL: *Well, in each of the cases, a decision is made according to the wishes of the majority.*

TEACHER: *Does democracy mean deciding things by majority rule?*

CARL: *Yeah, that's what a democracy is, like in our country when the people elect the president.*

TAMMY: *I disagree! I don't think case 4 is about democracy, because the few people who disagree with the majority have no freedom to express their beliefs.*

TEACHER: *But doesn't democracy mean majority rule?*

TAMMY: *Well, yeah, but the people have to have freedom of speech, too, or there is no democracy.*

TEACHER: *Does democracy mean both majority-rule and freedom of speech?*

MARGIE: *Democracy means that the people rule. But it also means that the rights of individuals are protected by law.*

KATHY: *Right! Only cases 1 and 3 are descriptions of democracy. Only in these cases do the people participate in government, and only in these cases are the rights of the minority protected.*

TEACHER: *Why do you think cases 2 and 5 are not examples of democratic political behavior?*

MARK: *Case 2 is about a dictator. He makes all the decisions without caring what the people want. And case 5 is a story about people who get sent to a concentration camp because they criticize the government or because they're just different.*

TEACHER: *Mark, why did you decide that the cases about the dictator and the concentration camp were not examples of democracy?*

MARK: *Well, in the case about the dictator, he just decides everything. There is no majority rule. The people don't get a chance to participate in government. In the other case, there is no freedom of speech, and no one has the right to openly criticize the government. And the leaders are prejudiced against minority groups.*

TEACHER: *According to what has been said thus far, what do you think are the basic characteristics of a democracy?*

MARK: *I guess that a democracy means to have majority rule and at the same time to protect the rights of minorities or individuals, to protect their freedoms, and to give them equal opportunities—even when most people don't agree with them or don't like them in some way.*

TEACHER: *Does anybody disagree with Mark? Well, it appears that everyone in this group has the same basic concept of democracy that you have, Mark. Now, let's move to the next lesson and try to learn more about the meaning of democracy. Let's try to enrich and extend our use of this concept.*

The preceding classroom dialogue is an example of instruction aimed at helping students to learn a concept, democracy. The teacher required students to apply a definition of democracy and to organize and interpret an array of information about various types of political behavior. In terms of their definition, or criterion, students selected the instances of political behavior that belong to the category labeled democracy. Figure 5.1 illustrates the intellectual moves of the students in the classroom discussion.

FIGURE 5.1.

Categorization of political behavior. Students determined instances and noninstances of democracy in terms of this gross definition: Democracy is the practice of majority rule with protection of the rights of minorities.

Examples of political behavior	TYPES OF POLITICAL BEHAVIOR	
	Democratic category	Nondemocratic category
1	X	
2		X
3	X	
4		X
5		X

The teacher asked the students to tell the criteria they used to decide what is and what is not democratic political behavior. As they responded, the teacher told them whether they were using correctly their culture's criteria for deciding what is democratic. Thus, students were involved in a lesson requiring them to look at data in a particular way and to see meaning in terms of a particular concept (Fig. 5.2).

As a definition, a means to categorize objects or events, the concept of democracy used by the students influenced the way that they saw or interpreted an array of factual statements or assertions about reality. These facts did not speak for themselves; they had no significance apart from the meaning given to them by an observer. By applying the concept of democracy to the ordering and interpreting of the facts, the students gave the facts a "voice"; they made them meaningful in a particular way. This relationship

FIGURE 5.2.
*The relationship between
concepts and data.*

ULUSCHAK, COURTESY OF THE EDMONTON JOURNAL

"Depends on how you look at it!"

between concepts and facts is illustrated by cases of individuals of different cultures who tend to think about the same phenomena in various ways due to differences in traditions and needs. For example, Eskimos distinguish several varieties of snow, although we typically make few, if any, distinctions. These differences in concept mean that the "facts" pertaining to a snowfall "speak" somewhat differently to a typical Eskimo living within the Arctic Circle than to a typical resident of Chicago.

A most useful outcome of concept-learning activities in the social studies is possibly acquiring the ability to simplify and standardize one's environment so that the potentially overwhelming stimuli which bombard one's senses can be viewed more meaningfully and validly. By learning in the social studies such concepts as democracy, students develop the ability to see certain objects and events more easily and clearly. The foreign guests, whose visit was mentioned at the beginning of this chapter, were confused by the football game because they were unable to apply a meaningful order, or set of valid concepts, to the objects and events of the game.

Another useful outcome of learning concepts in the social studies is acquiring the ability to construct, communicate, and comprehend statements about social reality. For example, the students in the preceding classroom dialogue must know, and be able to connect, the concepts of democracy and public policy before they can either construct or communicate meaningfully this valid statement about social reality: The process of public policy making in Great Britain is more democratic than it is in Spain. To extend their knowledge of democracy, these students must learn how to relate this concept to a vast array of relevant concepts. For example, students need to know the concepts of political behavior, varies, socioeconomic status, and society, to think, talk, and write about generalizations such as this: Political behavior varies with socioeconomic status in both democratic and nondemocratic societies. The foreign visitors of the early example were unable to comprehend or to make meaningful, valid statements about the football game they were viewing because they had not learned the concepts relevant to significant thinking and communicating about the game.

An additional utility of concept learning in the social studies is freeing thought and expression from a restriction to particulars in the social world. As the basis for abstraction, concepts enable thinking and learning in the absence of concrete referents. Students who learn the concept of democracy, for example, can think, learn, and communicate about democracy and related concepts without having instances of the concepts before them. Thus, they do not have to discover directly from experience in the social world every bit of knowledge they seek about democracy. Rather, concepts about the social world give students the ability to comprehend verbal communication that is detached from the concrete instances that the verbal communication describes or explains.

Human thinking and learning is tied to concepts, to organizing objects into categories and naming the categories. Categorizing enables management of the potentially confounding array of perceptions that assault our senses daily. Naming the categories makes possible efficient thinking and communicating about our ordered perceptions. Thus, concept learning is basic to all effective, high-level thinking and learning about social studies or anything else.

GOOD AND BAD CONCEPTS

Our concepts determine the quality of our thinking and learning. The reliability, or accuracy, of observations, descriptions, and explanations is tied inextricably to the concepts used to make them. Good concepts can be compared to good roadmaps. A good roadmap can help a traveler reach his destination most efficiently, and a good set of concepts can help a student to answer questions about the world most accurately and efficiently. As a good roadmap helps a traveler to make logical and accurate moves from place to place, a good conceptual framework helps a learner to make logical and accurate intellectual moves. As a bad roadmap leads travelers astray, bad concepts confound the person who attempts to describe and explain his surroundings. A primary task of instruction in the social studies is to help students to accurately "map" the social world by helping them to acquire and apply concepts that enable them to view the social world more meaningfully and validly.

What is a useful, or "good," concept? How can one distinguish the more useful concepts from the less useful, or "bad," concepts in the social studies? Ability to answer these questions can contribute significantly to high-quality performance in the social studies classroom by both students and teachers.

To be considered good, or useful, for assisting inquiry and learning, a concept must be defined adequately.[3] An adequate definition enables the user of the concept to distinguish clearly instances of the concept from noninstances. For example, the definition of polyandry—the practice or condition of having more than one husband at one time—is a clearly stated criterion for determining instances of the concept polyandry from noninstances. If a concept cannot be used to organize and interpret information without dispute, then it is not very useful. For example, if observer A concludes that Mr. X is very cynical while observer B concludes from the same evidence that Mr. X is not very cynical, then the concept of cynicism is not adequately defined and is not a useful device for describing or explaining phenomena. To be a useful tool for inquiry and learning, a concept must be defined clearly in terms of critical attributes, or indicators, so that the essential meaning of the concept is standardized.

If definitions of concepts are "loaded," circular, or too general, then the concept is faulty and cannot yield valid descriptions and explanations. For example, each of the following definitions is flawed:

1. A bureaucrat is part of a bureaucracy.
2. A legislator is a public official.
3. A liberal is a person who has unrealistic ideas.
4. A conservative is a person who rigidly opposes social improvements.

The definition of a bureaucrat is tautological, or circular, and the definition of a legislator is too broad. Neither of these definitions provides much help in deciding who is or is not a bureaucrat or a legislator. The definitions of a liberal and a conservative are loaded; they are stated so as to slant the views of those who try to use them to organize and interpret information. These loaded definitions can only mislead and distort rather than serve as guides to reliable, accurate descriptions of social reality.

FIGURE 5.3.
A concept must be defined clearly to be a useful tool for learning.

Concrete concepts such as man, woman, vote, mayor, public demonstration, and courthouse need not be defined explicitly for practical purposes. They refer to directly observable objects or events and are commonly understood at a gross, common-sense level. However, some concrete, directly observable concepts must be defined precisely prior to use. For example, before discussing the Ainu with a person who has never seen or heard about an Ainu, one must explain the term, which involves specification of the attributes of an Ainu.

Most concepts used for specific scientific purposes are highly abstract, rather than concrete; they refer to things that cannot be observed directly.[4] While these concepts are connected ultimately to concrete experience, they cannot as entities be seen, felt, or heard. For example, culture, an abstraction used by social scientists, has no independent existence in the world of reality. Culture cannot be observed directly, although this concept refers to things that can be observed directly or indirectly, such as typical ways of thinking and doing among a group of people. Yet we cannot actually observe a culture in action. Rather, we observe human behavior and make inferences from this behavior about the content of the culture.

Because highly abstract concepts refer to features of our environment that are not directly observable, they must always be defined in terms of observable conditions from which one can infer the applicability of the concept. For example, a social scientist may wish to make a study of anomie, a condition characterized by lack of direction, norms, and effectiveness. Anomic individuals tend to feel powerless and to feel that authorities do not care about them. In order to create observable conditions from which to infer whether individuals are more or less anomic, a social scientist, John Schaar, has developed an "anomie scale."[5] Agreement of a person's thinking with the following four items, which constitute the scale, provides the observable conditions from which it can be inferred that the person is more or less anomic.

1. People like me don't have any say about what the government does.
2. Sometimes politics and government seem so complicated that a person like me can't really understand what is going on.
3. I have often had the feeling that it's no use to try to get anywhere in this life.
4. There's not much use for me to plan ahead because there's usually something that makes me change my plans.

The anomie scale represents a definition in use, or an operational definition. This definition specifies what one must do, or the conditions which one must observe, in order to apply the concept of anomie to the social world. For example, if a person agrees with all the items on the above scale, he expresses a high degree of anomie. If he disagrees with all the items, he expresses a zero degree of anomie.

In addition to adequate definition, a good concept must be significant.[6] Just as some facts are not worth knowing, some adequately defined concepts are not worth using. For example, we can precisely define a unicorn. But unicorn is not a useful concept in helping one to think about animal life on our planet because the common characteristics denoted by this label do not correspond to anything in reality. In order to assist in the generation, acquisition, and communication of knowledge, a concept must fit some facet of our experience with objective reality.

To be significant a concept must also be related to other concepts. The more relationships that can be established between one concept and other concepts, the more useful the concept is in assisting one to describe and comprehend the world. For example, socioeconomic class is a concept that is very useful to social scientists because it is related to many other concepts. Social scientists have demonstrated that socioeconomic class is related to, among many other things, a variety of religious, political, and economic attitudes. These relationships are expressed in these kinds of statements:

1. Individuals of lower socioeconomic class tend to express less political tolerance than individuals of higher socioeconomic class.
2. Individuals of lower socioeconomic class tend to express a lower sense of political efficacy than do individuals of higher socioeconomic class.

Concepts, such as socioeconomic class, which are related to many other concepts, have great utility in the construction of statements that describe and explain reality.

Significant, well-defined concepts that can be used to make "more-or-less" distinctions among phenomena are more useful for purposes of scientific inquiry than are concepts that can be used only to make "either-or" distinctions. For example, the concepts of anomie and ethnocentrism can be used to make relatively precise more-or-less judgments, while the concepts of monogamy or voter can be used only to make either-or judgments. A marriage is either monogamous or it is not; a person can be classified either as a voter or as a nonvoter. By contrast, a person can be thought of as more-or-less anomic or as more-or-less ethnocentric. The definitions of concepts such as anomie and ethnocentrism enable an observer to determine the extent to which instances of the concepts do or do not possess certain characteristics.

In the social sciences instruments such as various I.Q. tests and attitude scales are the means to measure degrees of difference yielded by the use of more-or-less type concepts. For example, to make a judgment about the relative anomie of two groups of young adults, one might administer to them the anomie scale that appears above. Through analysis of the scores made by the two groups on the scale, it is possible to make a more-or-less judgment about the relative anomie of each group. The anomie scale represents a precise specification of criteria, an operational definition, for determining the extent to which individuals do or do not express anomie.

Often more-or-less judgments must be qualitative rather than quantitative. For example, in contrast to studies of ethnocentrism and anomie among small groups, social scientists have found it difficult to make precise numerical judgments about the relative degree of democracy of nations. Usually they make judgments about the extent to which nations possess certain qualities indicated by their definition of democracy. Then, in terms of these qualities, they judge that nation A is either more or less democratic than nation B. However, they have no instrument that gauges the degree of democracy of nations A and B. Through use of the anomie scale, we can say that on the average the extent of anomie shown by group A is five degrees more than that of group B. In contrast we may conclude grossly that nation A is more democratic than nation B. We have no instrument by which to gauge the degree of difference.

Concepts that enable one to make precise, more-or-less distinctions are more useful for scientific inquiry than are concepts that merely allow for either-or judgments. Judgments of more-or-less provide the bases for explanation and prediction, for theory building. In contrast, judgments only of either-or limit one to making descriptions.

In summary, good concepts are adequately defined and significant. And good concepts that enable more-or-less judgments are more useful for purposes of scientific inquiry than are those that merely enable either-or judgments.

Learning Concepts

Following are two very different approaches to instruction for concept learning. After you read the two portions of classroom dialogue, speculate about answers to these questions: What is concept learning? Which of these two classroom discussions is the better example of instruction for concept learning? Why?

CLASSROOM DISCUSSION 1

TEACHER: *I want you to name the two concepts which were discussed in your reading assignment.*

GEORGE: *Role and status.*

TEACHER: *Very good, George. Who can give a definition of role?*

MARTHA: *A role is a guideline for human behavior.*

TEACHER: *Yes, Martha, you're correct. But I want you to give the definition of role that is written in your text.*

MARTHA: *Just a minute. I'll look up the definition in my book.*

ALEXANDER: *I remember the definition. A role is comprised of the rights and duties associated with a status. That's what it says in the book.*

TEACHER: *Excellent, Alexander. Now who can give me the definition of status?*

NICK: *Status is how important you are.*

TEACHER: *You're wrong, Nick! Elaine, give us the right answer.*

ELAINE: *Well, ah, it said in the book that status is the position that a person holds within a social group.*

TEACHER: *That's not exactly what it said in the book. But I guess it's close enough. I'll accept your answer.*

CLASSROOM DISCUSSION 2

TEACHER: *You have had an opportunity to read a discussion of the meaning of sense of political efficacy. Now, I want to find out whether you can apply this idea to the five examples of political behavior described on the page which I have just distributed. Take ten minutes to classify these examples.*

TEACHER: *I think everyone is ready to discuss this exercise. Max, how do you classify the examples?*

MAX: *Mr. Peters, Ms. Stevens, and Mr. Carlson obviously were low in sense of political efficacy. The others were higher in sense of political efficacy.*

TEACHER: *Why do you think so, Max?*

MAX: *Well, Mr. Peters doesn't even care whether he votes or not. And Ms. Stevens believes that ordinary people like herself have no influence at all on government officials. And Mr. Carlson has a very poor self-concept, and he doesn't trust his fellow man, especially politicians. He thinks that the politicians don't care what people like him think.*

TEACHER: *Stanley, do you agree with Max?*

STANLEY: *Yes, these three people are low in sense of political efficacy. They don't believe that they can or should try to influence the government. And people who have a high sense of political efficacy do believe that they can and should try to influence government officials. That's what sense of political efficacy means.*

TEACHER: *Does everyone agree with Stanley? All right, I am now going to require you to use sense of political efficacy in combination with social class, racial identity, and sex identity to organize and interpret the statistical data contained in this packet of worksheets that I am now handing out.*

WHAT IS CONCEPT LEARNING?

Concept learning is acquiring competence to respond to objects or events as a category.[7] The student acquires the ability to generalize about instances within a category and to discriminate between the instances of different categories. These two dimensions of concept learning—generalization within a category and discrimination between categories—are illustrated in Figure 5.4. (See page 172.) A person who has learned the concept of circle can look at an array of objects of different sizes and colors and discriminate all the circles, regardless of size or color, from the other objects. This is generalization from particulars within a category. The student also discriminates between particulars of different categories by distinguishing the instances of square, circle, and triangle and putting every instance in the correct box, or category.

Those who have learned a concept are able to discriminate instances from noninstances of the concept.[8] For example, the students in the second classroom discussion are discriminating instances of the concept sense of political efficacy from noninstances. In contrast, the students in the first classroom discussion are demonstrating verbal associations, not concept learning; they are merely regurgitating definitions in response to verbal cues. To demonstrate concept acquisition, a learner must do more than verbalize the concept or use it correctly in a sentence. Neither naming nor defining a concept indicates concept attainment. Rather, concept attainment is demonstrated by use of the concept competently to organize and interpret objects or events.

Concept learning is very transferable. Those who have acquired a concept through a particular learning experience should be able to apply the concept to different, related situations.[9] The students in the second classroom discussion are applying a concept studied in a previous lesson to a fresh group of instances. And the teacher tells them, at the end of the discussion, that they will be expected in the next lesson to apply their concept of sense of political efficacy, in combination with related concepts, to the organization and interpretation of new data, or instances. This stress on the positive transfer of concept learning is the ultimate test of mastery. Students who can generalize their use of a concept by readily applying it to the categorization

FIGURE 5.4.
Two dimensions of
concept learning.

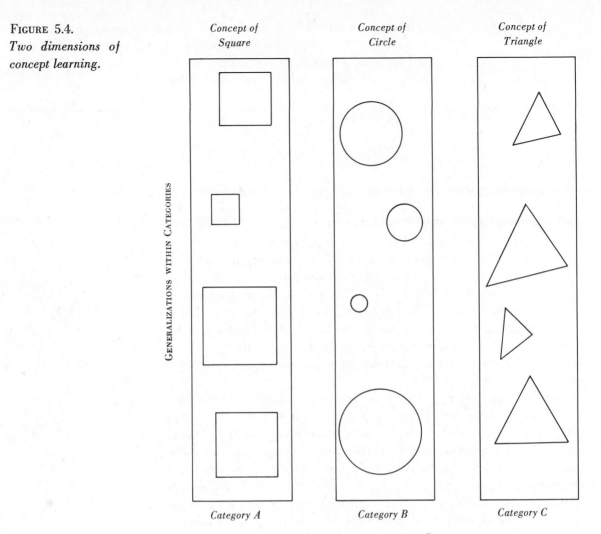

Concept of
Square

Concept of
Circle

Concept of
Triangle

GENERALIZATIONS WITHIN CATEGORIES

Category A   Category B   Category C

DISCRIMINATION BETWEEN CATEGORIES

of relevant new instances demonstrate that they have acquired the concept—
that is, it has become a part of their mental equipment.

Concept learning can occur at lower and higher levels of cognition.[10] Lower-
level concept learning is merely the ability to discriminate instances from
noninstances. The students in the second classroom discussion, for example,
are demonstrating lower-level learning of sense of political efficacy by identifying correctly examples and nonexamples of the concept. Higher-level concept
learning is using a concept, in combination with other concepts, to construct

descriptive or explanatory statements. The teacher in the second classroom discussion makes an assignment at the end of the discussion that will require the students to practice higher-level concept learning; they will use sense of political efficacy in combination with several related concepts to build descriptions and explanations from a packet of statistical data.

LEARNING CONCEPTUAL FRAMEWORKS

Higher-level concept learning involves the learning of conceptual frameworks (sets of concepts) that enable one to describe and explain. (See Chapter 6 for a discussion of the use of related concepts to build descriptive and explanatory statements.) A fundamental feature of recent curriculum reforms in the social studies has been the organization of curricula in terms of the conceptual frameworks of such social science disciplines as sociology, economics, and political science. For example, *Economics and Society*, a new high school economics course, has been designed in terms of a conceptual framework which has guided the selection and sequencing of subject matter. Facts, issues, and problems pertinent to fundamental economic concepts have been selected as the subject matter of the program. The subject matter has been sequenced so that the relationships between concepts are highlighted and so that students have an opportunity to apply the concepts again and again to the analysis of fresh information.[11]

One of the developers of *Economics and Society* has described the relationship between a conceptual framework and curriculum design:

We have tried to design a conceptual structure which not only guides curriculum design but which also becomes a pedagogical device in itself, helping students to learn economics more quickly. For these purposes, the conceptual structure has the following characteristics:
1. It defines economics so that students and teachers know what they are studying.
2. It is a simple diagram of the conceptual structure which gives a picture, or a Gestalt, of what economists study. It is a model which teachers and students can visualize and use as a frame of reference, a starting point for studying any economic problems.
3. It links economics to the study of society; showing economic organization as part of social organization and describing economic development as part of social change.[12]

The importance of learning in terms of conceptual frameworks, or structures, is illustrated by the following exercise (Fig. 5.5). Look quickly (no longer then two or three seconds) at the two groups of lines on page 174 and then answer the questions that follow without looking back at the figure.

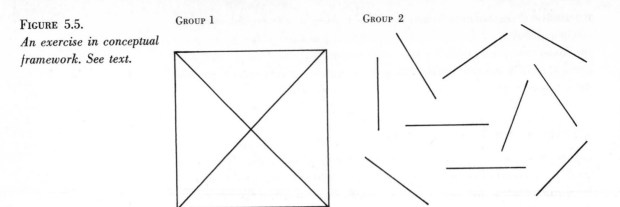

How many lines are there in group 1? In group 2? It is likely that you were able to recall easily the number of lines in group 1 and that you were unable to recall the number in group 2. Why? The answer is relatively simple. The lines in group 1 are ordered in terms of a meaningful structure, while the lines in group 2 are scattered randomly.

Relating facts in terms of some meaningful structure facilitates learning and retention. Numerous studies have indicated that students rapidly forget relatively isolated facts. Thus, it is efficient to design instruction which highlights the relationships between facts and concepts within an encompassing conceptual framework. The aim of this approach to instruction and learning is to develop a profound understanding of a few important tightly related ideas rather than to cover a large number of loosely related, or discrete, facts or concepts.

Jerome S. Bruner, a leading advocate of the importance of structure as an aid to learning, has said:

Teaching specific topics or skills without making clear their context in the broader fundamental structure of a field of knowledge is uneconomical in several deep senses. In the first place, such teaching makes it exceedingly difficult for the student to generalize from what he has learned to what he will encounter later. In the second place, learning that has fallen short of a group of general principles has little reward in terms of intellectual excitement. The best way to create interest in a subject is to render it worth knowing, which means to make the knowledge gained useable in one's thinking beyond the situation in which the learning has occurred. Third, knowledge one has acquired without sufficient structure to tie it together is knowledge that is likely to be forgotten.[13]

Following the urgings of Bruner and others, leaders of the recent reform movement for social studies curriculum have advocated the development of curricula, from kindergarten through high school, in terms of the most fundamental social science concepts—those that cut across disciplines. Substantive concepts such as culture, society, role, status, social class, socialization, and personality are used to build descriptive and explanatory generalizations in several disciplines. Methodological concepts such as hypothesis, induction, classification, and sample are used to facilitate and evaluate inquiry in every social science discipline. Students should encounter these fundamental concepts again and again; and as they move through a curriculum, they should be given the opportunity to attain a deeper comprehension of these basic concepts as they apply them to different facts and in different conceptual frameworks.

The conceptual frameworks, or structures, of the social sciences provide fruitful bases for instruction and learning. As particular ways of ordering and interpreting facts and of bringing a subject under control, they provide a teacher with the means for structuring learning activities. However, as teachers select and use concepts for social studies instruction, they must remember that although some appear to facilitate the interpretation of certain facts more than others do, no single set of concepts represents *the only* way to structure an inquiry. Teachers must instruct students in terms of conceptual structures in order to enhance learning; they must avoid any suggestion that they are imposing *the only* conceptual structure, the only way to organize and interpret particular phenomena.

Concepts must be appraised continually to determine their utility. A danger in the creation and use of concepts in curriculum development and instruction is ossified thinking due to unwillingness to alter concepts to accommodate new conditions and knowledge. Concepts are tools that we create to assist our thinking and learning. We must be ever ready to retool if we desire to protect our thinking and learning capability from stagnation. Concepts used to build curricula must be changed with advances in knowledge and the identification of new questions and problems. Since learning activities must be structured in terms of the most useful concepts, curriculum developers and teachers must be capable of modifying or discarding particular conceptual frameworks in favor of more productive conceptual tools whenever the need arises.

Designing Instruction for Concept Learning

Exposition and discovery, the two contrasting modes of instruction introduced in Chapter 4, can both be used to help students learn concepts. Neither mode of instruction is appropriate to all kinds of concept learning in the social studies. Good instruction for concept learning requires skillful orchestration of discovery and expository lessons. Thus, social studies teachers need to know how to use both expository and discovery approaches to concept learning and when to use one mode of instruction rather than the other.

TEACHING CONCEPTS THROUGH EXPOSITION

Expository instruction is a direct, efficient means to the learning of concepts that can be defined precisely and connected easily to experience. For example, these concepts can be efficiently taught through exposition: social class, alienation, random sample, law, public election, and gross national product.

Most secondary school students have the cognitive capacity and verbal ability to benefit from well-designed expository instruction for concept learning.[14] From about the age of 12 or 13, youngsters manifest the capability to acquire and use the more abstract concepts associated with social science inquiry. Older adolescents have the cognitive capacity to acquire and use abstractions without continual direct reference to concrete exemplars. However, one of the sad facts associated with public education is that many high school students do not realize their potential for higher-level conceptual learning and thereby remain disadvantaged relative to their peers who do fulfill their capacities. A major task of instructional designers is to create conditions of learning that can narrow the gap between learning potentiality and reality, that can enable as many youngsters as possible to achieve higher-level conceptual learning in the social studies.

Adequately designed expository instruction is a means to higher-level conceptual learning. This mode of instruction for concept learning, sometimes called rule-example instruction, consists of the following procedures:[15]

1. Indicate clearly that the objective of instruction is to learn a particular concept and tell why it is useful to learn the concept.
2. Present the definition of the concept, the rule for determining instances and noninstances of the concept.
3. Present positive examples to illustrate what the concept is, and clearly indicate these as instances of the concept. Present negative examples to illustrate what the concept is not, and clearly indicate these as noninstances of the concept. To be meaningful, positive and negative examples must be presented in language that students can understand and must pertain to the experiences of students. Also the examples must not include irrelevant or extraneous information, which impedes concept attainment. Direct, unadorned presentation of only obviously relevant information is necessary to efficient concept learning through expository instruction.

4. Require application of the concept to new instances to determine whether or not the student can discriminate instances from noninstances of the concept. Application exercises are essential to determine whether or not concept learning has occurred. Some students may present the appearance of having learned a concept by glibly spicing their conversations with the concept label. Others may seem to know the concept because they can parrot the concept definition. But unless ability to use the concept to organize and interpret fresh information is demonstrated, neither the student nor the instructor can be certain that concept learning has occurred.

5. Provide immediate feedback about the quality of the student's responses to the application exercise. Immediate positive feedback reinforces correct responses, and immediate negative feedback provides clues about mistakes that may enable the student to correct faulty responses.

Properly designed instruction for conceptual learning must require students to relate concepts, to use a concept introduced through a particular lesson in combination with other concepts to organize and interpret data and to construct descriptive and explanatory statements. Concepts learned and used alone provide little interpretive power. As they are linked in frameworks, or structures, they can provide the means to view the social world more meaningfully and validly.

Following is an example of expository, or rule-example, instruction designed for concept learning. Read the lesson carefully and answer these questions: What are the strong and weak features of this lesson? What is your appraisal of the teacher's use of the lesson? Would you in any way use the lesson differently? If so, how and why?

Learning the concept of political alienation. This lesson is part of a set of lessons about the meanings of political alienation and loyalty. Its purpose is to introduce the concept of political alienation in a direct, unadorned fashion. In subsequent lessons students are required to apply their concept of political alienation, in combination with related concepts, to the organization and interpretation of statistical data and several case studies. The object of instruction stated in Mehlinger and Patrick's *Teachers' Guide for American Political Behavior* is: "Students can classify examples of political behavior in terms of a definition of political alienation."[16]

The sample lesson about the meaning of political alienation appears below.[17] To what extent does this lesson, and the accompanying description of subsequent instruction, conform to the guidelines for designing instruction presented in this chapter and in Chapter 4?

*Lesson on the
Meaning of
Political
Alienation**

A person's loyalty to one group may exclude him from another group. For example, a person who joins a hippie clan may be expressing his feeling of isolation from other groups with whom he once associated. He probably has feelings of alienation.

An alien is a foreigner living outside his own country. We say that a person is alienated when he feels like a stranger even in familiar surroundings. An alienated person rejects, or feels rejected by, social groups with which he once had close attachments—family, friends, school, church, and the like.

A politically alienated person is one who rejects, or feels rejected by, his society and its political system. He has serious gripes about his government and does not think that his complaints can be corrected through the traditional machinery of government. The politically alienated person has lost faith in his government and the laws, customs, and beliefs which support it.

Some politically alienated individuals become political activists who seek to overthrow the existing political system. These radical political activists tend to have a high sense of power and personal efficacy. An alienated political activist may be willing to engage in conspiracy or violence to bring about the changes he seeks.

Other politically alienated individuals are political apathetics who seek to withdraw from the political system. These political dropouts tend to have a low sense of power and personal efficacy. They avoid activities that would show support for the established political system. However,

they are not interested in revolutionary political activity.

(1) Decide which of the following speakers are alienated from the political system or culture of the United States. (2) Then group the alienated speakers into two categories: (a) the alienated activist and (b) the alienated apathetic. Be prepared to defend your choices.

Speaker 1: Someone told me that the city government wants to add fluoride to our water. I think it has something to do with teeth. I don't know much about it. They will probably do what is best, and I will accept their decision.

Speaker 2: My friends and I are tired of this phoney society and the phoney politicians who run it. We're organizing our own commune on some wilderness land that my uncle left to me in his will. Living in the commune will give us a chance to be free from the corruption and insincerity of the straight world. Why don't you join us?

Speaker 3: I don't really care who gets elected to public office. I'm satisfied with my life. Whatever happens, it's not likely to affect me very much. I'll still have my job, my family, and my home.

Speaker 4: The whole society is sick. It has to be torn apart and rebuilt. Burn, baby, burn—that's the only political slogan that's worth anything.

Speaker 5: Some of my friends have tried to get me involved in politics, but I have resisted. I enjoy the Boy Scout group I work with. I like to work with the boys and think I am making a contribution to our society in that way. Boy Scouts and my family take up just about all my free time.

Speaker 6: The government and the

*From *American Political Behavior* by Howard D. Mehlinger and John J. Patrick. © Copyright 1972 by Indiana University. Published by Ginn and Company. Used with permission.

political big-shots in this country have always cheated people like me. But what can we do about it? We have to sit back and take their abuse. There's no sense in trying to overthrow the government, but don't expect me to cooperate with the public officials or obey the law if I can get away with it.

Speaker 7: Most public officials in this country are socialist traitors who have forgotten the true American heritage. No peaceful efforts can make these public officials change their ways. Therefore, I have started an underground organization of true patriots who will save this country from socialism. If necessary, we will violently overthrow the government in order to preserve the true American way of life.

Speaker 8: My friends and I have been working hard to elect Jones as governor of our state. We believe that he is a very able man who will begin to solve the serious problems of air pollution, traffic congestion, and unemployment that afflict our state. It appears that he has a good chance to win this election.

Following is an excerpt of a classroom discussion between a teacher and a group of twelfth-grade students. What is your appraisal of the teacher's use of the lesson?

TEACHER: *Now that everyone has completed the exercise about political alienation, let's talk about your answers. Barbara, which people in this exercise are expressing political alienation?*

BARBARA: *Speakers 2, 4, 6, and 7.*

TEACHER: *Why did you classify the examples as you did, Barbara?*

BARBARA: *The examples I picked are the ones that fit the definition of political alienation that was presented in this lesson. The speakers that I classified as alienated are in one way or another rejecting the system.*

TEACHER: *Does everyone agree? You do. Okay, you're right, Barbara. According to our definition, speakers 2, 4, 6, and 7 are the alienated ones.*

DAVID: *I'm really very disgusted with people like speaker 4. He says the whole society is sick. I think he's sick. If he doesn't like this country, he ought to get out and go someplace else.*

DON: *Wait a minute, David. You're all wrong. People have the right to . . .*

TEACHER: *Whoa! Hold on, Don and David. What you're saying sounds like it might be exciting, but the point of this discussion is to find out if everyone in this classroom knows what political alienation is. Rest assured that we'll get into some very deep discussions of issues about political alienation before we're finished with this unit. But before we do that, we have to be sure that everyone in the group knows what we're talking about. Unless we all have the same frame of reference about political alienation, we can't meaningfully study and discuss issues about alienation. Now let's move ahead with our discussion of this exercise. Pat, which of the speakers can be labeled alienated activists and alienated apathetics?*

PAT: *Speakers 4 and 7 are the alienated activists. Both of them reject the system as it is and believe that they ought to do radical things to change it. Both speakers are extremists. Speakers 2 and 6 are the alienated apathetics. They're against the system, too, but they've given up and dropped out.*

TEACHER: *Does anyone in the group disagree? All right, you're correct, Pat. If each of you used the concept of political alienation to classify these examples the way Barbara and Pat did, then you probably are starting to understand what political alienation is. But before we move to the next lesson, I'd like to make an additional check on your understanding of the concept. I want each of you to write one example of an alienated activist and one example of an alienated apathetic. Then write, in your own words, why you think your examples are appropriate. Hand in your papers, and I'll look at them right away so that I can give them back to you tomorrow, with corrections if necessary.*

The subsequent lessons about political alienation involved the students in a detailed and wide-ranging study. They examined statistical data to determine which groups in the society are more or less likely to express political alienation. They analyzed case studies of alienated people to identify the sources of political alienation in our society. Finally, they applied this concept of political alienation, in combination with related concepts, to the analysis of cases of political behavior for the purpose of interpreting these cases as meaningfully and validly as possible.

The previous lesson about political alienation can be rated highly in terms of our guidelines for appraising expository instruction for concept learning. The definition of political alienation is stated clearly and directly. The positive examples of the concept that are presented are likely to be meaningful to high school readers. Most importantly students are required to be active learners and to demonstrate mastery of the instructional objective by applying their definition of political alienation to the classification of fresh examples presented at the end of the lesson.

A weak point of the lesson is that negative examples, which could enhance comprehension of the concept, are not provided. Another weakness is that there is no provision for immediate feedback to indicate whether or not student responses to the application exercise are correct. However, the teacher provided this feedback during the classroom discussion.

The teacher's conduct of the classroom discussion was noteworthy in two respects. First, he focused the discussion clearly on the task to determine whether students could classify the examples of political behavior correctly in terms of a definition of political alienation. The teacher guided students efficiently to achievement of the lesson objective. Second, the teacher prevented students from digressing during the discussion, from pursuing interesting but irrelevant points. The teacher wisely indicated that issues pertinent to political alienation are important and are worth discussion but that it is necessary to acquire a useful concept of political alienation before one can fruitfully engage in the study of issues about political alienation.

TEACHING CONCEPTS THROUGH DISCOVERY

Social science concepts that are relatively amorphous and hard to define exactly or operationally are probably best taught through the discovery approach. Examples of such concepts are culture, freedom, justice, and political behavior. Teaching such concepts through discovery involves immersing the student in various instances of the concept prior to attempting formal definition and discussion of the concept. The student's task is to infer the defining characteristics of the concept from the instances, or data, that have been presented to him.

The discovery mode of instruction for concept learning consists of the following procedures:[18]

1. Inform the students of the objective of instruction and tell them why it is useful to achieve it.
2. Present various instances of the concept and associate the concept name or label with these instances. For example, suppose that you desire to teach the concept political behavior through the discovery approach. You might begin by posing the question "What is political behavior?" and by asking students to attempt an answer to this question based on information presented in several short case descriptions of human behavior. To cue students, you tell them that although the cases appear to be about very different

things, they have one common feature: Each case is an illustration of political behavior.

3. Require the student to infer, or discover, the defining characteristics of the concept from the array of instances that have been presented. For example, after reading several case studies that are positive examples of political behavior, students can be asked to speculate about what political behavior is.

4. Cue the students, if necessary, in order to prompt discovery. For example, in order to guide discovery of the defining characteristics of political behavior, you might ask the students to decide which individuals in the cases were behaving politically and which were not behaving politically. After making this distinction, you can ask the students to explain how they distinguished individuals behaving politically from individuals not behaving politically.

5. Require the students to apply the concept to new instances in order to reinforce and extend learning. For example, you might present additional case examples (in writing, on film, and on audio-tape) of political behavior that have been contrived to highlight certain basic features of the concept, such as conflict or public policy making. Students can be required to make additional inferences about the meaning of the concept from these pointedly contrived instances. Finally, to reinforce prior learning and to further refine student comprehension, you can present a formal definitional discussion, with numerous positive exemplars, of political behavior.

Following is an example of a discovery lesson designed for conceptual learning. Read the lesson before answering these questions. What is your appraisal of this lesson? How would you change this lesson, if at all, to improve it?

Learning the concepts of role and status. This lesson is the first in a series about the meanings of role and status.[19] Its purpose is to introduce students to the concepts of role and status through a "mind-grabbing" lesson which prompts insightful speculation about the dynamics of patterned human behavior. The objectives of instruction stated in *Teaching Plan, Studying Societies* are:[20]

1. Students should be able to suggest examples of specific clues that enable one to identify who someone is.

2. When given the name of a particular social position, for example, brother, students will be able to suggest several behaviors connected with that social position.

This lesson depends upon eliciting student responses to a series of pictures of human interactions which appear on a transparency and are presented via an overhead projector. Following is a description of the lesson that appears in *Teaching Plan*.[21]

The transparency, "How Do You Talk to Who?", has overlays of three figures facing right (a white teenager, a policeman, a woman) and three figures facing left (a black teenager, a white girl, a businessman). Pairs of situations can be created by placing various combinations of figures on the overhead projector deck. These are six pieces of dialogue on a separate sheet:

"Want to shoot a few?"

"Excuse me, but may I see your driver's license?"

"Darling, I'd love to stop and talk but I've got to go shopping."

"I wish you'd try to do something about your posture."

"That's a cute outfit you have on."

"Don't you have anthing better to do?" These "pieces of talk" can, of course, be shifted around and used in any combination, with any combination of the figures. The total result is a large number of possible conversations, some of them conventional, some shocking, and/or laughable. It will probably be best to start the exercise with some conventional dialogue [like] this conversation between two teenage boys. [See Picture 1 on page 184.] Nothing too surprising in that particular conversation. Next substitute the businessman for the black teenage boy. [See Picture 2.] Still nothing too surprising. Leave the dialogue and substitute the teenage girl for the businessman. [See Picture 3.] This dialogue begins to get into the inappropriate category

and some discussion can begin about the nature of the inappropriateness; why does it seem odd? Who is talking?

Clear the transparency and set up the following combination. [See Picture 4.] After the class has read it, switch the talk. [See Picture 5.] Now, leave the talk balloons but replace the two females with any other combination of figures. [See Picture 6.]

Discuss the reason for the laughter that will almost certainly occur. If students say it is "Silly" or "Goofy," ask why? What makes this situation funny when the last one, with the same talk, was not? (The effectiveness of this lesson and of those which build on it depends on students' exploring the basis for their laughter. Encourage them to probe their initial answers and to restate them as explicitly as possible.)

You may want to ask some students to set up some combinations, while others in the class discuss them. There are a great number of possible combinations, and discussion of all the permutations is not necessary or possible, given time limitations. The purpose of the exercise is to make visible the status-linked rules that guide everyday behavior. These rules are ordinarily not verbalized in a very direct fashion, but they are nonetheless rules. They become visible when, through this vicarious device, they are breached. When the students grasp this, they will be able, in their own language, to:

1. trace their laughter or other reaction

---

*Reproduced by permission of the American Anthropological Association from *Studying Societies* and *Teaching Plan, Studying Societies* (ACSP), 1971.

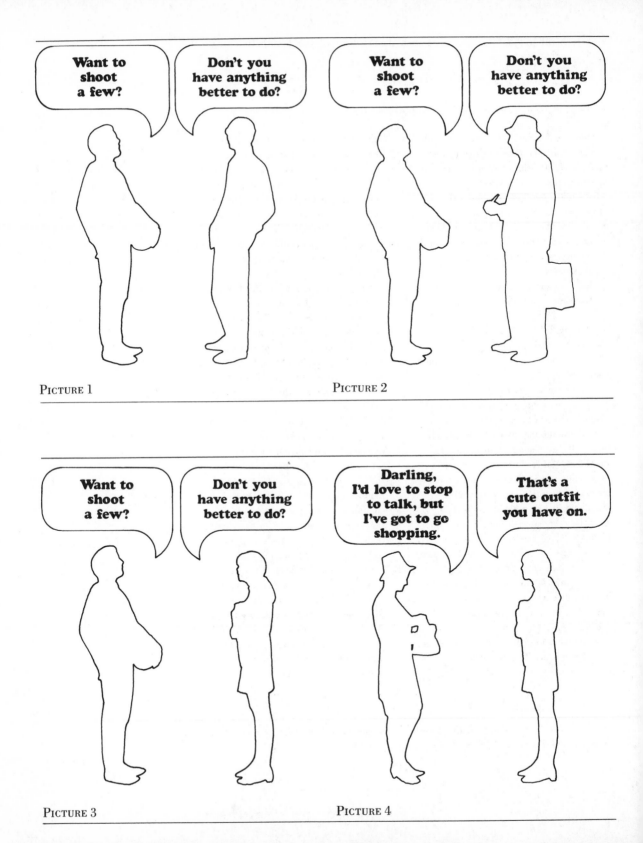

PICTURE 1

PICTURE 2

PICTURE 3

PICTURE 4

PICTURE 5   PICTURE 6

FIGURE 5.6.

Transparencies for learning the meanings of role and status.

to violation of their expectation of what was appropriate in the various situations,

2. specify the expectation and the situation represented,

3. pinpoint some specific clues they used to identify "who" someone was.

Several important insights seem likely to occur if you set up enough situations. First, a given individual has more than a single identity. Another, related to this, is that the identity is a function of "who" the *other* individual is. And students may realize that learning what behavior to expect of a certain "who" is something they've been doing for a long time. These ideas should not be dragged out of the discussion by brute force or insinuated into it by the teacher. If they appear, make them welcome. If they do not appear, well and good; they will be treated in subsequent lessons.

The social situations depicted on the transparencies can prompt student insights or discovery about the meaning of role and status, two related concepts that are basic to the inquiries of social scientists. It is anticipated that students will talk in terms of role and status without necessarily using these concept labels and without knowing or articulating a formal definition of the concepts. As students identify and discuss incongruous human interactions, such as those depicted in the third, fifth, and sixth pictures above, they are likely to talk about the rights and duties customarily associated with particular types of people, or role and status. Following is an example of the kind of classroom dialogue one might expect from a group of ninth or tenth graders who are responding to the third picture.

TEACHER: *What's odd about this picture?*

JULIE: *Most guys I know wouldn't go up to a girl and ask her to play basketball. That's something the guys do together.*

HERMAN: *Only some weirdo guy would want to go shoot baskets with a girl. It's just not the thing to do.*

LAURIE: *Most girls that I know wouldn't want to go shooting baskets with the boys. Most girls have something better to do.*

JILL: *I really disagree with what you're saying. I like to play basketball and so do some other girls I know.*

TEACHER: *Do you usually play with boys or with other girls?*

JILL: *Well, I am on the girls' basketball team here at school, and I guess I do play basketball with other girls most of the time.*

TEACHER: *Why do you think this is so?*

JILL: *I guess it's so because that's what everybody seems to think is right and proper. Some people even seem to think it's odd for girls to want to play basketball, and the majority of girls in this school aren't too interested in it or too good at it. They'd rather be cheerleaders or pompon girls or other dumb things like that.*

TEACHER: *Why do we expect girls and boys to behave differently in different situations?*

JOHN: *We're brought up that way. We learn certain customs and rules. We're told* how boys and girls are supposed to act, and those who don't conform are considered weird or odd.

JILL: *I agree with what you said, John. But you should realize that some of us are trying to change some of the customs about how girls ought to behave. We think the old ways are wrong and that we can find some better ways.*

TEACHER: *Very interesting discussion. Can someone tell us why no one in the class thought that picture number 1 was odd?*

JIMMY: *That picture shows very ordinary behavior. Guys are asking each other to play ball all the time.*

TEACHER: *What points do you think we have made so far about how we expect people to behave and why we have these expectations?*

As the discussion continues, the teacher behaves mostly as prompter and moderator of student interactions. The teacher avoids giving answers or making long didactic commentaries about role and status. The point of this introductory lesson is to attract the attention of students, to initiate serious thinking about role and status, and to spark discovery of the defining characteristics of the concepts of role and status.

Subsequent lessons involve students in a formal systematic study of role and status which is developed in terms of the frame of reference established by the initial lesson. To link the initial lesson to subsequent activities in this series, the teacher is offered this advice[22] for beginning the next lesson:

Ask the students for a quick description of one of the humorous dialogue combinations in the preceding lesson, and follow this with such questions as: Why was that funny? What did the laughter show about your expectations? What does the way a person is supposed to act in a situation depend upon? Then remind the students that whether or not the particular behavior was appropriate in a given situation has to do with "who" the individuals were. This should help the students recall the use of "particular behavior" and of "who" a person is.

Next, tell the students that there are technical names for both the "who" and the particular behavior associated with that "who." The technical name for "who" is status. The technical name for the behavior is role. Point out to the students that what they have been observing in the overhead transparency is behavior; that if you watch people, what you see is behavior (role) and from that you infer what [their] status is. (Behavior can include such things as clothes, posture, and facial expression.) Of course, one can be told the name of the status, but one cannot observe the status directly. One can only observe the behavior expected of someone occupying a status. Tell the students that from now on you will use the terms *status* and *role*.

The lesson about role and status can be rated highly in terms of the criteria for judging the discovery approach to concept learning which were discussed on pages 181 and 182. As required by the criteria, students were given an opportunity to infer the meanings of role and status from examples designed to facilitate discovery. The teacher properly prompted and guided student thinking without giving answers or judging student responses. Provision was made for extending and reinforcing comprehension by requiring continual application.

A possible weakness of this lesson is that the concept names, status and role, are not introduced until the next lesson. It can be argued that introducing the concept labels immediately and associating them with the initial learning experience would contribute to efficient concept acquisition. A second weakness is that the objectives of instruction are not stated as pointedly, or clearly, as possible. And students do not become aware of the point of the lesson until near the end of the learning experience. Telling them immediately what they are up to and why contributes greatly to the achievement of instructional objectives.

Instruction for concept learning ought to be a primary concern of social studies teachers. Youngsters who learn to structure their inquiries in terms of social science concepts have the potential to perceive the social world more meaningfully than those who view social phenomena with less powerful lenses. For example, a youngster who has learned the concepts of culture, socialization, role, and status has the capability to view more insightfully the social world than a youngster who does not possess this conceptual equipment.

Concept learning in the social studies has the potential to liberate thought, to free students from both the tyranny of intellectual anarchy and the tyranny of dogmatism. Individuals who are open-minded to the point of incapacity to think consistently in categorical terms cannot sustain rational thought. They are incapable of systematic inquiry. They are unable to relate or to make anything out of the events that they experience. Their cognitive style might be characterized as a "stream of consciousness" without continuity or consistency. Such individuals are cognitively unstable and are prey to fads and whims. However, individuals who think rigidly in terms of concepts, who are closed-minded to the point of incapacity to modify concepts to fit new experiences or changing conditions, are also incapable of fruitful inquiry. These individuals are the "true believers," the dogmatic idealogues. Their cognitive style is to mold every perception to a static mental structure and to resist any influence that would alter basic doctrines.

To guard against the sterility of both overly rigid and unstructured thinking, students should have the opportunity to learn to use and to appraise critically social science concepts. Thus, a main function of instruction in the social studies should be to help students acquire relatively definite meanings of basic concepts that have been useful tools of inquiry in the social sciences, to help them acquire the capability to think flexibly and critically about concepts, and to help students acquire the capability to form new concepts to apply to new situations. If these three elements of teaching social science concepts proceed simultaneously, students can acquire both the intellectual power of useful social science concepts and protection against stagnant thinking.

Summary

Concept learning is a primary goal of instruction in the social studies. A concept is a definition—a criterion or set of criteria—for categorizing—for grouping objects or events that have something in common.

Concepts serve thinking and learning in several ways. First, concepts simplify and standardize one's environment, permitting meaningful observation and interpretation. Second, concepts enable one to construct and communicate statements about reality. Third, concepts free thought and expression from restriction to concrete referents.

To serve thinking and learning, concepts must be significant and must be defined adequately. In addition, concepts that can be used to make more-or-less distinctions among phenomena are more useful for purposes of scientific inquiry than are those that can be used only to make either-or distinctions.

Concept learning is acquiring competence to respond to objects or events as a category. Those who have learned a concept are able to organize and interpret phenomena that fits the concept. Lower-level concept learning is merely the ability to discriminate instances from noninstances. Higher-level concept learning is using a concept in combination with other concepts to construct descriptive or explanatory statements. Higher-level concept learning involves the learning of conceptual frameworks, sets of concepts that enable description and explanation. Learning conceptual frameworks contributes substantially to transfer of learning and to retention.

Both the expository and discovery modes of instruction can be used to achieve effective concept learning in the social studies. Expository instruction is most applicable to the learning of concepts that can be defined precisely and connected easily to experience. Social science concepts that do not have clear-cut boundaries, that are difficult to define exactly or operationally, are probably best taught through the discovery approach. Claims for the efficiency of expository instruction for older children and adolescents are based on the development of verbal and abstract reasoning capability. As verbal ability increases, it is assumed that verbal cues can become stimuli for concept attainment. Given appropriate verbal capability, it seems educationally wasteful to require students to discover from direct experience all the concepts that we want them to learn.

In social studies instruction, concepts ought to be applied recurringly to fresh data in new contexts in order to ensure concept attainment. After a student is introduced to a basic concept, he should encounter it again and again. Additional encounters with the concept offer the possibility of heightened comprehension. Furthermore, the capability of a student to transfer the concept from the context of the situation in which he first encountered it to new contexts is evidence of concept mastery.

In planning and organizing instruction, teachers should provide for continual use of basic concepts. As students show evidence of concept attainment, teachers can rely solely on verbal cues when using the concept in instructional activities. For example, after a student has attained the concepts of socioeconomic status and sense of political efficacy, messages pertinent to these two concepts can be directly conveyed to students in formal statements. For example the statement "Individuals of upper socioeconomic status tend to have a higher sense of political efficacy than individuals of lower socioeconomic status" is immediately meaningful to a student who has attained the concepts of socioeconomic status and sense of political efficacy. However, teachers and curriculum developers must be careful not to confuse mere verbal facility with concept attainment. Students may spice their classroom dialogues with terms like *alienation, democracy, fascism* and *political power* and appear to the casual observer as profound or insightful social commentators. Yet they may be disguising ignorance with glibness. Neither naming a concept nor stating the concept definition demonstrates concept learning. The minimal demonstration of concept attainment is capability to distinguish instances from noninstances of the concept. Thus, instruction aimed at concept learning must stress application lessons, which require the student to use the concept to organize and interpret fresh information.

APPLICATION 5.1: TEACHING FOR CONCEPT LEARNING

Instructional objectives are the following:
a. Students are able to repeat, when called on, the formal definitions of these

words: social class, socioeconomic status, social mobility, social system.

b. Students are able to organize an array of raw statistical data in terms of these categories: racial identity and social class.

c. Students are able to compare and contrast the behavior described in a case study in terms of role and status.

d. Students are able to repeat the three examples of nationalism that appear on [specific] pages.

e. Students are able to identify examples of imperialism that appear in a series of historical case studies.

1. Which of the objectives are the better and worse specifications of instruction for concept learning? Why?

_____

_____

_____

_____

_____

_____

2a. Write a good instructional objective for concept learning.

_____

_____

b. Describe how you would design and/or implement the expository mode of instruction to achieve your objective.

_____

_____

_____

_____
_____
_____

c. Prepare a brief rationale in support of your instructional planning.

_____
_____
_____

3a. Write a second good instructional objective for concept learning.

_____
_____

b. Describe how you would design and/or implement the discovery mode of instruction to achieve your objective.

_____
_____
_____
_____
_____

c. Prepare a brief rationale in support of your instructional planning.

_____

_____

_____

4. Following are two statements about using concepts in building a social studies curriculum. Critically appraise these statements and indicate whether you would use each statement as a guide to curriculum development and instruction.

a. In the social studies concepts should be taught rather than facts. Students eventually forget most of the facts that they learn. However, concept learning is likely to endure. There are also too many facts to cover in a social studies curriculum. The only way a student can make sense of the complex modern world is to forget about learning a lot of facts and to learn concepts instead.

b. In designing social studies instruction, a teacher or a curriculum developer should permit each student to form concepts independently. To impose conceptual structures on students is a form of tyranny which must be resisted if we are to nurture free men. The imposition of social science concepts by the teacher results in the inhibition of inventiveness and open-mindedness; it can impede inquiry. Creativity and mental flexibility are fostered by a permissive approach to the use of concepts.

_____

_____

_____

_____

_____

_____

_____

Notes

1. Peter H. Martorella, *Concept Learning in the Social Studies*, Scranton, Pa.: Intext Educational, 1971, p. 5.

2. Lyle E. Bourne, Jr., *Human Conceptual Behavior*, Boston: Allyn and Bacon, 1966, pp. 1–3. Eugene J. Meehan, *Value Judgment and Social Science*, Homewood, Ill.: Dorsey Press, 1969, p. 19.

3. Vernon Van Dyke, *Political Science: A Philosophical Analysis*, Stanford, Calif.: Stanford University Press, 1960, pp. 61–70.

4. Ibid.

5. Lester Milbrath, *Political Participation*, Chicago: Rand McNally, 1965, p. 155.

6. Van Dyke, op. cit., pp. 61–70.

7. Robert Glaser, "Concept Learning and Concept Teaching," in *Learning Research and School Subjects*, ed. by Robert M. Gagné and William J. Gephart, Itasca, Ill.: Peacock, 1968, pp. 1–5.

8. Siegfried Englemann, *Conceptual Learning*, San Rafael, Calif.: Dimensions, 1969, pp. 13–15.

9. Robert M. Gagné, *The Conditions of Learning*, New York: Holt, Rinehart and Winston, 1965, p. 136.

10. Ibid., pp. 126–139.

11. Suzanne Wiggins, "Economics in the Curriculum," in *Social Science in the Schools*, ed. by Irving Morrissett and W. Williams Stevens, Jr., New York: Holt, Rinehart and Winston, 1971, pp. 93–107. (Suzanne Wiggins Helburn, John G. Sperling, and Robert Evans wrote *Economics and Society*, a high school economics course published by Addison-Wesley.)

12. Ibid., p. 100.

13. Jerome S. Bruner, *The Process of Education*, New York: Random House, Vintage Books, 1960, p. 31.

14. David P. Ausubel, *Educational Psychology: A Cognitive View*, New York: Holt, Rinehart and Winston, 1968, pp. 521–527.

15. Gagné, op. cit., pp. 145–157.

16. Howard D. Mehlinger and John J. Patrick, *Teacher's Guide for American Political Behavior*, Lexington, Mass.: Ginn, 1972, p. 56.

17. Howard D. Mehlinger and John J. Patrick, *American Political Behavior*, Lexington, Mass.: Ginn, 1972, pp. 142–143.

18. Glaser, op. cit., pp. 10–15.

19. Anthropology Curriculum Study Project, *Teaching Plan, Studying Societies*, New York: Macmillan, 1971, pp. 15–19.

20. Ibid., p. 15.

21. Ibid., pp. 15–18.
22. Ibid., pp. 19–20.

Suggested Reading

Beyer, Barry K., and Anthony N. Penna (eds.). *Concepts in the Social Studies.* Washington, D.C.: National Council for the Social Studies, 1971. This little volume is a collection of readings for social studies teachers about these four questions: (1) What are concepts? (2) Why teach concepts? (3) How can concepts be taught? (4) What are the implications of concept teaching? In response to these questions, the editors present commentary by psychologists, social studies methods teachers, and high school classroom teachers.

Bourne, Lyle E., Jr. *Human Conceptual Behavior.* Boston: Allyn and Bacon, 1966. The author reviews theories and research about concept learning. This commentary is technical, but highly readable and provides background for those who want to understand the theoretical and research foundations of current instructional practice for concept learning.

Engelmann, Siegfried. *Conceptual Learning.* San Rafael, Calif.: Dimensions, 1969. Engelmann has been a leader in designing instruction for conceptual learning of children. This book is a discussion of his instructional theory and practices. The emphasis is on systematic instruction to achieve precisely stated objectives. Although Engelmann's work has been with younger children, his ideas and practices are pertinent to concept learning among adolescents.

Martorella, Peter H. *Concept Learning in the Social Studies.* Scranton, Pa.: Intext Educational, 1971. Martorella has reviewed research and theories about concept learning pointedly for social studies teachers and curriculum developers. His writing is spiced with classroom examples and with practical suggestions for instructional design. The book is very readable.

6

Teaching the Use of Hypotheses

EVERYONE MAKES DECISIONS daily that are based on beliefs about what is true or false, likely or unlikely, possible or impossible. For example, suppose that you want to drive from Chicago to Milwaukee. It has, however, been snowing for the last five or six hours. You turn on the radio to get a weather report and learn that a blizzard is on. You start to reconsider your trip. You call a nearby state police headquarters to get a report of highway conditions and find that the roads are becoming icy and dangerous, and traffic is moving very slowly. You weigh the pros and cons of making the trip. "If I decide to go," you say to yourself, "it might take three or four hours to get to Milwaukee instead of the usual hour and a half. I'm supposed to meet my friend Tom for lunch at noon, and it's 9:30 now. I'll never get there on time because of the slow-moving traffic, poor visibility, and icy roads. In fact, driving conditions appear to be so bad I might not get there at all."

Based on particular beliefs about reality, you decide to postpone your trip to Milwaukee. Your line of reasoning can be described as follows:

I believe that driving conditions are bad.

I believe that the bad driving conditions make it impossible for me to reach my destination on time.

I believe that the bad driving conditions make it likely that I could have an accident.

Therefore, I decide that I won't drive to Milwaukee today.

The decision not to drive to Milwaukee is based on this hypothesis: If the roads are very icy, if visibility is very poor, and if traffic is moving very slowly, then it is impossible for me to arrive at my destination on time, and it is very likely that I would have an accident. In formal, abstract terms the line of reasoning is as follows: If A, B, and C are true, then D is certain to result, and E is likely to result.

Later in the day you hear and see evidence via a television news program that supports your hypothesis. The TV newscaster reports that numerous automobile accidents were caused by the bad weather, and you watch a video-taped traffic snarl that is projected to the television audience while the announcer continues to report details about the effects of the storm. You feel better than ever about deciding to postpone your trip to Milwaukee.

You can probably recall several actual decisions that you have made recently that involved the same manner of thinking as did the decision in the example about driving to Milwaukee. Indeed, much of everyone's behavior is based on hypotheses, beliefs about various relationships between conditions and consequences or between causes and effects. Somebody decides to do certain things because he believes that certain desirable consequences will result from these actions. He decides not to do other things because he believes that he can avoid certain undesirable consequences. Everyone, whether or not he thinks about it in such formal terms, is a formulator and tester of hypotheses. However, some are more competent than others in thinking about the relationships between events. A distinction of the highly competent person is the ability to determine the grounds for confirmation or rejection of a proposition, or hypothesis. This ability depends upon skills necessary to formulate hypotheses precisely and to marshall relevant evidence to test hypotheses. Thus, acquiring competence to formulate and test hypotheses about human behavior and social organization should be an integral feature of learning in the social studies.

Formulating Hypotheses

In order to teach students the skills for formulating and testing hypotheses, you must know what a hypothesis that can be tested empirically is. Of the following statements which are hypotheses that can be empirically tested?

1. The Republican party is better than the Democratic party.
2. Socialization is the process of learning how to become an acceptable member of a society.
3. Young adults are more likely than elderly people to participate actively in politics.
4. The president ought to support basic reforms in the federal income tax law.
5. A voter is a person who is legally qualified to cast a ballot in a public election.
6. Good citizens go to heaven when they die.

Statement 3 is the only hypothesis that can be tested empirically in the preceding list. This statement is an assertion about reality that can be confirmed or rejected on empirical grounds, that is, on the basis of sensory experience. Anybody can make observations of natural phenomena to judge the reliability of statement 3.

Statements 1 and 4 are value judgments, that is, assertions about what ought to be, about what is good or bad, better or worse. Statement 3, as a hypothesis that can be tested empirically, can be judged correct or incorrect according to public, replicable standards of confirmation. In contrast, statements 1 and 4, as value judgments, are ultimately viewed as right or wrong in terms of personal preference. When the personal preferences, or value judgments, of a group are very similar or the same, then it is relatively easy to obtain agreement about normative statements, or value judgments. For example, virtually everyone you know will agree that murder is bad. However, when the personal preferences of a group vary greatly, it is difficult or impossible for group members to agree about normative statements. For example, Americans have argued vigorously for years about whether busing of schoolchildren should be employed to achieve racial balances in public schools.

Statements 2 and 5 are definitional statements rather than assertions about what is. These definitions are criteria, or rules, for determining instances of the concepts voter and socialization. The definitional statements can be judged more or less useful in helping one to organize and interpret facts, but statements 2 and 5 cannot be judged true or false assertions about reality.

Statement 6 cannot be judged true or false on empirical grounds. It can be accepted or rejected only on faith, since it is not possible to make observations to confirm or disconfirm it in terms of sensory experience.

An empirically "testable" hypothesis such as statement 3 is a reasonable guess about reality which is stated exactly so that it can be measured in terms of the reality it is supposed to represent.[1] It is "testable" because it is possible to specify the kind of data which could confirm or reject it. For example, suppose you are interested in answering this question: Which political party do college-educated people tend to prefer in presidential elections? A social scientist might respond to this question by stating these alternative hypotheses:

1. People who have attended a college or university are more likely than those who have not experienced higher education to prefer the Republican party candidates in presidential elections.
2. People who have attended a college or university are more likely than those who have not experienced higher education to prefer the Democratic party candidate in presidential elections.
3. There is no discernible difference in the preferences for candidates in presidential elections of those who have and have not attended a college or university.

These alternative hypotheses are conflicting guesses and untested alternative answers to a question about variation in political behavior. To determine which of the alternative hypotheses fits reality, it is necessary to gather reliable data about the voting behavior of those who have and have not attended a college or university (Fig. 6.1).

The alternative hypotheses are guides to the organization and interpretation of evidence pertinent to the confirmation or rejection of the hypotheses. For example, political preference for a party's candidate, educational attainment, and presidential elections are the key concepts in the three preceding alternative hypotheses. These concepts direct attention to particular evidence to the exclusion of other evidence. Thus, the hypotheses are organizers for inquiry.

FIGURE 6.1.

The importance of testing beliefs against social reality.

To be useful guides to inquiry, hypotheses must be stated precisely, so that the relationship between the key concepts in the hypotheses are clearly indicated. In addition, the concepts from which the hypotheses are constructed must pertain to reality, must not be biased, and must be amenable to relatively precise measurement. (See Chapter 5 for an elaborate discussion about what is a useful concept.)

At this point you should be able to recognize easily that the hypothesis in the example at the beginning of this chapter about the contemplated automobile trip is a most useful guide to decision-making. It is a testable assertion about reality, a proposition that can be supported or rejected empirically. Indeed, the hypothesis was supported with evidence obtained from a television newscast.

Using what you have learned thus far, demonstrate your knowledge of hypotheses by identifying the empirically testable hypotheses among the following statements:

1. To be considered a good citizen, a person should participate in public elections.

2. Jim Johnson, a 45-year-old college graduate, does not participate actively in public elections.

3. Individuals of higher educational attainment are more likely than individuals of lower educational attainment to participate in public elections.

4. Younger individuals are less likely to participate in public elections than older individuals are.

5. Enculturation is the process of acquiring the culture of a society.

Statements 2, 3, and 4 are hypotheses that can be empirically tested. Can you explain why this is so? If not, you should reread the section Formulating Hypotheses beginning on page 197. Or you might refer to one of the books listed on page 255

Testing Hypotheses

How do we decide that our beliefs about reality are accurate guides to the world of objects and events that surround us? In the earlier example about the contemplated automobile trip, a combination of observation, reliance on authorities, and intuition was used to support the belief that driving conditions were too bad to allow a quick, safe trip from Chicago to Milwaukee. What techniques for supporting or rejecting or for testing hypotheses are mentioned in the examples below? Which of these techniques are more reliable? Which are less reliable? Why?

The setting for the following scene is the family dinner table. The cast is comprised of Mr. Marvin Morris; Mary Morris, his wife; the Morris children, Martha and Mike, who are teen-agers; and an out-of-town guest, Mr. David Douglas. They are talking about politics, in particular the political attitudes and behavior of young people.

MR. DOUGLAS: *Man, did you read the newspaper article about the wild demonstration at the state university yesterday? A group of leftist students were causing trouble. It seems that they're opposed to the new higher education law that the state legislature passed the other day. The students were so unruly that the police had to come to the campus to restore order.*

MR. MORRIS: *Yes, David, I read about the demonstration, and it really disgusts me. Most kids today aren't patriotic and law-abiding, like we were. And what amazes me is that the more educated kids, the college students, are the worst. Our college campuses today are infested with radical leftists, alienated youth who want to destroy the system and create some kind of crazy utopia.*

MARTHA: *I hate to disagree with you, Dad. But I think you're completely wrong. I think kids today care about their country, but maybe they show it in different ways.*

MIKE: *I have to agree with Martha. And I think you're very mistaken, Dad, about most college kids being leftists or radicals. I think most college kids, and high school kids too, are pretty much middle-of-the-roaders. I'll bet that no more than 2 or 3 percent of all the college kids in this country could be called radical leftists, revolutionaries, or alienated youth.*

MR. MORRIS: *Michael, Martha, I'm surprised at you. I expect you to be more informed about current events than this.*

MRS. MORRIS: *Calm down, Marv. I may not have the facts to settle your disagreement, but I do know that arguing around the dinner table won't help us decide who's right.*

MR. DOUGLAS: *Well, I may not be an expert in studying the political attitudes of youth, but I do travel quite a bit, and during the last three years I've been in several college towns. I've talked to many college students, and I've observed a few public demonstrations and political rallies. My personal experience has convinced me that today's young people are a new breed that opposes all the old values. I believe that they're a bunch of wild, leftist radicals.*

MR. MORRIS: *You'll be pleased to know, David, that Barney Burton, the editor of the local newspaper, agrees with you. I respect Mr. Burton very much, and I'm willing to believe what he says about the political attitudes of college students.*

MARTHA: *Dad, Mr. Michaels, my social studies teacher, showed us the data from three nationwide opinion studies. These studies were based on random stratified national probability samples, and they indicate that less than 1 percent of all college students can be labeled as radical leftists.*

MIKE: *Those results certainly agree with what we've found out in our social studies class. I've been working on a special project for the last two months which involves doing a survey research study of the political opinions of all the students in our high school. The results show that most kids in our school are middle-of-the-road in politics. Only a very few express any political alienation.*

MRS. MORRIS: *I don't know much about politics or current events. But my intuition tells me that the children are right, Marvin.*

MR. MORRIS: *Oh, bull! I just don't believe that polls are accurate. I think all pollsters are a bunch of crackpots.*

MARTHA: *Is it better to believe the results of scientific polling, or should we just believe what the editor of the newspaper says?*

MIKE: *Or should we merely trust our own experience. I've learned in school that science is a means for systematically extending our experience. I've learned a lot this semester about survey research, and I'd rather believe the results of a properly designed survey research study of political opinions than to trust my limited personal experiences or the words of some supposed authority like Mr. Burton, who is very biased.*

MRS. MORRIS: *Why don't we talk about the high school basketball game tomorrow night. David, did you know that Michael is a starting forward on the basketball team?*

COLLECTING AND USING DATA TO TEST HYPOTHESES

In the preceding example, four different techniques for confirming beliefs or testing hypotheses were mentioned. These can be called: (1) an appeal to personal experience; (2) an appeal to authority; (3) the practice of social science inquiry; and (4) reliance on intuition.

Both Mr. Morris and Martha tried to support their beliefs with appeals to authority. Mr. Morris relied blindly and uncritically on the authority of a respected person. In contrast, Martha relied on conclusions, supported by evidence, that were made by authoritative polling organizations which used public, replicable techniques to achieve their results. Thus, only Martha's appeal to authority was empirically based in terms of scientific inquiry.

Mr. Douglas used personal experience, an empirical approach, to support his hypothesis. However, his empiricism was very personal, impressionistic, restricted in scope, and unsystematic. In contrast, scientific empiricism is relatively objective, systematic, and extensive in scope. And scientific inquiry is based on public, replicable procedures. Indeed, as Michael pointed out during the dinner table discussion, science is a means of extending personal experience and of transcending the bias that can afflict parochial, limited experience.

Mrs. Morris appealed to intuition to support her beliefs. History documents the value of intuition, which has often led to brilliant political or personal decisions and even to scientific discovery. However, the scientist incorporates intuition into systematic scientific inquiry to guard against serious errors and merely fanciful beliefs.

Among the group at the dinner table, Michael was the sole practitioner of full-blown scientific inquiry. In his high school social studies course he was involved in a survey research study designed to test hypotheses about the political opinions of local high school students.

Social science is a way of knowing, a method of inquiry to support or reject hypotheses, that is designed to be more reliable than alternative ways of knowing about social reality. The social science way of knowing is empirically based; it depends upon controlled, systematic examination of natural phenomena. Through systematic collection and use of data, evidence is marshaled to support or reject hypotheses.

Ways of collecting data. Social scientists use three main approaches to data collection to test hypotheses: (1) direct observation of behavior, (2) indirect observation of behavior, and (3) examination of products of behavior.

The direct observation approach to the collection of data is based on firsthand experience; the social scientist collects data about human behavior that occurs in his presence. For example, Robert F. Bales, a social psychologist, used the method of direct observation to produce his studies of small-group behavior, such as "The Equilibrium Problem in Small Groups."[2] He presented a series of problems in human interaction to several small groups of people and observed the behavior of group members as they attempted to solve the problems. Margaret Mead based her ethnographic studies of nonliterate societies on direct observation. To produce her classic study *Coming of Age in Samoa*, she lived with Samoans and systematically observed the workings of their society.[3]

Studies of public opinion, such as those conducted by the Survey Research Center of the University of Michigan and Gallup poll, are examples of indirect observation through question-asking. The inquirers ask questions of samples of respondents to test hypotheses. From data collected through the use of instruments, such as questionnaires and attitude scales, hypotheses about human behavior are supported or rejected. These instruments are indirect indicators of behavior, since inferences are made from data recorded through use of the instruments rather than through firsthand observation.[4]

The third main approach to the collection of data to test hypotheses, examination of products of behavior, is based on the careful study of records of human behavior. Examples of this approach are the historian's examination of written documents and the archeologist's study of artifacts found in Egyptian pyramids and in digs of the remains of ancient buried cities. Through the examination of data found in behavior products, the inquirer develops and tests hypotheses.[5]

Sometimes social scientists combine the three main approaches to data collection in their attempts to formulate and test hypotheses. An example is

Robert A. Dahl's study of political life in New Haven, *Who Governs?* This classic was based on data gathered through the administration of a questionnaire to selected respondents, through direct observation of political behavior, and through the examination of the products of behavior such as newspapers and government documents.[6]

Types of systematic studies. Social scientists use three main types of studies to test hypotheses: (1) the sample survey, (2) the experiment, and (3) the case study.

The *sample survey* usually consists of obtaining the opinions or reports of behavior of a sample of individuals which is likely to represent the population from which the sample was drawn. From these opinions or reports of behavior, inferences are made about the population that the sample represents.[7]

Sample surveys of public opinion involve data collection through indirect observation. Respondents are asked to reply to questionnaires or attitude scales which yield the data. From these data inferences are made about the beliefs and behavior of the respondents. Judgments are made about human behavior indirectly through the use of an instrument—a questionnaire or attitude scale.

To test the three alternative hypotheses about educational attainment and voter behavior discussed earlier (page 198), students must use data gathered through sample survey methods such as the data in Table 6.1. These data[8] support hypothesis 1: People who have attended a college or university are more likely than those who have not experienced higher education to prefer the Republican party candidates in presidential elections. Hypotheses 2 and 3 are rejected by these data.

The data in Table 6.1 describe a sample, drawn by the Gallup organization, which was representative of the adult population of the United States. On the basis of this sample, we infer a factual judgment about the entire adult population. For example, when the Gallup organization does a sample survey

TABLE 6.1.

Candidate preferences by political party of voters of different educational attainments.

EDUCATIONAL ATTAINMENT	VOTER PREFERENCES IN PRESIDENTIAL ELECTIONS										
	1952		1956		1960		1964		1968		
	% D	% R	% D	% R	% D	% R	% D	% R	% D	% R	% I
College	34	66	31	69	39	61	52	48	37	54	9
High school	45	55	42	58	52	48	62	38	42	43	15
Grade school	52	48	50	50	55	45	66	34	52	33	15

SOURCE: The Gallup poll. American Institute of Public Opinion, 1968.

PART TWO / INSTRUCTOR

study, they ask questions of a nationally representative sample of 1,500 people. From responses given by this small group, the pollsters make inferences about the opinions of the entire population of our country. Because of the precise, systematic technique of selecting the sample of 1,500, the pollsters can claim an extremely high probability that their inferences are correct and accurate representations of the opinions of the total population. We tend to accept the inferences of the Gallup organization as "facts," even though they represent judgments about reality which extend beyond the available evidence. However, strictly speaking, these inferences are factual judgments; they are highly probable representations of reality.

The design of the sample survey study has been applied to the analysis of documents and other primary source material.[9] Random samples of pages, paragraphs, and types of source material have been drawn, and then writing has been analyzed quantitatively to test hypotheses about the substance of the writing. For example, content analysis has been used to test alternative hypotheses about the disputed authorship of such materials as portions of the Bible, the Dead Sea scrolls, and the plays of Shakespeare. Content analysis has been used also to generate and to test hypotheses about political decision-making and the behavior of national leaders in situations of crisis.

Experiments, although not as widely and easily used in the social sciences as the sample survey, are another means of testing hypotheses.[10] An experiment is a systematic study of cause-effect relationships under controlled conditions of observation and measurement. A common type of experiment consists of the comparison of two groups: an experimental group, which experiences some kind of treatment, and a comparable control group, which does not experience the experimental treatment. The outcomes of the experimental treatment are then measured. If the experimental group has been changed in some way, the experimental treatment is presumed to be the cause of this effect.

Following is an example of a social science experiment. A social psychologist wants to test this hypothesis: If a group of high school students experiences a particular series of films about the life of black people, these students will demonstrate a significant decrease in racial prejudice. To test this hypothesis, the social psychologist randomly assigns sixty high school students to experimental and control groups, thirty to a group. Next, he gives each group an attitude test to measure racial prejudice. Following the test the social psychologist administers a treatment to the experimental group which is a series of films about the life of black people in America. The control group receives no treatment. The experimenter then seeks to determine whether or not the experimental treatment had any effect on the experimental group by administering another attitude test to both groups.

Experiments may involve the collection of data through either direct or indirect observation. For example, some experiments require data collection through indirect observation—through the use of questionnaires or attitude scales. Other experiments require data collection through direct observation—through the use of tape recordings or through systematic observation and note taking. Some experiments may require the use of both indirect and direct observational techniques.

The *case study*, the third main type of study used to test social science hypotheses, is a detailed description and analysis of the human behavior of, for example, a person, a work group, a community, and a culture. Case studies usually depend on direct observation as the main technique for gathering data.[11]

William F. Whyte's *Street Corner Society* is a classic example of a case study based on direct observation. To do this study, Whyte, a sociologist, lived with a group of young working-class adults in a large city to observe and analyze their patterns of behavior.[12]

Hypotheses are tested on a limited scale through the case study method. This technique allows social scientists to study types of human behavior in depth. However, the data gathered in this manner usually have limited applicability since the point of the study is to find out as much as possible about one unit—a person, a work group, a community, a culture—rather than to find out a little about many units of the same kind—a nationally representative sample of people.

Case studies do not provide the grounds for rigorously testing hypotheses with general applicability. These studies are often abundant sources of insights and clues for further investigation and are the means for testing hypotheses about a particular unit that has been observed. However, case studies do not confirm social science generalizations.

The intensive study of particular past events, such as that by the historian or the archeologist, can be considered an extension of the case study approach. For example, J. C. Beaglehole, a historian from New Zealand, studied systematically all written accounts about the last years of Captain James Cook in order to test alternative hypotheses about the mysterious events surrounding the sea voyager's death. Beaglehole's work can be considered an intensive case study, conducted through the examination of behavior products, of a specific past event.[13] Erik Erikson's study of the life of Martin Luther, based on analysis of written materials in terms of psychoanalytic theories, is another example of a historical case study of related events that were part of an outstanding man's life.[14] Stanley M. Elkins' study of slavery in North and South America is an example of the case study approach applied broadly to the analysis of past events. Elkins examined behavior products of the slavery period in terms of social and psychological concepts such as role, status, personality, and self-concept in order to generate and test hypotheses about this question: What did slavery do to the slaves?[15]

Techniques for gathering and using data to test hypotheses are useful to those who want to become more competent thinkers and decision-makers about the objects and events of their own world. Those who acquire these skills are likely to have a high level of competence to deal with various personal and social problems. In contrast, those who fail to learn how to gather and use data systematically to support or reject alternative beliefs are severely handicapped in any serious attempt to think and learn about their social world. All who learn how to use social science as a way of thinking and knowing have the capability of thinking critically about the statements of significant people, such as politicians, newscasters, authors of books, newspaper reporters, interest group leaders, friends, and teachers. In contrast, those who do not learn how to determine the grounds for accepting or rejecting beliefs about reality are not able to think for themselves. They are relatively open to the appeals of propagandists and charlatans who would influence their beliefs for negative purposes.

THE PRODUCTS OF TESTING HYPOTHESES

In the social sciences the products of hypothesis testing are descriptive and explanatory statements about social reality that are more or less accurate and useful. These tested statements are considered to be facts (beliefs) about what is or what was that everyone, or nearly everyone, accepts as true on empirical grounds. Some of these facts are very specific; they describe or explain particular events. Other factual statements yielded by testing hypotheses are generalizations; they are broadly applicable and can be used to describe or explain many similar events. Some products of hypothesis testing are solidly supported by evidence and are indisputably accepted as facts. Other descriptive and explanatory statements are less solidly grounded and are more or less open to continuous critical appraisal and alternative factual judgments.

Which of the following statements are probably the products of hypothesis testing? Which are descriptive statements and which are explanatory statements? Which are specific factual statements and which are generalizations?

1. Manual laborers have tended to vote for the Democratic candidate in presidential elections during the period from 1932 to 1968.
2. Manual laborers are more likely than businessmen to vote for Democratic party presidential candidates.
3. Social change is the emergence of new patterns of relationships between people and groups.
4. Fascists ought to be prevented from holding public office.

5. If two groups of boys who feel hostile toward each other join their efforts to reach some common goal, their stereotypes of one another will become more favorable.
6. There was a political revolution in Russia in 1917.
7. Republicans are more likely than Democrats to vote in public elections.
8. One cause of the Russian Revolution of 1917 was the czarist regime's inflexible devotion to autocracy.

Statements 1, 2, 5, 7, and 8 are the products of hypothesis testing. Data have been gathered and used systematically to support these statements. For example, statements 1, 2, and 7 are products of sample survey studies of voter behavior. Statement 5 is the product of an experimental study. And statement 8 is the product of extensive examination of historical documents.

Statements 3, 4, and 6 are not products of hypothesis testing. Statement 3 is definitional; it is a criterion for categorizing objects or events that pertain to the concept of social change. (See Chapter 5 for a discussion of concepts.) Statement 4 is a value judgment. It may be a product of value analysis or merely an assertion of unconsidered preference. (See Chapter 7 for a discussion of value judgments and value analysis.) Statement 6, unlike statements 3 and 4, is indisputably empirical and descriptive of social reality. However, this type of statement is not a likely product of hypothesis testing. Rather it is, and has been, accepted universally as a fact that 1917 is the year when a sociopolitical upheaval occurred in Russia.

Statement 1, which is the product of hypothesis testing through sample survey studies, is a general description of past social reality; it is an assertion about the way concepts were related at a particular time.[16]

Statements 2 and 7, which also are products of hypothesis testing through sample survey studies, are very broad generalizations that describe past relationships between concepts and imply that these relationships will continue. Statement 2 comparatively describes the past patterns of voter behavior of manual laborers and businessmen and implies the prediction that these patterns will continue. However, one must be cautious about making predictions on the basis of such statements because they are based on past behavior patterns that pertain to particular social circumstances. If social conditions are very stable, there is a strong possibility that the descriptive generalizations will apply to events in the near future. However, if social conditions become volatile, then new patterns of behavior are likely to emerge. For example, statements 2 and 7 aptly describe voter behavior from 1932 to 1972, but changing social circumstances may lead to new voter behavior patterns in the future.

Statements 5 and 8 are explanatory; they are assertions about why concepts are related in particular ways.[17] Statement 5 is a product of an experimental study that was designed by the social psychologist Muzafer Sherif to establish causation precisely.[18] Through his ingeniously designed Robbers Cave experiment, Sherif attempted to specify particular social conditions that would result in particular social consequences about conflict and cooperation. He formulated and tested "if-then" explanatory statements: if X, then Y; or if a certain condition or a set of conditions exists, then certain consequences will occur.

Rigorously designed experimental studies are most appropriately suited to establishing causation, or explanations. However, social phenomena are not as amenable as natural phenomena to experimental study. Thus, the social scientist usually must try to build explanations on less solid empirical ground. For example, he often attempts to construct explanations through multifactor correlation. This technique, which is associated with sample survey studies, involves correlating several variables, or factors, that are the focuses of an investigation.[19] To demonstrate correlation between factors is to show that one factor increases or decreases with another factor. For example, political scientists have demonstrated through sample survey studies that the following factors are correlated with voter behavior: sense of political efficacy, strength of political party identification, political interest, socioeconomic status, and social involvement. Changes in these variables are related to changes in tendency to vote; for example, increases in these factors result in an increase in the possibility for participation in a public election.[20]

Most explanatory statements in the social sciences, unlike those in the natural sciences, are derived from multifactor correlational studies rather than through tightly designed experiments which exactly demonstrate causation. Social scientists tend to think in causal terms when constructing and using correlational statements. However, they acknowledge the tenuous quality of explanations based on multifactor correlation. Thus, when planning and executing social studies lessons about explanation, social studies teachers should remember that multifactor correlations merely describe variation, from which one infers the likelihood of causation. The correlations do not demonstrate causation rigorously. Social studies students should have the opportunity to learn about the limitations of social science explanations derived from multifactor correlational studies and to entertain viable alternatives to generally accepted viewpoints.

Statement 8 (one cause of the Russian Revolution of 1917 was the czarist regime's inflexible devotion to autocracy) is an explanation which is grounded even less solidly than statements established through multifactor correlation. This statement is derived from the study of behavior products, in this instance written documents and the oral testimony of those who witnessed the events of the Russian Revolution.[21] The statement is generally accepted as one of a set of statements that seem to account for the occurrence of the Revolution; but this explanatory statement, unlike the products of a rigorous experimental study, is very open to dispute or to alternative, viable explanations. Indeed, explanatory statements about historical events are usually based on extremely limited evidence which is subject to various interpretations. Thus, the student of history must combine artful speculation and intuition with systematic, scientific study of scanty and often loaded evidence in order to formulate and test hypotheses.[22] Teachers should encourage their students critically to appraise generally accepted explanations of historical events and to consider viable alternatives.

The goal of the social scientist is to produce descriptions and explanations that enable one to understand more fully the social world and to perceive and interpret social phenomena more clearly. Social science inquiry, a process of formulating and testing hypotheses, is designed to produce reliable descriptions and explanations. However, a cardinal rule of such inquiry is to view knowledge, or the products of inquiry, tentatively and probabilistically. The process of social science inquiry yields more or less accurate descriptions and explanations, not absolute substantiation for our beliefs. Hullfish and Smith have described the tentative quality of scientific knowledge very aptly:

It is a basic principle in science that every belief about matters of fact must be held subject to possible modification or rejection. No matter how fully warranted an accepted belief may be, new evidence may develop to indicate that, though it may still be said to be warranted in terms of the former evidence, it must now be judged to be incorrect.

A belief is warranted or unwarranted (and thus taken to be correct or incorrect) only in relation to a particular body of evidence at a given time. It is sometimes possible that two or more contrary beliefs may each have considerable warrant in terms of different bodies of evidence based on differing theories or conceptual schemes. In this case, scientific investigation may proceed on parallel fronts, so to speak. Usually it turns out that all but one of the approaches prove to be unfruitful, unnecessarily complicated, or the like. In any event, there is no such thing as an absolute or perfect warrant for any belief about matters of fact. Recognition of this is sometimes known as *the principle of continuous control*. It is in this sense that it is sometimes said that our knowledge of matters of fact is at best only highly probable knowledge.[23]

The tentative, probabilistic quality of social science descriptions and explanations is inherent in the scientific process of formulating and testing hypotheses. Inductive inferences are fundamental to the process of formulating and testing hypotheses empirically. And the distinguishing feature of an inductive inference is indeterminateness.[24] Note the indeterminate quality of the following inductive inference.

Statement 1: George is a man.

Statement 2: George is 40 years old.

Statement 3: George has rheumatism.

Statement 4: George will not run a four-minute mile tomorrow.

Given the evidence, the inductive inference, or conclusion, is highly probable but not necessary. The premises may be true, but they do not imply the conclusion.

The following syllogism illustrates the difference between an inductive, or indeterminate, inference and a deductive, or determinate and positive, inference.

Statement 1: All men are mortal.

Statement 2: Elmer Snodgrass is a man.

Statement 3: Therefore, Elmer Snodgrass is mortal.

If you believe that the premises in statements 1 and 2 are true, then you *must* conclude that statement 3 is true. Statement 3 is a deduction from, or implication of, statements 1 and 2; it is a determinate inference.

In contrast to a deduction, an induction is indeterminate and tentative. Turning the syllogism around as follows will illustrate.

Statement 1: Elmer Snodgrass is a man.

Statement 2: Elmer Snodgrass is mortal.

Statement 3: Therefore, all men are mortal.

If you believe that statements 1 and 2 are true, you can guess that statement 3 may be true. If you identify numerous other individuals who are both men and mortal, you increase your confidence in the conclusion that perhaps all men are mortal. But you can never know that an induction is absolutely, or positively, correct.

Deduction is the means for establishing the proofs inherent in purely logical systems, such as calculus or geometry. In contrast, induction is a primary means for establishing confirmation of hypotheses in the natural and social sciences. For example, the hypotheses about educational attainment and voter behavior (page 198) must be confirmed or disconfirmed through inductive reasoning—the process of deciding, on the basis of a sample, what is probably true of the population that the sample represents. Inductive reasoning involves extrapolations from what is known to what is probably true about the unknown. It is well to remember that many of the social science hypotheses that are accepted as facts are products of sound inductions. They are highly probable but indeterminate and tentative conclusions.

The process of formulating and testing hypotheses in the social sciences involves an interlacing of inductive and deductive inferring. Figure 6.2 illustrates the circular interplay between induction and deduction which is part of any effort to confirm a social science hypothesis. As shown in the figure,

FIGURE 6.2.
Formulating and testing
hypotheses.

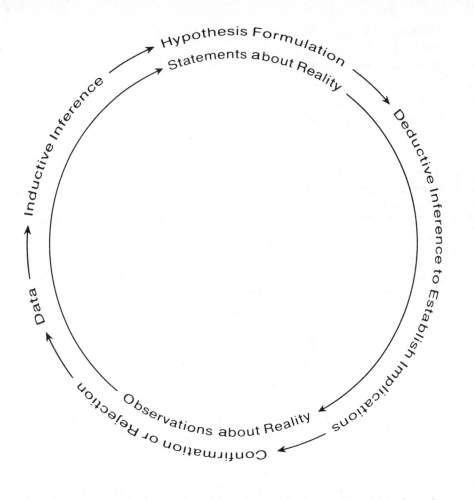

hypotheses are inductively inferred from bits and pieces of data. The hypotheses go beyond the available data; they are assertions about the unknown that are based on what is known. These hypotheses are then stated precisely, in provable form, which involves drawing deductive inferences from the particulars that are implied by the hypotheses. Relevant data is then gathered for the purpose of determining whether the implication of the hypotheses can be found in the real world. If these implications are found, then the hypotheses are confirmed. The process of confirmation requires inductive reasoning of the kind that initiated the circular process.[25]

The social science mode of inquiry is an attempt to cope with the problem of indeterminateness which is inherent in an induction-based system of thought. Essentially, the social science method is pragmatic; if the implications of a hypothesis are demonstrated through the observation of phenomena, then the hypothesis is accepted, at least until evidence gathered through other observations indicates that the hypothesis is untenable. In other words, the social science method is based on the successful application of assertions about reality to the real world. Hypotheses that work, that appear to be borne out by real world events, are accepted. Hypotheses that violate the observation of phenomena are rejected.

A basic rule of scientific inquiry is to view knowledge as tentative, as more or less probable, and never as absolute. As Richard B. Braithwaite says:

Since the conclusion of an induction is a general hypothesis there is no time at which it is conclusively proved. The hypothesis may, of course, be established by the induction, but its establishment at one time will not prevent its refutation at a later time if contrary evidence occurs.[26]

Another limitation of the products of social scientific inquiry is that most of the hypotheses and factual judgments of the social sciences, in contrast to the propositions of natural science, are tendency statements. Typical examples of such statements, which are products of the sample survey type of study, are:

1. Black voters in the United States have tended to support Democratic party candidates in recent elections.
2. Upper-class individuals are more likely to participate actively in civic affairs than lower-class individuals are.

By definition, there are always exceptions to the tendency generalizations of social science. However, these are the "exceptions that prove the rule," since the preponderance of positive examples substantiates, or confirms, the tendency that the generalization symbolizes.

The social science method of inquiry is the most powerful means available for formulating and testing hypotheses about the social world. Those who know the most reliable descriptions and explanations of social reality, which are products of hypothesis testing through use of the social science method of inquiry, have tools that can help them to understand more fully the objects and events around them. This knowledge is the key to effective intellectual and physical moves and to wise decisions about what to do, how to do it, and why. In contrast, those who are ignorant of the best available knowledge and of the process by which it is produced are relatively handicapped in their efforts to think and act. However, the products of social science inquiry must be used with appropriate caution and qualification, as indicated in the preceding discussion. Social studies teachers have the obligation of helping students to learn about both the power and the limitations of inquiry in the social sciences. Thus, critical appraisal of descriptions and explanations should be an essential ingredient of social studies instruction.

Teaching the Skills of Formulating and Testing Hypotheses

Traditional instructional materials in the social studies have stressed factual learning to the minimization, or even exclusion, of learning the intellectual skills that enable the production and use of facts. Many new instructional materials, especially those designed by the special development projects for social studies curricula, emphasize both the products and the process of social science inquiry.[27] The innovative materials include many lessons adapted from the studies of social scientists. Data yielded by sample surveys, experiments, and case studies are presented to students who are required to use the data to confirm or disconfirm hypotheses. Students are asked to make critical judgments about conflicting hypotheses and about the techniques of inquiry used to test them.

Lessons designed to teach students to formulate and test hypotheses should facilitate positive transfer of learning. For example, teachers should hope that a student who has learned how critically to appraise a public opinion poll in a social studies class will be able to *transfer* this set of skills to the successful appraisal of any public opinion poll.

Instruction for positive transfer of learning should feature task similarity and task variety.[28] *Task similarity* is correspondence between initial learning tasks and subsequent transfer tasks. For example, instruction that features task similarity requires students to practice directly for their tests and to demonstrate mastery of objectives by applying successfully what was learned in one situation to fresh similar situations. *Task variety* occurs when instruction features systematic variation in materials and techniques. The appropriate blending of expository and discovery lessons to teach problem-solving skills is an example of task variety. Another example is the use of both case study analysis and statistical data analysis to practice formulating and testing hypotheses.

To encourage transfer, instruction should be designed to require *active learning,* the application of knowledge and skills to the mastery of exercises and problems.[29] Most students need to experience instruction which pointedly requires them to apply knowledge and skills in order to develop a propensity to transfer learning. For example, students who are required to formulate and test hypotheses are more likely to be able to transfer learning to a broad range of situations and problems than are those who are required to absorb and repeat facts.

Instruction for higher-level learning can enhance the likelihood of general positive transfer.[30] For example, learning conceptual frameworks and descriptive and explanatory generalizations is a means to general positive transfer.

In particular, the intellectual skills acquired through mastery of higher-level learning tasks, such as formulating and testing hypotheses, are so basic as to be potentially applicable to various and unforeseen academic and practical problems.

Teaching for transfer of learning requires teachers to be highly selective and systematic when organizing the content of instruction for a social studies course. Teachers must focus on a few of the most important concepts and generalizations and on data relevant to these organizing ideas, or they will flounder in a swamp of unconnected information. They must have the courage to exclude, or they will have to develop the courage to endure the boredom and indifference of students who are unable to see relevance and purpose in their social studies assignments. Teachers who emphasize profound studies of a few basic ideas, facts, and skills are more likely to produce positive transfer of learning, an enduring educational benefit, than are those who try to cover too much ground.

The most important possible outcome of instruction for transfer of learning is learning how to learn. Individuals who are skilled formulators and testers of hypotheses have learned how to learn, how to become independent thinkers and learners. Those who have acquired a learning set possess skills that are fundamentally applicable to the solving of a wide variety of problems. In order for students to acquire a learning set, they must be taught to use basic intellectual skills such as constructing and applying conceptual frameworks, formulating and testing hypotheses, and critically appraising factual and value statements.

Good instruction designed to teach the skills of social science inquiry features a blend of expository and discovery lessons.[31] Throughout our discussion of instructional procedures, it has been stressed that no one best mode or technique of instruction exists; certain instructional modes and techniques are more suitable to particular instructional objectives than they are to others. The applications of discovery and exposition to instruction about the process and products of social science inquiry are illustrated in Chapter 4, pages 125 to 149. The Site Map Lesson (Application 4.1, pages 129 to 139) is an example of the discovery approach applied to the development of hypothesizing skills. The Voting Behavior Lesson (Application 4.2, pages 142 to 148) is an example of the expository approach applied to the teaching of generalizations about voter participation in public elections.

Discovery lessons are most appropriate in introducing students to the need to develop skills of hypothesizing and hypothesis testing. The discovery mode of instruction is also well suited to application lessons, those that require students to use facts, ideas, and skills introduced in previous lessons to solve a fresh problem.

Expository lessons are most appropriate in presenting products of social science inquiry and sources of systematically organized information to be used to support or reject quickly hypotheses formulated in prior lessons. These lessons are particularly well suited to introducing, in a step-by-step fashion, certain skills of critical thinking and inquiry, such as table reading and map reading. In order fully to develop and retain these skills, they must have ample opportunity to practice them and to apply them to a variety of problems and contexts that require the use of discovery lessons.

Good instruction stresses the weaknesses as well as the strengths of the social science method of inquiry. Students must be taught both its uses and abuses in order to learn how to use the social science method of knowing properly. They need to learn about the problem of induction (discussed on pages 210 to 213). They must also learn when and when not to use social science inquiry. For example, students must learn that while social science is our most powerful means for coping with empirically based problems, it is not sufficient to achieve solutions to other kinds of problems such as those in the purely metaphysical and moral realms of thought.

Good instruction about formulating and testing hypotheses in the social studies provides ample opportunities to explore relevant topics, even those that are highly controversial, and to examine unorthodox, as well as typical, points of view. Cool, systematic, science-based study of controversial subjects is necessary to the honest implementation of programs that purport to feature social science inquiry.

TWO LESSONS ABOUT TESTING HYPOTHESES THROUGH SAMPLE SURVEY

Following are descriptions of two lessons which require students to formulate hypotheses and to test them with data gathered by means of the sample survey.[32] A careful reading of the lessons will prepare you to discuss these questions:

1. What is your evaluation of the design of the two lessons?
2. What is your evaluation of the teaching techniques recommended for the implementation of these lessons?
3. Would you use these lessons in your social studies class? Why?
4. How would you change the lessons, if at all, in order to make them most effective with the students whom you expect to teach?

   *Lesson 1** is designed to elicit the formal statement of several hypotheses

---

*Adapted from *American Political Behavior* by Howard D. Mehlinger and John J. Patrick. © Copyright 1972 by Indiana University. Published by Ginn and Company. Used with permission.

about voter behavior. In order to do this lesson, students must have mastered prior lessons applying the skill of relating variables to construct hypotheses that can be tested empirically.

The objective of instruction for this lesson is: Students can hypothesize about the relationship of the following variables to political party preference, to voter choices in public elections, or to both:

1. Sex identity
2. Educational attainment
3. Occupation
4. Racial identity
5. Age group
6. Area of residence
7. Income

The teacher begins the lesson by presenting, via overhead projector, seven pictures of pairs of individuals (Fig. 6.3, page 218) who symbolize the seven variables just mentioned.[33] Each transparency includes this question: Which political party is each individual likely to prefer?

The teacher challenges students to decide what are the variables in each picture and to construct hypotheses that can be tested empirically and that relate these variables to political party preference, voter choices in public elections, or both. An example of a hypothesis that students might state is: Younger individuals are more likely than older individuals to vote for Democratic party candidates.

The role of the teacher in this lesson is to manage an open-ended discussion among students about the likely behavior of the types represented in the pictures. The teacher should anticipate lively disagreement in the students' responses to some of the variables. However, he should refrain from settling the disagreements at this point and should indicate that such disagreements are properly settled by gathering and interpreting relevant data.

Lesson 2 is designed to present to students statistical data relevant to the hypotheses that they have formulated about voter behavior in lesson 1. In order to do lesson 2, students must have mastered prior instruction on how to read tables and how to make inferences from data describing a nationally representative sample of voters.

The instructional objective for this lesson is: Students can infer the following generalizations from the data presented in Table 6.2[34,35] (page 219):

1. Individuals of upper socioeconomic status are more likely than individuals of lower socioeconomic status to vote for the Republican candidates. Individuals of lower socioeconomic status are more likely than individuals of upper socioeconomic status to vote for the Democratic candidates.
2. Individuals with professional, business, white-collar, and farm occupations

A

B

C

D

E

F

G

FIGURE 6.3.
Individuals symbolizing seven variables in political party preferences. "Which political party is each individual likely to prefer?"

TABLE 6.2.

*Percentage of vote by
groups in presidential
elections, 1952–1968.*

	1952		1956		1960		1964		1968		
	D %	R %	D %	R %	D %	R %	D %	R %	D %	R %	Wallace
National	44.6	55.4	42.2	57.8	50.1	49.9	61.3	38.7	43.0	43.4	13.6
Men	47	53	45	55	52	48	60	40	41	43	16
Women	42	58	39	61	49	51	62	38	45	43	12
White	43	57	41	59	49	51	59	41	38	47	15
Nonwhite	79	21	61	39	68	32	94	6	85	12	3
College	34	66	31	69	39	61	52	48	37	54	9
High school	45	55	42	58	52	48	62	38	42	43	15
Grade school	52	48	50	50	55	45	66	34	52	33	15
Professional and business	36	64	32	68	42	58	54	46	34	56	10
White collar	40	60	37	63	48	52	57	43	41	47	12
Manual	55	45	50	50	60	40	71	29	50	35	15
Farmers	33	67	46	54	48	52	53	47	29	51	20
Under 30	51	49	43	57	54	46	64	36	47	38	15
30–49	47	53	45	55	54	46	63	37	44	41	15
50 and older	39	61	39	61	46	54	59	41	41	47	12
Protestant	37	63	37	63	38	62	55	45	35	49	16
Catholic	56	44	51	49	78	22	76	24	59	33	8
Republican	8	92	4	96	5	95	20	80	9	86	5
Democrat	77	23	85	15	84	16	87	13	74	12	14
Independent	35	65	30	70	43	57	56	44	31	44	25

SOURCE: Estimates from a national survey by the Gallup poll, 1968.

are more likely than manual workers to vote for the Republican candidates.
Manual workers are more likely than professionals, businessmen, white-
collar workers, and farmers to vote for the Democratic candidates.

3. Blacks tend to vote for the Democratic candidates.

4. College graduates are more likely than noncollege graduates to vote for
the Republican candidates. Individuals of lower educational attainment tend
to vote for the Democratic candidates.

5. Younger individuals are more likely than older individuals to vote for
the Democratic candidates. Older individuals are more likely than younger
individuals to vote for the Republican candidates.

6. Farmers are more likely to vote for the Republican candidates than other
manual workers are.

The teacher begins this lesson by asking students to infer generalizations
about voter behavior from Table 6.2. His role in this lesson is to prod students as directly and efficiently as possible to construct warranted generaliza-

tions from the data in the table. He should require them to support their conclusions with evidence from the table. Disputes about correct answers should be resolved by appealing to the evidence in the table and to the rules for using such evidence.

The teacher concludes this lesson by asking students to determine which of their hypotheses, formulated during the previous lesson, are confirmed or disconfirmed by the data in the table. They should be encouraged to think about testing their factual judgments about voter behavior with data from upcoming elections. They should terminate these lessons by thinking about these future-oriented questions: (1) Will past patterns of voter behavior characterize upcoming elections? (2) Will peculiar circumstances lead to unusual voter behavior? (3) Will cataclysmic social forces influence a basic realignment of political party preferences and voter behavior?

A LESSON ABOUT TESTING HYPOTHESES THROUGH EXPERIMENT

The materials developed by the Sociological Resources for the Social Studies (SRSS) project include many lessons that are reports of experiments or are based on experiments. Read the following lesson, based on an experiment by Gregory Razran, a social psychologist, and prepare to discuss these questions:

1. What is your evaluation of the design of this lesson?
2. What is your evaluation of the teaching techniques recommended for the implementation of the lesson?
3. Would you use this lesson in your social studies class? Why?
4. How would you change this lesson, if at all, in order to make it most effective with the students whom you expect to teach?

The Girl Watchers experiment, which is part of the SRSS unit *Images of People,* is an example of a lesson based on a social science experiment.[36] The instructional objectives of the experiment are:

1. To help students identify any images (stereotypes) they hold or may be aware of concerning different groups of people
2. To stimulate student understanding of stereotypes by reflecting on attitudes about minority groups prevalent in their own community and elsewhere in the United States.

The Girl Watchers experiment was designed to find out the extent to which ethnic stereotypes influence one's evaluations of different people. Razran hypothesized that one's images, or stereotypes, of different ethnic groups influence one's ratings of individuals who are identified with particular ethnic groups.

	TRAIT OR CHARACTERISTIC				
GIRL	Intelligent	Beautiful	Dependable	Fun-loving	Ambitious
"A"					
"B"					
"C"					
"D"					
"E"					

FIGURE 6.4.
Girl Watchers experiment: ranking worksheet without names. (Handout 1 from Sociological Resources for the Social Studies Episode: *Images of People.*)

The lesson about the Girl Watchers experiment is initiated by carrying out the following procedures*:

1. Randomly divide your students into two equal groups. Send one group out of the classroom so they will not be able to hear what is taking place in your room.

2. Distribute a copy of the Girl Watchers ranking worksheet *without names* to each student. A copy of the worksheet is shown in Figure 6.4.

3. Show the pictures of the five girls without names (Fig. 6.5, page 223). Direct your students to rank the girls "1" through "5" for each of the traits, based on their intuition or personal judgment. Highest ranking is indicated by "1," lowest by "5." They are to mark the numbers in the spaces provided on the worksheet without names.

4. Collect the completed worksheets and instruct the students who have completed them to remain silent about what they have done until you tell them they can talk about it. Either send them to the back of the room or send them out of the room.

5. Call back the other group of students and distribute to each a copy of the Girl Watchers ranking worksheet *with names* (Fig. 6.6, page 224).

6. Show the pictures of the five girls with names (Fig. 6.7, page 226). Direct the students to rank the girls "1" through "5" according to each trait on the worksheet with names.

7. Collect the completed forms and have all students return to their usual seats.

8. Appoint a student committee to tabulate the responses on the worksheets.

---

*Adapted from *Images of People* and the *Instructor's Guide for Images of People* by Sociological Resources for the Social Studies, an agency of the American Sociological Association (Boston: Allyn and Bacon, Inc., 1969). Reprinted by permission.

This should be done out of class. The tabulation worksheet on which the results are to be recorded is shown in Figure 6.8 (page 227).

9. After the committee has completed tabulating the data, determine the over-all rank order from the scores on each part. The results are to be recorded on the tally chart shown in Figure 6.9 (page 229).

The results of the Girl Watchers experiment are the basis for a lesson about stereotyping. The teacher should show the results of the experiment to the students and then ask them to identify and discuss the patterns of responses of the two groups. The discussion can be initiated by asking them to try to explain any differences in the responses of the two student groups: those who responded to the pictures without names and those who responded to the pictures with names.

Following is a commentary about likely patterns of response to the pictures which appears in the *Instructor's Guide* to the lesson:

We can't predict how your students will evaluate these girls. Students in different regions, of different ethnic backgrounds, of different socioeconomic classes, etc., will react differently. They, themselves, may not hold the particular images we've used in this exercise. But, in general, you could expect that a fairly heterogeneous class, responding only to the pictures unidentified by name, to rate the white girls somewhat higher in most categories than the black girl. (A predominantly black class might do just the opposite.) When you introduce the element of ethnic group identification by name, you might expect a heterogeneous group to rate the Jewish and Polish girls (along with the black girl) lower than the "old" American and Nordic girls, depending on local ethnic conditions.

If your students differ markedly from the projected patterns suggested above, you'll have to try to explain it in terms of local conditions and practices.[37]

The findings of the Girl Watchers experiment conducted by Gregory Razran are reported to students in an expository lesson which follows the lesson about the conduct of the experiment in the classroom. Students can compare and contrast their findings with those of Razran and can try to interpret similarities and differences in the findings. On pages 224 to 225 is the exposition lesson about the finding of the Razran experiment.[38]

A

B

C

D

E

FIGURE 6.5.
*Five girls to be ranked on work-
sheet without names in Girl
Watchers experiment.*

FIGURE 6.6.

Girl Watchers experiment: ranking worksheet with names. (Handout 2 from Sociological Resources for the Social Studies Episode: *Images of People.*)

TRAIT OR CHARACTERISTIC

GIRL	Intelligent	Beautiful	Dependable	Fun-loving	Ambitious
Peggy Swenson					
Betty Johnson					
Sally Wilson					
Sarah Goldstein					
Irene Kowalski					

The Razran Experiment*

Our "Girl Watchers" experiment (with the pictures of the five girls) was patterned after a research project on images of people conducted in the late 1940's—known as the Razran experiment. It considered how the categories in which we place people affect attitudes toward them.

Some Americans believe that Jews are brainy, pushy, unfair, sly and that Italians are dumb, vulgar, ill-mannered. Gregory Razran, a social scientist, wanted to find out if these images or impressions influenced the way people reacted towards Jews and Italians. He conducted an experiment in which he showed photographs of thirty pretty girls to fifty Columbia College students, fifty Barnard College students, and fifty middle-aged people. One life-size photograph at a time was projected upon a screen. Each subject in the experiment rated the girl in the photograph on various traits: general liking, beauty, intelligence, character, ambition, and entertainingness. To rate the girls, the subjects marked on a sheet of paper

whether each girl seemed to be (1) much above average, (2) above average, (3) average, (4) below average, or (5) much below average for each of the six traits. In other words, the rating was done for each trait on a five-point scale.

Two months later Razran conducted the experiment again with the same people and the same photographs. But this time he put a name under each photograph. Five girls were given "Jewish" names (Rabinowitz, Finkelstein, Goldberg, Cohen, and Kantor); five, "Italian" names (Scarano, Grisolia, Fichetti, D'Angelo, and La Guardia); five, "Irish" names (McGillicuddy, O'Shaughnessy, O'Brien, Kelley, and Flanagan), and the remaining fifteen girls were given "Old American" names (Adams, Clark, Chase, Davis, etc.).

Razran wanted to know if the subjects would change their minds about a girl, depending on whether she was "Irish," "Italian," or "Jewish." He thought that by putting a girl in a category ("Irish,"

*From *Images of People* and the *Instructor's Guide for Images of People* by Sociological Resources for the Social Studies, an agency of the American Sociological Association (Boston: Allyn and Bacon, Inc., 1969). Reprinted by permission.

Type of Name	Rating Group	Changes in Ratings					
		General liking	Beauty	Intelligence	Character	Ambition	Entertainingness
JEWISH	Columbia	−1.5	−0.3	+0.3	+0.3	+0.1	+0.1
	Barnard	−1.3	−0.3	+0.3	−0.8	+1.1	−0.3
	Middle-aged	−0.8	−0.3	+0.4	−0.6	−1.0	−0.1
ITALIAN	Columbia	−0.8	−0.3	−0.3	−0.5	+0.3	−0.2
	Barnard	−1.0	−0.4	−0.4	−0.5	−0.5	−0.5
	Middle-aged	−0.6	−0.3	−0.3	−0.3	−0.4	−0.2
IRISH	Columbia	−0.3	−0.1	−0.1	−0.2	−0.2	0.0
	Barnard	−0.4	−0.2	−0.2	−0.4	−0.2	−0.3
	Middle-aged	−0.1	−0.1	−0.2	−0.3	+0.1	0.0
Average,* Jewish names		−1.2	−0.3	+0.4	−0.8	+1.0	−1.0
Average, Italian names		−0.8	−0.3	−0.4	−0.5	+0.4	−0.3
Average, Irish names		−0.3	−0.1	−0.2	−0.3	+0.2	−0.1

TABLE 6.3.
Average changes in the ratings of photographs of 15 American college girls when Jewish, Italian, and Irish names were added to the photographs (scale 1 to 5).

SOURCE: Gregory Razran, "Ethnic Dislikes and Stereotypes: A Laboratory Study," *Journal of Abnormal and Social Psychology*, 45 (1950), p. 12. Copyright 1950 by the American Psychological Association. Reproduced by permission.

*"Average" refers to average overall change in ratings.

"Jewish," "Italian," or "Old American"), different ideas might come to the subjects' minds about what the girl was like. For example, Razran hypothesized or guessed that if people thought the girl was Jewish, they would think she was more "brainy" (intelligent) than they had two months earlier. In brief, Razran wanted to learn if images would influence the way people rated the girls.

The results of the study clearly showed that the ideas people had about the girls influenced their perception. Using a five-point scale, Razran found that photographs labeled with Jewish names dropped on the average of 1.2 points in general liking, 0.8 in character, and 0.3 in beauty, and went up 1.0 in ambition and 0.4 in intelligence, with little consistent change in entertainingness. The photographs with Italian names went down 0.8 points in general liking, 0.3 in beauty, 0.4 in intel-

ligence, 0.5 in character, and 0.3 in entertainingness, and went up 0.4 in ambition. Overall, the photographs with Irish names dropped less than those with Jewish and Italian names.

[Table 6.3] presents these findings. (The changes in the ratings of photographs with "Old American" names are not given because they were insignificant.) Although the changes indicated may seem minor, in percentage terms they may be large since the scale runs only from 1 to 5. They are important because they reflect a tendency to change our behavior in accordance with ideas we hold in our minds about other people.

What percentage of change is indicated by the increase of +1.0 under "Ambition" in the row for "Average, Jewish Names"? (Assume that the rating rose from 3.5 to 4.5.)

PEGGY SWENSON

BETTY JOHNSON

SALLY WILSON

FIGURE 6.7.
Five girls to be ranked on work-sheet with names in Girl Watchers experiment.

SARAH GOLDSTEIN

IRENE KOWALSKI

FIGURE 6.8.

Girl Watchers experiment: tabulation worksheet. (Handout 3 from
Sociological Resources for the Social Studies Episode: *Images of People.*)

NAME OR RANK LETTER		TRAIT OR CHARACTERISTIC					TOTAL OVERALL
		Intelligent	Beautiful	Dependable	Fun-loving	Ambitious	
	1	× 5 =	× 5 =	× 5 =	× 5 =	× 5 =	
	2	× 4 =	× 4 =	× 4 =	× 4 =	× 4 =	
	3	× 3 =	× 3 =	× 3 =	× 3 =	× 3 =	
	4	× 2 =	× 2 =	× 2 =	× 2 =	× 2 =	
	5	× 1 =	× 1 =	× 1 =	× 1 =	× 1 =	
	1	× 5 =	× 5 =	× 5 =	× 5 =	× 5 =	
	2	× 4 =	× 4 =	× 4 =	× 4 =	× 4 =	
	3	× 3 =	× 3 =	× 3 =	× 3 =	× 3 =	
	4	× 2 =	× 2 =	× 2 =	× 2 =	× 2 =	
	5	× 1 =	× 1 =	× 1 =	× 1 =	× 1 =	
	1	× 5 =	× 5 =	× 5 =	× 5 =	× 5 =	
	2	× 4 =	× 4 =	× 4 =	× 4 =	× 4 =	
	3	× 3 =	× 3 =	× 3 =	× 3 =	× 3 =	
	4	× 2 =	× 2 =	× 2 =	× 2 =	× 2 =	
	5	× 1 =	× 1 =	× 1 =	× 1 =	× 1 =	
	1	× 5 =	× 5 =	× 5 =	× 5 =	× 5 =	
	2	× 4 =	× 4 =	× 4 =	× 4 =	× 4 =	
	3	× 3 =	× 3 =	× 3 =	× 3 =	× 3 =	
	4	× 2 =	× 2 =	× 2 =	× 2 =	× 2 =	
	5	× 1 =	× 1 =	× 1 =	× 1 =	× 1 =	

NAME OR RANK LETTER	TRAIT OR CHARACTERISTIC					TOTAL OVERALL
	Intelligent	Beautiful	Dependable	Fun-loving	Ambitious	
1	× 5 =	× 5 =	× 5 =	× 5 =	× 5 =	
2	× 4 =	× 4 =	× 4 =	× 4 =	× 4 =	
3	× 3 =	× 3 =	× 3 =	× 3 =	× 3 =	
4	× 2 =	× 2 =	× 2 =	× 2 =	× 2 =	
5	× 1 =	× 1 =	× 1 =	× 1 =	× 1 =	

Record the number of choices for each ranking (one through five), for each trait, and for each girl.

Multiply the number of choices by the factor beside it (5–1).

Add the products together to obtain the score for each trait; the highest score indicates the "winner."

Add the scores for each trait to obtain the overall total for each girl.

DESCRIPTION OF LESSONS ABOUT TESTING HYPOTHESES THROUGH CASE STUDY

The materials developed by the new social studies projects include many lessons that have been adapted from the case studies of social scientists. These case study lessons are used as stimulators of questions and hypotheses and as grist for the analysis of human behavior.

The case study lessons described below are part of a unit, "Studying Societies," designed by the Anthropology Curriculum Study Project.[39] The lessons utilize information written by anthropologists and presented in a case study about the Bushmen, "People of the Kalahari," and in a filmstrip, "The Bushmen in the Kalahari Desert."

These anthropology lessons are aimed at teaching students about the basics of social organization, as revealed by the behavior of a nonliterate, hunting-and-gathering people, and about some strengths and limitations of direct observation as a technique for gathering reliable data.

Read the description of these case study lessons and prepare to discuss the following questions:

1. What is your evaluation of the design of the lessons?

2. What is your evaluation of the teaching techniques that are recommended for the implementation of the lessons?

3. Would you use these lessons in your social studies class? Why?

4. How would you change these lessons, if at all, in order to make them most effective with the students whom you expect to teach?

The main objective of these lessons are:

1. Students should be able to recognize the difference between an objective

FIGURE 6.9.

Girl Watchers experiment: tally chart for ranking each trait. (From
Sociological Resources for the Social Studies Episode: Images of
People.)

NAME OR LETTER	Intelligent	Beautiful	Dependable	Fun-loving	Ambitious	TOTAL

description and a description that includes an implicit judgment or an
evaluation.

2. Students should be able to give examples of passages from the "People of
the Kalahari" that reflect the writer's subjective opinions or cultural perspective and to explain why they are subjective.

3. Students should be able to articulate some of the reasons for studying
hunter-gatherers in the context of the course and some of the risks in using
them as analogues of early men.

4. Students should be able to give several examples of differences in information supplied by the two accounts (written case study and filmstrips). They
should note not only disagreements but also differences in the categories
of information covered. For example, do both accounts give information
on leadership?

5. Students should be able to describe the Bushmen of the Kalahari in some
detail, including at least three aspects of their life (for example, kinship,
cooperation, food sources).

This set of lessons is initiated by projecting frame 18 of a filmstrip about
the Bushmen. The teacher is instructed to tell the class: "I want you to look
at a picture and write a description of what you see." Next the teacher is
supposed to conduct a class discussion about student responses to the picture.
The main point of the lesson is to indicate how difficult it is to make objec-

tive descriptions. The following points are to be highlighted during the discussion: (1) pattern of attention (what is noted and reported), (2) patterns of omission in the descriptions, (3) variations in the amount of detail reported, (4) variations in the accuracy of observations, and (5) distinguishing between inferences and observable facts.

The second lesson in this set is based on student reading of the case study "People of the Kalahari."[40] This case was adapted from an ethnographic study of the Bushmen by Elizabeth Marshall Thomas. The nomadic way of life of this "hunter-gatherer" society is described in this case through direct easy-to-read prose and drawings that illustrate behavior patterns. The case study includes several interesting anecdotes about events in the lives of both typical and extraordinary members of this society that reveal widely distinguishing characteristics of the Bushmen culture. The following questions are specified to structure class discussion of the case.

1. According to the opening paragraphs of the reading, what are some of the reasons for studying hunter-gatherer societies of our own times?

2. What are some of the cautions that we should observe?

3. There is a story about a wounded wildebeest and some lions. The story begins "Once, Short Kwi, John . . ." What can be learned about the Bushmen from the story alone? Does it seem to be an objective description?

4. Another quotation immediately follows that story, beginning "Sometimes, as on these occasions . . ." and ending "for once the Bushmen forgot their jealousy . . ." Compare the objectivity of this excerpt with that of the preceding story of the wildebeest and lion.

The third lesson in this set is based on the filmstrip "The Bushmen in the Kalahari Desert" by Richard B. Lee (see pages 231 to 232 for a short excerpt from the transcript) and on the written case study used in the second lesson. Students are asked to compare the two accounts in terms of these exercises:

1. Do these observers respect the Bushmen? What would be the evidence that they do or do not?

2. Give an example of an aspect of Bushmen life described by Mrs. Thomas that is not included by Mr. Lee.

3. Give an example of an aspect of Bushmen life described by Mr. Lee that is not mentioned by Mrs. Thomas.

Next students are asked to make factual judgments about the Bushmen from evidence presented in the two case studies. Questions to guide this activity are:

1. What are some important characteristics of the Bushmen's environment?

2. How much land area is typically viewed by a Bushmen group as "theirs," as their territory?

3. Is kinship important in Bushmen life? Give evidence.

4. What personal qualities are honored by Bushmen? In men? In women?
5. What are some of the rules Bushmen live by?

The last lesson in this set is about the overall adaptation of Bushmen to their environment. Using evidence from the written case study and the filmstrip, students are asked to discuss these questions:

1. By what means have the Bushmen adapted to their environment?
2. Exactly what is the physical environment or environments to which the Bushmen have adapted?
3. What is the wider social environment with which the Bushmen contend?

Upon conclusion of this set of four lessons, the teacher should expect students to have developed several warranted conclusions, or confirmed hypotheses, about the way of life of the Bushmen. Students should also learn from these lessons something about the utility and limitations of direct observation as a method of gathering information to test hypotheses. Finally, the lessons should develop understanding of some ideas about social organization that can be generally applied to mankind and of other ideas that are specifically applicable to similar preliterate, hunter-gatherer societies.

FRAME 1, 2, 3 Title, Credit, and Copyright notice.

FRAME 4 One of the great deserts of the world, the Kalahari, is a high plateau about 3,000 feet above sea level. Several different groups of people live in the Kalahari, including cattleherders and agriculturalists of Bantu stock, but our concern today is with the earliest inhabitants of the Kalahari, the Bushmen, a remarkable folk who live by hunting and gathering in the most inaccessible regions of the Desert. The Kalahari in midwinter is, as you can see, a dry, parched, sandy

place, where dust storms such as this one may occur rather frequently.

FRAME 5 In October or November comes the rainy season. Several months of rain may fill this dry lake bed with water, which can remain for weeks after the rains are over.

FRAME 6 There is much more green vegetation, and a sparse growth of grass covers the sandy earth. The vegetation doesn't grow very tall, however, and the one tall tree in the distance is a 75-foot palm.

"The Bushmen in the Kalahari Desert," a Filmstrip Narrative

---

*Excerpt from a transcript of a record to accompany a filmstrip, "The Bushmen in the Kalahari Desert" by Richard B. Lee.[41] Reproduced by permission of the American Anthropological Association from *Studying Societies* (ACSP), 1971.

FRAME 7 My name is Richard Lee, and I am an anthropologist at Harvard University. I am in this picture, bearded, chatting with a group of Bushmen gathered around their campfires in the evening.

FRAME 8 The Bushmen do a lot of hunting. One of the hunters is helping me to identify what a group of Bushmen ate from the scraps of bones they left behind when they abandoned this campsite.

FRAME 9 There are no medical facilities within 90 miles of the area where these people live, so during my stay I spent an hour or two each morning treating the sick who came to my field station from miles around. This child burned herself in the cooking fire and I am applying ointment and a dressing to the wound.

FRAME 10 The Bushmen are famous for their likable personalities. They enjoy laughter and good company, and they seek to avoid conflicts and disputes in their daily lives. They are noted for their friendliness and hospitality, so that I enjoyed working with them immensely.

FRAME 11 A Bushman village consists of a circle of grass huts, which can be constructed in the course of a morning's work. The frames are made from saplings which are set firmly into post-holes dug in the ground, with the earth tamped down around them. Then the framework of saplings is covered by sheaves of grass. The huts are most important as shelter during the rainy season.

FRAME 12 These camps are occupied for a period of one to five months. Frequent visiting among relatives living in different camps causes the membership of any particular group to change from week to week.

FRAME 13 A mother and her daughter stand in front of their hut.

FRAME 14 Nluhka is about fourteen years old, and, as is the custom with most hunting and gathering peoples, she will be married in a very few years.

FRAME 15 Nluhka's mother, Tinlay, is a woman in her forties. They are resting today because at this season it is easy to find food.

FRAME 16 Nluhka's grandfather, Toma, was a great hunter in his younger years. Nowadays he is greatly respected as a man of medicine whose successes in ritual curing have long been known amongst his people.

FRAME 17 One of the favorite pastimes of the Bushmen is smoking their pipes, which they make of scraps of metal or of wood, or they may get real smoking pipes in trade from their neighbors.

FRAME 18 Because the Bushmen live in the desert, it is often thought that they live a perilous existence, always flirting with starvation, but this isn't at all the case. They normally spend only two or three days a week on subsistence activities —hunting and gathering food. Much of their time is given to socializing.

FRAME 19 When it is hot, which is often, it isn't hard to find groups resting in the shade and discussing the events of the day.

TWO LESSONS ABOUT FORMULATING HYPOTHESES FROM PRODUCTS OF BEHAVIOR

Innovative programs in American and world history include numerous lessons that require students to formulate hypotheses from behavior products in response to questions about people and events of the past. These lessons challenge the student to reconstruct main features of past situations from bits and pieces of evidence contained in records or remains of human endeavor, such as documents, pictures, diaries, and various types of artifacts.

Following are descriptions of two lessons included in the course in American history designed by the Education Development Center and published in *From Subject to Citizen*.[42] The first lesson requires students to develop hypotheses from pictures, maps, and a journal, which are records of the first English settlers of North America. The second lesson consists of instruction about the process of building theories from behavior products.

Study the two lessons and prepare to discuss these questions:

1. What is your evaluation of these lessons?
2. What is your evaluation of the teaching techniques that are recommended for the implementation of the lessons?
3. Would you use these lessons in your social studies class? Why?
4. How would you change these lessons, if at all, in order to make them most effective with the students whom you expect to teach?

The main purpose of the two lessons is to teach students how to use evidence to form a theory about a past event. The first of the two lessons is titled The Mystery of Roanoke Island. Students begin the lesson by reading a context-setting commentary about how and why the English established a small settlement on Roanoke Island, off the coast of North Carolina, between 1586 and 1587. The commentary indicates that John White, the governor of the colony, returned to England in 1587 to obtain more supplies and people for the Roanoke settlement. It concludes with the information that in 1590 John White returned to Roanoke Island with a shipload of people and supplies, but he found that the settlers had disappeared.

The next part of the lesson consists of these behavior products: a portion of the "Journal of John White" which is dated August 17 and 18, 1590; two maps of the North Carolina coastal area (Figs. 6.12, 6.13); and nine pictures (Figs. 6.14 to 6.23), drawn by John White, of various aspects of the life of the Indians in the area of and around Roanoke Island. These primary source materials are presented on pages 236 to 238 and 240 to 245.

Students are asked to use evidence in the primary source materials to formulate hypotheses in response to these questions: (1) Why might the colony succeed or fail? (2) What happened to the colonists? List clues to support your theory and the sources of the clues.

Students are challenged to deal with these questions as a historian might by making inferences from different types of primary source materials. Worksheets (Figs. 6.10, 6.11) are given to students to help them systematically examine, organize, and interpret the evidence in the primary source materials.

FIGURE 6.10.

Students' worksheet for The Mystery of Roanoke Island. (From From Subject to Citizen developed by the Social Studies Program of Education Development Center, Inc.)

GROUP REPORT

Why the colony might . . .

Succeed	EVIDENCE IN THE PICTURES	Fail

The following excerpt from the section for the teacher indicates how teachers might have students use the worksheets and the primary sources. It suggests some possible student responses to the basic questions of the lesson.

After reading "Englishmen Claim a Part of America" and "Journal of John White," the class as a whole may make some tentative hypotheses about the fate of the colony and then for further evidence turn its attention to the picture of Indians in sixteenth-century Virginia painted by John White. This part of the exercise was designed for groups of no more than five students. Each group may study two or more pictures and complete the "evidence" chart "why the colony might . . . succeed—fail."

The evidence chart encourages students to look carefully at the pictures and

What happened to the colonists?

FIGURE 6.11.
*Students' worksheet for
The Mystery of Roanoke
Island.* (From *From
Subject to Citizen*
developed by the Social
Studies Program of
Education Development
Center, Inc.)

SOURCE* OF CLUE	CLUES SUPPORTING YOUR THEORY	YOUR THEORY

Source means J. White's Journal, pictures, or map or any other account, person, or thing from which you find evidence for your theory.

to use what they see to support the likelihood of the success or failure of the Roanoke colony. A single piece of evidence noted in the center column may well be indication of success *and* of failure. The worksheet seems to be most useful in helping students see this.

For instance, from the picture of the Indians fishing, some students have noted ample supply of fish as food. In the success column other students noted the large supply of food to keep all the colonists alive. The picture also could be evidence of failure: the colonists might have invaded the Indians' fishing territory. There might have been a squabble over who fished where, or the colonists may have taken too many fish. Either of these acts might have angered the Indians who would then have turned against the colonists. After the investigation, each group reports its findings to the class as a whole.

On the worksheet "What Happened to the Colonists?" . . . students explain the disappearance of the colony [and] the sources of their conclusions. Students' theories are judged on the basis of their ability to use evidence well.[43]

Journal of John White, Governor of Roanoke Colony*

17 August 1590: Our boats and company were prepared again to go up to Roanoke. But Captain Spicer had then sent his boat ashore for fresh water: by means whereof it was ten of the clock aforenoon before we put from our ships, which were then come to an anchor within two miles of the shore. . . .

At this time the wind blew at Northeast and direct into the harbor so great a gale that the sea brake extremely on the bar, and the tide went very forcibly at the entrance.

. . . Captain Spicer came to the entrance of the breach with his mast standing up, and was half passed over but, by the rash and indiscreet steerage of Ralph Skinner, his Master's Mate, a very dangerous sea broke into their boat and overset them quite.

The men kept the boat, some in it, and some hanging on it, but the next sea set the boat on ground, where it beat so that some of them were forced to let go their hold, hoping to wade ashore. But the sea still beat them down so that they could neither stand nor swim. And the boat twice or thrice was turned the keel upward, whereon Captain Spicer and Skinner hung until they sank, & were seen no more.

But four that could swim a little kept themselves in deeper water and were saved by Captain Cooke's means, who, so soon as he saw their oversetting, stripped himself, and four other that could swim very well, & with all haste possible rowed unto them, & saved four. They were 11 in all, & 7 of the chiefest were drowned. . . .

This mischance did so much discomfort the sailers that they were all of one mind NOT to go any further to seek the planters.

But in the end, by the commandment & persuasion of me and Captain Cooke, they prepared the boats. And seeing the Captain and me so resolute, they seemed much more willing.

Our boats and all things fitted again, we put off from Hatorask [Hatteras], being 19 persons in both boats. But before we could get to the place where our planters were left, it was so exceeding dark that we overshot the place a quarter of a mile.

There we espied, towards the north end of the island, the light of a great fire through the woods, to the which we presently rowed. When we came right over against it, we let fall our grapnel [anchor] near the shore, & sounded with a trumpet a call, & afterwards many familiar English tunes of songs, and called to them friendly; but we had no answer.

18 August: We therefore landed at daybreak and, coming to the fire, we found the grass & sundry rotten trees burning about the place. From hence we went through the woods to that part of the

*The Mystery of Roanoke Island from "Queen Elizabeth: Conflict and Compromise," *From Subject to Citizen*, developed by the Social Studies Program of Educational Development Center, Inc., Cambridge, Mass. Copyright © 1966, 1967, 1969 by Educational Development Center, Inc., Cambridge, Mass. Published by Denoyer-Geppert, 5235 Ravenswood Ave., Chicago, Ill. 60640.

island directly over against Dasamonque-peuc, & from thence we returned by the water side, round about the north point of the island until we came to the place where I [had] left our colony in the year 1586.

In all this way we saw in the sand the print of the savages' feet, of 2 or 3 sorts, trodden [in] the night. And, as we entered up the sandy bank, upon a tree, in the very brow thereof, were curiously carved these fair Roman letters:

C R O.

Which letters we know to signify the place where I should find the planters seated, according to a secret token agreed upon between them & me at my last departure from them. Which [agreement] was:

> that . . . they should not fail to write or carve on the trees or posts of the doors the name of the place where they should be seated.

For, at my coming away, they were prepared to remove from Roanoke 50 miles into the main [i.e. inland]. Therefore at my departure from them in *anno* [year] 1587 I willed them that, if they should happen to be distressed in any of those places, they should carve over the letters or name of Cross ✠ in this form.

But we found no such sign of distress. And, having well considered of this, we passed toward the place where they were left in sundry houses. But we found the houses taken down, and the place very strongly enclosed with a high palisade of great trees, . . . very fort-like, and one of the chief trees or posts at the right side of the entrance had the bark taken off, and 5 foot from the ground in fair capital letters was graven [cut]: "C R O A - T O A N"—without any cross or sign of distress.

This done, we entered into the palisade, where we found many bars of iron, two pigs of lead, four iron fowlers [gunshot], and such like heavy things thrown here and there, almost overgrown with grass and weeds. From thence we went along by the water side towards the point of the creek to see if we could find any of their boats or pinnaces, but we could perceive no sign of them. . . .

At our return from the creek some of our sailors, meeting us, told us that they had found where divers chests had been hidden, and long since dug up again and broken up, and much of the goods in them spoiled and scattered about, but nothing left (of such things as the savages knew any use of) undefaced.

Presently Captain Cooke and I went to the place, which was in the end of an old trench made two years past by Captain Amadas. Where we found five chests that had been carefully hidden by the planters; and of the same chests three were my own, and about the place many of my things spoiled or broken, and my books torn from the covers, the frames of some of my pictures and maps rotten and spoiled with rain, and my armor almost eaten through with rust.

This could be no other but the deed of the savages our enemies at Dasamon-quepeuc, who had watched the departure of our men to Croatoan; and, as soon as they were departed, digged up every place where they suspected anything to be buried.

But although it much grieved me to see such spoil of my goods, yet on the other side I greatly joyed that I had safely found a certain token of their [the planters'] safe being at Croatoan, which is the place where Manteo was born, and the savages of the island [were] our friends.

When we had seen in this place so much as we could we returned to our boats, and departed from the shore towards our ships with as much speed as we could, for the weather began to be overcast, and very likely a foul and stormy night would ensue.

Therefore, the same evening, with

much danger and labor, we got ourselves aboard, by which time the wind and seas were so greatly risen that we doubted our cables and anchors would scarcely hold until morning.

19 August: The next morning it was agreed by the Captain and myself, with the Master and others, to weigh anchor and go for the place at Croatoan where our planters were. For then the wind was good for that place. And also [agreed] to leave that cask with fresh water on shore in the island until our return.

So then they brought the cable to the captain. But, when the anchor was almost apeak [vertical], the cable broke, by means whereof we lost another anchor. Wherewith we drove so fast into the shore that we were forced to let fall a third anchor—which came so fast home that the ship was almost aground by Kenricks mounts, so that we were forced to let slip the cable, end for end.

And if it had not chanced that we had fallen into a channel of deeper water, closer by the shore than we accounted of, we could never have gone clear of the point that lieth to the southwards of Kendricks mounts. Being thus clear of some dangers, and gotten into deeper waters, but not without some loss (for we had but one cable and anchor left us of four), . . . the weather grew to be fouler and fouler, our victuals scarce, and our casks and fresh water lost.

It was therefore determined that we should go for St. John or some other island to the southward for fresh water. And it was further proposed that, if we could any ways supply our wants of victuals and other necessaries, either at Hispaniola, St. John, or Trinidad, that then we should continue in the Indies all the winter following with hope to make two rich voyages out of one, and at our return to visit our countrymen at Virginia. . . .

Wherefore the same night we parted, leaving the Moonlight to go directly for England. And the Admiral set his course for Trinidad, which course we kept two days.

Though Raleigh made later attempts to find the "Lost Colony," his efforts were fruitless. No one knows what became of these first colonists. They may have gone to the mainland or to Croatoan Island, where the Indians may have carried them off. Or, attempting to sail back to England in their one small vessel, they may have been lost at sea.

*How a Theory Is Formed**

Many times in this course you will use evidence to arrive at a theory or to support a position. The process of forming a theory is made up of several steps: deciding just what the question is you are trying to answer with the theory, collecting information related to the question, evaluating the information and, on the basis of the best information, interpreting the facts to answer the question. The

*How a Theory Is Formed from "Queen Elizabeth: Conflict and Compromise," *From Subject to Citizen,* developed by the Social Studies Program of Educational Development Center, Inc. Copyright © 1966, 1967, 1969 by Education Development Center, Inc., Cambridge, Mass. Published by Denoyer-Geppert, 5235 Ravenswood Ave. Chicago, Ill. 60640.

theory you form is tentative. It may change when new facts are discovered. But new facts can also strengthen the original hypothesis. The final step is deciding how to present your theory convincingly.

BEGINNING WITH A QUESTION How does starting with a question affect your research?

The question was: "What happened to the colonists?" What difference would it make in your research if the question was: "What happened to the Indians who had lived on Roanoke?"

EXAMINING THE EVIDENCE What are the facts?

We know that the colonists left the word CROATOAN carved on a tree. We do not know that the colonists reached Croatoan, because there is no evidence.

CONSIDERING POINT OF VIEW What difference does the point of view of the writer or source make in forming a theory?

For whom did John White write his journal? Would it have made a difference if it were a private diary or an official report?

If we had available an account of what happened when John White came back to find the colonists as told by an Indian of the island, how would you have changed your theory?

INTERPRETING EVIDENCE What assumptions about human behavior do you make in interpreting evidence?

To solve the mystery of Roanoke Island you made assumptions about human be-havior to give meaning to the facts you collected. For example, in one of the John White pictures you see fish traps built by the Indians to catch fish. If you assumed that the people who had worked hard to build the traps want to protect the results of their labors from others, how would you interpret the evidence? If you assume that the people who built the traps have enough provisions to share with others, how would you interpret the evidence?

TESTING A THEORY AGAINST EVIDENCE What decisions do you make in putting the evidence together to form a theory?

Once you looked at all the evidence you begin to put facts together to say: "This is what I think happened to the colonists." As a final check:

1. List the facts that support your theory.
2. Test the evidence to see that your facts hold up.
3. Ask: Have I remained open-minded in selecting evidence or do I have an affection for my theory that lets me avoid certain evidence?

PRESENTING A THEORY What steps do you take to strengthen the presentation of a theory?

Which argument is stated first? Which last? Is the strongest argument placed first or last?

What arguments might others raise? How can they be answered?

THEORIES AND ANSWERS When does a theory become a fact?

What would happen to your theory if historians knew what happened to the colonists? What kind of evidence would historians need?

The lesson How a Theory Is Formed is designed to help students think about how to build descriptions and explanations of past events from the necessarily limited evidence contained in behavior products. The lesson should

FIGURE 6.12.

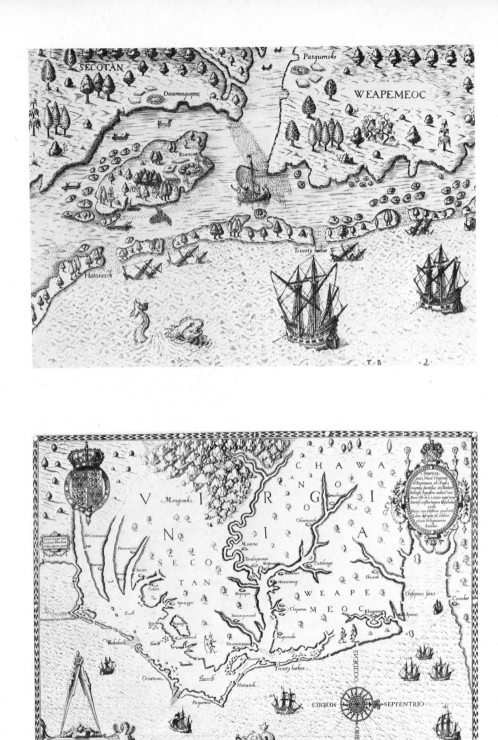

FIGURE 6.13.

240   PART TWO / INSTRUCTOR

FIGURE 6.14.

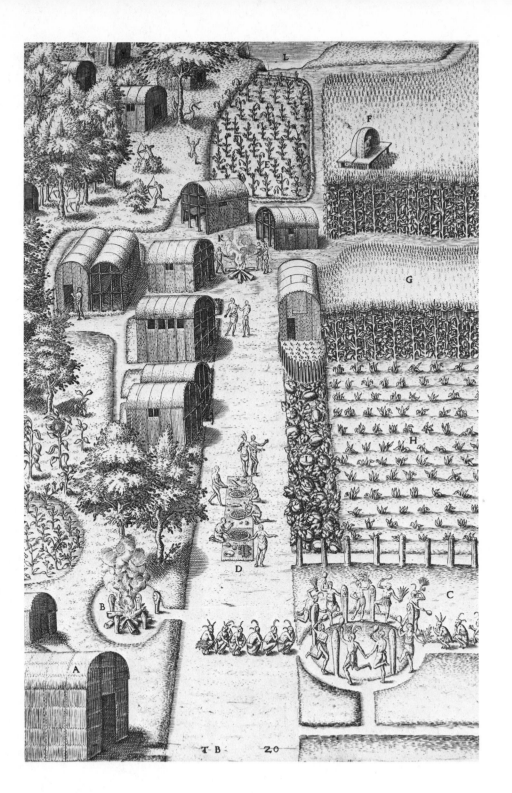

Figure 6.15.

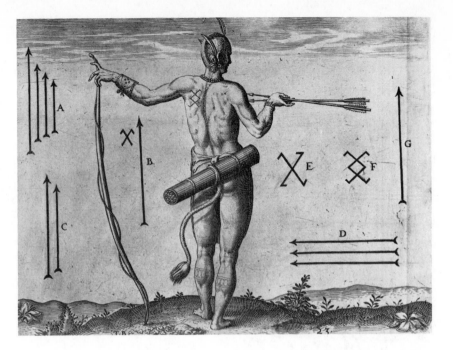

Figure 6.16.

242   PART TWO / INSTRUCTOR

FIGURE 6.17.

FIGURE 6.18.

6 / TEACHING THE USE OF HYPOTHESES

FIGURE 6.19.

FIGURE 6.20.

FIGURE 6.21.

FIGURE 6.22.
FIGURE 6.23.

encourage students to present and think about their own examples of how they proceeded to form a theory.

The preceding sample lessons illustrate how the intellectual skills of formulating and testing hypotheses can be developed among high school social studies students. These lessons are very representative of the quality of new materials which have been spawned by reformers in the movement for curriculum development in the social studies. While open to various types of criticisms, which you undoubtedly made while analyzing the materials, these types of lessons are symbolic of a firm belief among current social studies leaders that the main purpose of formal education is to develop the intellectual capacities of all students as fully as possible.

Summary

Learning to formulate and test hypotheses should be a fundamental outcome of instruction in the social studies. Those who master the skills of formulating and testing hypotheses acquire a learning set, the ability to learn how to learn. They are capable of independent thinking and learning and are equipped to make fruitful decisions and to solve problems.

Social science inquiry is a process of formulating and testing hypotheses empirically. An empirically testable hypothesis is a conjectural statement about the relationship between particular concepts that is stated exactly, so that it can be measured in terms of the reality it is supposed to represent.

Social scientists use three main approaches in collecting data to test hypotheses: asking questions about attitudes and behavior, direct observation of behavior, and examination of products of behavior. Social scientists have designed three main types of studies to test hypotheses in terms of data that they have gathered to use as evidence. These are the sample survey, the experiment, and the case study.

The products of hypothesis testing in the social sciences are more or less accurate and useful statements about human behavior. Some of these statements are descriptive while others are explanatory. A descriptive statement is an assertion about the way things are related at a particular time. An explanatory statement is an assertion about why things are related in particular ways.

A basic principle in social science inquiry is that knowledge claims, the products of inquiry, must be held tentatively and probabilistically. The possibility always remains that new evidence will develop that requires changes in factual judgments. The probabilistic quality of knowledge claims stems from the inductive foundations of social science inquiry. Induction is the process of making inferences about a population from a representative sample. As such, the distinguishing quality of an inductive inference is indeterminateness.

Social science inquiry is the most powerful means available to formulate and test hypotheses about reality. However, the products of this method must be used with appropriate caution and qualification. Social studies teachers must help students to learn both the strengths and the weaknesses of social science inquiry.

Instructional materials developed by the new social studies projects include many lessons about the formulation and testing of hypotheses which are adapted from the inquiries of social scientists. These lessons facilitate transfer of learning, that is, the capability to apply skills and knowledge acquired in a particular context to a fresh, related context. Acquisition of this ability is a function of well-designed instruction. It yields independent learners and thinkers, those who have well-developed decision-making and problem-solving skills.

APPLICATION 6.1: TEACHING THE SKILLS OF FORMULATING AND TESTING HYPOTHESES

The following are samples of instructional objectives:

A. Students are able to use tabular data to test this hypothesis: social mobility is more likely to occur in industrially developed countries than in undeveloped countries.

B. Students are able to list five causes for the Civil War that are presented in a standard textbook.

C. Students are able to formulate hypotheses from a packet of primary source material about why the Bolsheviks achieved victory in the Russian Revolution of 1917.

D. Students are able to identify at least two conflicting hypotheses, which are presented in reputable sources, about why urban development occurs.

E. Students are able to formulate at least two hypotheses about social change from a case study about social change in a preliterate society.

Answer these questions about the sample objectives:

1. Which of the objectives are better or worse? Explain.

_____

_____

_____

2. Which of the objectives would require students to make inductive inferences?

_____

_____

_____

3. Which of the objectives would require students to use social science techniques for data gathering and using evidence? What are these techniques?

_____

_____

_____

Following are hypotheses and data about the relationship of age and political party preference:

Hypothesis 1: Younger voters (under 21) are more likely than older voters (over 21) to be independents.

Hypothesis 2: Younger voters (under 21) are more likely than older voters (over 21) to prefer the Republican party.

TABLE 6.4.
Political party preferences of younger and older voters, 1971.

AGE GROUP	POLITICAL PARTY PREFERENCE		
	Republican	*Democratic*	*Independent*
21 and over	27%	45%	28%
18–21	16%	42%	42%

SOURCE: Gallup poll. The American Institute of Public Opinion, 1971.

NOTE: These data were derived from a Gallup poll taken in 1971. A nationally representative sample of 1,500 people constituted the group that was polled.

Discuss the following questions about how to use the data in Table 6.4 and hypotheses in the social studies classroom.

1. How could you use these hypotheses and data in a high school social studies class to teach something about social science method and techniques and about the strengths and weaknesses, or limitations, of social science as a way of thinking?

_____

_____

_____

_____

_____

_____

2. What would be your objectives of instruction? Why?

_____

_____

_____

_____

_____

3. How would you help students try to achieve these objectives? Why?

_____

_____

_____

_____

Table 6.5 provides data about social change. Use these data as the foundation for a lesson that you might teach about social change. Describe your lesson in terms of these questions.

1. What instructional objective, or objectives, would you try to achieve?

_____

_____

_____

_____

_____

2. What learning is prerequisite to the achievement of your objective(s)?

_____

_____

_____

_____

3. How would you use the data in Table 6.5 to achieve your objective(s)? Describe your proposed instructional techniques and strategy.

_____

_____

_____

_____

4. How can you justify your answers to the previous three questions? Apply what you have learned about instruction in the social studies to the writing of a brief rationale for your specification of instructional objectives, techniques, and strategies.

Characteristic	1910	1960
1. Total Population (United States)[a]	91,972,000	179,323,000
Urban	41,999,000	125,269,000
Rural	49,973,000	54,054,000
2a. Number of Urban Places by Size of Population[a]		
Total Urban Places	*2,262*	*6,041*
Of 1,000,000 or more population	3	5
Of 500,000–999,999	5	16
Of 250,000–499,999	11	30
Of 100,000–249,999	31	81
Of 50,000–99,999	59	201
Of 25,000–49,999	119	432
Of 10,000–24,999	369	1,134
Of 2,500–9,999	1,665	3,546
2b. Number of Rural Places by Size of Population[a]		
Total Rural Places	*11,830*	*13,749*
Of 1,000–2,500 population	2,717	4,151
Of under 1,000	9,113	9,598
3a. Percent of Population Living in Urban Places[a]		
Total Urban Population	*45.7%*	*69.9%*
Of 1,000,000 or more population	9.2	9.8
Of 500,000–999,999	3.3	6.2
Of 250,000–499,999	4.3	6.0
Of 100,000–249,999	5.3	6.5
Of 50,000–99,999	4.5	7.7
Of 25,000–49,999	4.4	8.3
Of 10,000–24,999	6.0	9.8
Of 2,500–9,999	8.7	9.7
3b. Percent of Population Living in Rural Places[a]		
Total Rural Population	*54.3%*	*30.1%*
1,000–2,500 population	4.6	3.6
Under 1,000	4.3	2.2
Other rural	45.5	21.3

TABLE 6.5.
Selected characteristics of urban and rural places and population, United States, 1910 and 1960.

TABLE 6.5. (*Continued*)

CHARACTERISTIC	1910	1960
4a. Percent of Population Urban by Race and by Region		
(A) *Race*		
White (total)	48.0%[b]	69.6%[a]
Negro	27.3	73.2
Foreign-born white	71.2	87.5
(B) *Region*		
Northeast	71.8[b]	80.0[a]
North Central	45.1	68.6
South	22.5	58.5
West	48.7	77.7
4b. Percent of Population Rural by Race and by Region		
(A) *Race*		
White (total)	52.0[b]	30.4[a]
Negro	72.7	26.8
Foreign-born white	28.8	12.5
(B) *Region*		
Northeast	28.2[b]	20.0[a]
North Central	54.9	31.4
South	77.5	41.5
West	51.3	22.3
5. Farm Population		
Number	32,077,000[c]	15,635,000[d]
Percent of total population	34.9%	8.7%
6. Percent of Population Employed in Agriculture (10 years and over, 1910; 16 years and over, 1960)		
Total	32.5%[b]	8.3%[a]
Males	35.2	10.2
Females	22.4	4.5

SOURCE:

[a]U.S. Bureau of the Census, *Statistical Abstract of the United States: 1969*, 90th ed. (Washington, D.C.: U.S. Government Printing Office, 1969), pp. 16, 29; adapted from pp. 17, 215.

[b]U.S. Bureau of the Census, *Population Trends in the United States: 1900 to 1960*, Technical Paper No. 10 (Washington, D.C.: U.S. Government Printing Office, 1964), pp. 18, 20, 22, 24, 140, 375.

[c]Vera J. Banks, Calvin L. Beale, and Gladys K. Bowles, *Farm Population Estimates for 1910–62* (Washington, D.C.: U.S. Department of Agriculture, 1963), p. 19.

[d]U.S. Department of Commerce, *Current Population Reports, Farm Population, Farm Population of the United States: 1968*. Series Census-ERS, P-27, No. 40 (Washington, D.C.: U.S. Government Printing Office, July 1969), p. 1.

Notes

1. H. Gordon Hullfish and Philip Smith, *Reflective Thinking: The Method of Education*, New York: Dodd, Mead, 1961, pp. 120–123.

2. Robert F. Bales, "The Equilibrium Problem in Small Groups," in *Working Papers in the Theory of Action*, ed. by Talcott Parsons, Robert F. Bales, and Edward Shils, New York: Free Press, 1953.

3. Margaret Mead, *Coming of Age in Samoa*, New York: Mentor Books, 1950.

4. A. N. Oppenheim, *Questionnaire Design and Attitude Measurement*, New York: Basic Books, 1966.

5. Edward H. Carr, *What Is History?* New York: Random House, Vintage Books, 1962.

6. Robert A. Dahl, *Who Governs?: Democracy and Power in an American City*, New Haven: Yale University Press, 1961.

7. Sanford Labovitz and Robert Hagedorn, *Introduction to Social Research*, New York: McGraw-Hill, 1971, pp. 28–47, 50–85.

8. American Institute of Public Opinion, The Gallup Poll, 1968.

9. Robert C. North, Ole R. Holsti, M. George Zaninovich, and Dina A. Zinnes, *Content Analysis*, Evanston, Ill.: Northwestern University Press, 1963.

10. Abraham Kaplan, *The Conduct of Inquiry*, San Francisco: Chandler, 1964, pp. 126–170.

11. Matilda White Riley, *Sociological Research*, New York: Harcourt, Brace & World, 1963, pp. 32–77.

12. William F. Whyte, *Street Corner Society*, Chicago: University of Chicago Press, 1955.

13. J. C. Beaglehole, "The Case of the Needless Death: Reconstructing the Scene," in *The Historian as Detective*, ed. by Robin W. Winks, New York: Harper & Row, Harper Colophon Books, 1968, pp. 279–302.

14. Erik H. Erikson, *Young Man Luther: A Study in Psychoanalysis and History*, New York: W. W. Norton, 1958.

15. Stanley M. Elkins, *Slavery: A Problem in American Institutional and Intellectual Life*, Chicago: University of Chicago Press, 1959.

16. Eugene Meehan, *Social Science and Value Judgment*, Homewood, Ill.: Dorsey Press, 1969, pp. 63–70.

17. Ibid., pp. 70–81.

18. Sociological Resources for the Social Studies, *Images of People*, Boston: Allyn and Bacon, 1969, p. 22.

19. Abraham Kaplan, op. cit., pp. 249–257.

20. William H. Flanagan, *Political Behavior of the American Electorate*, Boston: Allyn and Bacon, 1968, pp. 7–26.

21. John Lawrence, *A History of Russia*, New York: New American Library, Mentor Books, 1962, pp. 197–236.

22. E. H. Carr, op. cit., pp. 113–143.

23. H. Gordon Hullfish and Philip Smith, op. cit., pp. 66–67.

24. Ibid., pp. 110–117.

25. John J. Kemeny, *A Philosopher Looks at Science*, Princeton, N.J.: Van Nostrand, 1959, pp. 85–104.

26. Richard B. Braithwaite, *Scientific Explanation*, London: Syndics of the Cambridge University Press, 1968, pp. 265–266.

27. Among the major development projects for social studies curricula that produced materials featuring hypothesis formulation and testing are: (1) the High School Geography Project, materials published by Macmillan, (2) the Sociological Resources for the Social Studies Project, materials published by Allyn and Bacon, (3) the Anthropology Curriculum Study Project, materials published by Macmillan, and (4) the From Subject to Citizen Project, materials created by Education Development Center and published by Denoyer-Geppert.

28. Henry Ellis, *The Transfer of Learning*, New York: Macmillan, 1965, pp. 15–31, 44–45.

29. Ibid., pp. 39–47, 61–72.

30. Ibid.

31. Bryce B. Hudgens, *The Instructional Process*, Chicago: Rand McNally, 1971, pp. 30–34.

32. Howard D. Mehlinger and John J. Patrick, *American Political Behavior*, Lexington, Mass.: Ginn, 1972, pp. 214–216. *Teacher's Guide for American Political Behavior*, Lexington, Mass.: Ginn, 1972, pp. 73–74.

33. Ibid.

34. Ibid., p. 73.

35. American Institute of Public Opinion, The Gallup Poll, 1968.

36. Sociological Resources for the Social Studies, *Images of People: Instructor's Guide*, Boston: Allyn and Bacon, 1969, pp. 9–14.

37. Ibid., p. 13.

38. Sociological Resources for the Social Studies, *Images of People*, Boston: Allyn and Bacon, 1969, pp. 7–9.

39. Anthropology Curriculum Study Project, *Teaching Plan, Studying Societies*, New York: Macmillan, 1971, pp. 6–13. This teacher's guide is the source of the instructional objectives and discussion questions on pages 225 to 231 of this text.

40. Margaret C. Fallers, "People of the Kalahari," in *Studying Societies*, by

the Anthropology Curriculum Study Project, New York: Macmillan, 1971, pp. 8–11.

41. Richard B. Lee, "The Bushmen in the Kalahari Desert," in *Studying Societies,* by the Anthropology Curriculum Study Project, pp. 18–19.

42. Louis B. Wright, "Queen Elizabeth: Conflict and Compromise," in *From Subject to Citizen,* Cambridge, Mass.: Education Development Center, 1970, pp. 2–21.

43. Louis B. Wright, "Explanation and Guide to 'Queen Elizabeth: Conflict and Compromise,' " in *From Subject to Citizen,* Cambridge, Mass.: Education Development Center, 1970, pp. 14–15.

44. Ibid., pp. 52–53.

Suggested Reading

Carr, Edward H. *What Is History?* New York: Random House, Vintage Books, 1961. This is a highly readable, short discussion of history as a way of thinking and knowing. The highlight of the book is Carr's treatment of historians' approaches to deciding what is reliable evidence, and what is knowledge.

Greer, Scott. *The Logic of Social Inquiry.* Chicago: Aldine, 1969. Scott Greer is both a practicing social scientist and a philosopher of social science. From these twin perspectives he examines the rationale, methods, and techniques of social science. He discusses the social scientist's way of formulating and testing hypotheses in language suitable for the lay reader.

Hullfish, H. Gordon, and Philip Smith. *Reflective Thinking: The Method of Education.* New York: Dodd, Mead, 1961. Hullfish and Smith are philosophers of education who are concerned about teaching youth to be systematic, independent, reflective thinkers. In this book they specify what reflective thinking is, and they provide suggestions about how to teach for reflective thinking in the high school classroom. The book includes a discussion about formulating and testing hypotheses which can be very helpful to high school social studies teachers.

Labovitz, Sanford, and Robert Hagedorn. *Introduction to Social Research.* New York: McGraw-Hill, 1971. This book is aimed at the nonspecialist in social science and is designed to introduce the basic features of social research. The case study, experiment and sample survey are presented as basic types of research designs. Techniques of data collection and analysis are discussed.

7

Teaching
the Analysis
of Values

VALUE JUDGMENTS, TOGETHER with the process by which they are constructed, are a vital part of the social studies. Because young people are as concerned with value claims as they are with factual claims, social studies draws relevance from analysis of value judgments.

TEACHER: *Lynn, do you agree with government regulation of family size as a way to curb overpopulation?*

LYNN: *Yes, world population is growing so fast that some drastic action needs to be taken, or many innocent people will suffer through starvation and crowding.*

HARRY: *But it seems to me that the effects of government control over such a personal part of people's lives would be worse, in the long run, than possible starvation or overcrowding.*

LYNN: *Harry, that's just a value judgment. You can't prove it, and . . .*

HARRY: *(Interrupting) But I think I can support what I say with reasoning and facts, if you'll give me a chance. Mr. Miles said that's what's important in this class. Right, Mr. Miles?*

TEACHER: *Harry, Lynn hit it right on the head—you can't prove your position is better than hers because we're dealing with values. There's no point in arguing about different people's value judgments. It's different than with factual material, where there's evidence. Every one is equally entitled to his or her opinion—that's what democracy is all about. So just state your position, and let others do the same. It's just a value judgment, anyway.*

HARRY: *But you said a well-reasoned historical explanation with facts to back it up is better than one with no support. I think I can support my statement—what if Lynn can't?*

TEACHER: *Harry, everybody's entitled to an opinion. One isn't better than another. This is a democracy we live in.*

Teachers and students in social studies classrooms often echo the teacher's comments in this imaginary classroom dialogue.[1] Lynn's use of *just* in "that's just a value judgment" suggests that value statements are less important than factual assertions. The teacher in this dialogue suggested that there are no defensible grounds for value judgments but that there are for factual assertions. *We strongly disagree with the teacher.*

We disagree also with the position that there are no processes by which value assertions can be supported and compared. Each value judgment about a particular issue is, however, not equally defensible. Consider the following four value judgments about capital punishment:

1. Capital punishment is desirable because it deters individuals from committing the most serious crimes.
2. Capital punishment is desirable because it removes the misery caused by lifetime prison sentences.
3. Capital punishment is desirable because it results in less cost to government.
4. Capital punishment is undesirable because it represents sanctioned societal violence which is not necessary.

Each judgment is different, and some are better than others. Value judgment 2 appears to have very weak support. Eliminating a man's misery by killing him may be defensible under certain circumstances but certainly is not in the case of all prisoners. Judgment 1 might be tested by empirical evidence concerning the relationship between capital punishment and rates of serious crimes in different states or countries. Judgment 3 has to be analyzed in terms of the worth of human life. Judgment 4 is based on the principle that anything that contributes to unnecessary sanctioned violence in a society is bad. This principle can be weighed against those underlying the other value statements. The point is that there are ways of analyzing and comparing value judgments; these procedures will be more fully explained and illustrated later in this chapter.*

What Are Values?

Chapters 5 and 6 have been concerned mainly with teaching students how to make intellectual sense of the social world around them. Observing and classifying, describing and explaining, hypothesizing and generalizing—these intellectual processes are important. Students who do them well view the

---

*Although other chapters draw examples from materials for the new social studies curricula, this one will use mostly illustrations presented as though they came up spontaneously in the classroom or were made up by the teacher, rather than coming from some already-developed projects. There are numerous books and materials that social studies teachers can and do use to support their instruction in the analysis of values.[2] But in the area of values students themselves often raise the concerns, the problems, and

social world in a more objective, scientific way, and less in an uncomprehending folkway. When studying the empirical world of social studies, the social scientist and historian have been our models; they do best what we want students to do. But social scientists and historians do not provide much guidance in dealing with values and with processes of formulating and analyzing questions about them. Values are highly important to all people, however, and social studies teachers have special obligations to students in this area. Without values we are not human.

Values are standards used to decide whether some objects are good or bad, right or wrong, important or worthless, preferable or not preferable. The *objects* in this definition can take many forms; they can be ideas, decisions, persons, statements, actions, or physical objects. Compulsory universal education (an idea), a Supreme Court ruling to allow soldiers to protest wars in public demonstrations (a decision), President Nixon (a person), war is hell (a statement), stealing money from an old lady (an action), and Picasso's *Guernica* (an art object) are examples of these objects.

Because a value is intangible (you cannot see a standard), we refer to value statements as indicators of values. The following is a value statement: "I believe it is wrong to force racial integration on segregated school districts." This indicates to the listener or reader something about the values or standards that are held and used by the person making the statement. In this case the object of the belief is a governmental policy decision: the policy that imposes integration on school districts. The statement indicates that the speaker believes this policy is bad, or wrong. This, in turn, implies that some standard for judging is being used. In this case the standard may be the principle that the use of federal force to coerce local government is undesirable. On the other hand, the principle might be that racial segregation in schools is desirable. Determining which, if either, of these is the standard, or value, for judging is at the heart of value analysis. Determining what values underlie value statements is usually a difficult task. The standards are often not recognized and are not always accurately translated into value statements by the person holding the values, nor are accurate inferences about values always made from listening to value statements made by others.

---

the issues that become the focus for inquiry. Teachers should use students' concerns as a regular part of the instructional planning process. Using them is one way that relevance can be maintained. Social studies is different from almost all other subject fields in that it does place special emphasis on human values as well as on the empirical social world. This difference is an advantage. Chapter 7 will help teachers capitalize on that advantage.

DISTINGUISHING VALUE STATEMENTS FROM FACTUAL STATEMENTS

It is important for social studies teachers to be able to distinguish between value statements and other kinds of statements. (This is an example of one of our value statements!) Factual statements and value statements are often confused by both students and teachers in classroom discussion. In two independent surveys just less than 50 percent of several hundred social studies teachers judged the following to be a factual, rather than a value, statement: "The American form of government may not be perfect, but it's the best type of government yet devised by man."[3]

"Genoa County school system is segregated" is a factual statement; it can be checked out against observable data, assuming that a definition of *segregated* can be agreed on. Assume that a definition is agreed on and that after data from the Genoa schools are gathered, the statement is found to be untrue. It is still a factual statement, but it is simply an incorrect one. The statement is then changed to reflect empirical accuracy as the facts have determined it. But if the statement is changed to "The Genoa County school system should remain segregated," it becomes a value statement. There is no way to find out whether it is right or wrong empirically because the grounds or basis for the statement are not in the empirical world, as is the case with descriptive or explanatory statements, but are rather in the value system of the person making the statement. Value statements are often, but not always, distinguishable from factual statements by the inclusion in the former of rating words such as *should, ought, good, bad,* and *better*.

Values are not the same as personality traits or emotions, although both may be related to values. Personality characteristics and emotions refer to overt behavior of persons rather than to standards or beliefs. People are rigid, authoritarian, and dogmatic; they are happy, sad, and bewildered. None of these terms represent values, although from each, inferences about people's values and value systems can be made. The rigid person, for example, may believe that order and structure are more important for a happy life than any other qualities. He may apply this general principle to many value objects. Inferences about a person's values, therefore, can be made from his value statements as well as from other aspects of his overt behavior.

WHY VALUES ARE IMPORTANT

Values guide people in deciding how to live. They serve as standards for judging between alternative ways to expend time and energy and for judging the worth of decisions about how to live. Perhaps you have known persons who drift around in life without purpose or pattern. They are generally unhappy. Individuals with stronger and clearer values are steadier and more purposeful. Clear, coherent, constructed values contribute to happiness and relative freedom from serious personality problems.

Values are also tools for finding meanings in a complex social world. As it has become more and more troubled and complicated, the need for clear, well-grounded values has increased. Three relationships in life are profoundly influenced by our values; these relationships in turn affect and shape our values: (1) our relationship to ourselves, (2) our relationship to those persons closest in life to us, and (3) our relationship to elements of the wider society, such as the polity and the economy.

The intrapersonal connection. Values serve as guides and standards for making important judgments in personal life. These judgments affect the inner state of the individual. What a person views as social or economic or religious "success" indicates his values; whether or not he achieves success in these areas will feed back into his feeling about himself. With no values the individual is lost, as far as self-esteem is concerned. The lack of these values as personal standards means the person is completely adrift in life.

The interpersonal connection. Values serve important functions in close interpersonal relationships with others significant to the person. They help determine the nature of relationships with parents and siblings; they play a part in determining who friends will be and how they will react to the person; they influence the choice of a spouse and the nature of family life in adulthood.

The societal connection. Values also influence the extent and nature of relationships between individuals and the larger society. Take as an example the decision whether, and in what ways and direction, to participate in the political process. With no values to serve as guides, the decision-making becomes a random activity. Choosing to march in protest of a discriminatory election law is a decision that can be made for many reasons. It could result from careful thought in reference to a person's high value of political equality and justice; it could result from a desire to have one's picture in the newspaper; it could result from blindly following a mass of people, led by a charismatic speaker. Values are better guides for political and other social behavior than are emotions or mindlessness.

Values serve as perceptual screens in determining the range and kind of social phenomena that a person attends to and reflects upon. Values, like stores of concepts, also influence the interpretations made of these phenomena. Assume person A values his enjoyment of leisure time—his hobbies, sports, or reading—more than his work. He will likely respond differently to a political issue such as expanded federal support of recreational areas than will person B, whose value priority is the opposite. The two will also react differently to an issue involving a shorter workweek.

A person's concepts shape his perceptions and responses, and there is an interplay between concepts and values. Hard-working person B will define work in a way different from that of leisure-loving person A. B might define work as the essence of life itself, while A views work as something a person has to do to support himself economically. These different meanings of work assigned by the two persons will shape perceptions and actions. It is also clear that values shape the definitions. Values, as well as concepts, make it possible for an individual to make sense of his life and to chart new directions in which to move.

Analysis of Values in Social Studies Classes

We believe that the principal goal of dealing with values in social studies classes is to help students discover and ground a set of consistent values that can be used to form reasoned value judgments on a variety of social issues. Others emphasize different goals. Some assert that core values of the society should be inculcated into the young. Others believe that feelings, or emotional development, are the most important educational outcomes. Still others insist that schools should promote social action and not stop at promoting critical thinking alone.

The position on the goals of value-oriented social studies that is set forth in this book does not reject completely any of the three contrasting positions. There are parts of each that are accepted. The position stated here simply marks a different emphasis.

PURPOSES

To inculcate core values. There is a wide range of beliefs within the large group of educators who subscribe to the notion that some values should be inculcated in school students. On one side are "educational essentialists" who want students to learn the cultural heritage, which embodies actions, ideas, and objects that the wise men and women in the past have valued. Students should value the same actions, ideas, and objects. In this way the belief in and the practice of democracy, for example, can be transmitted from generation to generation. A quite different group of inculcators would teach students only one or two prime values—such as belief in the dignity and worth of individuals and belief in the democratic ideal of rational consent.[4] Using values such as these as the foundation, value positions are then clarified and strengthened.

The inculcation position has one inherent flaw: Who chooses the values to be inculcated and on what basis? Depending on who is choosing and on how effective the inculcation is, a range of radically different value outcomes is possible. Some teachers might teach that social change is always bad and should be fought at every turn; others might instill faith in violence as the answer to social ills. Worship of conformity to authority is another outcome that many might hold to be at the "core" of society's strengths.

But the inculcation argument is hard to reject from another standpoint. Before dismissing the position as indoctrination, the teacher has to search his own assumptions about inculcation or indoctrination. Do not teachers, for example, want students to appreciate, or value, the subject they study? There are procedural values, too, that teachers try to instill; respect for others' positions and allowing others a fair chance to express themselves are two such values. Seen in this way, most teachers do subscribe to the inculcation position in one way or the other.

To develop emotions and the self. Many educators believe that much of the heavily rationalistic approach of the school curriculum is irrelevant to the basic needs of youth. These needs, it is argued, have more to do with questions about the feelings of self and others than with intellectual abstractions. The questions "Who am I and why do I feel this way?" and "Who are they and how do they feel?" are of central concern. Self-awareness and emotions are the keys to affective education.[5]

Emotions and the self are important concerns for youth as well as for adults. These concerns have to be considered and used in choosing what to study in social studies classes. We believe, however, that there are other societal institutions that are also responsible for these concerns; the family, the church, and peer relationships are all expected to contribute toward emotional development. Schools have other objectives such as intellectual development and cannot serve all functions for all persons. We maintain that intellectual development should be the primary concern of educators and schools.

To encourage and practice social action. Some social studies educators argue that the mere study of social controversy and classroom analysis of values and value positions are not sufficient for meaningful "values education."[6] Because most school curricula emphasize thought without social involvement, they argue, youth tend to learn that good citizenship is passive citizenship and that democratic government will watch out for everyone's interests without citizen action.

We believe that there is merit in this argument, but for many school settings, student social action based on reflection in or out of class is unmanageable. Not only are there administrative problems in a broad implementation of the idea, but the resources to support adequately such a move are beyond the limits of a classroom teacher with 130 students. Acting on the basis of well-thought-out positions on social values should be part of a citizen's education, but the social studies classroom is only one of many arenas for that action. If they are to develop into competent citizens, young people must learn to act on their own and with groups outside of the context of the school. The intellectual foundation for thoughtful social action is, however, built partly in schools, and within limits thinking and action can be joined in social studies.

EFFECTS

Value analysis in the social studies classroom can result in better-grounded value systems. Although all people probably have some values, the most important differences in the value systems of individuals lie in the way these values are formed, changed, related to one another, and used by those holding them. For example, two persons could make the same value statement: "I believe it is right that the federal government compel the electricians' labor union to allow qualified black persons to become apprentices." Student A might believe this because: his parents told him it was the proper way to believe or because he read it in a newspaper editorial or because he liked the sound of it in class. On the other hand, student B might have derived this statement from some general values he holds, such as believing in the inherent rights of all individuals to be treated equally and to be afforded equal opportunities. Because student B considers equal job opportunities for black electricians to be more important than the negative effects that would ensue from the government's abridging the freedom of the union to restrict recruitment of apprentices, he concludes that the value statement is justified. Student B can give satisfactory grounds for the value statement; student A cannot. B can articulate his values much better than A can articulate his. B's whole system of values is well organized and perhaps forms a structure or philosophy that makes it easy to relate values to social issues. It is doubtful that student A has such a framework or philosophy. Student A can be changed so that he has student B's capabilities for dealing with value questions. This can happen in social studies classrooms directed by a well-prepared, thoughtful teacher.

Values form a bridge between the "knowledge world" and the "action world" in social education. In order to act intelligently and responsibly, people need both knowledge and values. Citizen Z, for example, knows through careful reading and attending political meetings that candidate P is running for the sheriff's office on a platform including the "need for preventive detention of arrested persons who have been previously convicted of certain crimes." Candidate Q is running on a similar platform *except* that he is against preventive detention. Citizen Z knows what preventive detention is and what position the two candidates have taken. But he still cannot decide how to vote without reference to his system of values. Can he relate this specific issue to broader values embodied in the Constitution regarding arrest and detention procedures? Can he trace the consequences of such a provision (and the lack of the provision) to the groups involved? Can he trace the effects on more general rights of citizens and the coercive power of government? These questions illustrate that values and the valuing process serve as links between knowledge and action. Both reliable knowledge and a consistent value system are necessary for thoughtful social action.

Before going on, see if you can use this notion of the "value bridge" in examining a social situation requiring a decision on action or inaction.

APPLICATION 7.1: KNOWLEDGE + VALUES = DECISION

Situation: Bob is approached by some friends who want him to march and carry a sign in a demonstration. The demonstrators are protesting a city voter-redistricting plan. The plan would change city voting from a ward system, in which each ward elects a member to the city council, to an at-large procedure, in which each voter votes for candidates to fill all the council seats. Bob's friends argue that this change would mean that minority groups, including both blacks and poor people, would lose their representation.

Problems: 1. What knowledge is required by Bob for an intelligent decision on whether or not to march?

_____

_____

_____

_____

_____

_____

2. What value considerations does he have to make?

_____

_____

_____

3. What are the larger values that this issue is related to?

_____

_____

_____

4. What are the consequences of marching or not marching?

_____

_____

_____

What are the consequences of excluding value analysis in social studies classrooms? The most serious consequences involve the way that young people would respond as citizens. They might not take any social action at all (apathetic response), or they might act without paying any attention to their values or to the ethical consequences of their actions (mindless response). Neither type of response is satisfactory.

The apathetic response can be avoided partly through value analysis in social studies. Forming and examining and changing value statements bearing on social questions in class necessarily involve students in thinking about taking action in the social sphere. What would *I* do if I were in that situation? How would I respond if I had to make that choice between conflicting actions? These are the kinds of questions that are raised, if not by student then by teachers, in analyzing value-laden problems. If students study social data solely for the sake of knowing, describing, explaining, and theorizing, this reinforces the notions that action is unnecessary and that knowledge alone is sufficient. This position educates people who know how to know but not how and why to act. The inclusion of value analysis is necessary to avoid this outcome.

The "mindless action" response is just as serious. Action without consideration of the values involved can be very dangerous. People who do what they are told by charismatic leaders illustrate mindless action. Violent action taken "because I felt like it" or "because it felt good" is another example. "I never realized that it would hurt anybody" is not an uncommon statement. All these approaches to social actions reflect the absence of values and a value system against which to measure and assess individual actions. That they also reflect lack of practice in relating possible actions to values suggests that just such practice, if carried out thoughtfully in school, can help prevent mindless action in the social world.

OBJECTIONS TO EMPHASIZING VALUES

Objections to emphasizing value analysis in social studies classes are varied. One common argument is that if all the empirical facts surrounding a social problem were known, then there would be no need for referring to values because the "single best answer" would naturally follow from the facts of the case. Thus, facts should be studied as carefully as possible, and nothing else need be done, since the solution will be obvious. This argument has been labeled the "naturalistic fallacy" and has been discredited by many thinkers in this area. A rather simplistic position, it ignores situations involving competing value positions, each of considerable merit. For example, there is a court case in British Admiralty law that involved men on a lifeboat with no hope for rescue. One was dying, and the men had the fearful choice of whether to kill the dying man so that they could eat him, thus holding out for possible rescue, or to die of starvation themselves. It is difficult to study the facts of this case without referring to some system of values in order to determine the best action that could have been taken. Most value-laden issues involve just this sort of dilemma. The position that "facts will determine the correct action" is not very helpful in cases involving two or more "good positions."

Another argument against dealing in the classroom with value-laden topics and issues is what might be labeled the "indoctrination" or "tender young minds" argument. This view assumes that students' value systems are very malleable and that raising value questions in schools can result in uncritical acceptance and internalization of whatever values are promoted at the time. Because of the dominant position of the teacher, it is held, students are likely to accept the values a teacher professes.

There are at least two ways of challenging these assertions. First, it cannot be concluded that a teacher is advocating a particular position just because value-laden issues are being dealt with in class. One study has asked the question of just how much classroom time is spent by social studies teachers in making value-oriented statements or asking value-oriented questions.[7] Observing sixteen hours of what fourteen teachers considered controversial topics yielded an average of only about 2 percent of the time devoted by teachers to talking in the "values mode." If the argument about indoctrination is taken seriously, one has to question how it can take place under such circumstances.

Second, studies have also been made to determine whether there is congruence between the political beliefs of students and teachers. If they think similarly on political questions, for example, one might suspect that indoctrination is taking place. In general, there is very little congruence; therefore, these studies provide no support for the indoctrination argument.[8] In fact, little congruence except for political party identification is found between students and their own parents. It seems that rather than having tender, young minds that are easily influenced by the arguments and values of adults, high school students tend to have belief systems that are fairly well solidified and more or less impervious to outside influences. Under these conditions little is to be feared from teachers trying to indoctrinate students.

From the preceeding arguments you might be led to conclude that if indoctrination fails to change students' belief systems, then there is no point in dealing with value issues in the classroom. But one important study has established that if these topics are dealt with intensely and systematically, high school students' abilities to analyze and work with controversial issues can be strengthened, with no corresponding loss in social studies "knowledge."[9] Another study suggests that junior high students' moral development can be influenced by similar systematic instruction.[10] It must be emphasized, however, that these outcomes have to do with ways of valuing or with orientations toward grounding moral questions, rather than with the specific values or morals themselves.

Another argument for keeping questions of values out of the classroom is that any one person's opinion is as good as another's. The tenability of this position was rejected earlier in this chapter. The grounds that a person has for making a value statement determine the merit of his position, not the simple fact that he said something. Unreasoned, ungrounded, poorly understood positions are not "equal" to well-reasoned, grounded, clearly understood positions. If teachers allow any sort of statement to be made and to go unchallenged in class during the analysis of a values question, regardless of the quality of the statement, simply on the grounds that "everyone is entitled to his opinion," these teachers understand neither the purpose nor the process of value analysis. Stating an initial position on an issue is only the first of a number of steps necessary before values are analyzed, clarified, and often modified by students. This first step—the sounding out of opinions—is often all that happens in social studies classrooms. When teachers have no procedures or strategies to employ in the further treatment of these initial opinion statements of students, it may be more a rationalization than anything else for them to claim that "people can't argue opinions." We offer productive methods of clarifying and analyzing initial statements of opinion.

There is another somewhat related argument against value analysis: the extreme moral relativistic argument. It holds that no person can judge or analyze the values of others because others' values can only be considered relative to their own culture and life experiences. A person cannot impose a negative value judgment on the polygamous marriage patterns of another society, for example, because the only grounds for doing so are the unique values of his particular society. This line of argument is perfectly sensible in this example, but it is often extended beyond reason. It is useful in defeating ethnocentric bias, but when used to cover all value judgments, it loses its power. The extreme relativistic argument might hold, for example, that a moral judgment against one who murders an innocent person is not possible, on the grounds that the murderer believes that murder is not bad. Similarly, the Nazis cannot be judged to have done wrong by murdering countless of their ethnic enemies because it seemed correct to them. These extensions of the relativistic argument are highly questionable in light of general moral standards used across a wide variety of cultures and times if not universally. Murder of innocents is and has been judged morally wrong by nearly all societies in most of recorded history.

Recent investigations of individual moral development suggest that there are several moral "stages" that apply across all cultures.[11] Persons in any particular stage are similarly oriented toward moral values and principles. These stages range from the lowest, an "obedience" orientation (consequences of actions are judged in the light of punishment or avoidance of it), to the highest, a "universal ethical" orientation (right actions follow from conscious references to self-determined ethical principles). The existence of such stages of moral orientation, which are independent of any specific values or ethical principles, constitutes another argument against the morally relativistic position. In fact, the goal of value analysis in social studies can be stated in terms of these stages: we should work to move students from lower to higher stages.[12]

Some people object to value analysis because there are not enough facts known about controversial, value-laden topics to settle the issues, so that discussion of these issues represents only a "pooling of collective ignorance." However, all the facts are never available on any topic, and often crucial decisions in life have to be made on the basis of scarce facts. We are not opting for ignoring facts in deciding value problems—students should become skillful in seeking out and considering as much relevant evidence as possible before making decisions. Even discussion based only partly on facts and partly on individual value positions does not constitute pooling ignorance, unless the discussion is badly handled by the teacher. Because value positions cannot be proved in the same way that empirical statements can be is no reason to assume that value positions are based on ignorance, as is implied in the argument of pooling ignorance. Value statements and issues represent a mode of discourse different from, but no less important than, empirical questions.

Finally, it is argued that because no models are generally agreed on for systematically dealing with values, it is better to concentrate on empirical discourse and learning, which are generally accepted models for generating and verifying knowledge. While there is no systematic framework for values analysis agreed on by large numbers of scholars and teachers, attempts to produce at least partial methods for handling value analysis have been and are being made. Some of these methods will be explained later in this chapter.

Elements of the Analysis of Values

TEACHER: *Some of you have probably heard of the bill in Congress which will set an annual guaranteed income for all families. What do you think about it? (Pause) Bill?*

BILL: *About what?*

TEACHER: *The bill—the guaranteed income for all families.*

BILL: *I don't know. It's okay, I guess.*

TEACHER: *Do you agree, Joe?*

JOE: *Yeah, I guess so, but some people would never work, that way.*

TEACHER: *What do you mean?*

JOE: *Lots of poor people are just lazy, and a deal like that would just give them an excuse to sit around. I don't know.*

TEACHER: *Sue, what do you think?*

SUE: *I agree.*

TEACHER: *Henry?*

HENRY: *Yeah, I guess they're right.*

TEACHER: *Well, let's move on to discuss the chapter for today . . .*

This classroom dialogue is certainly not a model to copy. It may help to illustrate certain problems in value inquiry, however. Although no claim about its representativeness is made here, many similar sessions have been observed. The overall type of discussion might be labeled opinion polling. The teacher does very little more than solicit vague opinions on an issue from several students in class then goes on to a new subject.

APPLICATION 7.2: DIALOGUE OR POLL—THE TEACHER'S ROLE

Before you go on with the discussion of the analysis of values, jot down briefly what you think the teacher left out in conducting the classroom dialogue.

For the next few pages we will explain our answer to the application. The answer outlines some of the major elements of the analysis of values that you, as a social studies teacher, will want to promote and teach in your classes. First, a general observation: The teacher's goal in the dialogue did not seem to include stimulating students to think in ways different from those in which they had thought before. They had only to say anything—perhaps only nodding their head or mumbling would have sufficed—in order to satisfy the teacher. But no student had to think, except to remember something about how he or she stood on a bill in Congress. The teacher's goals here seem to lack any substance beyond forcing students to verbalize ungrounded opinions.

Here are general goals that can help to fill this vacuum:

1. Stimulating thought about some value concern or policy matter that poses a *problem for students*
2. *Identifying* and *clarifying* the *central value issues* and conflicts embedded in the problem
3. Identifying and *defining key concepts*
4. *Relating* specific issues to general values or philosophical positions
5. Projecting and testing the *consequences* or action implications of holding a specific position on the issue
6. Testing for *completeness* of data and arguments
7. Testing for *relevance* of data and arguments
8. Testing for *consistency* and logic of data and arguments.

All these operations have one overall goal as a focal point. This is the process of stimulating (or perhaps forcing) students to give the grounds, or an acceptable defense and reasons, for holding a particular value position. This is the general goal that the teacher in the dialogue seemed to lack.

No attempt to impose a sequence on value analysis is implied by listing the above operations in a particular order. Value analysis involves switching back and forth between operations as classroom situations require. After you have worked at several of the steps in the list, it might be necessary to respecify and clarify the value issue or to define important new terms whose key places in the discussion were not at first anticipated. Or, after a short definition of the policy issue in question, students might skip ahead to the real-world consequences of particular actions related to the issue. This jumping around in instruction is necessary; there is no recipelike order in any serious instructional process, least of all in value analysis. But this is not to say that students should do anything they please in value analysis, with limits set as to how sloppy and ungrounded it may be.

STIMULATING THOUGHT

A common problem in the analysis of values rests in the fact that often few students in a class ever sense a problem at all. The teacher in the above dialogue had that problem. Another teacher might start by asking, "How many of you saw that TV special last night on the pros and cons of government-financed guaranteed annual income?" Four or five raised hands, some nods. "Well, what do you think the Congress should do?" After a few minutes this discussion peters out for lack of knowledgeable response. The teacher wonders why. The answer is not too difficult: Very few students started out by sensing that there was any problem beyond keeping the teacher happy. The teacher was playing to a very limited segment of his class; the others had not seen the TV program and lacked information. They were unlikely to become excited. Opening a discussion can be tricky and certainly requires careful planning and execution. Some excellent discussions may start spontaneously, but more often they must be carefully planned, just as they must be in other facets of teaching. Here is another teacher's opening:

TEACHER: *Okay, class, I've handed out a fact sheet which summarizes the pro and con arguments made on the TV program I asked you to watch last night. Study the sheet in groups of three for a few minutes and be prepared to judge whether it is complete or not. If a group says it is not complete, that group can fill in the missing arguments from their notes from the program. (Several moments of silence) Okay, the group with Bob, Jim, and Mary in it, have you decided?*

BOB: *It's okay, we think.*

TED: *Our group doesn't think you included the part about people being encouraged not to work because of this program.*

JOE: *Yeah, and you also missed the argument that it's wrong for people who work and pay taxes to have to support people who don't work.*

BOB: *But what if they can't work—like if the father is disabled from the war?*

This teacher is off to a solid start. What did he do besides trying to make sure the whole class saw the TV program and took notes on it? He did something essential in any opening of value analysis: the conflict or problem situation was quickly set up with students involved in completing the summary of arguments. In this case he left critical arguments out of the fact-sheet summary, hoping that the holes would be discovered and filled in by the students. Not only does a move such as this get students involved in the basic arguments, but it gives the teacher critical information on how much they know about the issue at this point. If the issue is not well understood, the fact will be revealed through this opening exercise, and the teacher must remedy the information gap, probably with some contingency plan developed beforehand. Going on as though the students understand, when they really do not, is usually disasterous—as the first example illustrates.

There are, of course, many ways of stimulating thought on a value issue. Dramatic presentation, pictures or films, records, tapes, articles, role-playing, outside speakers, field trips, stimulations—all can serve as effective points of departure for the analysis of values. The basic idea, though, is to get the students into the problem so that it is their problem rather than a teacher problem. Often the students themselves are the most fertile sources of value issues. Using their concerns, their moral dilemmas, their moral indignation— rather than the teacher's—avoids many of the pitfalls of "teacher problems" which are not perceived or felt by students.

IDENTIFYING AND CLARIFYING CENTRAL ISSUES

At some point in an analysis of values, the core issues must be highlighted. Although this might occur at any point, or at several points, in a discussion, specifying and clarifying the issues is useful during the beginning phase. It is then that potentially irrelevant and distracting digressions can be avoided by referring back to some central point or points of reference. The process of clarifying the issues can also set up other necessary elements which may follow, such as identifying key concepts, abstracting general values from the specific issues, and inferring consequences of actions. Without the key issues clearly agreed on, discussions can and often do wonder aimlessly. Not all relevant issues might be identified during the initial phases; it might be effective to have students uncover important but overlooked questions as they move through the process. But starting on something concrete and commonly understood is imperative. Let's pick up on the previous discussion.

TEACHER: *What seem to be the most important issues or conflicts involved in this controversy? We have to have a clear idea of the general problems before we can come to some defensible arguments and conclusions.*

TED: *One problem seems to be that by trying to help people you can hurt them at the same time.*

TEACHER: *What do you mean by that?*

SUE: *Oh, I see what he means! By guaranteeing an income to some families, you might kill their incentive to help themselves.*

JOE: *But you sure won't help them by letting them starve because they can't . . .*

TEACHER: *Wait a second, Joe. We've got to get some clear issues out in the open before we debate. Ted and Sue are suggesting that there's a possible conflict between society's efforts to aid a poor family and the long-range self-interest of that family. Doesn't that seem reasonable to you?*

JOE: *Yeah, but what do you mean by "the family's self-interest"? What you said really isn't an issue until we know what that term means.*

BOB: *And we've got to define aid here, too! There can be lots of different kinds of aid given . . .*

In this excerpt the teacher is using fairly heavy-handed tactics in trying to get one of the issues in this general area stated and clarified. He cuts off argument by Joe, apparently thinking that Joe's argument will detract from the process at this stage. This is generally not a bad thing to do if the purpose is to keep discussion from flying off in all directions. The teacher can make this up to Joe later by incorporating his point into a later operation, perhaps when implications or consequences are being drawn. Alternatively, the teacher might have shifted at that point to a discussion of consequences, especially if Joe is a more reticent student and this is one of the few times he raises a point. But in general a teacher has the responsibility to make these decisions and not to let anything that might happen pull discussion off into a dead end or chaos.

The particular issue raised by Ted and Sue in the dialogue might be further clarified and sharpened; it might possibly be recorded on the blackboard or an overhead projector transparency. You could see in the dialogue that the teacher probes Ted's initial response, but that Sue actually clarifies it for Ted. This is a situation that requires another decision and action on the teacher's part. Apparently this teacher decided that it required no unusual action, but often such a situation might require the teacher to interrupt Sue and insist, politely of course, that Ted be allowed to clarify for himself. You have seen many Sues ruin an otherwise productive discussion by monopolizing at the expense of other Teds. Too many teachers seem to believe that the situation will take care of itself and that these things will balance themselves out. But a problem like this rarely solves itself. More commonly, after two or three instances of this phenomenon, Ted will become angry and remain quiet; often others in the class will follow suit. Sue will talk all the more (she gets her way), and the discussion becomes a tête-à-tête between Sue and the teacher, who wonder why no one else seems interested. There is another possible reason for insisting on Ted's, rather than Sue's, clarification. Ted might not be able to clarify that statement because he has not thought it through, or he is not good at clarifying. In any case the teacher needs to know these things so that he can give Ted more time to think or more practice or some other help. Sue stands in the way of this important information, and some teacher action is needed if the teacher is to gain that information. As soon as Sue starts talking in Ted's place, he can stop thinking if he wants to, and this presumably is contrary to the teacher's objectives.

IDENTIFYING AND DEFINING KEY CONCEPTS

It is clear from the previous dialogue that stating and clarifying issues often leads to definitional operations. This might be a matter of teaching various concepts not already understood by students, requiring operations described earlier in this book. Or it may be simply agreeing on a common meaning for a term. In the example, *aid* is easy to agree on; it means whatever the congressional bill calls for in the form of income supplements to needy families. The definition of *long-range self-interest* of the family obviously is a more difficult idea to pin down. But the term must be defined if the issue in question is to have any meaning and be solved. If the teacher in response to Joe's request for a definition says, "Oh, Joe, you know what I mean," or avoids the question, he is dooming the issue to a quick death.

APPLICATION 7.3: DEFINITIONS AS CORNERSTONE

Write a dialogue of your own on guaranteed income for families, ending with a brief meaningful definition of *long-range interest* in this context. To start out, assume that you as teacher decide to reflect Joe's question back on him (it could be reflected toward another student) and he responds: "Well, I think one part of family long-range self-interest in this case could be their ability to support themselves without anybody's help." Include in your definition of *long-range self-interest* the elements you think are necessary before the class can work intelligently with the issue.

The two intellectual skills discussed so far—identifying and defining key concepts—are basic parts of any analytic task in social studies. It is assumed that the teacher has these skills and that one of his principal objectives is to teach students how to perform these operations when approaching a social issue or problem. The two skills are just as important when engaging in non-value areas. One reason for the superficial "opinion polling" illustrated at the beginning of this section might be that teachers fail to recognize the applicability to values discussions of the same intellectual operations they insist on in value-free inquiry.

RELATING SPECIFIC ISSUES TO GENERAL VALUES

Another mark of an educated individual is the ability to relate issues of different levels of generality. To be able to fit a specific political issue into an overall framework of values or to be able to move from a general economic philosophy to a specific instance of that philosophy in practice—these are examples of this kind of relating skill. Students should develop the capacity to fit specific value problems, such as the proposal for a government-financed annual income in our example, into larger, more general value systems.

TEACHER: *Now that we've defined some of the important items in this problem, what general values of our society are involved?*

JOE: *As I was trying to say earlier, it's sort of a matter of going against a system of people helping themselves. Of not taking handouts or . . .*

SUE: *The political conservatives call that something, uh, rugged . . . something.*

TED: *Rugged individuals or something like that.*

TEACHER: *Rugged individualism, I guess that's what you're thinking of. Sue?*

SUE: *Uh huh. Well, anyhow, that's the name for the idea that it's just good if people help themselves; that's the way the country became great. So this individualism is a kind of value which is involved in the guaranteed-income issue, at least that's one argument against it.*

TEACHER: *Right. What are some other values or principles here?* (Long silence) *Well, suppose two politicians were debating this bill in Congress, and one argued against it on the basis of rugged individualism. How would the other counter that argument?* (Pause)

TED: *Well, the other one might say that some families might have sickness or injury or other bad luck, so they can't be so rugged and all that stuff.*

TEACHER: *But why have the annual income?*

TED: *The thing is that everybody has a right to exist—we can't just let down-and-out families suffer or die. They have the right to at least have enough food and clothes and stuff.*

BOB: *If you don't have those things, you're not even human, really. You turn into a part animal or something, like in the concentration camps.*

TEACHER: *So the principle or value here is that all people have the right to . . . to what?*

KAREN: *Self-respect. If you don't have those basic things, you lose self-respect, you are ashamed, like some kids don't come to school because they don't have the clothes or anything to eat at lunch. They have pride and won't show others they don't have those things, else they'd lose their pride. But if you don't have anything, you even lose your pride. Your dignity, I guess.*

TEACHER: *That's a very good example, Karen. So, we are talking about two ideas that our society thinks are good—individualism and the basic self-respect or dignity of the people.*

BOB: *We've seen those values being argued about before in history.*

TEACHER: *Yes, and they crop up in other issues today. Can you think of any?*

JOE: *In the school busing controversy. There they . . .*

Here the class is engaged in the process of applying the specific welfare issue at hand to more general societal values. In the discussions some new concepts surfaced, and their meanings were worked through. This is what is meant by the interplay between components of value inquiry.

First, *individualism* was named rather quickly in the discussion. But the teacher had to work harder to arrive at the second value: the inherent worth in the dignity or self-respect of the individual. He resorted to having his class imagine a hypothetical debate, and stimulated thinking in that way. This tactic needed some patience, but it did work out after some probing.

Karen brought in an analogous case involving the value of self-respect, and the discussion ended with other examples of the general value being discussed.

One opportunity to relate different sides of the issues to general political philosophies was apparent. After Sue mentioned that conservatives talk about rugged individualism, the teacher might have used that as an entry into linking political conservatism and liberalism to the general values being discussed. This teacher might have avoided that particular topic for several reasons, or he might be planning to raise the subject at another time. It might have confused the issue at this point, or he might think that the class doesn't generally understand the concepts liberal and conservative and that teaching these concepts at this point would constitute too serious a digression to warrant such a linking operation.

APPLICATION 7.4: FROM SPECIFIC VALUES TO BROADER ISSUES

Can you discover in the dialogue other opportunities to move from specific to broader issues that weren't taken up? How would you have acted on them? Also, how would you have continued after Joe trailed off at the end of the dialogue?

TESTING THE CONSEQUENCES OF A POSITION

One way to assess the merits of particular value positions is to project the real-life consequences that would stem from actions implied by the position. The students have been doing this at certain points in the dialogue above. When the objection to guaranteed annual income is raised on the grounds that it would tend to promote dependence of families on the government, the student is testing the worth of a particular value position (guaranteed annual income is good) against one possible consequence (it will promote dependence). If the statements of consequence can be made specific enough, they can be tested with evidence and therefore either supported or rejected. Making the consequence statements clear and provable usually involves concept definition. In the example the concept dependence has to be clarified. One way that students might define *dependence* is shown here:

SUE: *I think that one thing that will happen if the government pays everyone a minimum income is that some families will lean on the government too much. It will get to be a habit for them, especially for families where the father doesn't have too good a job anyway.*

TEACHER: *Now Sue is suggesting that the program might promote dependence on the government and that's bad. What kind of dependence do you mean, Sue?*

JOE: *Oh, I know! They won't try to get jobs; they'll just live off the government checks instead.*

TEACHER: *Are you sure that would happen?*

SUE: *Sure, that's just natural.*

TEACHER: *Would you do that, Sue?*

SUE: *No, but that's different. Anyhow . . .*

TEACHER: *How could we find out if that's really true?*

TED: *Well, there are some countries—like Sweden and I think Denmark—which have these programs. Maybe we could find out if it happened there when they started their guaranteed annual income.*

TEACHER: *Good idea. We'll test this with some evidence. Now, how could we state this so we could give it a clear-cut test?*

TED: *Compared with countries which have no guaranteed income, those countries that do tend to have a higher proportion of persons who don't try to get jobs.*

TEACHER: *That's pretty good. We might try to find out if that's true or not. I think I have some data in a book which will help us. What do you think of this, Sue?*

SUE: *It will tell if I have a good argument. What if it turns out to be false?*

TEACHER: *Well, maybe there are some other good or bad outcomes of this program. Can anybody come up with another?*

We can see the teacher moving the class from a rather vague consequences argument to a more clearly defined and provable proposition. From that point on, the process is identical with that of hypothesis testing discussed in Chapter 6. The main point is that it is often helpful to think of testing value statements in terms of their consequences. If this path is followed, it should include a wide range of possible consequences. One job the teacher has, then, is to make sure that a complete set of consequences, rather than just one, is considered. Once several consequences have been explored in this way, the relative merits of a value position should be clearer and more meaningful.

TESTING FOR COMPLETE INFORMATION AND MULTIPLE POINTS OF VIEW

One problem often encountered in value analysis is that a class will look at a problem from a limited perspective. Students might all agree on one position and see no second or third side to it. This might mean that a teacher has to take a drastically different position in order to stimulate student thinking. Either new information or new viewpoints may have to be injected. Assume that the class in the example dialogue has emphasized only harmful outcomes that may stem from the guaranteed-income program. If, after trying to promote other views, the teacher still cannot shake the class from the single perspective, he must be more forceful. Excerpts from the testimony of persons helped by welfare programs might help. Or arguing that some assistance to poor families might actually stimulate independence, rather than dependence, might open up a new viewpoint.

Preparing to combat a class situation in which there is only one viewpoint or only a limited set of information is one of the most difficult tasks facing a social studies teacher. But some thought (and experience) can be applied to this problem. Some teachers practice values discussions on their families or friends outside just to find out what ranges of arguments and evidence are needed and to anticipate problems. You might argue that no preparation of this nature is useful or even desirable. You might think that a free discussion is best and that prior thinking or planning by the teacher would stultify the class. We believe that this is wrong. What often happens, unfortunately, is that the free discussion ends up by going nowhere because of too little preparation. Plans can always be disregarded if the discussion moves in unforeseen but fruitful directions. But if the reverse happens—nothing moves, or students start to drift from idea to idea in an unreasoned fashion— preparation can be invaluable.

TESTING FOR RELEVANCE

Arguments in discussions of social studies values sometimes include irrelevant assertions and information. It is important for students to become skillful at distinguishing the relevant from the irrelevant. The teacher plays an important part in their developing this skill. If the teacher does not point out instances of irrelevant contributions made by students, it is unlikely that anyone will, at least during the first few value discussions. The teacher has to perform this function, even though it might seem unpleasant. After some modeling of this skill by the teacher, students may pick up this job on their own, judging the relevance of each other's statements and evidence. The teacher, of course, may be subjected to the test of relevance. Care must be taken, however, that you do not mistake as irrelevant a student's sincere but confused effort to contribute to the discussion. Students often need to verbalize a point or argument more than once before it begins to make sense. They sometimes have to be prodded or coached before making themselves clear. Students' responses have to be judged closely, then, before you conclude that the response is irrelevant and should be ignored.

TESTING FOR LOGIC AND CONSISTENCY IN ARGUMENTS

Logic and consistency are another pair of criteria for testing certain elements of value inquiry. One general class of illogical assertions is the statement of a position given with evidence or reasoning that supports the opposite or another conclusion. Inconsistency in argument often occurs when a student tries to draw two opposing conclusions from the same evidence. Or he might try to use conflicting evidence to support a single contention. As with the criteria of completeness and relevance, the teacher is obliged to do most of the early work on these dimensions, hoping that his modeling will result in students' starting to apply the same tests themselves.

APPLICATION 7.5: RECOGNITION AND RESPONSE TO ILLOGICAL ARGUMENT

Using the following dialogue, see if you can pick out instances of irrelevant, illogical, or inconsistent operations in argument. For each example you find, describe how you, as the teacher, would have responded.

TEACHER: *Yes, Ted?*

TED: *Some of us have been listening to the news about all this school busing problem, and we'd like to discuss it in class sometime.*

TEACHER: *Discuss what about it? Anything in particular bothering you?*

TED: *Yes, some of us think it's wrong to force kids to go in a bus to a school far away when there's one close by in the neighborhod.*

JANICE: *But blacks have got to get a chance to . . .*

BOB: *That doesn't have anything to do with it. It's just got to do with freedom, that's all. People ought to be free to go to the school that they want to. Nobody should stuff kids on a bus and drag them off where they and their parents don't want them to go to school.*

TEACHER: *Now, Bob, what specific freedom are you talking about? As I understand this issue . . .*

TED: *My dad told me that before World War II the Nazis in Germany used to bus kids to different schools, and look how they came out! We can't afford to have this kind of thing going on in the United States. Think of what might happen!*

BOB: *About this freedom business, well, uh, I think everybody ought to be free to choose his own school.*

SUE: *But not many blacks are free to choose their schools, are they? Isn't that what the whole argument is about? Some black parents want their kids going to schools that are better than the ones they go to now.*

BOB: *Look, anybody knows those colored are happier together in schools, not mixed in with whites. They shouldn't be able to horn in on others' schools just because some politician or judge says they can. Those colored are just trying to cause trouble. I say we keep them in their schools, and we'll stay in ours. That's the fair way.*

TEACHER: *Maybe there are some other points of view that should be on the floor. Does anyone else want to give his opinion?*

Problems in Teaching the Analysis of Values

The eight elements or goals of the analysis of values explained in the previous section should provide teachers an operating framework on which to work in value analysis. Intelligent application of these elements should result in well-stated value positions to be taken by students. Some classroom problems connected with value analysis still remain. How can students' positions be challenged even further, if that is desired? Should a teacher try to remain neutral, or take a partisan stance in value-laden discussions? How can teachers speed up or slow down discussions when they want to? How does the teacher avoid drifting, disconnected discussions? How can a teacher handle highly sensitive issues? What if a student takes positions that are morally unacceptable? It is to these questions that we now turn.

HOW TO CHALLENGE STUDENTS' POSITIONS

One of the most difficult problems of teaching in the domain of values is how to challenge students' positions.[13] Some suggestions have already been made in explaining the eight elements. But there are other tests of value positions which a teacher can use with students. It is to be hoped that students will begin to use them without the teacher's intervention.

The first two tests are extensions of the task of *consequences projection* explained before. One unique consequences test, *role reversal*, asks the student to place himself in the position of the person *most negatively affected* if the value position was acted on. Such a test might look like this:

Teacher: Now we've discussed this proposal to grant amnesty to all draft re-sisters, and Jim has given some well-reasoned arguments and some evidence against such an amnesty. Jim, we all know that you are in favor of our involvement in the Vietnam War. But put yourself in the position of a man who is against killing under any circumstances. You are not exempted from service, even though you try. Then, to avoid serving, you go "underground." The war ends; there is no amnesty granted; you can't return to a normal life because you'll be caught and jailed. In that position, does your conclusion about amnesty still appear to be a good one?

Sometimes the role-reversal test does not apply or is difficult to use. Another consequences-oriented test, *universal consequences*, may be used in such a case. To apply it, the teacher or a student challenges a position by asking what consequences would ensue if everyone acted on the basis of a value position. The test might look like this:

Teacher: Sally, you've taken the position that it's all right for a person not to obey traffic laws in his automobile as long as he doesn't do harm to anyone. That might work out if only one or a few drivers act this way. But the law is supposed to apply to everyone. What would happen if every driver disregarded traffic laws?

The use of *analogies* is a third means of challenging a student position. The teacher first helps the student establish a principle underlying the value judgment. Then the teacher imagines a new case to which the principle does not apply. This may force the student to alter or reject the principle, and this in turn may require him to reformulate the original value position. Here is an example of the use of an analogy to challenge a values position:

TEACHER: *Now, Sally has taken the position that grand juries should not compel reporters to divulge their confidential sources of information relating to criminal investigations. What more general principle does this involve, Sally?*

SALLY: *Freedom of the press. I don't think we should restrict it in any way.*

TEACHER: *Under any circumstances?*

SALLY: *That's right.*

TEACHER: *What if a reporter writes a false account which involves a drugstore owner with a criminal drug ring? If it is published, it may ruin the man's business and whole life, even though it isn't true.*

SALLY: *I guess the reporter shouldn't be able to do that.*

TEACHER: *Then there are some restrictions on freedom of the press?*

SALLY: *Yes, maybe. But your case is much different than the one we're studying. I don't think we can compare them. For criminal proceedings, I still think that freedom of the press should never be restricted.*

TEACHER: *What if the reporter's source is the only link to a killer who continues his pattern of murder? More murders may result if he isn't tracked down. Shouldn't the capture of the killer be considered more important than freedom of the press in this case?*

SALLY: *Yes, I guess so. Maybe the protection of confidential sources in these cases shouldn't be absolute. If there is grave danger to people, then maybe that's justification enough to restrict this part of press freedom.*

In this example the teacher uses two analogies. The first doesn't work because Sally sees that it is not parallel to the original case. (Attacking the parallelism of others' analogies is a desirable intellectual skill to be promoted in value analysis.) Then the teacher constructs a new analogy which is more parallel, and Sally modifies the principle. Constructing analogies in the middle of discussions requires quick thinking of teachers. But before-instruction planning can produce a set of analogies which the teacher has ready if the situation calls for them.

All three tests described here have as their goal challenging the value conclusions of students. They often serve to lead students to view the value problem from fresh perspectives rather than from the same viewpoint. This is an important part of value analysis.

SHOULD THE TEACHER TAKE A POSITION?

Social studies teachers are concerned with the problem of whether or not to take positions in value-oriented discussions. Many argue that a neutral stance is best, because it steers away from indoctrination or more subtle persuasion of students to the teacher's viewpoint. Teacher neutrality is held to allow balance in discussion, allowing the teacher to make sure that all points of view are given fair hearing. Proponents of this view consider also other problems that might arise if the teacher takes strong positions in class. These problems might include parental and school administrators' disfavor and unfavorable student reactions.

But others reason that a partisan role might be better than a neutral one, at least sometimes. The teacher can never really be neutral on issues, they argue; positions can only be hidden more or less cleverly. Rather than hide partisanship behind a neutral mask, it is better to be openly partisan, so that students can understand and take into account the teacher's bias. Another argument comes into play: if the teacher models neutrality, he is likely to have student neutrality as an outcome. If, on the other hand, the teacher models a defensible partisanship, subjecting his position to the same tests of value analysis as those to which the students are accountable, then his behavior is more apt to convey precisely what he intends to teach them and what they are more likely to learn.[14]

Both lines of argument have merit; there is no single correct posture for a teacher to adopt. The defensible partisan role requires more care in development because students might be more easily confused as to the teacher's purpose. But used correctly, it is a powerful means of liberating the classroom so that each person respects others' positions and subjects their positions to a fair test. Because the teacher is subjecting himself to the same tests, and his arguments are openly evaluated according to their merits rather than to his position of authority, the atmosphere is more likely to be open and characterized by a free spirit of inquiry. But that condition obviously requires careful and skillful work on the part of the teacher.

Some situations might dictate the use of neutrality; others suggest defensible partisanship. Most important, however, is the idea that the teacher should be aware of which position he takes. A deliberate choice should be made, based on the class situation and knowledge of the probable outcomes of making that choice. Sometimes the teacher will have planned this well in advance; at other times an on-the-spot decision will have to be made to assume one posture or to change quickly from one to the other because of the pattern of student responses. In any case, the teacher should make a conscious and thoughtful choice, rather than letting this decision go by default.

Another condition of classroom climate in values discussions that can be varied by the teacher is the directness or indirectness of teacher control. We assume that one goal of all value analysis in social studies is that students should become more responsible for control of what goes on during the analysis. If this autonomy is not promoted, then students will continue to be dependent on teachers and other authority figures, rather than being able to perform value analysis on their own. Given the general goal of student autonomy, teacher indirectness of control is to be strived for. This means that, in general, students' ideas, rather than teachers', are to be used and incorporated into the discussion when there is a choice.

Students should be encouraged to make their points rather than having the teacher make them. Rephrasing of student ideas, often performed almost unconsciously by teachers, should be avoided. Student-to-student interaction should be encouraged and rewarded when it occurs; one primary means of promoting indirectness of teacher control is to let students talk to and especially *question* each other. Very often a student asks another student a question, but *through the teacher*. Student A asks the teacher if sudent B meant this or that; the teacher asks student B; and so on. To shift control to students, each has to be modified so that the teacher does not always mediate between students. A physical change in the classroom might help; the teacher might arrange the desks in a circle or other arrangement so that he is no longer at the focal point of attention.

Another means of shifting the burden of control onto the students is to insist that they be responsible for evaluating discussion by the criteria, such as relevance and consistency, outlined in the previous section. Individual students might be asked to take over the teacher's role, giving them a chance to practice application of these formal criteria. Small group discussions, with or without leaders, can also decentralize control, and they also afford opportunities for more students to become involved during a given period.[15] These suggestions assume that the elements of value inquiry are understood by the students; it will do little good to give students control of a process they do not understand or are not able to carry through.

HOW TO "HEAT UP" A DISCUSSION

How can a teacher "heat up" a discussion that is dragging? We will suggest three different actions you might take if you have that problem. They are: individualizing questions, personalizing issues, and role-playing.

One problem involving teacher questions is that they are often too general. They can be too general in the sense that the student does not have to answer from his own perspective. Rather, he can respond as if he were someone else. An example is: "Do you think it's right for some young men to object to military service on moral grounds?" The student may or may not be stimulated by this question, but if he is not, it might be because he does not have to relate *his own views* to the question. He can think about the problem in the abstract or not at all. The teacher can change this by individualizing the question. "Would *you* consider objecting to serving in the military on moral grounds?" is pointed much more clearly at the student; it gives him his own personal problem to work on, rather than someone else's. This might seem like an overly simple solution to the problem of the slow discussion, and it will not always work, of course. But it is one technique that can pick up the pace of discussions.

The second action, personalizing issues, involves linking general problems to students' perspectives, often through student-related examples and analogies. A discussion of a court case involving unreasonable search and seizure, for example, might be dragging badly. Inclusion of an analogy centered around the privacy of school lockers or desks or belongings at home, however, might be enough to demonstrate the relevance of the more general or abstract issue to student experiences. These examples or analogies are usually not difficult to think of, especially if advance planning included listing one or two for each part of the values issue to be considered.

A third means of picking up interest and quickening the pace of values inquiry is role-playing. This is particularly effective with junior high students, who probably need more frequent opportunities for physical and emotional release than do their high school counterparts. Situations involving the value issue or dilemma can be acted out, giving students more insight into the human dimensions and implications of the problem. Role-playing can be repeated by different individuals, or even by the same ones, often with different results. It is a means of engaging the talents of some students who might otherwise not be involved in the inquiry at all. In any case, role-playing affords the opportunity to generate more data and insights into the question of values, and can be used to increase the tempo of value inquiry.

HOW TO "COOL DOWN" A DISCUSSION

At times discussions have to be slowed down, not speeded up. If feelings run too high in value analysis, emotions can block rational thought and result in undesired outcomes. In an earlier discussion it was suggested that speeding up a discussion could be achieved by injecting personal feeling; just the opposite operation can slow it down. Moving to generalize questions and depersonalize examples can lower the emotional level and pace of the discussion.

Two other techniques might also be considered when highly volatile topics are approached. One is the exercise of a very high level of teacher control with students' feelings carefully checked by teacher intervention. Another is a very strong method of keeping discussion at a deliberate emotional and intellectual pace. This involves operating the discussion under a strict rule: The next person to speak must restate the previous speaker's ideas to that person's satisfaction.[16] This simple device will quickly slow down a discussion; it has other positive functions as well. The teacher takes a very indirect posture, only intervening to enforce the rule and to choose the next speaker. Students have to listen to one another very carefully in order to satisfy the rule. The common "talking right past each other" mode of irrational discourse almost automatically ceases, and less forceful speakers have an equal chance to have their ideas considered. Finally, relevance of statements is very high in such a discussion. This device should not be overused, however, because it is very time-consuming and requires considerable patience. But it can be used as a tool in the hands of a teacher who wants to vary systematically certain characteristics of discussions.

HOW TO REDIRECT A DRIFTING DISCUSSION

A constant problem is that of drifting discussions. Students and teachers may drift from one topic to another in a seemingly meaningless pattern. Irrelevant statements and data are introduced, and no one seems to know where the class is going. We believe that this condition is usually the fault of the teacher and that it can be corrected by positive and firm action on his part. Using a device like the restating rule, explained above, is one way of focusing a discussion, increasing awareness and understanding of others' points of view, and ensuring relevance of contributions.

Drifting discussions are often symptomatic of poorly thought-out topics on the teacher's part. If the teacher himself does not clearly understand the point or direction of the discussion, it is unlikely that he will provide accurate feedback to discourage irrelevant or tangential statements. He is also unlikely to provide leadership so that discussion has purpose and clear direction. This is why advance planning and thinking through value topics is crucial. The teacher who has no clear idea of the dimensions of the problem beforehand will often be faced with drift.

SENSITIVE ISSUES

In our view this problem is somewhat overplayed by teachers and school administrators. There are topics that might evoke repercussions from various elements in some school districts, and there are instances of dismissals and reprimands of teachers because they dealt with oversensitive topics, usually those involving sex or pornography, race, and direct challenges to patriotic ideals. But in the main, school persons seem overcautious in this problem area. Often a simple explanation to administrators, parents, and students is enough to defuse potential problems. One of us once had students who wanted to conduct an in-school survey of attitudes toward various facets of premarital sex; an explanation to the principal and a brief, direct note to parents at the beginning resulted in no problems with the class work. Adults often express concern over poisoning or damaging impressionable young minds by dealing with highly controversial and sensitive topics, but the maturity and range of knowledge in adolescents today tends to be underestimated by these critics.

INHUMANE STATEMENTS

Perhaps one of the stickiest problems in value analysis is that some students will take a moral position that is completely outside the bounds of what the teacher considers human. "Well, if I caught that kid stealing my hubcaps and wheels, I would just pick up his lug wrench and kill him—I would beat him to death." A statement very much like this one was heard by one of us from a very serious youth in a senior high classroom discussion of law and the role of the police. What does the teacher do with that idea? What if, in a discussion on schoolwork, students insist it is all right to cheat and steal from others' lockers because many in society do the same kinds of things? Some argue that morals are completely relative and that it is wrong to change another person's serious beliefs. On the other hand, it is difficult to rationalize not trying to get the first boy, who would kill over a relatively trivial incident, to view the problem in a different perspective and perhaps from a different moral position.

We believe that simple moralizing as a response to a morally unacceptable position of a student is unlikely to be successful. That amounts to a contest of will: "You're wrong. It's wrong to kill except in self-defence." With persons who strongly believe in their positions, such a frontal attack of moralizing is inappropriate. Rather, a less direct tactic seems in order. Analogies may be helpful: "Let's say *you* are the one stealing the hubcaps; if the owner comes along, would you expect him to kill you?" or "Let's say a policeman, and not the owner, finds you stealing the hubcaps—would you expect him to kill you?" or "What if the kid is stealing your hubcaps and someone else, a policeman or somebody, catches the kid in the act; would you hope that they'd kill him for you?" From the answers he gives to these analogies, the student is likely to expose inconsistencies or lack of previous thought which can in turn be converted into a reexamination of his values position.

There is no simple solution to this tricky problem. But we believe the teacher is responsible for taking positive and thoughtful steps so that the student will be confronted by the moral dilemmas that his position implies. Social studies classrooms are places in which students (and teachers) should be able to reexamine and perhaps change ungrounded beliefs and values. Otherwise what goes on in those classrooms seems to be little value.

Summary

Values are standards used to judge or rate objects. They are important to all people for the function they perform as tools in perceiving the social world. Personal well-being and fulfillment stem from well-developed and integrated value systems.

Four views of the place of value analysis in social studies classrooms include: inculcation of core values, development of emotions and the self, encouragement of social action and its practice, and the view of value analysis expressed in this book. Although none of the first three views is rejected completely, our view of social studies in secondary education places particular emphasis on cognitive, rational development.

Eight elements or goals of value analysis include:

1. Stimulating thought about value issues
2. Identifying and clarifying central value issues
3. Identifying and defining key concepts
4. Relating specific issues to general values
5. Testing the consequences of a position on an issue
6. Testing for complete information and multiple points of view
7. Testing for relevance of data and arguments
8. Testing for logic and consistency in arguments.

Also, specific tests to challenge the value conclusions of students are the role-reversal test, the universal consequences test, and the use of analogies. Other problems in the classroom related to value analysis include the teacher's position on value issues, stimulating slow discussion, slowing down overheated discussion, redirecting a drift in discussion, and controlling over-sensitive and controversial issues.

Notes

1. For a provocative statement on the topics of importance and defensibility of value judgments, see David J. Bond, "The Fact Value Myth," *Social Education*, vol. 34, no. 2 (February, 1970), pp. 186–190.
2. Space precludes a comprehensive description of all value-oriented social studies materials. The Appendix refers to the Social Science Education Consortium *Data Book*, which is an excellent place to look for such materials. The November, 1972, issue of *Social Education* contains a thorough description of many materials. Especially aimed at value analysis are the following materials:

    U.C.L.A. Committee on Civic Education:
    Your Rights and Responsibilities as an American Citizen
    Conflict, Politics, and Freedom
    Voices for Justice
    All are published by Ginn and Company, Lexington, Mass., 1967–68.

    Carnegie-Mellon University Slow Learner Project:
    The Americans: A History of the United States
    Living in Urban America
    Both published by Holt, Rinehart, and Winston, New York, 1970.

    Harvard University Social Studies Project:
    Public Issues Series (28 booklets on controversial topics)
    Published by American Education Publications, Columbus, Ohio, 1967–70.

Law in America Society Foundation:
Justice in Urban America (6 booklets on urban legal topics)
Published by Houghton Mifflin Company, Boston, 1970.
Utah State University Social Studies Project:
Analysis of Public Issues (32 packages of materials)
Decision-Making in a Democracy
Both published by Houghton Mifflin Company, Boston, 1973.

3. Byron G. Massialas, *Structure and Process of Inquiry into Social Issues in Secondary Schools*, vol. 1, *Inquiry into Social Issues*, Ann Arbor: University of Michigan, 1970, p. 74. Harmon Ziegler, *The Political World of the High School Teacher*, Eugene, Ore.: Center for Advanced Study of Educational Administration, University of Oregon, 1966, pp. 130–131.

4. For a compelling rationale and instructional approach for this position of inculcating only a few prime values, see Donald W. Oliver and James P. Shaver, *Teaching Public Issues in the High School*, Boston: Houghton Mifflin, 1966.

5. One of the most appealing presentations of the position of affective education for social studies is found in Louis A. Raths, Merrill Harmin, and Sidney B. Simon, *Values and Teaching*, Columbus, Ohio: Charles B. Merrill, 1966.

6. Fred M. Newmann with David W. Oliver, *Clarifying Public Controversy: An Approach to Teaching Social Studies*, Boston: Little, Brown, 1970. See especially Chapter 11, "Education and Community," pp. 313–345.

7. Lee H. Ehman, "Normative Discourse and Attitude Change in the Social Studies Classroom," *High School Journal,* vol. 54, no. 2 (November, 1970), pp. 76–83.

8. M. Kent Jennings, Lee H. Ehman, and Richard G. Niemi, "Social Studies Teachers and Their Pupils," in *Families, Schools, and Political Learning,* ed. by M. Kent Jennings and Richard G. Niemi, Princeton, N.J.: Princeton University Press, forthcoming, 1974.

9. Oliver and Shaver, op. cit., pp. 262–285 (note 4).

10. M. Blatt and L. Kohlberg, "Effects of Classroom Discussion upon Children's Level of Moral Judgment," in *Recent Research in Moral Development*, ed. by Kohlberg and Turiel, New York: Holt, Rinehart and Winston, 1972.

11. Lawrence Kohlberg, "Moral Development," in *International Encyclopedia of the Social Sciences*, New York: Macmillan, 1968.

12. June L. Tapp and Lawrence Kohlberg, "Developing Senses of Law and Legal Justice," *Journal of Social Issues*, vol. 27, no. 2, 1971, pp. 65–91.

13. This discussion on challenging students' positions on values is partly based on Jerrold R. Coombs and Milton Meux, "Teaching Strategies for

Value Analysis," in *Values Education: Rationale, Strategies, and Procedures*, ed. by Lawrence E. Metcalf, National Council for the Social Studies, 41st Yearbook, Washington, D.C., 1971, pp. 54–61.

14. Byron G. Massialas and C. Benjamin Cox, *Inquiry in Social Studies*, New York: McGraw-Hill, 1966, pp. 174–177.

15. There are a number of specific suggestions for the discussion of strategies in value analysis in Fred M. Newmann, op. cit.

16. This idea of slowing down and cooling off a discussion is demonstrated in a film entitled "Experiment in Understanding," featuring Neil Postman, part of a television film series, *Communication Now*, Los Angeles: County of Los Angeles Schools, 1968.

Suggested Reading

Lawrence E. Metcalf, ed. *Values Education: Rationale, Strategies, and Procedures.* Washington, D.C.: National Council for the Social Studies, 41st Yearbook, 1971. This is a short, practical book with a solid, thoughtful foundation. Each of four chapters outlines useful ideas which can be applied directly to the classroom. Beginning with a simple value analysis model, several classroom strategies are developed. The philosophy of this work is close to that of the present volume.

Fred M. Newmann, with Donald W. Oliver. *Clarifying Public Controversy: An Approach to Teaching Social Studies.* Boston: Little, Brown, 1970. This exciting book presents a well-grounded case for secondary social studies curricula based on the analysis of public controversy. At its foundation are the two core values of rational consent and individual freedom. It is built around the use of the texts of the Harvard University Social Studies Project's *Public Issues Series,* mentioned in the chapter. Many practical, powerful ideas, which a teacher can use immediately, are contained in the several chapters. In addition to the basic value analysis teaching model, from which the present volume draws extensively, there are separate chapters on how to deal with several substantive values, such as morality-responsibility, equality, welfare-security, and property. Ideas for conducting discussions and evaluating value analysis outcomes are very helpful.

Sidney B. Simon, Leland W. Howe, and Howard Kirschenbaum. *Values Clarification: A Handbook of Practical Strategies for Teachers and Students.* New York: Hart, 1972. This book presents a brief rationale for clarifying mainly personal, rather than public, value problems. The rationale is followed by seventy-nine specific classroom procedures which can be employed in personal value clarification. Because of its emphasis on personal values, its philosophy differs significantly from that of this book. It presents a clearly alternative view of the valuing process in social studies. It is much less heavily rational and cognitive and is more affective-oriented than this book. Many of its procedures can be used, however, to attain goals or subgoals suggested in this chapter; see especially strategies 8, 9, 23, 24, 26, 40, 45, 48, and 50.

John Wilson. *Language and the Pursuit of Truth*. London: Cambridge University Press, 1960. Wilson explains the semantic underpinnings of this and other chapters in a style readable by high school students and by teachers as well. This short book is a must for social studies teachers.

EFFECTIVE INSTRUCTION REQUIRES careful sequencing or integrating of instructional events for these reasons: learning some things is prerequisite to learning others, and motivating and facilitating student learning requires that certain types of lessons precede others. Students must learn certain lower-level cognitions before attempting certain higher-level learnings. For example, students need to learn the concepts socialization, varies, and social class before being able to work with this hypothesis: socialization varies with social class. Before using data in contingency tables to confirm or disconfirm this hypothesis, students must have learned how to read the tables. The need to motivate and facilitate learning requires that certain types of lessons precede others. For example, lessons that provoke speculation, generate questions or trigger formulation of conflicting hypotheses about a controversial subject are motivators to subsequent study and should be used to initiate a set of lessons.

An instructional strategy is a scheme for sequencing lessons that integrates instructional objectives, modes, and techniques. Following is a discussion of an instructional strategy that fits a competency-based approach to instruction about social reality. However, the strategy discussed is only one of several appropriate ways that might be used to integrate social studies instruction.[1]

Categories of Instructional Strategy

The instructional strategy shown in Figure 8.1 has four categories: confrontation, development of knowledge and intellectual skills, analysis of values, and application for assessing achievement.

Confrontation initiates a set of lessons by focusing attention on the instructional objectives, raising questions, and prompting speculative answers to the questions. These initiating lessons are also supposed to motivate students, to arouse curiosity and attract their attention, and to provoke them to subsequent study to check their speculative answers against available evidence.

The discovery mode of instruction is appropriate to confrontation lessons. Examples of instructional techniques that can be used during the confrontation category are educational games that raise questions and hypotheses, in-class opinion surveys that provoke questions and speculations about public opinion and behavior, open-ended case studies that raise provocative questions or present conflicting viewpoints, and primary source materials that serve as grist for hypothesis formulation about past events. Examples of instruction presented in this book that could function as good confrontation lessons are: (1) the Site Map Lesson (page 129), (2) the Voting Behavior Lesson on hypothesis formulation (page 143), (3) the lesson about status and

FIGURE 8.1.
An instructional strategy.

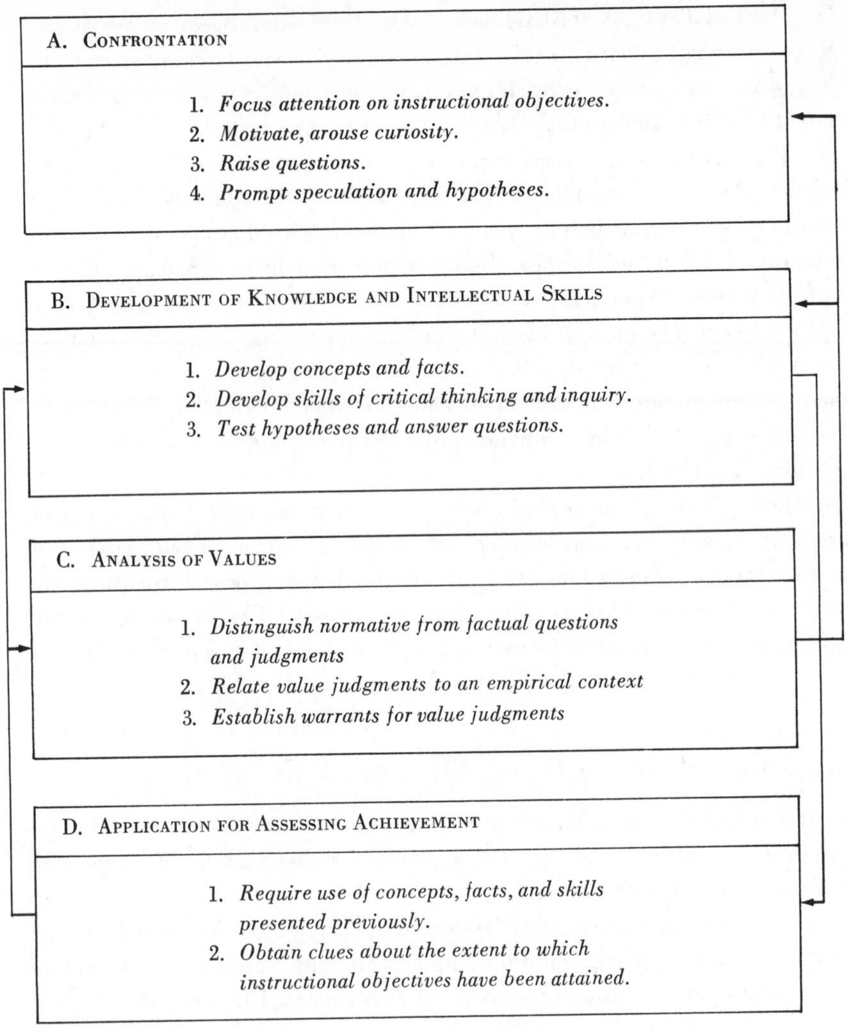

A. CONFRONTATION

1. *Focus attention on instructional objectives.*
2. *Motivate, arouse curiosity.*
3. *Raise questions.*
4. *Prompt speculation and hypotheses.*

B. DEVELOPMENT OF KNOWLEDGE AND INTELLECTUAL SKILLS

1. *Develop concepts and facts.*
2. *Develop skills of critical thinking and inquiry.*
3. *Test hypotheses and answer questions.*

C. ANALYSIS OF VALUES

1. *Distinguish normative from factual questions and judgments*
2. *Relate value judgments to an empirical context*
3. *Establish warrants for value judgments*

D. APPLICATION FOR ASSESSING ACHIEVEMENT

1. *Require use of concepts, facts, and skills presented previously.*
2. *Obtain clues about the extent to which instructional objectives have been attained.*

role (page 182), the first part of the Girl Watchers Experiment (page 221), and (4) the first part of the lesson reconstructing a historical event with John White's Journal (page 236).

The teacher of a confrontation lesson is supposed to conduct open-ended discussion, to provoke students to respond to stimuli presented in the lesson, and to provide cues to sustain discussion. The teacher is to refrain from judging student responses because the point of this type of lesson is to generate speculation, to raise questions, and to provoke inquiry. Thus, the teacher is primarily a discussion manager, rather than a giver of answers or a judger of student responses.

Lessons that systematically help students to master relevant facts, concepts, and skills should follow the confrontation category in a well-designed instructional sequence. The purpose of these lessons is to provide for recall and reinforcement of relevant prior learning and for appropriate practice toward achieving cognitive instructional objectives. Students are provided with opportunities for the *development of knowledge and intellectual skills* needed to test hypotheses and answer questions raised during the confrontation category of instruction. For example, answering a question raised by a confrontation lesson might depend on mastery of the concept of social change. If this is so, then the category of the development of knowledge and intellectual skills should be used to present rule-example lessons designed to teach the concept social change. Or, for another example, answering a question raised by a confrontation lesson might require mastery of skills needed to interpret certain types of statistical tables and graphs. If this is the case, students should then experience instruction designed to teach skills in reading tables and graphs. Finally, testing hypotheses and answering questions generated by confrontation lessons require systematic examination of evidence, which should be an integral feature of the lessons of category B of the instructional strategy.

The expository mode of instruction is usually most appropriate to the development of knowledge and intellectual skills. Following are three examples of instructional techniques appropriate to such development. First, programmed instruction lessons can be designed to teach specific skills such as table reading, map reading, and graph reading. Second, written exposition, enriched with examples and exercises that require active learning, can be used to introduce and develop concepts, facts, and skills. Third, lectures by the teacher or audio-visual demonstrations can be employed to present information systematically or to develop concepts, facts, and skills. Examples of lessons presented in this book that are designed to facilitate student mastery of concepts, facts, and skills systematically are: (1) the expositional lesson about patterns of participation in public elections (pages 142 to 148), (2) the rule-example lesson designed to help students acquire the concept of political alienation (pages 177 to 180), (3) the case study of the Bushman way of life (pages 231 to 232), and (4) the latter parts of the Girl Watchers Experiment (pages 224 to 225).

The teacher's role in the category of the development of knowledge and skill is to assist students in the mastery of particular skills, ideas, and information. The teacher is expected to help them make judgments about the quality of their responses to questions and exercises. The outcome of these lessons should be the mastery of skills, concepts, and facts relevant to the answering of questions or to the testing of hypotheses formulated during the preceding confrontation lesson. While doing a set of these lessons, students should have the chance to answer questions, either conclusively or tentatively, and to test hypotheses.

Analysis of values, category C of the instructional strategy, provides students with opportunities to distinguish normative from factual questions and judgments and to analyze warrants for value judgments. This category of instruction requires them to relate particular descriptions and explanations to value judgments. Through these lessons, students have the opportunity to relate their studies of what is and what has been to consideration of questions about what ought to be.

Lessons using the discovery mode are usually most appropriate to the analysis of values because these lessons require divergent thinking in response to open-ended questions. Examples of techniques that fit this category of instruction are open-ended case studies about highly controversial public issues, debates about public issues, and in-class opinion surveys which generate opposing value judgments which students can be required to analyze. Examples of lessons that fit the category of the analysis of values were presented in Chapter 7.

The role of the teacher is to conduct open-ended discussions, to provoke student responses, and to influence students to engage in rational consideration of value claims. Rational consideration of value claims means assessing the consequences of particular value judgments and determining the consistency between preferred means and valued ends.

As shown in Figure 8.1, lessons requiring students to demonstrate the mastery of learning through application follow the lessons of category B, development of knowledge and intellectual skills, and those of category C, analysis of values. The purpose of the lessons of category D, *application for assessing achievement,* is to require the use of concepts, facts, and skills presented previously to obtain clues about the extent to which learning has occurred. If students show that they can apply concepts, facts, and skills developed in one context to the solution of a fresh, related problem or exercise, then they provide evidence of the achievement of instructional objectives.

Among the kinds of lessons that would fit the application category are case studies for analysis, classification exercises, problems of data processing and interpreting, and educational games. Examples of application lessons for high school students presented in this book are: (1) the three educational games described in this chapter, and (2) the classification exercise about political alienation presented in Chapter 5.

The teacher's role during the application stage of instruction is to help students assess the extent of their learning and to determine whether or not they have attained particular instructional objectives. Teachers should give special attention to those who cannot demonstrate mastery. Students who demonstrate mastery of application lessons provide evidence of particular capabilities. If these capabilities were not realized prior to instruction, then one can assume that mastery of application lessons demonstrates learning. Inability to master application lessons indicates deficiency in terms of particular instructional objectives. Careful appraisal of inadequate student performance may provide clues about student incapacity that can be overcome through remedial instruction.

Although the four categories of the instructional strategy are depicted in block fashion in Figure 8.1, there can be dynamic interplay between the categories as they are used to design and implement lessons. The arrows in the illustration suggest possibilities for flexible, dynamic relationships between categories of instruction. For example, application for assessing achievement can occur not only at the end of a set of lessons, as suggested by the arrangement of the categories, but also within other categories, as shown by the arrows. Also, as indicated by the arrows, analysis of values is applicable to each of the previous categories of the instructional strategy. Sometimes students may move back and forth between two categories before moving ahead.

Instructional Variety

Instructional variety, the use of various kinds of techniques, modes, and materials, is a central feature of the instructional strategy. The use of variety in planning and implementing lessons is based on these assumptions:

1. No one instructional mode or technique should be used exclusively in social studies instruction. The teacher who only lectures or who only conducts class discussions is undoubtedly much less effective than the teacher who uses various techniques.[2]

2. Instructional modes and techniques should be varied in terms of instructional objectives. Some objectives are most efficiently or effectively achieved through educational games. Other objectives can be achieved best through class discussion. The successful teacher carefully considers the fit between instructional objectives and instructional techniques.[3]

3. Variation in instructional modes and techniques contributes to student motivation and interest in learning.[4] Students who are asked *only* to discuss or to complete programmed exercises or to play educational games are likely to become bored. By contrast, those who experience an artful blend of different types of lessons are more likely to be motivated and interested.

Following is a discussion of when and how to use four common types of instructional techniques in terms of the instructional strategy discussed previously. The techniques are lectures, class discussions, educational games, and textbooks.

LECTURES

A lecture is any oral presentation of information, whether it is lengthy and formal or brief and light.[5] The primary purpose of any lecture should be to present information and ideas pointedly and efficiently. The printed page can serve a similar purpose and in many cases is more efficient than the lecture. However, whenever it is important to communicate feeling, a lecture may be the most appropriate instructional technique.

The lecture is an example of expository instruction. Some educational reformers are quick to deride lectures in the same way that they oppose other forms of expository instruction. They have labeled the lecture an ineffective and inappropriate teaching technique for precollege students. In particular, they claim that a lecture cannot hold the attention of young people, that it is an authoritarian instructional technique, and that it contributes to rote learning—to thoughtless repeating by students of the lecturer's words. However, *lectures, as well as other forms of expository instruction, must be judged good or bad in terms of the instructional objectives they are employed to achieve.* It is inappropriate to label the lecture unsatisfactory merely on ideological grounds or because it has been fashionable in some educational circles to dismiss it as a traditionalist or authoritarian technique.

Lectures can be used effectively for certain purposes during each of the categories of the instructional strategy. One obvious example of the pervasive use of the lecture is to give directions for classroom activities. For example, you can tell students the rules for conducting a classroom debate, or you might orally present instructions for playing a game.

Another potentially effective use of the lecture is to introduce a topic or problem during the confrontation category of instruction in order to set the stage for subsequent study, to provoke inquiry, or to do both. Background information about a topic or question might be vividly and interestingly presented in the lecture. And questions to guide subsequent study might be raised provocatively, with rich illustrations and feelings, through a well-done classroom lecture.

A third use of the lecture is to summarize, to link topics, problems, or ideas, or to do both. For example, you might highlight, to promote retention, the main conclusions that have been established through previous lessons. Or you might indicate how a previous set of lessons is connected logically to a set of lessons that the students will study.

Lecturers should plan their presentations carefully to preclude rambling, disorganized talks. Students should have a clear sense of direction and purpose while listening to lectures. Whenever possible, the overhead projector should be used to help present remarks systematically and to maintain student attention. For example, main ideas of a lecture can be written on transparencies and projected during important points in a lecture. Data can be arranged in tabular or graphic form and shown via transparencies and the overhead projector. Maps and simple line drawings which help you to illustrate ideas also can be put on transparencies and shown via the overhead projector.

Long lectures should not be used daily in the classroom. They would bore students and be inefficient and ineffective instruction. However, the lecture, used sparingly and pointedly, is appropriate to the achievement of certain instructional objectives. Teachers should remember that the lecture per se is neither good nor bad. Rather, questions about when and how to use this instructional technique must be answered in terms of purpose. The lecture is the right instructional technique whenever you can demonstrate that it fits your instructional objectives and helps students to achieve them efficiently.

CLASS DISCUSSIONS

Class discussion is an instructional technique that can be used to advantage during each category of the instructional strategy. The class discussion is, however, more suited to the achievement of certain instructional objectives than to others. For example, discussions that are highly directed and structured in terms of particular exercises, questions, and outcomes can be used to advantage during the category of the development of knowledge and skills. Relatively open-ended discussions are most suited to the categories of confrontation and analysis of values.

The class discussion is most appropriate to the achievement of instructional objectives that concern divergent thinking. Controversial factual questions and problems, for which there are no clear-cut right answers, are probably best presented through the class discussion. For example, you might present the controversy among scholars about the impact of the mass media on political attitudes, beliefs, and behavior. Some scholars and commentators contend that the impact of the media, particularly television, can be very extensive under certain conditions. Others minimize the effect of the media on attitude development and behavior. They tend to emphasize the influence of affiliations and identifications with a social group as the main shapers of beliefs and behaviors. Through a pointed and lively discussion an issue such as this can be presented to students who can spark each other's thinking as a prelude to substantial investigation of pertinent data.

Normative questions and problems, those that require value judgments as answers, are most suitably introduced and developed through classroom discussion. For example, questions about public policy and public issues, such as busing as a means to achieve racial balance in public schools, are appropriate subjects for classroom discussion. (See Chapter 7 for an elaborate presentation of value analysis through classroom discussion.)

It is appropriate to use class discussion both in the initiating and culminating stages of the study of controversial factual and normative questions. This technique provides opportunities for students to stimulate one another and to generate the widest array of reasonable alternative responses to questions that cannot at present be answered exactly or definitively.

David P. Ausubel describes very well when and why to use discussion to facilitate effective divergent thinking:

Discussion is the most effective and really the only feasible method of promoting intellectual growth with respect to the less established and more controversial aspects of subject matter. It provides the best means of broadening the pupil's intellectual horizons, of stimulating his thinking through cross-fertilization, of clarifying his views, and of measuring their cogency against the viewpoints of others. Interaction with peers, furthermore, helps the pupil overcome both his egocentricity and his childhood perception of adults as the absolute source of truth and wisdom with regard to all value judgments. He learns the extent to which both his ideas and those of the teacher represent idiosyncratic positions along a broad spectrum of opinion whose validity is indeterminable.[6]

Relatively open-ended class discussions are necessary to promote divergent thinking, the type of response appropriate to the study of controversial factual and normative questions. The teacher should create a nonthreatening, open classroom atmosphere in which students feel free to speak their opinions and in which the answers of both students and teacher are judged according to scientific and logical standards known and accepted by everyone in the group.

Arranging the students' seats in a circular or semicircular pattern can facilitate communication in class discussions. When students are seated in straight rows, they have more difficulty seeing and hearing one another than they do when seated in a circular pattern. By sitting among students in a circular arrangement, the teacher can help to create the open atmosphere so necessary to fruitful class discussions. Seated among students in the discussion circle, the teacher is saying symbolically "For discussion purposes, I am one of you, and I am subject to the same rules for discussion and confirmation of answers that apply to you." This posture does much to ease student anxiety and to promote free-flowing communication.

The class discussion is an appropriate vehicle for teaching valuable human interaction skills and concomitant attitudes pertaining to bargaining, cooperation, task leadership, respecting the rights and opinions of others, and observing common rules and procedures. Through class discussions about controversial topics, a student can learn to give and take, to respect reasonable alternatives, to tolerate diversity of opinions when it is impossible to establish a "best" answer, and to accept the "best" answer when scientific and logical methods demonstrate correctness, even if this answer conflicts with his viewpoint.

Class discussions can be used profitably in combination with many kinds of lessons and with other instructional techniques. For example, students might profit from discussing the main ideas or questions raised in a teacher's lecture. Students can stimulate one another productively through group discussion in preparation for the formulation of hypotheses. Case study analysis can be carried out effectively through class discussion. However, the successful teacher remembers that class discussion is not *the* instructional technique; it is neither good nor bad as such. Rather, questions about when and how to use this technique must be answered in terms of purpose. The class discussion is the right instructional technique whenever you can demonstrate that it suits your objectives and helps students to achieve them efficiently. (See pages 283 to 290 in Chapter 7 and pages 384 to 399 in Chapter 11 for additional treatment of the class discussion as an instructional technique.)

EDUCATIONAL GAMES

Educational games are a recent addition to the array of instructional techniques available to the social studies teacher. An educational game "is an activity among two or more independent *decision-makers* seeking to achieve their *objectives* in some *limiting context.*"[7]

Educational games in the social studies usually simulate, or at least approximate, real-life situations for the purpose of helping students more fully to understand human behavior. Thus, these games focus on human interaction within a social structure, that is, a system of rules that constrain human behavior. Within a social structure participants are faced with choices pertaining to various objectives. The games require them to make decisions that may or may not help them to win or to achieve their objectives.

Games in the social studies often stress cooperation, bargaining, and compromise—the key features of human interactions in societies. These games usually do not require one-against-one competition. As in real life, winning is often relative and social; some groups may win more than others. And it is necessary in some social studies games, as in real life, for all the players to cooperate to attain some common goal. Everyone either wins, more or less, or everyone loses, absolutely.

Educational games can effectively serve the purposes of each of the four categories of our instructional strategy. Games can be used during the confrontation category to raise questions and to generate hypotheses. They are applicable to the category of the development of the understanding of concepts and the testing of hypotheses. Games are especially valuable during the application category of instruction as indicators of transfer learning. Students who can transfer concepts, facts, and skills learned in one context to a fresh context, the gaming situation, indicate mastery learning. Finally, educational games may require students to make value judgments and to act in terms of their values. Thus, they can be used to teach value judgment and value analysis.

The two main types of educational games are board games and role-play games. Board games in the social studies graphically represent some social process through a game board and other game equipment which might include cards, dice, numbered spinners, and score sheets.

Role-play games require participants to assume realistic social roles and to interact with one another in terms of a common social situation. Role-play games are designed to teach the dynamics of human behavior in response to particular social problem situations. Thus, these games require participants to negotiate, bargain, compromise, and make decisions.

Role-play games usually consist of these materials:

1. Role cards, or profiles, which describe the role behavior to be performed during the game
2. A scenario, or case study, which describes the social situation in terms of which the roles are to be performed
3. Rules which specify the conditions under which the game is to be played and which indicate how winning and losing are to be determined.

Ninth Justice is an example of a board game designed to teach students about the judicial process at the Supreme Court level.[8] Three major aspects of the process are highlighted in the game: recruitment of a ninth justice through presidential recommendation and Senate ratification, decision-making on major cases presented to the Court, and the impact of Court decisions on society. Students are asked to answer a series of questions about each aspect of the process. They are also asked to formulate combinations of answers that demonstrate the various ways judicial recruitment, decision-making, and impact on society are related under different political conditions. Teams answering the most questions correctly win the game. Through the questions and answers in game play, students study the judicial process and its effect on society as a whole. The president may not get his choice of a justice on the court because the Senate will not ratify his nominee. The ninth justice may not make a difference in Court decisions because the majority of the court is of an opposite opinion. Decisions may or may not have an impact or enduring effect on people in society. Through playing the game, students understand the import of each aspect of the judicial process and the effect of each aspect on the process as a whole.

City Hall is a good example of a role-play game.[9] It deals with the problem of electing a mayor of a fictional town in midwestern United States and is a reflection of a typical real-world election campaign. The purpose of the game is to demonstrate how citizens make voting decisions in choosing their elected officials. During five class periods, players participate in an election campaign between Democratic and Republican candidates. Students attend party meetings, hold bargaining sessions, go to campaign rallies, and finally vote on election day. Students play roles of voters, candidates, party or interest group leaders, newspaper reporters, and radio commentators. While playing these roles, students must make choices among party loyalties, issue positions, and candidates. While making these choices, they develop strategies for using their political resources most effectively.

Educational games require the teacher to play a relatively nondirective and nonmanaging role. In a gaming situation he should behave like a consultant, a referee, or both. He behaves in a directive fashion when introducing the game and when debriefing students in a postgame discussion session about what happened during the game. While students play, the teacher should circulate among the participants so as to be readily available as a consultant to those who need assistance in interpreting the rules or in making moves in the game. The teacher should, however, exercise appropriate restraint in order not to inhibit the participants.

The teacher should be the central figure during the postgame discussion or debriefing. During the discussion, he helps students to determine the extent to which they understand the main ideas that structure the game. The teacher should ask questions that require students to focus on the key features of the game and that help to reveal what they have learned or not learned from the game.

Educational games are used most appropriately in the social studies classroom to develop intellectual skills associated with decision-making and problem-solving, to develop understanding of social processes, and to help students to learn and to appraise their culture's norms for group interaction. These games require students to make decisions from among alternatives in order to achieve a particular objective. For example, in the role-play game City Hall, students who play the roles of voters must decide how to use their political resources in order to achieve particular political objectives. They must decide when and how to declare support for a particular mayoral candidate. The candidates and their campaign managers must decide how to conduct their campaigns in order to achieve voter support and win the election. Interest group leaders must decide how to use their political resources to achieve particular objectives. In order to make the decisions required by this game, students must apply various intellectual skills in such ways as using evidence to build reasonable political arguments, analyzing the political arguments of others, and clarifying and making value judgments.

Many educational games are designed to teach effectively the dynamics of behavior that constitutes particular social processes. For example, the board game Bottleneck is designed to teach students about the legislative process.[10] The game focuses on the problems of passing bills into law; the game board simulates the basic stages of bill passage. Students acting as senators and representatives sponsor bills for which they must build support in their constituencies, in congressional committees, on the floor of the Congress, and with the president. Students must also try to block opponents' bills by using amendments, bury-bill motions, filibusters, and vetoes to do so. Playing cards are used to simulate these various aspects of congressional activity. Throughout the game, students are shown the complexity of pressures on congressmen, the intricate politics of bargaining, and the variety of relationships that have grown up between senators and representatives, congressmen and the president, and congressmen and their constituents.

If the teacher merely wants to impart information about the legal steps by which a bill becomes a law, a textbook description or an instructional program is the appropriate instructional device to use. However, if he wants to teach the dynamics of the legislative process, the human interaction that constitutes the real-life legislative process, then it is appropriate to use a game such as Bottleneck.

Role-play games can help students to learn what are the norms for various types of human interaction in our society. Through participation in realistic situations, these games can teach them the rights and duties associated with various roles and statuses in our society. In addition, they help to impart respect for rules. Thus, educational games can buttress the socialization process which takes place in schools. Since socialization in games usually occurs in the context of adult roles, this type of instruction helps to bridge the gap between social study and social reality, which gap often plagues formal instruction about human behavior.

Educational games embody some key features of good pedagogy as suggested by psychological research and classroom practice. For example, games require active learning rather than the passive reception of information. They require participants to use information to make decisions and to solve problems—to function at higher levels of cognition. Participants in educational games receive immediate feedback about their decisions, since their intellectual moves in the game have consequences which influence the moves of other players and the outcome of the game.

Educational games have enormous value as motivators. Students report that they enjoy participating in this type of activity and that they consider games to be interesting and relevant. Used in combination with other instructional techniques, educational games appear to have great value as developers of intellectual skills, teachers of social processes, and imparters of social norms.

TEXTBOOKS

In the social studies, printed exposition, in the form of the textbook is usually the dominant instructional device.[11] The best typical textbooks in the social studies have been rich sources of key definitions and facts pertinent to an organized field of study, such as American history. Thus, these typical texts can be used during category B of our instructional strategy (Fig. 8-1) to help students acquire concepts and facts relevant to questions and hypotheses formulated during category A, confrontation. However, since the typical, traditional textbooks have not been designed in terms of an instructional strategy with different categories of instruction, they usually do not include lessons that can be easily adapted to the purpose of our categories: confrontation, application for assessing achievement, and analysis of values. And most of the typical, traditional texts provide little or no instruction about the intellectual skills necessary to the formulation and testing of hypotheses.

Many social studies teachers are required to rely on the standard, traditional textbooks. In order to provide a variety of learning experiences, which are systematically integrated by an instructional strategy, teachers must creatively adapt and supplement the standard textbooks. For example, teachers who use the instructional strategy discussed on pages 295 to 299 must design confrontation and application lessons to supplement the standard fare of the typical textbook. (See pages 312 to 316 in this chapter for an example of how to supplement the traditional text in terms of an instructional strategy.)

In contrast with the typical, traditional textbooks, a number of the newer, innovative text materials, especially those created by the national social studies curriculum projects, have been designed in terms of some kind of instructional strategy that provides for variation in teaching techniques, lessons, and types of learning. Printed materials, such as textbooks, are used in combination with other materials, such as filmstrips, transparencies, educational games, and recordings. For example, text materials designed by the High School Geography Project, the Sociological Resources for the Social Studies Project, and the Anthropology Curriculum Study Project include various types of

FIGURE 8.2.
*The textbook helps stu-
dents acquire concepts.*

lessons for the purpose of matching instructional procedures with different types of objectives or learning.[12] Text materials are the core of these programs; but various other types of materials are designed for use with them, and the various lessons and instructional materials are integrated in terms of an overall instructional strategy.

Some of the most important distinguishing qualities of these innovative text materials are described below.[13]

1. Textbook content is presented systematically in terms of basic concepts and generalizations.

2. Lessons are presented systematically in terms of a viable concept of instruction, such as some type of competency-based approach to instruction or some other concept of how to teach effectively.

3. Higher-level learning is stressed. For example, students have ample opportunity to organize and interpret data in terms of useful conceptual frameworks, to formulate and test hypotheses, and to make and analyze value judgments.

4. Active learning is stressed. For example, students are continually required to use concepts, facts, and skills and to think as deeply as possible about the content of the instructional materials.

5. The content of the instructional materials is accurate and realistic. Students have the opportunity to learn the best available knowledge and ways of knowing about social reality.

6. The textbook or other printed materials are used in combination with a variety of instructional materials. The various lessons and materials are integrated in terms of an instructional strategy.

Lee J. Cronbach has provided a very apt description of the place of the innovative textbooks in classroom instruction:

The modern textbook is more and more thought of as an "assistant teacher in print" . . . [The author] sets up as clearly as possible the aims which his teaching is to accomplish.

. . . [He] does this, not on the spur of the moment, nor in any catch-as-catch can impromptu way, but thoughtfully and deliberately, with time to check and recheck, test, revise, and actually try out his materials.

. . . He assumes that [classroom teachers] will cooperate with the teacher in print, using all their teaching ingenuity to make it work for them and for their pupils.

This calls for no sacrifice of responsibility on the part of the teacher. With all they have to do, there is no reason for them to plan the organization of the course in detail. The author of the textbook can do that for them.

The author, however, can never fully . . . provide for individual differences [nor capitalize] on opportunities in a particular locality. He can only set the stage, assuming that . . . the teacher will be the director . . . and use his script sympathetically.[14]

Well-designed text materials can be a very valuable instructional tool for social studies teachers. But, as Cronbach says, the best textbooks require good teachers who can properly implement the text lessons. Good teachers can adapt text materials to fit the particular conditions of their classrooms, and they can artfully orchestrate textbook lessons with other instructional techniques and devices in terms of a viable instructional strategy.

Planning Lessons

Social studies teachers who are required to use a standard, traditional textbook must imaginatively adapt and supplement it in order to provide the rich variation in learning experiences that is necessary for good instruction. The instructional strategy discussed in the first section of this chapter is the type of framework that has guided instructional design in major curriculum-development projects. The strategy can also be used to structure lesson planning for the imaginative use of a standard, traditional textbook with ancillary materials.

Suppose that a teacher of a course in United States history for eleventh graders is required by his school system to use *The American Experience,* a competently written, typical textbook for high school history.[15] It is the latter part of the school year, and the students are studying topics in recent American history. The teacher is planning a series of lessons about social change associated with the black civil rights movement and Black Power. The required textbook contains fifteen pages of descriptive writing with graphs and pictures about the civil rights movement, Black Power, and the lifestyles of black Americans. In order to plan lessons in terms of the instructional strategy discussed in the beginning of this chapter, the teacher must adapt and supplement the textbook material.

Suppose that the teacher has in the classroom fifteen copies of each of two additional textbooks which have been used for supplementary readings throughout the year. These textbooks are *The People Make a Nation*[16] and *Discovering American History*.[17] Both books are collections of edited primary sources about various topics in American history, and both contain material about social change and black Americans.

APPLICATION 8.1: LESSON PLANS GUIDED BY AN INSTRUCTIONAL STRATEGY

Following is a series of five lesson plans that the teacher has created to teach about aspects of the experiences of black people in modern America. These lesson plans are the teacher's guide to classroom action, and they represent his expectations about what will happen in the classroom during a particular span of days. Read this series of lesson plans carefully and prepare to discuss these questions:

1. What is your appraisal of these lesson plans? Discuss the strengths and weaknesses of the plans in terms of the main ideas about learning and instruction that have been discussed in previous parts of this book.

_____

_____

_____

_____

_____

_____

_____

_____

_____

2. Would you change these lesson plans in any way? How? Why?

_____

_____

_____

_____

_____

_____

_____

The first lesson is a confrontation activity which is designed to generate speculations about social change related to the black civil rights movement and Black Power in America. The teacher needs to prepare this lesson as a supplement to the required textbook, which is not designed in terms of an instructional strategy with various types of instructional techniques and learning experiences. To implement this lesson, the teacher must prepare a packet of primary source materials for each student in the class.

Lesson Plan One: Confrontation

OBJECTIVES Students are able to speculate about answers to these questions from a packet of primary source material:

1. What were major changes in the living standards and sociopolitical opportunities of black Americans from 1950 to 1970?
2. Why did these changes occur?
3. What were the responses of various blacks and whites to these social changes?
4. How can you explain these responses?

MATERIALS A packet of brief mimeographed excerpts from primary source materials which includes: (1) brief excerpts from the Civil Rights laws of 1957, 1960, 1964, and 1968 and the Voting Rights acts of 1965 and 1970; (2) statistical tables that comparatively describe these aspects of the behavior or lifestyles of blacks and whites from 1950 to 1970: voter participation, income levels, occupations, and educational attainment; (3) brief excerpts from comments about race relations and the status and roles of blacks in American society by these blacks: Martin Luther King, Jr., Malcolm X, Shirley Chisholm, Stokely Carmichael, H. Rap Brown, Roy Wilkins, and Whitney Young, Jr.; (4) brief excerpts from commentaries about race relations and the status and roles of blacks in American society by these whites: John F. Kennedy, Lyndon B. Johnson, Richard M. Nixon, George C. Wallace, and Daniel P. Moynihan.

ACTIVITIES FOR CLASS PERIOD 1

1. Introduce the assignment and tell students they are expected to make speculative answers to the questions listed in the objective, answers to be based on the evidence in the packet of primary sources. Answer questions about the assignment.
2. Divide the class into five subgroups so that the students can work easily together to read and interpret the primary sources. Ask students to use the balance of the period to study the evidence in their packets and to prepare speculative answers to the basic questions.

HOMEWORK Tell students to complete their assignment with the packet of primary source materials before coming to class tomorrow.

ACTIVITIES FOR CLASS PERIOD 2

1. Ask students to sit together in their subgroups. Tell them to use the first ten minutes of the period to review their work with the packet of primary sources. Encourage them to discuss their work with one another if they want to.
2. Use the balance of the period to conduct a full class discussion of the three basic questions about blacks and social change. Conduct the discussion in a discovery lesson style. Encourage student interaction.

HOMEWORK Assign pages 587 to 592 and

637 to 645 in the textbook *The American Experience*. Ask students to find out the answers provided by the authors of the text to the basic questions that they have been discussing: (1) What were major changes in the living standards and socio-political opportunities of black Americans from 1950 to 1970? (2) Why did these changes occur? (3) What were the responses of various blacks and whites to these social changes? (4) How can you explain these responses?

The next two lessons in this series are for the purpose of developing knowledge relevant to the questions raised during the confrontation lesson. Students first consult their textbook to check their speculative answers against the textbook commentary. Students are next directed to two additional sources of evidence because the textbook coverage is very brief and does not present a range of explanations of the changes that are being studied.

Lesson Plan Two: Development of Knowledge

OBJECTIVES
1. From the textbook reading assignment, students are able to state these descriptive generalizations about major changes in the living standards and opportunities of black Americans during the period 1950 to 1970:
   a. The median income of black families has increased from $2,500 in 1950 to over $5,000 in 1968.
   b. The median school years completed by blacks has increased from 8.5 in 1950 to almost 12 in 1968.
   c. The percentage of blacks in high-status professional and technical occupations increased from 3 percent in 1950 to 7.4 percent in 1967.
   d. Racial segregation of public facilities was ended by federal legislation.
   e. Voter registration practices that unfairly discriminated against blacks were ended by federal legislation.
   f. There was a large decrease in the percentage of black families living in substandard housing during the 1960s.
   g. Blatant discriminatory practices in the armed forces were ended.
   h. The percentage of black public offi-cials, elected and appointed, increased markedly from 1960 to 1970.
2. From commentary in the textbook, students are able to make these explanatory generalizations about social change associated with black Americans:
   a. Black Americans achieved an end to many racially discriminatory practices through a combination of tactics which depended on organized group action, such as public protests, negotiation and bargaining by interest group leaders, and legal action in the courts and legislatures.
   b. Lower-status white groups in cities tended to resist the progress of blacks because both groups competed for the same limited opportunities.
   c. Many blacks were dissatisfied with their status and roles in American life despite obvious gains because relative to most whites, most blacks remained in an inferior position in regard to living standards and social opportunities.
3. Students are able to recognize the in-

complete commentary of the authors of the textbook by citing at least these limitations:

a. Opposition to black progress on the part of whites other than by lower-status urban dwellers is not mentioned.

b. Explanation of black progress is rather shallow and brief.

MATERIALS Pages 587 to 592 and 637 to 645 of the textbook.

ACTIVITIES

1. Conduct class discussion about the answers to the basic questions that can be found in the text. (Use the entire period.)

2. Pointedly manage the class discussions in terms of the basic questions about social change and black Americans.

3. Judge the quality of the student answers in terms of the knowledge objectives for this lesson.

4. Stress the limitations of the textbook commentary to set the stage for the next assignment.

The next assignment is aimed at developing further knowledge about social change and black Americans by requiring students to look at the two additional textbooks, which are available to the class as supplementary readers. These books are collections of primary source materials.

Lesson Plan Three: Development of Further Knowledge

OBJECTIVES

1. Students are able to state at least four descriptive generalizations (which were not stated in the previous lesson) about major social changes in the living standards and opportunities of black Americans during the period 1950 to 1970.

2. Students are able to support their descriptive generalizations with evidence.

3. Students are able to make at least two explanatory statements about social change associated with black Americans that were not stated in the previous lesson.

4. Students are able to support their explanations with evidence.

MATERIALS The supplementary readers: (1) *The People Make a Nation*, pages 612 to 659; (2) *Discovering American History*, pages 727 to 742.

ACTIVITIES FOR CLASS PERIODS 1 AND 2 Discuss with students their need to consult additional sources to obtain more information about the basic questions. Tell students that they will work with the classroom sets of the two supplementary textbooks that they have been using this year. Inform students that they can use the balance of this first period and the next class period to find evidence for additional descriptive and explanatory generalizations about social change and black Americans during the period from 1950 to 1970.

ACTIVITIES FOR CLASS PERIOD 3 Conduct class discussion about the basic questions in terms of the students' examination of the supplementary texts.

The next lesson requires students to make and analyze value judgments. Since this type of lesson is not included in the standard textbook, the teacher needs to create a lesson to fit the category of analysis of values.

Lesson Plan Four: Analysis of Values

OBJECTIVES

1. Students are able to identify conflicting value judgments of black leaders about how best to achieve equality of opportunity and overall progress for black Americans.
2. Students are able to identify at least one value judgment about black Americans and their aspirations that is presented by the textbook authors.
3. Students are able to appraise value judgments that they identify in the text.
4. Students are able to make warranted value judgments about the efforts of black people to achieve social change.

MATERIALS pages 587 to 592 and 637 to 645 of the textbook.

ACTIVITIES

1. Begin the class discussion by asking students to identify, in the reading assignment, conflicting value judgments of black leaders about how best to achieve their objectives. Students should note the differences in the views of Malcolm X and Martin Luther King, Jr., which are highlighted in the text.
2. Ask students to identify at least one value judgment about social change and black Americans that is made by the authors of the textbook. For example, on page 645 they state that in order for the United States to "survive as a peaceful, open society," blacks must be able to achieve equality. Note the authors tend to couch their value judgments in statements that appear to be factual assertions.
3. Use the remainder of the class period to allow students to state their views about the value judgments of black leaders and the textbook authors about the progress of black Americans.

HOMEWORK Require students to read a three-page, mimeographed position paper about the progress of black Americans and to evaluate this paper in terms of the knowledge they have acquired in the previous lessons of this series.

The final lesson in this series is an application lesson, which requires students to use knowledge acquired in previous lessons to criticize a position paper. The teacher created the position paper especially for this lesson. Thus, he included some factual errors and some dubious interpretations in order to test the critical thinking abilities of the students.

Lesson Plan Five: Application

OBJECTIVES Students are able to criticize a position paper about the progress of black Americans during the period 1950 to 1970. They are able to demonstrate their critical thinking abilities and their knowledge by identifying two unwarranted interpretations in the paper and seven factual errors.

MATERIALS A mimeographed position paper titled "The Progress of Black Americans: 1950 to 1970."

ACTIVITIES Conduct class discussion about the position paper. Require students to identify the unwarranted interpretations and factual errors that appear in the paper.

The preceding lesson plans are the teacher's expectation about what will happen in the classroom. They are guides to the teacher's behavior during particular class periods and serve as a record of his performance which can be consulted when preparing lesson plans in the future. Although the lesson plans are lean and general, they provide sufficient help to the teacher who is secure in his ability to teach about the subject matter. Teachers who lack knowledge about this subject would probably feel the need to write much more elaborate notes about answers to the planned discussion questions.

The format of the teacher's lesson plans appears to be quite adequate in that they contain these four essential components:

1. A precisely stated instructional objective or objectives. (See Chapter 3 for an elaborate discussion of objectives.)
2. A brief description of instructional materials. For example, are students to read an instructional program or are they to play an educational game?
3. A description of classroom activities with an estimate of the time to be devoted to each activity. For example, are students to hear a lecture or to participate in a class discussion? If they are to participate in a class discussion, what questions will be asked to guide the discussion?
4. A description of the homework assignment, if any.

The substance of the lesson plans include more strong than weak features in terms of the main ideas about learning and instruction presented in the textbook. However, the substance of the lesson plans might be open to several criticisms. What is your evaluation of this series of lessons?

Summary

Effective teaching requires an instructional strategy, that is, a scheme for sequencing lessons that integrates instructional objectives, modes, and techniques. The instructional strategy presented in this chapter consists of these categories: (A) confrontation, (B) development of knowledge and intellectual skills, (C) analysis of values, and (D) application for assessing achievement. Figure 8.1 (page 296) illustrates the purposes of these categories and shows how the categories mesh to provide a well-integrated approach to instruction.

Instructional variety—the use of various kinds of techniques, modes, and materials—is a central feature of our instructional strategy. The use of instructional variety is based on these assumptions: 1) There is no one instructional mode or technique that should be used exclusively in social studies instruction. 2) Instructional modes and techniques should be varied in terms of instructional objectives. 3) Variation in instructional modes and techniques is necessary to the motivation of students and to their interest in learning. Lectures, class discussions, educational games, and textbooks are four widely used instructional techniques that can be used effectively in terms of the four categories of instructional strategy.

When planning lessons, teachers should provide for a blend of various types of instructional techniques and materials that are integrated in terms of the instructional strategy. Lesson plans should reflect the teacher's ideas about what and how to teach and about what will happen in the classroom during a particular time. These plans should include the objectives of instruction and the materials and techniques to be employed to achieve them.

When planning lessons, teachers should remember that: (1) learning some things is prerequisite to learning others, (2) motivating and facilitating learning require that certain types of lessons precede others, (3) instructional modes and techniques should be varied in terms of instructional objectives, and (4) various objectives, modes, and techniques should be integrated by a viable instructional strategy.

APPLICATION 8.2: INSTRUCTIONAL OBJECTIVES AND HOW
TO ACHIEVE THEM

1. Following are four instructional objectives. Indicate what teaching techniques you might use to achieve each objective.
   a. Students are able to read bar graphs and line graphs.

   _____

   _____

   b. Students are able to identify the concepts of gross national product and national income.

   _____

   _____

   c. Students are able to play the roles of public policy makers and interest group leaders.

d. Students are able to make rational value judgments about a current public issue.

2. Construct a set of lesson plans for one week of social studies instruction that could take place in your classroom. Write a brief rationale for the set of plans that justifies your selection of objectives, your selection of instructional techniques, and your design for sequencing the lessons.

Notes

1. This instructional strategy is adapted from the strategy used in Howard D. Mehlinger and John J. Patrick, *American Political Behavior*, Lexington, Mass.: Ginn, 1972. See their *Teacher's Guide for American Political Behavior*, Lexington, Mass.: Ginn, 1972, pp. 4–6. For discussion of alternative approaches to sequencing instruction, see Doris A. Trojcak, "Developing a Competency for Sequencing Instruction," in *Developing Teacher Competencies*, ed. by James E. Weigand, Englewood Cliffs, N.J.: Prentice-Hall, 1971, pp. 131–165.
2. Ivor K. Davies, *The Management of Learning*, New York: McGraw-Hill, 1971, pp. 160–162.
3. Ibid.
4. Ibid.
5. W. James Popham and Eva J. Baker, *Systematic Instruction*, Englewood Cliffs, N.J.: Prentice-Hall, 1970, p. 92.
6. David P. Ausubel, *Educational Psychology: A Cognitive View*, New York: Holt, Rinehart and Winston, 1963, pp. 421–422.
7. Clark C. Abt, *Serious Games*, New York: Viking, 1970, p. 6.
8. Judith Gillespie, *Ninth Justice*, Lexington, Mass.: Ginn, 1972.
9. Judith Gillespie, *City Hall*, Lexington, Mass.: Ginn, 1972.
10. Judith Gillespie, *Bottleneck*, Lexington, Mass.: Ginn, 1972.

11. Bryce B. Hudgins, *The Instructional Process*, Chicago: Rand McNally, 1971, p. 177.

12. Other instructional materials developed by national social studies curriculum projects that feature particular instructional strategies are: *The American Political Behavior* project, published by Ginn and Company, Lexington, Mass., 1972; the *From Subject to Citizen* project of the Education Development Center, published by Denoyer-Geppert, Chicago, Ill.; and *The Harvard Public Issues* project, published by American Education Publications, Middletown, Connecticut, 1967.

13. Bryce B. Hudgins, op. cit., pp. 178–186.

14. Lee J. Cronbach (ed.), *Text Materials in Modern Education*, Urbana: University of Illinois Press, 1955, p. 196.

15. Robert F. Madgic, Stanley S. Seaberg, and Robin W. Winks, *The American Experience*, Reading, Mass.: Addison-Wesley, 1971.

16. Martin W. Sandler, Edwin C. Rozwenc, and Edward C. Martin, *The People Make a Nation*, Boston: Allyn and Bacon, 1971.

17. Allan O. Kownslar and Donald B. Frizzle, *Discovering American History*, New York: Holt, Rinehart and Winston, 1970.

Suggested Reading

Davies, Ivor K. *The Management of Learning*. London: McGraw-Hill, 1971. Davies is a leading instructional theorist who advocates systematic, competency-based instructional design. In his book, he discusses the various components of instruction and how they fit together, such as objectives, strategies, and techniques of instruction. Davies presents an especially helpful analysis of the fit between instructional techniques and objectives.

Gagné, Robert M. *The Conditions of Learning*. New York: Holt, Rinehart and Winston, 1965. Gagné is a leading learning theorist who is very concerned about instructional practices in schools. In this book, written for educators, he discusses eight different types of learning which range from the lowest to the highest levels of cognition. Gagné shows how his hierarchy of types of learning can assist one to plan and implement sequences of lessons.

Hudgins, Bryce B. *The Instructional Process*. Chicago: Rand McNally, 1971. This is a very thoughtful book about instruction and learning in school. Hudgins discusses the relationships between research, instructional theories, and classroom practices. Throughout the book guidelines are presented to aid in planning and implementing lessons.

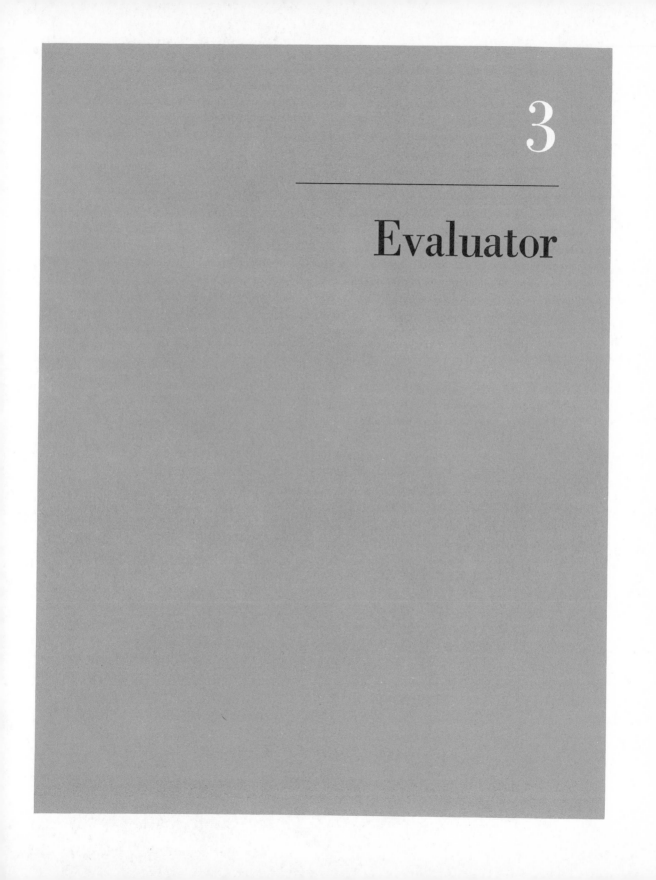

3

Evaluator

PART THREE aims two chapters at developing understandings about evaluation in social studies teaching. Compared with other books in the subject area, this allotment of space is much greater. We believe that because evaluation of students and teaching is such an important part of a teacher's profession, this extensive treatment is warranted. New concepts and knowledge in the evaluation field will help teachers to carry out successful instruction.

Just as Chapter 4 presented the foundational ideas of a mastery teaching strategy, Chapter 9 develops key evaluation ideas necessary to the implementation of mastery teaching. Chapter 10 presents testing problems and principles that are more technical and that should result in better essay and objective social studies tests.

The principal objectives of Chapters 9 and 10 are to prepare the teacher to:
1. Understand key terms and ideas that must be applied to a mastery teaching strategy
2. Understand the different functions of tests and grades and be able to apply these understandings in the analysis of "grading policies"
3. Understand and apply key principles used in constructing essay and objective tests at different levels of thinking
4. Understand some diagnostic applications of standardized tests.

I N THIS CHAPTER we will delve into what many teachers believe to be the heart of school evaluation—student learning. Did students learn what the objectives specified or not? Without answers to this question, student problems cannot be diagnosed and remedied, nor can the teacher decide whether or not to be concerned about teaching quality.

Purposes of Testing

Scene 1.   Thursday evening, the night before the first United States history test in the class of Homer Jones, social studies teacher. Homer is talking to his wife, Helen.

HOMER: *Helen, I don't know what to do about the test I'm supposed to give in class tomorrow.*

HELEN: *You mean you haven't even written up the test yet? Can I help?*

HOMER: *No, I guess not. I've just been having problems deciding what kind of a test to give and what it should cover.*

HELEN: *Why not just give a nice multiple-choice test over what they've read so far? That'll be easy to grade, and we can have more time this weekend to spend by ourselves.*

HOMER: *I thought of that during my study hall today and started to work on it. But they're kind of hard to write. It took me an hour to write only five items that I thought were good.*

HELEN: *Well, I thought the essay exams I used to take were easy. I just wrote a lot, and the teachers thought I knew more than anybody. I got good grades, you know!*

HOMER: *But that's 135 tests to grade. It'll take the whole weekend.*

HELEN: *Why not copy the fifty most important sentences from the text,* change half of them to be wrong, and use all of them as a true-false test? That's easy. Come on, I'll type while you choose them. We can grade them together tomorrow night and be done with it.

HOMER: *I don't know. Mr. Allen, the department chairman, seemed to think that was a bad way to test.*

HELEN: *Oh, he can't tell you what to do. Who does he think he is, anyhow? You've got academic freedom.*

HOMER: *You're right. The only other problem is that some of the other things I covered won't get tested that way. Oh well, maybe that will be in the semester exam . . .*

Scene 2.   Same evening, at the local teen club. Several of Homer Jones's students are gathered around a huge pizza, eating and talking.

SAM: *This sure beats studying for old Jonesey's test. Nobody could figure out what to study for anyhow, after those queer quizzes he gave.*

SHARON: *The one I remember best was when he just read a question and wouldn't even write it on the board. Nobody understood it, but he said writing it would give away the answer. Then June started crying, and he just said skip the whole thing.*

MIKE: *What gets me is that he gives the quizzes on stuff we haven't even covered in class. It's like someone's making up his tests who doesn't know what he teaches in class. His teaching is sure better than his testing.*

SUE: *I just wonder what grade I'll get in his class. He won't tell us how he's grading. Remember how he curved that one easy quiz? I got seventeen out of twenty right, and he gave me a C. Boy, that burned me.*

TOM: *What really gets me is that I think I'm learning a lot in the class—he does teach us a lot—but he gave me a D on my report because I've been late a few times and I didn't type the paper. He said it was one of the best reports he'd seen, but his grade sure didn't seem fair.*

SUE: *Yeah, he sure uses those grades as a whip. I guess we'd better get home and guess what he's got up his sleeve. I heard him say to the other U.S. history*

These two scenes reveal testing problems that many social studies teachers create. Why test? When and how often to test? What kinds of test items to use? Whether or not to grade on a curve? How long does it take to grade tests? How to make tests valid, reasonable, and fair? All these questions are crucial but difficult to answer. Mr. Jones, the beginning social studies teacher, is not doing a good job in meeting these problems.

The night before a scheduled examination is not a good time to confront the problems for the first time. In order to plan the evaluation of students intelligently, three important terms need to be understood. They are *diagnosis*, *formative evaluation*, and *summative evaluation*.

DIAGNOSIS

Diagnosis, as it is used here, means the collection and use of information to solve teaching problems. Most commonly, it involves student data that, when interpreted, point to underlying problems in the learning processes of students. For example, if a student does not read his history assignment, some sort of diagnosis is called for. The teacher might either ask the student why he does not read, or consult his school record to determine his reading scores. The teacher could ask the student to read aloud, either in or out of class, to determine whether or not he is able to understand the words in the assignment. The student's home situation might be considered in order to find out if he has personal problems that might be interfering with his schoolwork. All of these factors might be consulted together, and then some action taken on the basis of the diagnostic conclusion.

Diagnosis does not always involve students. If the teacher finds that all the students in a class are not comprehending an assignment, he will have to look at his own work—perhaps the assignment—rather than at the students. The teacher might also have to diagnose problems in his own instruction. In all of these examples, diagnosis, as in medicine, involves finding out what is wrong with the patient—in our examples the student or the teacher himself—before trying to solve the problem. Just as in medicine, sources of evidence in addition to the patient have to be consulted. Diagnosis takes place during all teaching phases. But the diagnosis of the learning problems of students usually takes place during or after, rather than before, regular classroom instruction.

Another use of diagnosis is finding out before setting instructional objectives whether or not students have certain knowledge, skills, or attitudes. This implies pretesting in some form to avoid redundant instruction or instruction that erroneously depends on and assumes prior knowledge, skills, or attitudes. This kind of diagnosis obviously occurs before classroom instruction on the particular topic in question.

FORMATIVE AND SUMMATIVE EVALUATION

The difference between formative and summative evaluation is that *formative evaluation* refers to evaluating something in its beginning stage or as it is developing. *Summative evaluation* refers to evaluating at the end, at the summing-up point in instruction. The applications in this book are intended to be formative evaluation tests. They can help both you and the instructor to determine if the intended learning has taken place. If it has not, the problem can be diagnosed and remedied before study of the book is completed.

Assume you are planning for the senior sociology class a fifteen-day teaching unit on the topic of institutions. After diagnosing the students' prior knowledge and developing the objectives for the unit, you will want to figure out how to tell, in the postinstructional phase, whether or not these objectives have been met. You might decide to give an examination at the end of the unit or to base your evaluation on a project or some kind of report. These are examples of *summative* evaluation: at the end of instruction, they give indications of how well you met the objectives. The problem with depending entirely on summative evaluation is the lack of earlier information on how students are doing; through early evaluation you might be able to modify the unit to head off problems that show up. Early evaluating might be done in the form of a quiz at the end of the week, through informal observation, or by assessing the quality of some homework done during the unit's early stages. This evaluation is *formative*—accomplished early enough to allow you to intervene and change the instruction for the benefit of the students before it is completed.

Finding out whether there is a problem is done through formative evaluation; how to solve the problem is one function of diagnosis. Assume that one of your instructional objectives in the unit is: The student will be able to explain in a written essay the interdependence of two societal institutions by citing three examples of this interdependence that have not been discussed in class or treated in the readings. After testing for this objective in the first week's formative quiz, you find that the students do very poorly on this particular item, although they do well on the rest of the quiz. At this point you have an evaluation of your success in meeting the specific objective:

you failed. The diagnostic task is explaining what the problem is and what its solutions are.

You might look back at the readings and class sessions to find gaps. Perhaps no examples of institutional interdependence have been brought out in class. There might be some kind of confusion in terminology or a sloppy discussion of interdependence that led to the lack of understanding. Perhaps the students had no prior practice in forming examples of interdependence, even though they would recognize any examples that they encountered in readings. The students may have been completely apathetic about learning. Whatever the case, finding out why they had not met the objective and inventing remedial solutions are the diagnostic task.

Evaluation is multistaged: diagnosis can inform the teacher about students' knowledge before instruction; then formative evaluation is followed by diagnosis (if a problem is encountered) and remediation; this is followed by successive formative evaluations, diagnoses, and remediations until the end of instruction. Then summative evaluation is carried out to determine whether the objectives finally have been met.

It is clear that for Mr. Jones his test was summative, although he did not think about it in that way. Another question he did not consider was: What other functions can tests and grades have besides those suggested in the preceding discussion? Are they and should they be to reward and punish? Do they and should they convey information?

OTHER FUNCTIONS OF TESTS AND GRADES

Tests have several uses in the classroom. As has already been seen, they can be used for diagnosis, formative evaluation, and summative evaluation, and they can sometimes be used for more than one purpose at once. Tests and grades can be used both to motivate and to inform. It is important to understand the difference between these two functions. The *motivation function* implies that tests and grades are used as rewards and punishments. For those who do well, praise, good marks, teachers' special favors, parents' dollars, peers' admiration—all of these and more—reward the successful test taker. For those who do poorly, failure, teacher's glares, parents' admonitions, and peers' smugness are the punishments that are handed out. This use of tests and grades is sometimes justified, wrongly we believe, by asserting that without the whip of tests and grades, students will not study.

Tests and grades are supposed to serve an *information function* as well as a motivation function. Students receive feedback on what they do and do not learn so that they can remedy weaknesses. The teacher needs to have the same information, and he must make evaluations about his objectives, instruction, and materials, based on how well students do. Information can motivate, but in a way different from that of rewards and punishments. With the latter the source of motivation comes from *outside* the student, from such as parents, teachers, and peers. These sources can be called *extrinsic*. But with information, the student can either be personally satisfied with a good performance or be driven on to correct mistakes and weaknesses, provided he is afforded more opportunities to succeed. These sources of motivation can be called *intrinsic*, coming from within the student himself.

The *extrinsic* motivation function and the information function are independent of one another. In a particular classroom setting these can be situations in which motivation is the only function being attended to by teacher and students. A Monday morning pop quiz on the chapter assigned the previous Friday is an example. The students already know that the only "information" that the teacher might gain is whether or not they read the chapter. Students will most often see this device as simple reward (if they had read it) or punishment (if they had not). What useful information does the teacher gain? It depends. He might be looking for reading comprehension. In that case the test could be a reasonable diagnostic device for the purpose. But if he only wants to know if the students had read the material, it seems a prohibitively expensive way to find out. Some students may be able to bluff enough on the quiz to give him wrong information on what they learned. Finally, the teacher may become angry at the class, perhaps for misbehavior, and give them the pop quiz. In this case the sole testing function is punishment, except for those students who do well on tests without having read the assignments.

Another situation might involve a teacher who is giving a formative test after a week's instruction on labor economics. He wants to determine how many of the several unit objectives the students have mastered, and also wants them to know how many. No grades are recorded, but a "satisfactory" level of performance has been established, and each student is rated either satisfactory or not. Those who do not reach the satisfactory level are given specific study suggestions and, if desired, remedial instruction. They can repeat different forms of the test until they reach the satisfactory level. In this case the motivation is *intrinsic*—it comes from within the student. The teacher's concern is solely with information. He positively supports each student, whether that student succeeds or not. In addition, the teacher can modify instruction on the basis of how well the class performed as a whole.

Teachers should recognize the difference in function of tests and grades and should analyze their own reasons for testing and grading. We believe that the information function should be maximized and the *extrinsic* motivation function minimized. One reason is that prolonged emphasis on the rewards and punishment function will tend to limit the amount of information gained both by students and teacher. The negative feeling associated with tests and grades will tend to mask the information available. Students will not ask, "How much did I learn?" They will ask, "What grade did I get?"

Giving frequent formative tests is a technique for maximizing information for students. Rather than two or three summative tests in a semester, which tend to give little information too late for remediation, teachers should provide students a constant stream of short tests to aid instruction and learning. If students have the opportunity to work on such tests until they perform satisfactorily, the formative tests can be as instructional as any other part of regular classroom teaching. The rapid feedback provided in this way helps students pinpoint their own problems. Testing as students progress through a unit, rather than waiting to test only at the end of the unit, is a powerful teaching strategy.

Another argument for the information function and against the extrinsic motivation function is that if tests and grades are used to punish, as in the earlier example of the pop quiz, students will react negatively. They will trust the teacher less, especially if the "tests for punishment" action is erratic and bears little relation to learning the subject. This is seen in Mr. Jones's students at the opening of this chapter. Such erratic and nonsystematic behavior, which seems only aimed at punishing and controlling, will diminish trust and confidence in the teacher. Similarly, attitudes toward the subject matter are likely to become more negative with this kind of teacher behavior.

Care must be taken that the information conveyed by grades is not confused by factors other than learning performance. Student behavior aside from learning often causes grades to go up or down. Attendance and tardiness, participation in discussions, working on projects irrelevant to objectives, good or bad deportment in class or school are examples of such extraneous behaviors. Put yourself in the place of a parent who comes to the teacher after his son received an F in United States history:

PARENT: *Gosh, Allen got this F, the first he's ever received. I'm really surprised, especially since he's always gotten B's and A's in social studies before. Just last semester he got a B in this course.*

TEACHER: *Well, Allen just didn't do very well. Here are his marks for the semester. (Shows parent the grade book)*

PARENT: *But Allen said he did quite well on all the tests. What was the problem?*

TEACHER: *Well, you can see that Allen did do okay on the tests, but he never participates in class, and I base one-third of the grade on that. Allen just got nothing for that. He also missed eight days of class and was late for six other days. I also had to knock off one letter grade for that. I also had to give him points off for several instances of sleeping in class and for writing on his desk. If my students don't keep interested, they get it in the grade book!*

PARENT: *Did Allen learn some United States history or not?*

TEACHER: *Of course he did—he knows more than many of the students here. But we've got to have standards in this school, and if kids misbehave, they get punished. Sorry.*

The parent gets the information he wants: Allen learned in the class. But the grade reported did not reflect that information. We believe it should. Because it is the only indicator of learning that others (like college officials, prospective employers, and parents) will have, it should be accurate.

The prolonged emphasis on information—rather than on rewards and punishments—from tests and grades should have positive outcomes. The student should become less dependent on extrinsic rewards and more able to channel intrinsic motivation into continued perseverance to learn. This approach, in turn, will lead to more autonomous learners—ones who learn outside of school and after they leave school as well as in school. This independent learning is an important educational goal. Excessive reliance on extrinsic rewards in school will tend to defeat its accomplishment.

Two Philosophies of Grading

Should student grades be based on how well a group of students perform or on a predetermined set of standards? One view holds that a group of students should be the reference point for assigning a single student's grade. This method of grading implies the use of the "normal curve." The teacher puts all students in order of rank according to their scores. Of a teacher's 150 students, perhaps 20 had total semester scores above 285—they get A's. Similarly, 10 students had below 165—they get F's. Similar "cutting points" are chosen to assign B's, D's, and C's. Perhaps this teacher gave 25 B's, 25 D's, and 70 C's. This method uses *other students'* scores in the group as a norm, against which individual student scores are compared to determine a grade. We will refer to this grading philosophy as *norm-referenced grading*.

Another philosophy suggests that absolute standards be used as the reference for evaluation. These standards are the objectives specified for instruction. Each student's grade is determined by how well he satisfies the objectives. For example, before a unit began, the teacher may have decided that three objectives were essential; a student had to satisfy each in order to receive a passing grade. Also, a group of seven objectives were in an "important" category, and each must be satisfied in order to gain a C. Finally, the remaining ten objectives were in a "desirable" category but were used only to gain a B or A. This system differs from norm-referenced grading. All students can earn A's. One student's grade is not determined by the other students but by his own work. We will refer to this philosophy as *criterion-referenced grading;* instead of using other students as the standard, the instructional objectives are used as criteria for judging success or failure in learning.

NORM-REFERENCED GRADING

These two approaches to grading are related to basic assumptions about the function of education in our society. *Norm-referenced grading* assumes that some students will learn less than others. In fact, it assumes (and ensures) that *some* students will fail. When the normal curve idea is used, the last 5 or 10 percent of the students' scores typically are assigned F's, and these students fail. Usually, these students fail repeatedly, and many drop out of the educational system at one level or another. Throughout the system these marginal students are systematically clipped off the bottom end of the distribution of grades. Some leave before finishing grade school and others on reaching the legal school-leaving age (usually 16 years), others fail to finish high school, and some do not go to college. This is a *selection* process. Those who can keep their test scores above the bottom end of the distribution succeed; the others fail and drop out.

The normal distribution curve, used by scientists in all fields, is based on the idea that for any randomly distributed trait, such as height, there will be a large number of scores near the average of the distribution and relatively few scores as the scores move away from the average. Taking the distribution of height of men in the United States, for example, most men are near the average of 5′ 10″, very few are as tall as Kareem Abdul-Jabbar at more than 7′ 2″, and a similarly small number are under 5′. This is a good illustration of a randomly distributed characteristic. An examination of the measure of intelligence like the one for height would show a distribution of scores similar to the one for height.

Why not use a normal distribution curve to grade learning in school? If learning in school is expected to be randomly distributed, with some students always learning nothing, then it is an appropriate tool. But learning results are not supposed to be random. All children in schools are supposed to learn, and teachers are paid to help bring about this learning. Because of this explicit purpose in learning, the closer the distribution of learning is to a normal, and random, distribution, the more the schools have failed to bring about learning. It makes little logical sense to set about the work of helping all to learn and then to consign to automatic failure some students because of a misused grading tool like the normal curve.

The normal curve method of grading sometimes causes teachers to behave strangely. One teacher, because his class is performing on tests at a much higher level than in past years, deliberately loads subsequent tests with very difficult and trick questions so that the scores will spread out more on a grading curve. Another teacher, because scores are much lower than usual, writes his tests for the curve, too. He makes them much easier. In both cases, the teachers are forcing the scores to conform to a predetermined distribution through the manipulation of levels of difficulty in the tests. The more basic issues of how to give accurate information about learning and of how to remedy low learning levels are not being met. But they are the true educational problems, not the problems of grade distribution that these not-so-hypothetical teachers have invented.

APPLICATION 9.1: A CRITIQUE OF GRADING POLICY

Read the following grading policy of an actual school for the year 1969–70. Using concepts presented so far, write an evaluative response of two or three paragraphs that you, as a classroom teacher in this school, might make at a faculty or school board meeting. Include references to stated and unstated assumptions, and criticize unwarranted conclusions you find in the policy.

It is the strong feeling in the Public School District that each child work as near to his capacity as possible. The student and the teacher have a *mutual* responsibility in achieving this concept. We believe the district has a responsibility, actually a moral obligation, to provide a curriculum for each student that is designed to give him the most meaningful and the most realistic education that our resources will permit. It is our responsibility to place that child in those class sections designed to enable him to achieve the nearest to his potential; however, we are not always able to do this, especially in the secondary area. When this occurs, it is incumbent upon the teacher to modify first of all her expectations of that pupil and, second, *to modify that pupil's course work insofar as possible.* With this concept of mutual school and pupil responsibility, we should have very few failures because of lack of ability. The resourceful teacher is cognizant of these individual differences and makes adjustments and allowances accordingly. On occasion it is possible to reschedule a misplaced pupil, if attempted in time, but frequently this is impossible; therefore the responsibility for the pupil's course work rests with the teacher. The failures that would occur, then, would be the result of lack of effort, application, and poor attendance on the part of the pupil, not because of lack of scholastic ability.

Normally we expect a teacher to give few failures, and these for the reasons already listed. Every time a failure occurs, it has to be a failure on the part of the teacher and school as well as the pupil. A pupil should never enter a classroom with a "built-in F" awaiting him because of his lack of ability.

School marks should not be used as a disciplinary device to punish a child. Usually the pupil who is a disciplinary case lowers his own marks automatically by his inattention, poor attitude, and other aspects of social misbehavior; the teacher, however, should not specifically lower a child's grade further because of poor discipline. Poor behavior is a matter of counseling, a matter of guidance, not one of giving a misconception of scholastic ability in an effort to bring about better habits of conduct.

It shall be the policy in grades K–6 to give no marks above a C in those classes designed as remedial for our slower students. In this type of class situation, the pupil is not doing the type or quality of work we would expect of him in his normal grade placement; therefore it is not being realistic to him or fair to the other pupils to give him a grade that would falsely indicate that he was better than average in that particular subject area. It would appear that the giving of a B to a pupil working below grade level just because he does this work quite well would make other B's and A's relatively meaningless. It does not seem advisable to weaken the basic grading policy in order to please a few students. In the areas of junior high and senior high, pupils in remedial-type classes are not to be given A's, and the giving of a B should be an extremely rare incident. We would assume that we would have a preponderance of D's and C's in the low-ability groups.

The retention policy on the elementary level shall remain as it has existed in the past; that is, a pupil is retained only after a meeting involving the teacher, principal, supervisor, and parent would indicate that retention is favored. Social development, physical size, and, lastly, mental ability are the basic factors considered; other extenuating factors, peculiar to each case, are brought in for consideration also.

In relation to pupils in accelerated classes as commonly found in grades 7–12, we would expect a high incidence of A's and B's with an occasional C. The C would largely be the result of imperfect grouping.

Marks given for reporting achievement in classes for the accelerated and the remedial shall be designated as such on the cumulative folders. By "accelerated," we are referring to high-ability groups in our homogeneous grouping. The teacher is reminded that a natural tendency is to scale marks from low to high, even in ability groupings. This is an error but certainly is understandable. For instance, a teacher with a group of high-ability students is prone to categorize the students into low, medium, and high plateaus of achievement because of their relationship to each other. He then grades accordingly, frequently from A to D, whereas actually the slowest student in the high-ability group might conceivably do outstanding work in a middle-ability group. By the same token, the best pupil in the low-ability grouping might appear by comparison to be a fine student and, as a result, might be given an unrealistically high mark.

CRITERION-REFERENCED GRADING: FOR MASTERY LEARNING[1]

The "selection" philosophy in education, based on norm-referenced grading, assumes that the ability to learn is randomly distributed, that some will fail at any educational level, and that teachers should weed out students who tend to learn less well than their peers. But if education is truly universal, if the responsibility of teachers is to help as many students as possible to learn, then the selection philosophy has to be discarded. An alternative philosophy might be called mastery learning.

The phrase "mastery learning" suggests that the reference for evaluating learning is not the school peer group. Instead, to make a judgment about student learning, you have to decide whether or not each student has *mastered* the particular instructional objective. This decision involves the use of *criterion-referenced grading*. Of course, there is no way directly to measure mastery. However, if objectives are well stated and if the measurement items are closely congruent with these objectives, inferences about mastery should be reasonably sound. If you test repeatedly for specific objectives using several different means, confidence in inferring mastery will increase.

The mastery learning idea cannot be realized without assuming that all students—except those with physical, mental, or emotional handicaps—can master the objectives. If you fall back on the old belief that some will fail, you accept a set of educational assumptions that do not fit mastery learning. The assumption that all students can learn is based on the work of several educators, including Benjamin S. Bloom and John B. Carroll.[2]

Bloom has educational research evidence that the mastery learning approach has positive intellectual and emotional outcomes.[3] In one study at the college level, students under mastery learning in 1966, 1967, and 1968 were compared with students in 1965, before the experiment with mastery learning began. The number of A's increased from 20 percent in 1965 to 80 percent in 1966 and to 90 percent in 1967 and 1968. Standards were not lowered, nor was content changed; the teaching and evaluation strategy was all that changed.

Likewise, attitudes toward the course work improved; students began to like the subject and to explore it further. Similarly, Bloom predicts increases in student self-esteem if students are evaluated throughout their school years in this manner. Competition with other students under the more traditional norm-referenced approach, often resulting in hurt feelings, is eliminated in a mastery learning situation. Similarly, unstated pacts among students to "keep the curve low"—obviously harmful to students and to the learning process as well—are nonexistent. Slower students feel that they have a chance—that they are not doomed to failure by the curve. Most important, perhaps, is that the entire system focuses the teacher's attention on the important question "Did the students learn?" and if they did not, "What can I change in order to remedy that?" The blame for educational failure is shifted from the students to the persons responsible for instruction, the teachers.

Mastery learning in practice. Bloom has suggested a practical strategy for mastery learning that will work in social studies classrooms. First, students are told what standards are to be used in grading. This means that objectives are made clear to them, as is the system for assigning grades. Next, the instruction is broken down into units and subunits. A Civil War unit, for example, might be broken down into several subunits, including origins and causes of the conflict, the North and South during the war, the military history, and the immediate results of the war.

Each of these subunits might have a formative evaluation of some kind to provide feedback to both teacher and student. Bloom sees a diagnostic-remedial function in these formative evaluations, allowing the teacher to suggest specific direction and assistance to the student. Formative quizzes would not be graded, except that the student would know if he met the minimum criterion established by the teacher. Thus, by the time the student reaches the final, or summative, evaluation, he has had considerable feedback on his progress and opportunity for success.

The system involves allowing the student to try to learn as long as he wants to, within some reasonable bound. That is, if a formative quiz or examination or report is judged unsatisfactory by the teacher, the student can try again. More instruction, perhaps with remediation, is followed by a parallel but different test or other formative measuring device that assesses performance on the same objectives. Thus, the work is reassessed, and if the student and teacher are satisfied, the student proceeds to the next unit of instruction. If they are not satisfied and want to continue on the same work, the student does so. Only the scores from summative tests are considered for the student's grade.

The description of the mastery learning system may have raised questions about feasibility. How, for example, could a teacher manage the degree of individualized instruction implied by the system? Some students may be able to pass a mastery test on a topic *before* receiving instruction; some may pass it the first time after instruction; others may have to spend much more time with it.

The truth is that no one has solved these problems satisfactorily. But students who go faster than others can go in a number of directions. First, in a school with a flexible schedule in which the student can decide how much time to spend on his different subjects, he can devote time to those he finds more challenging. Second, a student may find areas of particular interest within a subject that he might explore alone. Another alternative is to put the rapid learners to work as peer tutors. If students who are having difficulties are given *specific suggestions* as to what to work on and are placed in small groups of one or two students with similar problems, the quicker students who have already mastered the material may be able to teach the others. This tutoring is not likely to be a waste of time, either; most experienced teachers find that when they teach a subject for the first or second time, they learn more than they teach. Other solutions to the problem of individualized instruction include regular leaderless small-group work, individual tutoring by the teacher, alternative texts, and self-pacing programmed instruction.

Some argue that the mastery learning approach lowers standards and reduces the amount of learning expected of students. These persons assume that the objectives that students attempt to master define a "ceiling" of learning and that no other learning will take place after mastery. We believe that a more useful way of looking at the problem is in terms of a performance "floor." The objectives define a level of learning that the teacher believes nearly all the students can and should gain. Many students may learn more—they will perform at a level higher than the floor—but nearly all will meet the basic objectives set forth for the course. These accomplishments leave room for individually determined and creative directions for learning but also assure a basic level of competence for the class as a whole.

Examples of diagnosis and evaluation in mastery learning. With the mastery learning idea as a base, diagnosis and evaluation of students can be fitted into the instructional sequence. First, a teacher must have some idea of how the student will have changed as a result of instruction. It is hoped that this will be clear from the objectives specified by the teacher as he plans. These objectives later become operational definitions of evaluation items used to assess student performance.

In a sociology class the following instructional objective might be included in a unit: The student will be able to explain in a written essay the interdependence of two societal institutions by citing three examples of this interdependence that have not been discussed in class or treated in the readings. Given this example, it is obvious that the means of evaluation at the end of the unit are defined by the objective. Even the test question and form is defined.

Either before or after specifying the objectives, a teacher must *diagnose* students' levels of knowledge and skill relative to the topic. The teacher should not make unwarranted assumptions at this point. One such assumption might be that all students are totally ignorant of the topic or subject matter.

Another questionable assumption is that all students know what the concepts institution and interdependence mean in the context of the unit. Further, it is often erroneously assumed that whatever the level of entering knowledge, it is the same for each student in class. This is obviously false for most social studies topics. Assumptions about such as reading ability and motivation also have to be examined. Diagnosis, then, is a key task for the teacher as he plans and performs instruction.

As the teacher proceeds through instruction, it is necessary to gather information in order to judge how instruction should be changed before the end of the unit and to give students information on how well they are progressing in relation to the objectives. As has been stated before, this process is called formative evaluation. This ongoing process also feeds back into diagnosis and may serve to suggest changes in objectives, methods, and materials. Summative evaluation can also serve this feedback function, but it comes too late to make any changes for the students who have completed instruction. It may, however, be a part of the diagnostic information used for subsequent instructional units.

Taking the objective on institutional interdependence, you must first choose instructional materials and methods. Using three written case studies of individuals, you will have students read these and discuss them in class, focusing first on which institutions impinge on each individual and then moving on to interrelationships between the institutions. Next you will ask each student to write a sketch of his own case study, identifying those institutions impinging on his own life. The unit will end with a discussion of these sketches and will attempt to generalize about the kinds of institutions that influence individuals and about the interrelations among them.

As mentioned before, you should find out from the students whether they know what the concepts institution and interdependence mean. Later in the unit, you will have to know if they understand the concepts economics, politics, family, church (or religion), and other institutional labels. You might know whether they are familiar with these concepts from previous experience. If so, there is no problem. But if that is not the case, some sort of information is needed. One way of getting this is simply to ask in class for the meanings of the terms. They could be given orally or in writing. The danger in the more informal oral questioning is that only a few students respond, and they are likely to be those who do understand. If this is the method you are using, it would be better to choose the weakest students in order to get a more accurate picture. If the concepts are not understood by any or all of the students, some sort of concept-teaching sequence must be provided. It could be in-class explanation, a homework assignment, or another kind of instruction.

Another diagnostic question would be: Will the average students in the class be able to read the case materials? If not, some change must be made. One way to find out is by applying a reading formula to the case materials to find out their reading grade level. Then the reading scores for the students can be examined to determine whether the materials are suitable. Although this may sound like a great deal of trouble, it may be the most efficient means if many varied sets of reading materials will be used in a semester or year.

An alternative to this procedure is to give an informal reading test to the students or to a subsample which will give the needed information. An informal test could consist of presenting ten or twenty of the most difficult words from the readings and asking students to pronounce them. One way of inferring whether or not they comprehend words is to test for their ability to pronounce them correctly. This is obviously not a foolproof method, but it is one quick indicator. A student who can pronounce does not necessarily comprehend the meaning of a word, but one who *cannot* pronounce words is very likely not to understand them.

Another method of diagnosing reading ability relative to specific materials is to devise a short comprehension test, which might be part of a pretest for the unit. An excerpt from the case materials—perhaps two or three paragraphs—could be given to the students to read. Then, after they have given it back or without their referring to it, they can respond to comprehension questions about the materials. Their responses should be an indication of their ability to read the materials.

What if the diagnosis shows that many students cannot read the materials or even that none can? One answer is to choose other, less difficult reading materials. But films or tape recordings might be better. Perhaps the students could generate other case studies by interviewing individuals and could then report on and use these as the data for the unit.

Diagnosis of reading ability is one important factor that interacts with other instructional decisions. Knowing about students' motivation to read is similarly important; this knowledge will have to be generated through experience with the students. In the example, having the students write their own case is an attempt to capitalize on motivation inherent in that task. If motivation is crucial, it might be wise to change the sequence of the unit, having the students write their cases first and then asking them to compare themselves with others by reading different cases. If this was the situation, the case studies should probably involve adolescents.

As instruction unfolds, information for formative evaluation is needed. The focus should be on elements of the objective that are necessary for the final student performance. If instruction in the several concepts mentioned above is included, this focus would be an element. Choosing examples of institutions from instances and noninstances of these concepts might be a skill that could be evaluated formatively. Recalling an example of interdependence from class activities could be another element. These and other subtasks implied by the objective could be assessed as instruction proceeds. By these means the teacher finds out what has and has not been accomplished and what has to be changed or repeated. Similarly, students can gauge their progress and can repeat parts of the unit or receive other remediation in cases in which they do not meet criterion levels on the formative tests.

Finally, at the end of the unit, the summative test is given. Based on the objective, you might compose the following essay question:

Essay (20 minutes)
Choose two institutions and describe at least three ways in which they are interrelated. Do not use examples of interrelationships in the readings or brought up in class; use new ones that you have found in your study or ones that you think up now.

It is important to note that this task is just what was implied by the objective. As will be seen in the next chapter, *congruence* between the objective and evaluation item is very important.

Summary

Three basic concepts in evaluation of student learning are diagnosis, formative evaluation, and summative evaluation. *Diagnosis* refers to a teacher's anticipation or discovery of the nature of and remedy for the learning problems of students. *Formative evaluation* refers to the process of making judgments about how well students are learning during an instructional segment. This form of evaluation implies that teachers and students can go back and correct ineffective instruction and learning before proceeding to the next segment. *Summative evaluation* refers to the process of making final judgments about student learning after instruction has ended. It has been stressed in this chapter that frequent, brief formative evaluation is a key to successful social studies instruction.

Tests and grades have at least two possible functions. The first is *motivation function*. Grades and tests can be used to reward or punish. If grades and tests are used in this way, motivation can come from outside the student. This is called *extrinsic motivation* and can consist of free time in class, five-dollar bills for A's, peers' scorn, or double homework assignments. *Intrinsic motivation,* coming from within, consists of self-satisfaction or determination to try again until success is achieved. It does not depend on outside sources. One important task for the teacher is to help move students from extrinsic to intrinsic sources of motivation in learning.

The second function of tests and grades is to provide *information*. They can inform students how well they are learning, so that more or less effort can be released, as required. The teacher can use information derived from tests to modify the instruction or to question the objectives. Parents, prospective employers, and colleges, for example, can also gain information about student progress. But if grades and tests are used as rewards or punishments, the information they convey can be all wrong. Teachers must guard against this common problem.

Two grading philosophies are diametrically opposed, and a teacher must choose between them. *Norm-referenced grading* pits each student against the relative standard set by his peers in class. The normal curve is used to assign grades, so that the highest grades are A's and the lowest F's. This assumes and ensures that some will fail. *Criterion-referenced grading* measures each student's progress against agreed-on standards that are the instructional objectives. All students can succeed under such a system. If many fail, the teacher must take responsibility for this and change the objectives or the instruction. Norm-referenced grading, in contrast, leads to the conclusion that it is the student's fault when he fails, even though use of the normal curve makes failure for some a certainty.

Mastery learning is an instructional strategy based on the philosophy of criterion-referenced grading. It also depends on the successful and frequent use of diagnosis, formative evaluation, and summative evaluation. Research evidence supports the idea that almost all students can master instructional objectives if the teaching is well arranged and performed.

APPLICATION 9.2: A TEACHER'S TEST FLUNKS

Turn to the beginning of the chapter and read the description of Mr. Jones and his students. In outline form, note what he was doing wrong and why. After each point, jot down what he could do to improve his diagnosis and evaluation procedures.

_____

_____

_____

_____

Notes

1. This section on criterion-referenced grading closely follows Bloom's work on this topic in Benjamin S. Bloom, J. Thomas Hastings, and George F. Madaus, *Handbook on Formative and Summative Evaluation of Student Learning*, New York: McGraw-Hill, 1971, chap. 3.

2. John B. Carroll's thinking on criterion-referenced grading is represented in James H. Block (ed.), *Mastery Learning: Theory and Practice*, New York: Holt, Rinehart and Winston, 1971.

3. For a summary of 40 research studies that add support to these findings on the outcomes of the mastery learning approach, see Block, op. cit. (note 2).

Suggested Reading

Bloom, Benjamin S., J. Thomas Hastings, and George F. Madaus, *Handbook on Formative and Summative Evaluation of Student Learning*. New York: McGraw-Hill, 1971. This comprehensive volume gives an extended rationale and description of the mastery learning concept. It also discusses in detail the other principal concepts set forth in this chapter, such as formative and summative evaluation and diagnosis. An excellent chapter is included on evaluation for the social studies curriculum of the secondary school.

AT THE BEGINNING of Chapter 9, you met Mr. Jones who was struggling with a common teaching problem: how to construct a test. This is always a problem whether the test is formative or summative. Turn back to Mr. Jones and reread that scenario. It will help to orient you to this chapter, which discusses how you might solve testing problems.

Two Principal Types of Tests

As the predicament of Mr. Jones suggests, there are two principal types of tests: the essay test and objective test. The former usually poses a question to which the student responds by writing an essay. This essay is then judged by the teacher who posed the question. The objective test, on the other hand, is composed of many questions to which various answers are suggested or to which brief answers are to be supplied; students choose or supply the most likely answers or the correct ones.

In addition to the difference between writing an original essay and choosing or supplying a brief answer, another distinction separates the two types. This is the way in which tests are scored and by whom they can be scored. Essay tests are scored by the expert—the teacher—who judges the essay according to certain principles and against criteria he has generated. There is no absolutely correct or incorrect answer; rather, the essay is judged to have degrees of "goodness" or strength and receives a grade on some scale, often A, B, C, D, or F or from 0 to 100. Objective tests, in contrast, require no expert to score them; a machine, a student, or a teacher's aide can do this work with great accuracy because comparing test answers with a key is easy. The term *objective* presumably arose because any two observers scoring the same group of tests against the key would generate the same set of scores, and this is one way of defining the word *objective*. With this understanding of objective tests, it follows that essay tests are less objective and more subjective because different graders would usually generate different sets of scores for the same group of essay responses.

Another basic difference between the two types of tests is crucial to a teacher. Objective items test for knowledge, comprehension, application, and the analysis level of Bloom's taxonomy discussed in Chapter 3, if there are single, best answers or outcomes of these intellectual operations. Objective tests therefore tend toward *convergent* knowledge or intellectual ability—that which converges on right answers. Essay examinations, although they can be used in assessing convergent knowledge and skills, can also be given to test for *divergent* thinking skills; objective items do not generally do this.

Examples of divergent intellectual skills include synthesis and evaluation as well as some of the lower-level skills. Asking students to hypothesize the reason for a phenomenon new to them would involve a divergent response; the answers given might vary considerably, and the teacher would not be able to predict all answers, especially if the students are creative. Another example of a divergent question would be to ask for specific types and sources of information that could be used to test the hypotheses. Convergent questions could include those testing for the meanings of specific concepts, the application of an economic principle to a problem, and the recall of a specific generalization.

This difference between the two types of tests suggests the first step in deciding between them for a specific testing application. Do you want to test for convergent or divergent thinking? If it is the latter, an essay test is called for. If the former, either type might be used.

Assume that you want to test for divergent thinking, and the unit in United States history under study emphasizes critical thinking in evaluating or verifying the authenticity of historical evidence. You might formulate the following essay question:[1]

A historian was given some letters, found in an old house, which seemed to have been written by a soldier during the American Revolution. The soldier said that he thought the British troops were poorly trained and were reluctant to fight. Before he could include the letters in his book, the historian tried to find out if the letters were actually written during the war and if the soldier's statements could be correct.
Write an essay describing some possible tests the historian could use to verify the authenticity and accuracy of the letters. Include both internal and external authentication procedures, labeling each of your suggested procedures as either internal or external authentication.
Time limit: 15 minutes.

Given the same introduction, an objective item for convergent thinking might be:

What is a relevant procedure for the historian to use in authenticating the letters? (Check as many as are correct.)
a. Finding out if the soldier's name appears on lists of those who fought in the American Revolution
b. Determining the age of the house in which the letters were found
c. Sending the letters to a laboratory to determine their age
d. Checking on the training and morale of British troops during the Revolution
e. Checking the family tree of the person who gave him the letters to determine if the soldier was related to him

From these two examples you can see that if a divergent response is desired, an essay is appropriate; if you want to know whether a student can discriminate between a relevant and an irrelevant test of authentication, which is a convergent thinking task, an objective item can do this job.

Suppose all you want to know is whether students understand the difference between internal and external authentication. In this case, an essay question would appear to be an unnecessarily time-consuming type of test. You could write an essay question, of course:

Point out the differences between internal and external authentication of historical evidence by giving contrasting definitions and examples of each.
Time limit: 5 minutes.

But the same job could be done more effectively with one or more multiple-choice items such as:

A day-by-day, first-person account of a farmer's life in Kentucky was discovered in an attic. It was dated 1842. Historians said it was not authentic (trustworthy) because it included a description of President Lincoln's inauguration in 1864. This procedure is an example of:

a. Historical classification
b. Internal authentication
c. External authentication
d. Causal inference

WRITING ESSAY QUESTIONS

How does a teacher write a good essay question? Part of the answer lies in the creative and intellectual powers of the individual teacher. We cannot change those qualities, but we can present some tested prescriptions for making everyone's initial attempt better. First, the question must fit the objectives you have for instruction. Drafting the question at the time you decide on objectives, rather than waiting until the end of a unit, will help avoid essay questions that are unrelated to your objectives.

The essay type was chosen to test for deeper understandings and higher-order thinking. Do not, therefore, write a question that asks only for the recall of specific information—such as the outlines of Chapters 16 and 17 covered in class last week, or what you have said in lectures for the past three weeks. Rather, test for higher-thinking skills: application, analysis, synthesis, and evaluation. To avoid memory testing, create, with the essay question, a problem similar to what has been done in class but one in which the student works on an unfamiliar situation or uses new data. Here is an example essay question from a senior high sociology course:

Consider the following situations.

a. A black mayor is elected in a medium-sized city.

b. A neighborhood playground is located near a river. There have been several near-drownings of small children. A committee of white and black parents is formed to work for the erection of a fence between the river and the playground.

c. The local council of churches initiates a program encouraging white and black families to exchange visits in each other's houses.

Which of the three situations would you expect to be most effective in helping reduce interracial tension? Which would you expect would be least effective? Support your choices with reasons. In your discussion you might consider such ideas as social class, manifest and latent function, stereotypes, formal authority, and informal power, as well as ethnicity.

Time limit: 20 minutes.

If this question had been asked after discussing this specific set of situations in class or after a lecture or reading on these situations, the exercise would be one of memory and composition only. But if the principles and concepts have been taught but never applied before to these situations or to ones closely parallel to them, then the students must apply the concepts and principles to the problem situations. That is quite different from a question such as:

Discuss the following concepts and ideas in relation to interracial tension: social contact, social class, stereotypes, formal authority, and ethnicity.

For many students (and teachers) this "discuss" question really means "write everything you can remember."

Another characteristic of good essay questions is that they are well focused and not too broad or diffuse. The sample essay question above, with the three situations, shows sharp focus; this usually will be true of essay questions with a problem situation. In addition to the focus provided by the problem, the question suggests (but does not limit the student to) several concepts that can be used in the answer. This is good for at least two reasons. First, the student is not put in a potentially vague situation in which he has to guess the teacher's true intent. Second, suggesting key concepts *avoids* reliance on memory. The objective of the essay question is to have the student demonstrate his ability to apply concepts to the problem. If he has forgotten the *labels* for the concepts (which are themselves relatively unimportant, compared with the ability to apply the understood concept), they are provided for him. Thus,

FIGURE 10.1.
Better essay questions would test Peppermint Patty's higher-thinking skills rather than her memory.

the question does not necessarily test for recall of the concept labels but for the application objective.

Another prescription for writing good essay questions is for the teacher to write a model answer within the time limit imposed by the directions. Doing this will serve several functions. It will consign to the wastebasket many questions that are unreasonably long or complex. It may result in helpful modifications to the question or directions. It will avoid questions written in great haste, questions that are likely to be weak. Finally, it will provide one standard against which to grade each student's paper. In addition to this "content" criterion, the teacher can specify other criteria he will use in assessing the response, such as organization, supporting evidence or reasoning, and others unique to the teacher and situation. The criteria can then be incorporated in the test directions so that each student will understand the standards being applied.

A model answer (in outline form) to the essay question discussed before might be:

Guide for Grading Essay Question

Situation (b) has the greatest potential for the reduction of interracial tensions.
1. The manifest function is to obtain the fence, but regardless of whether this effort is successful, there is an important latent function of whites and blacks working together on a common problem.
2. A common enemy (those in formal positions of authority) will tend to unify people who would not otherwise have much to do with each other or get to know each other as real people.
3. Roles ascribed on the basis of race have little value in attacking specific problems of this nature. People are therefore caused to shift somewhat to basing their evaluations of each other on skill and competence.

4. Informal power in the group will emerge on the basis of the contribution a person can make to the achievement of the desired goal.

Situation (c) has the least potential for success.

1. This program poses a personal, one-to-one kind of relationship. It does very little to alter the social conditions that generate the attitudes.
2. The contact will probably be between middle-class people of both races and will not touch high- or low-class whites or lower-class blacks, the groups in which most animosity lies.
3. The situation is somewhat artificial. Each will be self-conscious in his behavior, and the old stereotypes can as easily be reinforced as otherwise.

Situation (a) has both positive and negative features.

1. Persons working with the mayor, if he is competent, may begin to see him as a competent person, regardless of race. If he blunders, many will point to his blunders to reinforce negative stereotypes of the black person.
2. Again, there is a new person in the role, but the role or its social context is changed little.
3. The presence of a black mayor might be pointed to by some as a great advance toward equality and therefore used as an excuse for not taking other steps.
4. A black mayor might have considerable difficulty eliciting cooperation from whites who are reluctant to work with him or suspicious of his motives *and* from blacks who regard him as having sold out to the whites in power.

In evaluating student answers, greater weight should be given to the cogency of the reasons used than to the particular situations chosen.

Two other suggestions for constructing good essay questions are often neglected. We believe that the review by a colleague and the pretesting of questions with students would improve sharply the quality of first or second drafts. As has been observed elsewhere in this book, fellow teachers are often overlooked as sources of criticism and helpful suggestions. Doctors consult one another, sharing problems and experiences; so should teachers. A fresh, professional point of view, applied to your essay questions by one or more of your colleagues, can spare you embarrassment and your students the agony of overlooked errors and ambiguities. Fellow teachers may give you valuable new ideas regarding how to construct or phrase a particular question. Give them the opportunity to help you.

Pretesting questions with students presents greater problems. You may not have access to students you can ask for help in this way, and you may be afraid of "information leaks" to the other students in your classes, which would bias the test results. On the other hand, some ingenuity and trust can be combined in many situations so that pretesting can be achieved. Even if students in a pretest do not actually answer but only give feedback on such features as clarity, specificity, directions, and time limit, this is better than trying out the test for the first time on your students during the actual examination!

Use adequate numbers of essay questions, especially when relying solely on this type of test. Having only one essay question for measuring a whole unit with many objectives may be a less powerful device than having three or four shorter ones. It is a matter partly of coverage and partly of fairness to the student. With only one question—one opportunity to demonstrate his learning—he will suffer greatly if he botches it or forgets essential ideas or has a mental block. With several shorter questions, the likelihood of this is reduced.

Finally, we have some specific suggestions for grading answers to the essay exam. Use a predetermined set of criteria for assessing the answer. This will help you to avoid changing criteria during the grading. Research studies have shown that essay graders tend to be tougher in grading toward the end of a set of papers than at the beginning. The criteria may help to avoid this problem. Standardize the procedure used in grading as much as possible. We suggest that instead of having students write their names on papers, have them write code numbers which they have obtained by signing their names opposite a list of numbers on a sheet of paper you had handed around the class at the beginning of the test. This procedure will help you to avoid the personal bias that creeps into essay grading. If more than one essay question is answered on a test, grade the exams by question, not by the individual paper. That is, grade all the number 1 questions, then all the number 2 questions, and so on. Between each run through the papers, reshuffle them so as to obtain a random order of grading. If possible, have each response on a separate page so that you do not see the score for the previous question before grading the next one. Knowing who the writer is can bias you for or against the answer. Knowing the score from preceding questions on a paper can bias your grading of subsequent questions. The suggested steps can help to reduce the effect of these sources of systematic bias on your grading.

WRITING ITEMS FOR OBJECTIVE TESTS

Many teachers and students react to objective tests just as Linus does in Figure 10.2 on the following page. He is right in one sense. When answering a true-false question, a student has a 50 percent chance of being correct; random guessing tends to yield a 50 percent score. But there are other types of objective test items. Much of what can be accomplished with essay tests can be accomplished with good, objectively scored items, except for those aimed at divergent-thinking objectives.

The four main types of objective test items are: (1) fill-in or supply-the-

© 1968, UNITED FEATURE SYNDICATE, INC.

FIGURE 10.2.

True-false questions give a scholar a fifty-fifty chance.

answer type of question for which the student is supposed to recall and write a very brief answer, (2) true-false items, (3) multiple-choice items, and (4) matching items. Specialists in measurement tend to speak against the use of fill-in and true-false items. Fill-ins reflect memory operations at the lowest level of the cognitive taxonomy; unless your objectives lie only in this area, it is best to avoid fill-ins. Objections to true-false items take two forms. The already-mentioned 50 percent chance of responding according to the scoring key is one serious drawback. There will always be doubt as to whether the results from a test mean that students demonstrated mastery or whether they made lucky guesses.

We will therefore disregard those two types of items and turn to the other two, multiple-choice and matching items. Multiple-choice items have several forms,[2] but our discussion will focus on two kinds, the statement-completion and question-response forms. In both cases the item consists of a *stem* (the statement to be completed or responded to), an *answer* (the correct choice), and one or more *distractors* or *foils* (the incorrect choices). Here is a multiple-choice item of the completion type:

Stem   Sociologists call movement from class to class in the social system:
Answer   a. Vertical mobility
Distractor b. Horizontal mobility
Distractor c. Social change
Distractor d. Status seeking

Changing the stem to a direct question (What do sociologists call movement from class to class in the social system?) and leaving the answer and distractors as they are make this item a question-response type. This type may be the easiest to write and the least error prone for teachers just beginning to construct multiple-choice items.[3]

Matching items should not be overlooked. Many of this type are only tests of memory, but creative efforts can result in items like the following:[4]

Directions: In the following items you are to judge the effects of a particular policy on the distribution of income. In each case assume there are no changes in policy that would counteract the effect of the policy described in the item. For each item print the appropriate letter in the answer space provided:

a. If the existing policy described would tend to *reduce* the existing degree of inequality in the distribution of income
b. If the policy described would tend to *increase* the existing degree of inequality in the distribution of income
c. If the policy described would have no effect, or an indeterminate effect, on the distribution of income

1. Increasingly progressive income taxes __*a*__
2. Confiscation of rent on unimproved urban land __*a*__
3. Introduction of a national sales tax __*b*__

As can be seen, this type of item can be used to test higher-order thinking such as hypothesizing, inferencing, explaining, and applying principles.

What are the criteria for writing good objective items, and what are the mistakes to be avoided? Many problems can be avoided by the application of the following prescriptions.

Use clear, precise wording. Tests should not challenge a student's ability to decipher poorly worded or awkward items and to contend with ambiguous terms. Consider the effect on a student of the following item:

Sociological studies have shown that people tend to identify the social class to which they belong with:
a. Moderate accuracy
b. Perfect accuracy
c. Considerable accuracy
d. Little accuracy

How could a student choose between "moderate accuracy" and "considerable accuracy" and "little accuracy"? These terms are so vague that they are useless. Try to rank order the terms yourself. Is the order "perfect," "moderate," "considerable," and "little," or is it "perfect," "considerable," "moderate," and "little"? It is difficult to determine.

Avoid long, complex sentences. Sentences with many phrases and qualifiers should be broken down into short sentences. Conflict in meaning can often be spotted in this way.

Use enough qualifying words. Consider the following:

In a caste system occupational roles are:
a. Achieved
b. Ascribed
c. Overlapping
d. Identical
e. None of the above

It is most likely that the writer of this item would key b, "ascribed," as the correct response. But not *all* occupational roles are ascribed in *all* societies labeled as caste systems. The student might well choose e, "none of the above," as the proper answer, since none of the other possibilities seem accurate. In fact, students who have studied more—who have more examples of caste systems for their use in answering this item—will probably do worse on the item than those who do not know as much. Changing the stem to "In a caste system occupational roles are *usually*" qualifies the statement enough to allow students to make a correct application of the concept of ascribed roles. In this case it is not an absolute situation in which there may be known exceptions.

Avoid unnecessary words, phrases, and introductory sentences. These distractions can add to confusion about the item's meaning, and they may add enough necessary reading time so as to hinder students who have reading difficulties.

Television is an important and powerful medium in today's society. It may influence one group differently than other groups. Much study has been devoted to the impact of television on the values of different groups in our society. Which of the following statements best summarizes what is known about the impact of television?

This stem is very long and wordy. Most words add no clarification to the item, yet the student has to read them all, perhaps worrying about possible clues embedded somewhere. It would be better to ask:

Which of the following statements best summarizes what is known about the impact of television on the values of different groups in our society?

Sometimes introductory sentences are necessary. Make sure, however, that they add to the clarity of the item before using them.

Avoid accidental clues. As you probably know, objective tests often contain clues to right answers which can be used by "test-wise" students. Because the whole point is to measure learning rather than clever test-taking, you should avoid these clues.

One such clue is that the *answer* is consistently longer than any of the distractors. Here is an example:

High, positive correlations have been found between the results of two occupational prestige studies done sixteen years apart. What is the important meaning of this?
a. It proves that both studies are reliable.
b. It means nothing important.
c. It shows that facts do not change.
d. It indicates that the relative prestige ranking of occupations changed little in that time.

Standing by itself, this item may not indicate that the writer makes answers longer than distractors, but if a student taking the test finds that this is true after ten or twelve items, he can get better scores on the next forty items than he would have without this knowledge.

Another clue can be the systematic placement of the answer. Study of the positions of correct multiple-choice answers has shown that they are most often placed second in the list of possible ones. To avoid this and any other systematic clue, place the possible responses for each item in random order *after* the items have been drafted, so that when the items are typed, most responses are in an order different from that in which they were drafted.

Another type of clue is the interrelating of items. This means that the answer to one item is contained in the stem and answer of another:

1. Which of the following statements best reflects what is known about rates of high school graduation?
   a. Black children are more likely to graduate from high school than white children.
   b. Black children are just as likely to graduate from high school as white children.
   c. White children are more likely to graduate from high school than black children.
   d. None of the above is known.
2. In general, black children are less likely to graduate from high school than white children. Of the following reasons, which is *not* supported by the evidence?
   a. Less money per capita is spent in educating black children than white children.

b. Black children feel less opportunity to achieve social success than white children.

c. Educational institutions reflect, and tend to perpetuate, social inequalities.

d. Education is less valued in the lower social classes in which a greater proportion of black persons are represented.

Clearly the stem of item 2 gives the answer to item 1. One can imagine *another* interrelated item, beginning:

3. In which social class is the proportion of black persons likely to be higher than white persons?

By giving unnecessary clues in this way, teachers enable students to obtain higher scores than their actual knowledge and learning would earn them.

The fourth kind of clue to be avoided is the use of rigid qualifying words such as *never, always, all,* and *none.* For students who have learned the tentative nature of history and the social sciences, these words will probably signal an automatically incorrect response, thus making this item easier than intended. Here is an extreme example:

The family serves as a unit of economic production in:
a. Most times and places in the world
b. Only in the modern city
c. No known place in today's world
d. Older urban areas only

The student can eliminate all answers except a, deciding on the basis of the qualifying words ("only" in b, "no" in c, and "only" in d) rather than on any knowledge of the correct answer. These rigid qualifying words make their distractors so implausible that the item measures little or nothing more than "test wisdom."

Have a colleague check the test. In the best situation you would have a colleague respond to the test within the time limit you plan to allow your students. Without the key the knowledgeable colleague should be able to produce a very high score. He may be able to spot poorly worded or ambiguous items and other difficulties. He can help you find serious errors in the key itself. You may discover that you have not allowed enough time for the test. Most important, you will find out if the items are clear and if the answers are acceptable to more than one expert person—in this case, to you and your colleague. If there is disagreement, then the items in question cannot be called objective at all; they are peculiar to your point of view and are subjective. It should be clear that these items will not be considered fair by most students, and you should either change them or throw them out. The process of review by a colleague should be used whenever possible; it will improve your tests.

Above all, make certain the test items are congruent with the testing objectives. If you become inspired with engaging text questions, write them out as they come to you. Then go over them carefully and objectively to ensure that they are suitable for your testing objectives.

APPLICATION 10.1: WRITING TEST ITEMS CONGRUENT WITH OBJECTIVES

Study the following test items and relate them to this instructional objective: The student will be able to explain in a written essay the interdependence of two societal institutions by citing three examples of this interdependence that have not been discussed in class or taken up in the readings.

1. Compare and contrast two institutions that influence you.
2. Explain three examples of interdependence between institutions that we discussed in class.
3. Which of the following are examples of parts of institutions that influence our lives? (More than one can be correct.)
   a. A policeman directing traffic on a busy corner
   b. A schoolteacher teaching students how to read
   c. An unemployed man trying to get a job through a state unemployment agency
   d. A priest taking confessions.
4. Discuss institutions and their interdependence.

Determine whether or not each item is congruent with the objective. If not, explain.

_____

_____

_____

_____

_____

_____

EXAMPLES OF ITEMS FOR OBJECTIVE TESTS

The examples of objective items in this section are organized according to the categories of Bloom's taxonomy of educational objectives, discussed in Chapter 3. Before these examples are given, it should, however, be mentioned that rich sources of social studies examples are readily available. The original volume by Bloom and others contains many such items.[5] In their recent work Bloom, Hastings, and Madaus have added considerably to that original pool of specimen items, with entire chapters devoted to items in the various categories of the cognitive taxonomy plus a chapter solely devoted to social studies test items.[6] Sanders' very helpful book is focused almost exclusively on social studies and is another source of stimulating ideas for test items.[7] Wesman's chapter in Thorndike's *Educational Measurement* is also helpful in this regard.[8]

Items in the knowledge and comprehension categories are very common in social studies tests, and are not difficult to invent.

Knowledge. This category describes a student's ability to recall or reproduce information. The student need not transform or use the information to demonstrate this ability.

Which of the following is the best-recognized vehicle for achieving upward mobility in the American social structure?
a. Politics
b. Family
c. Education
d. Religion

The student has only to recall a particular bit of knowledge in order to answer the item correctly. It should be noted that the last phrase in the stem is necessary to qualify the item, so that it does not refer to all societies. If the context is not specified, the answer might depend on the particular society the student has in mind, so that several correct answers are possible.

Comprehension. This category describes a student's ability to make simple transformations of information, as in translating information into one's own words or in reading a set of data for specific information (see the following example).

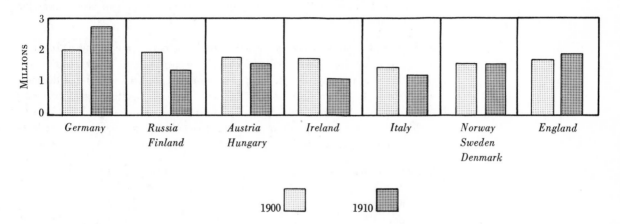

FIGURE 10.3.
Foreign-born population of the United States in 1900 and 1910.

1. Which country had contributed the most people to United States population in 1900?
   a. Germany
   b. Russia, Finland
   c. Italy
   d. Ireland
2. Which country appears to have had the largest drop in contribution to United States population between 1900 and 1910?
   a. Germany
   b. Russia, Finland
   c. Italy
   d. Ireland[9]

In this item the student is required to be able to select correct facts based on the information in a graph. This ability to use tables and graphs correctly is one example of the meaning of comprehension.

Application. At this level of the cognitive taxonomy, the ability to apply principles or generalizations to new problem situations not previously encountered by the student is tested. Imagine that you have been teaching a unit on the experimental method in the psychology of learning, emphasizing basic principles such as avoiding confounding variables and reducing sampling error. One way to test students' ability to apply these ideas is by using a set of items exemplified by the following.[10]

Directions: Read the following paragraph and choose the *single* best answer for the question following.

A psychologist wants to find out whether students learn more in the morning or in the afternoon. He gives a spelling lesson and a spelling quiz to one eighth-grade class in the morning. In the afternoon just before the students will attend the most important football game of the year, he gives the same spelling lesson and quiz to another eighth-grade class. Since the afternoon class did much worse on the spelling quiz than the morning class, the psychologist concluded that students learn better in the morning.

The error in this research is:
a. Inadequate data for conclusion
b. Sampling error
c. Confounding variable
d. None of the above

Analysis. At this level the student is asked to break down into its component parts some communication or body of material, or to find relationships among the parts and the ways in which they are organized. In the following example, the student is asked to locate an unstated assumption underlying an argument in a historical document.[11]

Passage A (written in 1789): "A plural Legislature is as necessary to good Government as a single Executive. It is not enough that your Legislature should be numerous; it should also be divided. Numbers alone are not a sufficient Barrier against the Impulses of Passion, the Combinations of Interest, the intrigues of Faction, the Haste of Folly, or Spirit of Encroachment. . . .

"Hence it is that the two Branches should be elected by Persons differently qualified; and in short, that, as far as possible, they should be made to represent different Interests. Under this Reasoning I would establish a Legislature of two Houses. The Upper should represent the Property; the Lower the Population of the State. The Upper should be chosen by Freemen possessing in Lands and Houses one thousand Pounds; the Lower by all such as had resided four years in the Country, and paid Taxes. The first should be chosen for four, the last for two years. They should in Authority be coequal."

—An anonymous author writing on the
Pennsylvania Constitution

Directions: The following questions refer to Passage A. For each question blacken the answer space corresponding to the one best answer or completion.

1. Of the assumptions that the writer of the passage makes, one is that:
   a. Decisions made by a government in which there is a heavy representation of property will always be wise decisions.
   b. The principle basic to politics is that various groups strive to achieve their own economic ends.
   c. Under a good form of government, "factions" will be eliminated.
   d. Under a good form of government, the drives that people have of using government to promote their own economic ends will be eliminated.

It is likely that several test items, perhaps including comprehension, application, and evaluation on cognitive levels, would be included in a set based on this document. It would not have been studied before in class but would be linked to the main ideas and skills in the teaching unit.

Synthesis and evaluation. As was pointed out before, objective items are not suited to the synthesis and evaluation levels at which the student is asked to form a new and complete communication from several previously unconnected parts or at which the student has to evaluate. An essay question for the synthesis level might be based on the historical document used in the previous item:

Compare and contrast the position taken in this passage on the desired form of government with the views of two members of the Constitutional Convention. Include consideration of unstated assumptions in the passage as well as the stated arguments.

Here is a sample essay question for the evaluation level:

Issue: A respected scholar of human intelligence concludes that as a group, black Americans have lower average intelligence than white Americans. He presents evidence that would ordinarily convince his scholarly colleagues. In this case, however, the colleagues do not want him to publish these findings. They argue that even if true, the findings are racist and immoral and would lead to increased social prejudice and possibly to violent confrontations.

Directions: Write an essay in which you advocate either publishing or not publishing the findings. Include in it the values that are involved in this issue, plus reasoning and evidence that supports your position. (30 minutes)

ESSAY TEST OR OBJECTIVE TEST?

Which kind of test is better? It depends. Many teachers have been heard making ungrounded statements such as "Objective tests don't measure anything worth knowing" and "Essay tests only measure ability to shoot the bull." These and similar statements usually signal a biased and emotional response, perhaps reflecting the unsuccessful personal experience of the speaker rather than any special knowledge in this area. There are specific considerations a teacher can take into account to make an intelligent choice of type of test. The abilities of the students, the time available to invent and score the test, the nature of the teaching objectives—all these are factors to be considered.

Students' reading and writing abilities should be considered. In an essay test most time will be spent thinking and *writing*; in an objective test most time will be spent thinking and *reading*. Thus, if you know that students are very weak as writers, it may be desirable to use the objective form, so that their learning rather than writing ability is assessed.

Another difference between the test forms is that with essay tests the student has to plan his answer and express it in his own words. If these organization skills (synthesis level of cognitive operations) are most important, essay tests may be better. But analytic skills—requiring the student to distinguish between strong and weak assumptions, for example—may be better tested with objective tests when the ability or lack of ability to organize an answer does not mask the analytic ability that you are trying to assess.

Beginning teachers often misjudge or fail to think through the problems involved in inventing and scoring tests. Prospective social studies teachers have often been heard asserting that they will give only essay examinations, but later it was found out that many of them gave only one or two such tests, abandoning them for objective tests. The reason?

The time necessary to grade an essay test for 150 students is great. This task becomes a heavy burden, and even with prompt and hard work on the part of the teacher, it often lasts many days and nights. Another disadvantage is that students do not receive the immediate feedback on the results that is usually the case with objective tests.

Another problem plagues objective tests. Whereas essay questions are relatively easy to write, the invention of objective tests is difficult and demanding. It will take many hours to generate enough good-quality items for a thirty-minute test. An advantage accrues over the long run, however; items can be reused, cutting down on the *overall* time for preparing test items. But the advantage is gained over years, not days, and teachers are often so pressed for time that other solutions have to be found. Perhaps using a combination of a few multiple-choice exams with essay exams at first, later adding slowly to the stock of objective items, is a reasonable compromise. Some social studies departments have pools of objective and essay items for beginning teachers to use to avoid the heavy original investment of time.

One other point should be remembered in choosing between essay and objective tests. This is the teacher's conscious or unconscious influence over the scores of students. With objective tests little such influence can be exerted, and the distribution of scores will reflect the difficulty of the test and the knowledge of the students, not the teacher's manipulation of scores. But with essay tests the teacher can actually produce any distribution of scores he wants simply by "adjusting" scores as he goes through the grading process. The procedures for reducing bias discussed in the earlier section on essay tests should reduce this possibility, but a teacher can still "kid himself" into thinking that his students did very well (a range of scores from 75 to 100 out of a possible 100) or they did very badly (a range of scores from 30 to 70 out of a possible 100), *based on the same set of answers.* Thus, a teacher might try to trick himself into thinking that his students are learning more (or less) than they actually are. This would subvert the entire process of assessing realistically the accomplishment of the teacher's objectives. If a mastery learning philosophy and procedure are followed, this potential weakness in the essay examination dictates limitations in its use. Essay questions do not have to be eliminated in mastery learning situations, but other forms have to be used as well.

Before discussion of this topic is completed, it is important to note that types of tests other than the objective and essay can be used to assess student learning. An essay paper prepared outside of class, oral reports on specific topics chosen by teacher or student, experiments conducted by student groups, and other devices can be used to measure progress. At times the best indicator may be the response of the student to the question "Have you learned this?"

Using Standardized Tests for Diagnosis

Using standardized tests for diagnosing the learning problems of students in social studies has been discussed in Chapter 9. In this section more detailed information on the topic will be presented. First, however, a note of caution is in order. Great care must be taken when using standardized test scores. Scores can be misinterpreted and misused, perhaps with results that are harmful to students. Whenever one is dealing with these test scores, it is best to take time to read through the brief manuals that accompany the tests. The persons in your school system who administer the tests have these, and the publisher of the tests can provide what are referred to as specimen materials. If considerable weight or reliance is to be placed on test scores, take the little time required to take the test yourself. Doing so will refresh your memory concerning the students' approach to tests and will give you a clear picture of what the test actually tries to measure. The manual and scoring material should be examined for information about assumptions, specifications, field testing, reliability, and norms. For an independent evaluative commentary on a standard test, a ten-minute consultation of the most recent edition of *The Mental Measurements Yearbook,* edited by O. K. Buros, will give added insights into the uses, strengths, and weaknesses of a test.

Not understanding test scores or making unwarranted use of them is a relatively easily remedied problem. More serious, however, is the possibility, documented by educational researchers, that knowledge of the test scores of individual students may cause teachers to behave differently toward the students.[12]

Students scoring higher on standardized tests may receive more attention and higher-quality instruction than their low-scoring counterparts do. This situation would directly circumvent the intent of the present section, which calls for diagnosing the learning problems of students and then giving remedial attention to those having such problems. When standard test results for diagnosing relevant student characteristics are used, this last point must be kept in mind. You must avoid labeling students slow learners or dummies and then consigning them to predetermined failure. This phenomenon of self-fulfilling prophecy does occur in school at various levels throughout education. Chapter 9 discussed a school policy of normal curve grading creating such a situation. It is to those students who have the greatest learning problems that we owe our greatest attention, work, and creativity.

A CRITICAL THINKING TEST

Many spokesmen for and critics of social studies education consider critical thinking to be a high-priority goal for social studies teaching. Assume that you hold that goal for your own teaching. How do you find out what your students' capabilities are in this domain in order to plan appropriate instruction? There are standardized tests that purport to measure this trait, and one, chosen as an example for discussion here, is the Watson-Glaser Critical Thinking Appraisal.[13] This test is particularly relevant for the content areas of social studies. It has been used as a norm-referenced instrument for comparing local class or school student performance with national norms. It has also been used extensively by educational researchers in social studies education. We suggest its use as a source of diagnostic information on which to base instruction planning decisions.

Watson and Glaser conceptualize critical thinking as having three general parts: (1) positive attitudes toward scientific inquiry, including recognizing problems and the nature of scientific evidence that can solve these problems, (2) understanding generally accepted scientific proof processes and components, and (3) ability to employ these attitudes and understandings in scientific thinking. The test, which is recommended for students from grade 9 through college and for adults, takes about one hour to administer. It has five parts: (1) recognizing valid inferences, (2) recognizing assumptions, (3) making valid deductions from given premises, (4) interpreting conclusions from given evidence, and (5) evaluating the strength of arguments. Each part uses roughly the same form: mostly social science or historical statements are followed by inferences, assumptions, deductions, conclusions, and arguments, depending on the particular test section. The student is asked to distinguish between: inferences that can or cannot be made, assumptions that are made or not made, deductions or conclusions that do or do not follow, and arguments on a position that are strong or weak. Here is a sample item* from the directions to the *inference* part of the test:

In this test each exercise begins with a statement of facts that you are to regard as true. After each statement of facts, you will find several possible inferences—that is, conclusions that some persons might make from the stated facts. Examine each inference separately and make a decision as to its degree of truth or falsity.

For each inference you will find spaces on the answer sheet labeled T, PT, ID, PF, and F. For each inference make a mark on the answer sheet under the appropriate label as follows:

T If you think the inference is definitely *true*; that it properly follows beyond a reasonable doubt from the statement of facts given

PT If, in the light of the facts given, you think the inference is *probably true*; that there is better than an even chance that it is true

ID If you decide that there are *insufficient data*; that you cannot tell from the facts given whether the inference is likely to be true or false; if the facts provide no basis for judging one way or the other

PF If, in the light of the facts given, you think the inference is *probably false*; that there is better than an even chance that it is false

F If you think the inference is definitely *false*; that it is wrong, either because it misinterprets the facts given or because it contradicts the facts or necessary inferences from those facts

Example: Two hundred eighth-grade students voluntarily attended a recent weekend student forum conference in a midwestern city. At this conference the topics of race relations and means of achieving lasting world peace were discussed, since these were the problems the students selected as being most vital in today's world.

Test 1 / Inference

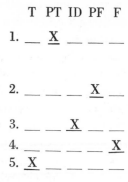

T PT ID PF F

1. As a group the students who attended this conference showed a keener interest in humanitarian or broad social problems than have most eighth-grade students.

1. __ X __ __ __

2. The majority of these students were between the ages of 17 and 18.

2. __ __ __ X __

3. The students came from all sections of the country.

3. __ __ X __ __

4. The students discussed only labor relations problems.

4. __ __ __ __ X

5. Some eighth-grade students felt that discussion of race relations and means of achieving world peace might be worthwhile.[14]

5. X __ __ __ __

Given scores on this or a similar test, some judgments about student abilities can be made. Assume, for example, that four of your eleventh-grade United States history classes have taken the test and that you have the results. If all the class averages were very high—perhaps in the top 20 percent range for that grade level—and the ranges of scores were low, you might decide that despite your objectives in the area of critical thinking, little or no special efforts need be made, and other objectives deserve more attention. If all the class means were relatively low and the ranges of scores low, perhaps a shift to materials and methods specifically oriented toward developing skills in critical thinking would be warranted. For example, materials of the American Educational Publications Series were designed and developed with these skills as objectives. Much of that series is applicable to subject matter in United States history and might be substituted in place of the regular text. If there are clear differences between the classes or within classes, differentiated materials and methods may be called for. Extra instruction and practice in reading newspapers and magazine articles, for example, might be adopted for those with indicated low ability in critical thinking.

The Watson-Glaser test can also be used to diagnose *particular* problems in critical thinking, since each of the five test areas has been found to measure somewhat different skills. Using subtest scores (a score for one part of the test, such as *inference* or *deduction*, rather than the total test score) can point out even more clearly where to focus instructional attention. Suppose that students who achieve high scores on the test as a whole make almost all their mistakes on one subtest, such as evaluation of arguments. The other areas can then be largely ignored, with help concentrated in just that particular area.

One potential problem with the Watson-Glaser test is its heavy dependence on reading ability. In this respect it is much like all paper-and-pencil tests of mental maturity, personality, aptitude, and so on. If a person scores high on the Watson-Glaser, it is reasonable to assume that he can read at a level necessary to take the test. But for a person who scores low, you cannot always tell what the proper conclusion is. It might be the lack of critical thinking abilities. (We certainly hope this is a reasonable conclusion; if not, we would not use the test.) But there are other possible conclusions, including the one that holds poor reading ability, not the lack of critical thinking ability, to be the cause of the low score. As has been pointed out, however, ability to read and critical thinking are definitely related but not identical. Therefore, care and intelligence must accompany the interpretation and use of this test.

DIAGNOSTIC READING TESTS

References to reading difficulties have been made earlier in this chapter. Teaching students to read is not a commonly held goal for social studies teachers. Nevertheless, they are in part responsible for this aspect of education as it relates to reading special social studies materials. And the problems that complicate the life of a social studies teacher often revolve around reading. Some students simply cannot read what is assigned in school. Others, probably constituting a much larger share of students in the "problem" category, *will not* read for a variety of reasons. Among these reasons might be boring reading material, dislike of a class or teacher, rebelliousness, peer norms, and lack of conditions conducive to reading (both in school and at home). These problems have to be diagnosed and solved, given the fact that much of the social studies curriculum is print oriented. Breaking completely away from this situation is very difficult.

First, you must separate those who *cannot* read from those who can but perhaps *will not*. A few simple devices were suggested earlier, but more reliable tools are available. Of the many standardized reading tests in wide use, only two need be used as examples here. (Detailed description and explanation are beyond the scope of this book and can be found in references elsewhere.[15])

The Iowa Silent Reading Tests (for grade 9 through junior college) contain seven sections. In the sections on rate-comprehension, word meaning, sentence meaning, paragraph comprehension, and location of information, social studies content is well represented. This suggests that results from the tests do reflect reading abilities in your subject area, rather than solely in such as science and literature. Information from the tests can be used to modify or replace materials being used in social studies classes; the tests suggest differential assignments, in-class remediation, or special assistance from school reading specialists. Many school systems have trained persons and special reading materials, and often depend partly on classroom teachers for referrals of students.

Another more specialized test of reading ability in social studies is found in the Iowa Tests of Educational Development, Grades 9 through 12. Test 5 in that battery of tests measures ability to interpret reading materials in the social studies. It consists of eight written passages taken from, among others, tests, newspapers, and books on social problems, each followed by a set of multiple-choice response items. The major skills tested are comprehension of what is presented, interpreting the implications or conclusions, and analyzing and evaluating. In some respects the functions of these tests overlap those of the Watson-Glaser Critical Thinking Appraisal, although the latter does not purport to assess comprehension but assumes it. The results from the Iowa Tests of Educational Development can be used in the same general ways as suggested for the Iowa Silent Reading Tests. One difference between these two, however, is that the latter focuses on reading as a skill; the former is a more general survey test of educational abilities.

Summary

Social studies tests usually consist of essay questions and objective items. Multiple-choice and matching items, as well as essay questions, are useful in testing for learning and thinking at the first four levels of the cognitive taxonomy—knowledge, comprehension, application, and analysis. To test for higher-level thinking, at the synthesis and evaluation levels, essay questions are most effective.

Writing essay questions can be improved in several ways. You should include information and concepts to free students from recall problems. This encourages performance at higher-thinking levels. Constructing a model answer and other grading standards in advance, providing several short questions rather than a single long one, and having a colleague review the questions are also key steps.

Writing objective items is difficult, but they allow for more rapid and objective scoring, and feedback to students is apt to be quicker than it is for essay items. Several steps in writing objective items help to avoid problems:
1. Use clear, precise wording.
2. Avoid long, complex sentences.
3. Use enough qualifying words.
4. Avoid unnecessary words, phrases, and introductory sentences.
5. Avoid accidental clues.
6. Have a colleague check the test.
7. Make certain that the test items are congruent with the testing objectives.

Standardized tests are available for several purposes in social studies.

They have to be used with caution, and the principal function they should play is diagnostic, not summative. Tests for general critical thinking, reading ability, and content knowledge are introduced in the chapter.

APPLICATION 10.2: WRITING AND GRADING OBJECTIVE AND ESSAY ITEMS

Using five of the following nine instructional objectives, write a test with both objective and essay items. Write grading models for the essay parts, and describe what grades would be assigned to the range of possible scores from the test.

1. Given a list of questions regarding a public issue, identify the factual questions, the definitional questions, and the value questions.
2. Given a series of advertisements or descriptions of advertisements, identify which best exemplify a status appeal, a sex appeal, and a youth appeal.
3. Given three examples showing conflict between the adolescent's need for independence and his need for dependence, explain how the two needs conflict.
4. Given the thesis that conflicting groups will have their conflict limited if they (a) agree on a common goal, (b) accept a set of rules, or (c) never come into direct contact, match each of these conflict-moderating factors with an example of it in action.
5. Given an imaginary market economy producing only bread and cheese, identify the effects on the economy if people start to spend a larger proportion of their incomes on cheese than they had in the past.
6. Given an account of how the Nazis treated the Jews between 1933 and 1945, analyze the similarities and differences in an account of another oppressed minority.
7. Given a list of military conflicts involving the United States and a list of postwar problems, match each problem with the conflict that produced it.
8. Given several areas of life (for example, marriage, law, and longevity), identify how the level of a person's social status is related to his life chances for a good life in those areas.
9. Given conflicting interpretations of a historical event, determine the facts or assumptions that created points of difference between the two interpretations.

Notes

1. This and other test items in this chapter have been adapted from W. James Popham, *Development of a Performance Test of Teaching Proficiency*, Washington, D.C.: U.S. Department of Health, Education, and Welfare,

Office of Education, 1968, p. C-5. (Final Report of Project No. 5-0566-2-12-1, Contract No. OE-6-10-254.)

2. For a comprehensive discussion of the different forms of multiple-choice items, see Alexander G. Wesman, "Writing the Test Item," in *Educational Measurement*, 2d ed., ed. by Robert L. Thorndike, Washington, D.C.: American Council on Education, 1971, pp. 81–129. Parts of this section are based on that work.

3. Ibid., p. 113.

4. Ibid., p. 99.

5. Benjamin S. Bloom (ed.), *Taxonomy of Educational Objectives*, New York: Longmans, Green, 1956.

6. Benjamin S. Bloom, J. Thomas Hastings, and George F. Madaus, *Handbook on Formative and Summative Evaluation*, New York: McGraw-Hill, 1971, chaps. 7–9, 16.

7. Norris M. Sanders, *Classroom Questions, What Kinds?* New York: Harper & Row, 1966.

8. Wesman, "Writing the Test Item," in Thorndike, op. cit. (note 2).

9. Adapted from Popham, op. cit., p. B-5 (note 1).

10. Ibid.

11. Bloom, *Handbook on Formative and Summative Evaluation*, p. 184 (note 6).

12. Interested readers may want to consult Robert Rosenthal and Lenore Jacobson, *Pygmalion in the Classroom*, New York: Holt, Rinehart and Winston, 1968. This is a controversial and stimulating report on the topic of the unanticipated effects of teachers' knowledge of "testing results."

13. Goodwin Watson and Edward G. Glaser, *Watson-Glaser Critical Thinking Appraisal*, New York: Harcourt, Brace and World, 1964.

14. Ibid., p. 2.

15. O. K. Buros, *Reading Tests and Reviews*, Highland Park, N.J.: Gryphon, 1960. This is an excellent source of information on reading tests. Other texts in reading instruction are available.

Suggested Reading

National Council for the Social Studies, Bulletin Series, Washington, D.C.: National Council for the Social Studies. Bulletin No. 6 (rev. ed., 1964), *Selected Test Items in American History*, by Howard R. Anderson and E. F. Lindquist, rev. by Harriet Stull. Bulletin No. 9 (rev. ed., 1960), *Selected Test Items in World History*, by Howard R. Anderson and E. F. Lindquist, rev. by David K. Heenan. Bulletin No. 15 (rev. ed., 1964), *Selected Items for the Testing of Study Skills and Critical Thinking*, by

Horace T. Morse and George H. McCuve. Bulletin No. 40 (1968), *Teacher-made Test Items in American History: Emphasis Junior High School*, by Dana Kurfman. These bulletins contain large numbers of test items in the areas indicated by the titles. Even if they might not be used in a particular test, they provide direction and ideas for teacher-made tests of your own.

Sanders, Norris M. *Classroom Questions, What Kinds?* New York: Harper & Row, 1966. This is a readable and helpful guide to question asking and writing for social studies teachers. Based on Bloom's cognitive taxonomy, it has many examples for various subject areas in social studies.

Wesman, Alexander G. "Writing the Test Item," in *Educational Measurement*, 2d ed. Ed. by Robert L. Thorndike, Washington, D.C.: American Council on Education, 1971. This chapter is an excellent source on writing good test items. Thorough and clear, it contains extensive examples which will be useful for social studies teachers.

4

Professional
Teacher

Part Four concerns a teacher's participation in his social setting and provides the larger context for his roles as curriculum planner, instructor, and evaluator. This book was designed to help prepare social studies teachers for active participation in the "new social studies" which requires a wide range of competencies. These teachers must be able to select goals and develop instructional objectives consistent with the method of inquiry. They must be able to select materials and devise instruction that will enable students to acquire and apply concepts, to formulate and test hypotheses, and to engage in value analysis. In fulfilling all of these tasks, the teacher must design instruction that permits students to achieve instructional objectives efficiently while maintaining their interest in the subject. Finally, a competent teacher must be an able evaluator, both of student achievement and of the instructional process itself.

Up to this point of the text, we have approached instruction primarily from the perspective of a single teacher interacting with students in one classroom. But instruction does not occur in isolation, nor are a teacher's associations limited to contact with his students only. A social studies teacher is a participant in the social system called school—a society that has its own norms, ideology, opinion leaders, decision-makers, sanctions, rewards, and institutional structures. The school system itself has an effect on the way teachers perform their tasks.

The teacher who practices the method of inquiry will find some school settings more congenial than others. The number of teachers and schools practicing this method is growing steadily. On the other hand it is possible that a new teacher may find employment in a school where the faculty treats his instructional ideas with suspicion and hostility. A teacher must then attend to his own survival while seeking ways to help the school to change in positive ways.

Chapter 11 discusses in observable terms key teaching characteristics that have been linked to student learning outcomes. Methods are presented for using these characteristics as the basis for the evaluation of teaching.

The principal objectives of Chapter 11 are to prepare the teacher to:

1. Understand and identify in dialogue key teaching characteristics
2. Understand the different sources of information for teaching evaluation and the instruments used to collect that information
3. Assess teaching performance from written classroom dialogue.

Chapter 12 provides a number of suggestions for helping a new teacher adjust to his position. It also provides guidelines for introducing change in a social studies department that seems lethargic and nailed to the past.

The principal objectives of Chapter 12 are to prepare the teacher to:

1. Become informed about the various roles within the high school and the norms accompanying these roles that can significantly influence teacher success
2. Acquire some ways for coping with people in these roles in order that the teacher can begin work with the greatest possible advantage
3. Acquire some understanding of the factors to be considered when introducing planned change into a school system
4. Learn ten specific ways to help a social studies program change in a positive way and to devise a strategy to carry through the successful achievement of at least one of the ten innovations.

ONCE THERE WAS a young man who aspired to become an expert diemaker. To learn this exacting and prestigious craft, he apprenticed with a master, read and observed much, and practiced until he, too, was a master. In fact, he outshone his old teacher and everyone else with whose work his was compared. As with all craftsmen, however, some of the dies he manufactured were less than perfect. Rather than blame poor materials or the lathe, he took full responsibility for these failures. Carefully analyzing every part of his work, he solved each problem and improved on his procedures, contributing new concepts and techniques to his fellow craftsmen. Often others, looking over his shoulder, would make suggestions for changes that he had not thought of. The high quality of his work distinguished him throughout the country.

Finding that he could reach no higher plateaus in diemaking, the man turned to teaching others the secrets of his skill and knowledge. At first this was an exciting enterprise. His students were greatly awed by his expertise. As time passed, however, it became obvious that the great master's students were not learning the trade; they began to leave him for other teachers. Some came and complained to him, "We're not learning from you, master. You seem unable to teach your craft as well as you practiced it. Perhaps some other master could help you change your teaching." In a rage the master threw all the students out, screaming, "All you young fools are stupid and can't learn! The manuals we use are awful! Don't complain about my teaching! I'm not just a craftsman anymore, I'm a professional!" No more students came to learn from the master's teaching.

One part of professionalism is assessment by self and peer. Rather than depending on others for constant supervision and evaluation, professionals are expected to monitor and assess the quality of their own work. This is as true of teachers as it is of physicians and lawyers. In the parable the master as a craftsman acted as a professional when he learned from his own mistakes and from his own observations and the suggestions of others. But as a teacher he refused to review his own performance, blaming his failure on other factors. Some teachers make the same mistake in schools today. Some use academic freedom as a means of ducking the responsibility for self-evaluation and for having others help them to evaluate their instruction. Teaching will not continue to be a profession if teachers do not take responsibility for assessment.

Unfortunately, one of the problems contributing to this shortcoming of some teachers is the lack of knowledge about teaching evaluation. In this chapter we will present suggestions for systematically evaluating instruction. We will examine instructional variables which researchers have related to important learning outcomes. The nature of these relationships will be discussed, focusing on their implications for social studies teaching in secondary schools. A variety of approaches and specific techniques for assessing instructional variables will be explained, including devices that use information from students, colleagues, and the teacher himself.

This approach assumes that quality of instruction can be observed and assessed in certain ways and that instruction can be changed at will by the teacher. Both of these assumptions must be true for the teacher who qualifies as a professional. Of all the components that help determine student achievement, it is quality of instruction over which teachers exert most control. To control it, you must understand its nature and possible outcomes and use this knowledge in manipulating instruction so that student learning is raised as high as possible. Any goal short of this one signals a serious lack of professionalism.

Research on Teaching Effectiveness

Answers to the question "What characteristics of instruction are more or less effective?" have to be framed in terms of some reference point. Effective with respect to what? Many agree that the most reasonable and meaningful reference point is student learning. Comparatively little research has been done to investigate the relationships between various teaching characteristics and student outcomes, especially in comparison with a field like medicine, in which much is known about the effects of medical practices and medicines on patients' health. But some teaching characteristics have been linked to student outcomes, and knowledge of these linkages is what has to be used in devising instructional evaluation procedures.[1]

To refer to student learning as the criterion in research studies is to oversimplify somewhat. These distinct components of student learning are often used in research on the teaching-learning process: (1) student cognitive understandings, perhaps of historical or political concepts, or generalizations in a particular area of study; (2) student cognitive skills, such as general critical thinking skills, or reading skills; and (3) student attitudes toward the subject (does he like it or not,), toward school in general, and toward himself (self-esteem). The research reported here focuses on cognitive understandings and skills.

TEACHING CHARACTERISTICS RELATED TO STUDENTS' LEARNING
Eight teaching characteristics will be discussed; they will be split into two groups. The first group includes the four characteristics most clearly and consistently related to student learning: clarity, variety, enthusiasm, and businesslike behavior.

Clarity. This characteristic refers to the extent to which a teacher's presentation, questioning, and answers, for example, tend to be easily understood by students and are not distracting or confusing. Higher clarity leads to positive learning outcomes, as evidenced by several studies. Several specific attributes of clarity, which can be controlled by a social studies teacher, are identified by these studies. Teachers who explain clearly in their first attempt spend little time answering questions calling for clarification and are more likely to have students who do learn. This makes available one indicator you can use to control your performance. By analyzing the extent to which students do ask for clarification or interpretation of your explanations, you can spot a potential teaching problem and then correct it.

Another specific attribute of clarity is the ability to phrase questions clearly and succinctly and not to repeat or rephrase the questions. Some teachers ask a question and, before anyone can answer, add more information and then reask the question or add another question. These are called *add-on* or *run-on questions.* They detract from clarity and tend to inhibit learning.

Another, but less specific component of clarity, is organization. This refers to coherence of the lesson or teaching unit, meaning that the parts fit together in a logical and understandable fashion so that the relatedness of the parts is obvious to the students. This is not necessarily an indicator of overt teaching behavior in the classroom, but it can also represent the teacher's skill and efforts in *planning* for instruction. Well-organized lessons or units, as opposed to poorly thought out and unconnected ones, tend to promote student learning because of their clarity and organization. Some learning can, of course, result from completely spontaneous and unplanned instruction. But over the long run, we believe, clarity and organization will produce the most positive and significant outcomes.

APPLICATION 11.1: CLARITY VERSUS OBFUSCATION IN THE CLASSROOM

Examine the following dialogue excerpted from a real social studies class. Identify instances of lack of clarity as described in this section. Then invent clearer explanations or questions that might correct the difficulties.

T: *Okay, the question is, is the American electoral system democratic? Now, uh, first I've got to explain democracy. One of the basic principles of democracy is popular control. Now is there anybody who can tell me what that means?*

s1: *It's where they vote, and the one who gets the most votes gets the office.*

T: *Any other ideas? The most votes, the person who gets the most votes.*

s2: *The most popular person is elected to be the representative . . .* (Trails off into inaudibility)

T: *Would you repeat that?*

s2: *Popular vote wins, and the people vote for who they want to be in office.*

T: *Okay, how does control fit into this, though?*

s3: *Control?*

T: *Popular control.*

s2: *Well, the people with the most popularity are who everybody wants to be the representative . . . except I don't know if that's what you are talking about . . .*

T: *Okay, so the person who gets the most votes wins, right? Okay, but behind those votes are the people, and by popular control what we really mean is the people participate in the decisions that are going to be affecting their lives. Okay?* (Long pause) *Okay, so on the basis of this, how many of you think we have a democratic system?* (Pause) *Just by a show of hands.* (Pause) *How many think it's democratic?*

s2: *What is the electoral vote? That, you know . . . In the presidential vote, do the peoples' votes really count?*

T: *That's what we're going to find out. Whether or not it really does, whether or not they're represented. This is the question that we're going to ask.* (Pause) *Okay, so how many think it's an undemocratic system? Our way of electing representatives? How many of you think it's unrepresentative—undemocratic?* (Pause) *We have two who think it's democratic. One?*

s4: *I don't understand . . . um . . . the electoral system.*

T: *Okay, this is the system . . . how we vote . . . how we elect the candidates that will represent us in government—you, the voter.* (Pause) *The elections, you know—like we just had in November.*

sl: *Oh, you mean how we feel personally, or how it is?*

T: *Whether or not you think our system as it stands now, not, you know, whether you think there's room for improvement, but is our system, our way of electing representatives right now, do you think it's democratic or not?*

sl: *I do.*

_____

_____

_____

_____

_____

_____

Variety. The concept of variety refers to the extent to which there is instructional variation in what the teacher does and uses—in the material, activities, tests, and teaching modes. On the cognitive level of classroom teaching, variety is important. When there is variety in these instructional factors, student learning increases. Dropping into a routine mode of teaching—assigning six pages from the text, the next day having students recite in a discussion of the assignment, then assigning the next six pages, and so on—may lead to little student growth. Similarly, staying at one cognitive level constantly may be stultifying. The clear implication for social studies teachers is that variety must be built into teaching.

Enthusiasm. This rather vague term, made specific by different researchers in different ways, has been consistently related to student achievement. Several adjectives help to describe the meaning of enthusiasm—stimulating, exciting, original, alert, vigorous, interesting, involving. A few more helpful, behavior-specific characteristics have been identified. They include movement, gestures, and the use of voice inflections, as well as variety in the teacher's questions so that they call for both facts and the interpretation of facts. These are behaviors that teachers can and do control. Part of enthusiasm is personality based, and some might argue that this is beyond control. But even low-keyed, soft-spoken, and reserved teachers can "act" enthusiastically, and this very acting might spell the difference between effective and ineffective teaching.

Businesslike behavior. The teacher characteristic of being businesslike might be called task-oriented or goal-oriented behavior. It is the quality of keeping students "on task," and the ability to convey to students that the teacher is serious about helping them to learn. "There is something to be learned and we're going to learn it" is the hoped-for impression that businesslike teachers strive for. This, too, has been shown to be related to student cognitive achievement. The research done in this area is not very helpful in defining specific behaviors that teachers can control. But some can be hypothesized. The degree to which a teacher discourages or does not permit long, irrelevant discussion and digressions might be one factor in businesslike teaching behavior. Similarly, a prompt, energetic start into the day's work might help signal this orientation. Holding high expectations for students' learning might be a third factor. Rather than an attitude that conveys the message of "you probably won't be able to learn all this, but we'll give it a try until you're lost," the teacher should get across the idea "you can all learn this and we're going to get right down to hard work in getting there." Setting that kind of mood, by whatever means, should help transmit to students the businesslike message which is related to student learning. The use of the mastery learning strategy may be one way to achieve businesslike behavior.

The second set of four teaching characteristics includes those that are not so strongly or consistently related to student learning as the first set of four. Nevertheless, they provide implications for evaluating social studies teaching.

Use of students' ideas; indirectness. These two factors are closely related and will be considered together. The first, use of students' ideas, can be thought of as one of several specific teaching behaviors, including the following: acknowledging the ideas of students by repeating or restating them in slightly different words; modifying an idea by changing it through adding to it; applying the idea to some relevant problem; comparing it to other ideas already expressed by the teacher or other students; alluding to it in a summary or while working with the ideas of other students; and basing a new question on it. This teacher behavior is related to positive student cognitive and attitudinal outcomes. Students apparently feel rewarded by this type of teacher action. It is not difficult to control, we have found, once the teacher is aware of its importance.

Teacher indirectness is a more general factor and subsumes use of the ideas of students. Indirectness refers to the extent to which teachers (1) recognize and accept the feelings of students; (2) approve of, praise, and encourage students' work or ideas; and (3) use students' ideas, as opposed to giving directions and criticizing. Taken together, these behaviors constitute a "classroom climate," or mood, in which learning is facilitated. The climate is one of warmth, acceptance of feelings such as frustration, tension, and anger, support of students, and recognition of the worth of students' thinking. Indirectness represents the extent to which the students', rather than the teachers', ideas and behavior dominate the classroom. In the indirect classroom the teacher exerts less influence and the students more. In the direct classroom teachers tend to dominate, with students exerting less influence. *Indirectness does not necessarily imply unstructured and unplanned instruction.* A teacher can closely structure a class session and be comparatively indirect by focusing on students' ideas. Another teacher can provide no organization or purpose and yet can be quite direct by concentrating on and valuing only his own ideas and feelings.

Research on indirectness has shown very interesting and complicated results, which might account for the weakness of the simple relationship between indirectness and student growth.[2] Different relationships have been found according to the cognitive level of the learning task. For low-level, concrete learning tasks, such as remembering simple facts or concepts, it was found that as *direct* teaching increased, student learning also increased. In the case of learning tasks requiring more complex and abstract intellectual skills, such as higher-order reasoning, as *indirect* teaching increased, student learning increased. Figure 11.1 summarizes, through the use of representative but hypothetical curves, this more complex but very important set of findings.

As seen in the figure, neither curve is a straight line. For the more concrete tasks (curve A), even though direct teachers tend to promote higher learning, there are limits. For *very* direct teachers, the curve begins to fall off toward lower learning levels, suggesting that even with this kind of task, teachers cannot afford to be too direct. For the more abstract learning task (curve B), *too high* a level of indirectness is dysfunctional for student learning. Perhaps this is true because at very indirect levels the structure of the learning situation becomes unclear. Devoting complete attention and effort to the feelings and ideas of students may, in the end, detract from learning because it so often leads away from the learning task at hand. Also, extreme indirect teaching behavior may leave students with no structured situation to which they can relate their efforts, and therefore they may simply drift, rather than continue to engage in purposive behaviors. Whatever the explanation, a balance between directness and indirectness must be struck, the nature of which depends on whether the teacher wants to optimize abstract and high-level learning or simple and concrete learning. A similar set of findings obtains for the degree of student participation in planning and controlling what goes on in the classroom.

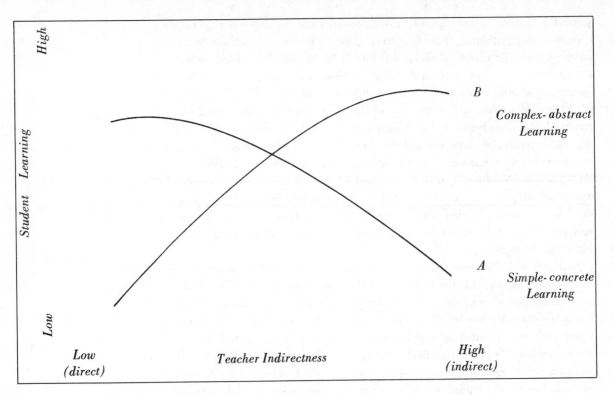

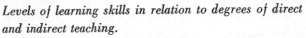

FIGURE 11.1.
*Levels of learning skills in relation to degrees of direct
and indirect teaching.*

APPLICATION 11.2: INDIRECT TEACHING AND CLASSROOM USE
OF STUDENTS' IDEAS

Go back to the dialogue in Application 11.1 and find instances of approval,
praise, and the use of students' ideas, as discussed in the above section. Also
look for opportunities for these behaviors that the teacher missed. Invent
statements that the teacher might have inserted to increase indirectness.

Criticism. Research studies have provided only mixed findings on the relationship between teacher criticism and student learning. The most important conclusion seems to involve a difference between harsh and mild criticism; harsh criticism is related to low learning, whereas mild criticism is only weakly related in this way. Several studies show mild criticism not to be related at all—or not positively related—to student learning. What is the difference between harsh or mild criticism? Harsh criticism often involves hostility and sarcasm, designed to hurt the person being criticized. ("Bob, that was a brilliant remark.") Mild criticism is more neutral; its purpose is to correct, rather than to hurt or to show hostility and dislike. ("Bob, your comment seems to miss the main point. Could you rephrase the idea so that it bears more directly on the subject?") Telling students they are wrong does not seem harmful, but there is evidence that sustained use of harsh criticism may be related to low learning levels.

Statements that structure information. Statements structured by the teacher provide organization for the students. They enable students to see how what is happening *now* in the class is connected to what has happened before and to what will happen later on. Examples include introductory comments, closing summaries or reviews, statements leading to pivotal questions, transition statements that signal the end of one part of a lesson and the beginning of another, and statements underscoring the importance of certain parts of a lesson. ("We're now going to turn to the subject of international trade, and we'll be linking the idea of comparative advantage, which we've just been learning about, to international trade.") Research results suggest a consistent positive relationship between the use of structuring statements and cognitive growth.

An example of a structuring statement can be seen in the continuation of the dialogue started in Application 11.1.

T: *You do. Okay, how many do we have who think it's democratic?* (Pause) *Okay, three, four? Okay, anybody think it's undemocratic?* (Pause) *You're abstaining?*

s1: (Chuckles) *Some people don't think at all.*

T: *Okay, so well, generally the consensus is that it is democratic, right?* Okay, well, in order to really answer this question, we're going to take our electoral system, break it down, and analyze it. And in order to do this, we need to establish also some conditions that we think are necessary in order for us to have a model, the perfect democratic electoral system. Okay? If we're wanting to set this up, you know, how we would go about it. *Okay. So let's first take the, uh, individual voter. We can't have an election without the voter. All right? Now, what do you think should be required of him? When that individual goes up to the voting machine and pulls that curtain and he's just about ready to pull down that little lever that makes his vote, what kinds of things should he be thinking about at that time?*

s1: *Will he really be able to handle the job?*

T: *Okay, his opinions of who he thinks is best able to handle the job. All right, anything else?* (Pause) *Okay.*

The structuring statement in this excerpt is not italicized. The statement frames for the students the next question and the subsequent analytical moves that the teacher intends to make. As often happens, the teacher launches into the set of moves he has structured by asking a question. The same thing occurs in lecturing, except that instead of a question, the first move is stating a principle or other core idea.

The excerpt also contains approval and use of students' ideas by the teacher. You should be able to spot them quickly.

Probing. Probing refers to teachers' reactions to students' answers, statements, or questions that try to elicit clarification or elaboration of what the student meant. A probe tries, in effect, to say to the student: "Tell the class and me more about what you just said. It sounds interesting." It encourages the student to carry on with the thinking he has initiated and not to drop it. Only three studies have connected this teacher behavior with student learning, but the little evidence available points to this as an important variable in promoting student learning.

The following excerpt, continuing the same dialogue as before, illustrates a probe by the teacher of student 3:

---

s3: *He shouldn't really be influenced by his friends if he really doesn't agree with the person.*

T: *The person.* What is it about this person, though? How are you judging this person; on what basis?

s3: *On the basis that he knows what he's talking about and that he will do what he says he will do.*

T: *Okay. So it's the individual and his policies, right? Whether or not he's informed about them.*

The probe is not italicized. As can be seen from the students' response, the teacher is successful in eliciting further thinking and explanation.

TEACHING CHARACTERISTICS NOT RELATED TO STUDENTS'
LEARNING

It is important to look at teacher behavior characteristics that have *not* been found to be related to student learning. A few of these will be mentioned here, in hopes that they will provide a perspective for viewing those behaviors that *are* related to student outcomes. Future research might contradict the lack of relationships, but at this point in time there is no evidence to support it.

Studies have not found consistent positive relationships between teacher praise and student learning. Both nonverbal (such as facial expressions) and verbal praise have been studied in this connection. As shown before, use of students' ideas is consistently related, and it might be inferred that a student finds the use of his ideas more rewarding than simple praise of those ideas.

The fact that simple praise is not related to student learning might be explained by an unexpected research finding. In studying the logic of teaching operations in secondary social studies classes, Arno A. Bellack closely examined the congruence between the logical operations a teacher *asked* a student to perform and the operations *actually* performed by the student.[3] For instance, if asked for a definition, does the student actually attempt a definition, or does he do something else such as give an opinion? Bellack also examined the kind of teacher assessment response to the students' answers—whether the teacher praised or criticized. Teachers praised about 80 percent of the time whether the answer was congruent or incongruent with the teacher's question.

The same finding obtained when the *substance* of the response was considered. The teachers praised an off-target response as often as when the response was on target. Perhaps teachers praise *any response* given, praise not depending on the *kind of response*. If this is the case, and students come to realize it, the lack of relationship between praise and student learning is not as surprising as it seems. If random behavior is rewarded, learning is unlikely to take place. In the Bellack study the teachers appeared to be rewarding randomly; perhaps this is why studies have shown the lack of relationship between simple praise and student learning.

Quantity of student participation in discussions does not appear to be related to cognitive learning. This fact raises the question of using the participation factor as a part of a student's grade. It depends on the assumptions being made. If the teacher assumes that participation in class discussions indicates student cognitive learning and is therefore similar to a paper-and-pencil test score, then the research seems to contradict such as assumption. But if the teacher is using participation level as an indicator of achievement on an oral discussion and an objective of analysis skills, then perhaps there is some logic behind the assumption. Considering only the *quantity* of participation, however, seems less worthwhile than assessing the *quality* of participation, given oral discussion objectives.

Finally, neither the length of the teacher's experience nor his knowledge of subject matter, indicated by college grades or the results of achievement tests, has been shown to be related to student learning!

METHOD OF INQUIRY AND METHOD OF AUTHORITY

In Chapter 2 the distinction between a method of inquiry and a method of authority was made. Three of the eight teacher behavior categories shown to be related to student learning illustrate this distinction in behavioral terms. In each case a method of authority leads to negative student outcomes. Concentration on teacher ideas and directness, use of harsh criticism, and not probing students' ideas are behaviors that characterize teachers using a method of authority. They lead to negative results. A method of inquiry, on the other hand, implies use of students' ideas and indirectness, lack of harsh criticism, and probing students for clarification and elaboration of their ideas. A method of inquiry involves more than just these behaviors. But limited knowledge linking student learning with these few characteristics lends empirical support to the method of inquiry.

How to Evaluate Instruction

Means of gathering and using information about these instructional factors that contribute to student learning are needed. That is the problem that will be taken up in the rest of the chapter.

Three sources of information can be used: students, other teachers or supervisors, and self-generated data. These sources will be discussed in turn, and ideas for instruments that might be used by each source will be suggested.

It should be noted that, in our view, self-analysis is the most important. Student or peer feedback is often very helpful, but in the end it is the individual teacher who must determine the need and direction for changing his own behavior, and self-analysis is always necessary.

INFORMATION FROM STUDENTS

Students constitute a large group that has a high level of contact with the teacher and therefore may be a richer source of information than the casual, infrequent observer. Students are perceptive about a number of important teacher characteristics; they can often uncover undesirable behavior patterns. On the other hand, they are relatively untrained observers and may key on traits that have little or no relationship to learning in classrooms. Personality and particular personal mannerisms, among others, are often attended to by students, but these factors are of secondary importance to the teacher who is trying to improve instruction. This suggests that student information has to be clearly structured if it is to be useful and not misleading.

One means of collecting information from students is by paper and pencil. These lend themselves well to structured responses. Student reluctance to answer questions about teaching is minimized through this device, assuming that the responses are anonymous. One kind of question on paper-and-pencil instruments is open-ended: "Are there particular things that you think should be changed about the way I teach or what goes on in class?" This kind of question may generate useful data, but it is rather general and unfocused. It might be used in conjunction with other, more specific questions that zero in on particular aspects of teaching: "Do you think I could help you learn more by changing the way I use the text, conduct discussion, give tests, or make assignments? Please explain your answer so that I will know why and how you think I should change any of these things."

When you frame an open-ended question for students, it is important to keep in mind your learning objective regarding the information you are asking for. We urge you to ask: "What helps or hinders you in learning in this class?" rather than: "Do you like me or the way I do things in this class?" If you ask the latter kinds of questions, it implies that your goal is that students should like you. That is not a bad goal, but it should not be equated or confused with that of student learning. Can students learn in a class whose teacher they do not like? Yes, they can. If students like the teacher very much, does this mean that they will learn? No, not necessarily.

If you do use open-ended questions of this type, we urge you to have some other person help you use the information from them. For example, before you look at the responses, have another teacher, a supervisor, your spouse, or some other person read and summarize the results for you, and then discuss them with you. There are two reasons for this suggestion. First, people all tend to be a bit defensive about others' evaluations of them, and this fuels the "selective perception" mechanism, which helps them unconsciously to refuse to attend to certain information that they do not like and to overreact to that which they do like. Another person's summary of the students' answers to open-ended questions can help you avoid this pitfall. Second, another person will contribute valuable insights and suggestions that you might not think of. The very process of discussing the results with someone else can be very beneficial just because it forces greater reflection and inquiry than otherwise might be the case.

Another kind of paper-and-pencil instrument that can generate student information is the closed-ended question. This type can be used to focus more sharply on specific behavior, but it is not as good as an open-ended instrument in allowing for very helpful student explanations and divergent comments. But if you want to aim student responses accurately at the factors to be improved, and desire an economical, less time-consuming instrument, the closed-ended questionnaire is useful. Questions can be followed by simple rating scales as shown in the following example.

Directions: Please answer the following questions by checking the one most accurate response. As you answer, think of the question as referring to how that part of teaching helps or hinders you in learning in this class, and *not* to whether you like or dislike the teacher.

a. How much attention does the teacher pay to student ideas that are expressed in class?

_____None

_____Very little—some, but not enough

_____About the right amount

_____Too much—so much is done with student ideas that we're often off the subject

b. Do you have the feeling in this class that we have things to learn and know how to do that, or does it seem as though we fool around a lot and don't get much done?

_____We have things to learn and get down to business.

_____There is too much emphasis on getting down to business and too little time in exploring interesting ideas.

_____We fool around a lot and don't seem to learn much.

Another kind of closed-ended item sets up a dimension with opposite but paired objectives, between which there is a rating scale. The following is an example.

Directions: Please check the place on the scale that represents your reaction to how this class stands. As you answer, think of the question as referring to how that part of teaching helps or hinders you in learning in this class, and *not* to whether you like or dislike the teacher.

The teaching is:

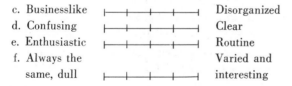

c. Businesslike   Disorganized
d. Confusing   Clear
e. Enthusiastic   Routine
f. Always the
    same, dull   Varied and interesting

This last kind of item is the easiest for students to answer and gives considerable information. The adjectives must be chosen with care, both because students might not understand them and because the adjectives should be opposites. It should also be noted that the direction of the scale is alternated, so that checking the extreme right-hand side of the first scale is a negative rating, while on the second it is positive. This is done to avoid the tendency to respond at the same place for all items, and to force a close reading of the adjective pairs.

These closed-ended data can be tabulated by you with much less danger of selective perception as discussed above. Nevertheless, we urge you to discuss the findings and their interpretations with another person. The last device, with the adjective pairs, can be used to check for change over a period of time, such as from lesson to lesson, from month to month, or across different years. It can also be used to focus on particular lessons, instructional modes, and techniques that you are interested in, simply by modifying the directions.

A third form of student feedback can be generated through open class discussion, either with you present, or with another teacher present and you absent. This is the most difficult information to get and use, both because of students' reluctance to be candid and because it is relatively unreliable—what students might say one day might change completely on another day. Despite these serious drawbacks, there are some advantages. Students tend to stimulate one another's thinking in a group discussion, and this can result in information that might not be gained using paper-and-pencil instruments. Also, students may be encouraged to become more active and autonomous as learners if they see that they have some input into the decision-making process in their classroom. This suggests that if you are not prepared to respond to students' suggestions, open discussions are probably a bad idea, since you will generate student disappointment and distrust.

In carrying on such an evaluative discussion, care must be taken that it does not dissolve into a meaningless bull session or random complaint department. To avoid this, you must have planned to lead a structured, businesslike discussion in which students understand that you are trying to find out their reactions in order to improve your teaching so that they will learn more. Similarly, they must be assured that no retribution will fall on their heads as a result of speaking out (fear of this is one reason a colleague, rather than you, might better be present) and that if the information is congruent with other data you have, you are prepared to change your teaching.

Again, if you are present, we urge you to use a colleague as another observer and to have him summarize and help interpret the results. If you lead the discussion, this is especially true because of your involvement in and lack of detachment from what went on.

When should student data be gathered? This, of course, depends on your objectives and the circumstances of your situation. But we can advise you not to wait until the end of the semester or year, when you are least likely to make any changes in your behavior. Think of student-generated information as contributing to formative rather than to summative evaluation. The earlier you start collecting such data, the better your opportunities for using it effectively.

INFORMATION FROM PEERS

Teaching colleagues should be insightful observers of teaching and may be better sources of information about your instruction than students. One problem with peers is that, unlike students, they are few in number, and you may have trouble persuading more than one or two teachers to observe you at the same time, so it is difficult to judge how reliable the observations are. Despite this problem the insights of another professional are usually valuable, and this source of data should be exploited whenever possible. Asking for data from peers has the added advantage of contributing to the solutions of problems that are uncovered. Whereas students are relatively unsophisticated about how to change what they see as wrong, colleagues may be able to help significantly in this regard.

One way to collect peer information is to ask for a simple, open-ended visit and postclass discussion. But it might be more helpful if you can focus the observations in particular targets of concern. The eight variables, found to be related to learning and described earlier in this chapter, might serve as categories for the observations. Similarly, you might ask your colleagues to observe other phenomena that you think are important or that students have identified as problems. Mannerisms of speech, length or complexity of questions, and clarity of directions in making assignments are examples of such factors that another teacher might be looking for.

Another potentially helpful device is to reverse the observation so that you visit another teacher's classroom, affording a comparison between your behavior and his and perhaps leading to insights that would otherwise be impossible.

One major problem concerning the collection of information from either students or peers may be norms that make such procedures difficult and perhaps impossible. In spite of its inherent professional nature, evaluation of teaching, even your own, is suspect by some teachers and even by some administrators. Even students may react negatively to what has been suggested. But we urge you not to *assume* automatically that such norms exist or that you will be ostracized by your peers if you try to evaluate and change your teaching. Teachers often imagine that certain behavior in schools is contrary to norms, when in fact there are no penalties attached to it at all. Some individuals might try to convince you not to do this or that because they feel threatened, when in fact the majority of teachers, if asked, would disagree with the few dissenters. It might take a bit of risk taking on your part to generate some new norms regarding evaluation of teaching. Do not give up before you try.

SELF-ASSESSMENT

Because self-assessment depends less on a public process in schools than on assessment by others, there are fewer problems with violating the norms of others while engaging in self-analysis. That is why we feel that it is especially important, and why we give it more extensive treatment than assessment by students and peers.

Self-assessment means the process of collecting your own evaluation information and using that information systematically to improve your teaching. Students and peers may or may not be used in this process, but you yourself are the principal agent in collecting, analyzing, and using the data to change your teaching. This process suffers from the disadvantages raised earlier; your biases and selective perception may distort the objectivity of information, and not having others' reactions and interpretations detracts from the full potential of evaluation. Still, it is most realistic to expect that if you must evaluate your instruction systematically in schools where contrary norms exist, self-assessment is the most likely and reasonable mode of operations open to you, since it is relatively private.

Recording instruction. For self-assessment to work, you will need means of recording class sessions. The possibilities include: audio-tape recorders, video-tape recorders, student observers and note takers, and teacher observers and note takers. Rather than using others' *interpretations* of your teaching behavior, as discussed in the previous two sections, you may now attempt to keep an accurate *record* of teaching behavior, and interpret it yourself. Thus, the term *self-assessment*. Some may argue that using such recording means in the classroom, whether mechanical or human, will alter what goes on to the extent that the results will not be worth the effort; some will say that the teacher's own memory is a more worthwhile "recorder." Reliance on memory has serious drawbacks. Selective perception may distort the interpretation of written responses of students, and this difficulty is probably even more severe when trying to reconstruct accurately a class session in which you yourself were teaching. Also, very few have the ability to remember accurately enough to reconstruct an entire class session. For these reasons we recommend the use of recordings in addition to memory in the self-assessment process.

Audio-tape recorders are often available in schools, and many teachers own one. Cassette recorders are the least obtrusive, and some machines now have built-in microphones, so that the usual object of distraction—the mike—is not a problem. Video-tape recorders are less often available, although an increasing number of schools own them. We have been in several schools in which social studies teachers did not realize that the school had such equipment and that it was available to them.

Video-tape equipment is particularly good if you are working on nonverbal dimensions of classroom processes which audio-tape recorders are not able to reproduce. Video-tape recordings can also help to identify individual students more easily. But if these last two factors are not important, audio-tape machines are in one important respect better: they are not distracting to students and teacher. We have observed, however, that after some exposure to the use of video-tape equipment, students and teachers act normally, and little if any disruption results.

Recording machines are faithful reproducers of verbal classroom discourse but may be impractical. Students and other teachers can be used in place of machines with some distinct advantages. They can be instructed to be selective is what is recorded, observed, or rated, and thus they can conveniently abstract long lessons into relatively useful forms, with the result that the self-assessment is not as time-consuming as it is with a mechanical recorder. For example, assume you want to know the proportion of time you spend talking in class. A student or teacher observer can be told how to get this information during class, rather than having you tape-record the lesson and then having to listen to the whole tape to get the information. Much more sophisticated coding tasks can be performed simultaneously by the same person or by others, saving you important time. Length and clarity of questions and types of teacher responses to student-initiated ideas, for example, are all easy for students to code, and they are often interested in helping teachers while doing something novel and interesting. Other teachers can be used in the same way, but they have much less time than students and will probably be used for relatively sophisticated tasks.

Analytic procedure. Whatever means of recording are used for your self-assessment process, systematic analytic procedures are necessary. For our purposes as social studies teachers, the term *assessment* implies that measurements of some teaching process are compared with some standards and that a judgment is made as to whether the observed process was good or needs improvement. We have discussed means of *recording* classroom verbal processes, and we have to establish systems of measurements with which to use these recordings. The standards to be suggested come from the earlier section in which the eight factors (clarity, enthusiasm, use of students' ideas, and so on), which seem related to student outcomes, were discussed. These will be used as standards for judgments in conjunction with the relevant objectives to be specified for a particular teaching situation. An example of the process may help to make this clear.

An eleventh-grade teacher of United States history is teaching a unit on the topic of migrations. One particular class session is devoted to the *consequences* of migrations in history, such as the American Indian migrations westward, the rural-to-urban migration, and the South-to-North migration of blacks. One of the teacher's principal objectives is to generate hypothesizing behavior in response to the general question: "What were the consequences of these migrations?" He is concerned about his use of students' ideas during the open-ended discussion he has planned because, after observing one of his earlier classes, one of his peers pointed out that he tended to focus the attention of the class on his own ideas.

The teacher makes an audio-tape recording of the class session and later listens to the tape. He tallies the number of times he, in some way, used students' ideas when they were offered and the number of times he ignored them. To his surprise, he could find only two genuine hypotheses that were offered; the rest of the talk by students seemed to be focused on asking questions of him and trying to clarify what he wanted them to do. Because of this there was very little use of students' ideas since few of their statements had to do with the substance of the lesson. He then decided that he had been unsuccessful in meeting his objective of generating hypotheses and in using students' ideas. He replayed the tape, listening closely to his structuring statements and the questions with which he had intended to elicit the hypotheses. He found that the questions were long and confused and that he repeated himself, often changing the question as he did so. He concluded that clarity of questions was a serious problem and began to practice forming succinct, clear questions; he resisted repeating himself, even if a student failed to answer immediately.

In this example the *standards* were: (1) Did the students hypothesize answers to the main question? (2) Did the teacher use students' ideas when they were verbalized? The *measurement* devices were a simple count of student hypotheses and the sorting of reactions to students' ideas into two categories: he either used an idea or did not use it. After comparing the measurements with the standards, the teacher made a negative judgment and *diagnosed* his problem as one of question clarity.

There will be occasions in the self-assessment process when the use of recordings of class sessions will be followed by impressionistic (nonsystematic) analysis. This could be bad or good. If your purpose is simply to listen to the verbal interaction of your class without having to think of other things at the same time, as is true when you are teaching, then open-ended, impressionistic analysis may be just the right tool for analyzing your teaching in a new light. If your analysis is to be focused sharply on particular variables, however, you should use more systematic analytic procedures. We have already suggested some of these: weighing teacher and student talk to determine the proportion of each, counting student statements of a particular type (hypotheses), counting the number of times the teacher uses students' ideas versus the times he ignores them, and measuring the length and style of question-asking. All of these simple measurements can be important, depending on your individual needs. Here are some other easy ways of generating data relevant to the standards discussed earlier in the chapter.

Clarity. Three specific clues to your clarity can be discovered by analyzing classroom recordings. First, you can count the number of times you have to answer student questions that ask for an interpretation of what you have said in a lecture, for an explanation in discussion, or an assignment you have made. There may be other cases in which you might expect such student requests for interpretation or clarification, but these are three principal ones. If you do allow for such student feedback and if you do observe it regularly, this may be a signal that you are not being as clear as you should be.

Second, you can count the number of times that students respond to your questions with requests for clarification or with expressions of not understanding. You can, if you code student responses to *all* your questions, figure a proportion of responses to your questions: the proportion of misunderstood teacher questions = misunderstood questions/all questions. There is no absolute standard for this proportion, but if it is from 0.20 to 0.25 or higher, representing one-fifth to one-quarter or more of your questions, it is probably serious enough a problem that you should work to correct it.

Third, an indicator of clarity that is fairly easy to spot on recordings is the number of times you repeat yourself by restating exactly or rephrasing remarks, questions, directions, and assignments, for example. Repeating may be a sign that you yourself are unsure of your clarity and are trying to make certain that the students understand you by saying or asking the same thing several times or in several ways. Unfortunately, the result is often more, rather than less, confusion, and repeating yourself should be wiped out of your teaching behavior as much as possible.

If you have diagnosed your teaching as less clear than it should be, one solution is to practice stating or questioning in more succinct ways. From the tape or from example statements that an observer might have written down, you can try to reformulate a clearer way of saying or asking the unclear part. Practice of this kind, although it sounds simple, will help. Another plan that can help is to wait before you explain an important point or ask a key question and to think out how you are going to say it. This plan may take an extra second or two, and it might cause your teaching to appear less smooth, but these are trivial concerns compared to that of clarity.

Another possible source of problems with clarity is a failure to understand and organize your lessons. If you have not done your homework completely and have not thought through your objectives or the topic, the result can be a rambling, disconnected lecture or discussion, with much jumping from idea to idea without coherence. This, too, can cause lack of clarity and can be solved by more attention to thinking about and planning instruction. You always have to "think on your feet" as a social studies teacher, but complete reliance on that mode in place of thorough preparation can prove disastrous in terms of students' understanding of what is going on.

Variety. A more difficult quality than clarity to capture directly from classroom recordings is variety. One factor does have to do with the cognitive level of operations in classes, however, and this can be coded according to a simple scheme. Try to categorize your own and students' verbal statements or questions into one of four possible types: (1) low-level *memory* or *recall* where the emphasis is on remembering ("During the Cuban Missile Crisis, what proof did we have that the Cubans had missiles?"); (2) *convergent thinking* where the emphasis is on a higher level but will result in a single right answer ("What historical analogies are there for President Kennedy's blockade of Cuba, and what are the differences between the analogies and the Cuban Missile Crisis?"); (3) *divergent thinking* where there is higher than recall-level thinking should result in an unpredictable number of "grounded" or "justified" answers ("What were some alternative actions that President Kennedy could have taken in the Cuban Missile Crisis?"); and (4) *evaluative thinking* where the thrust is on a normative or values level rather than on a factual one ("Was President Kennedy right in using United States military power to bluff the Russians when there was substantial danger of world war?"). After categorizing the classroom discourse into these cognitive levels, do you have a picture of the class at a single level of thinking, or is there variety? Conducting entire sessions at one level—recall or convergent thinking, for example—can be boring to students and may be why variability is related to student learning. Intelligent mixing of cognitive levels is not difficult after you have decided that it is necessary.

Variety in the use of materials and instructional modes, among others, is also important, although information about it is best not acquired through analysis of classroom records. Perhaps a simpler way of determining variability in this regard is to ask yourself: "Do you use written and other materials besides your regular text? Do you vary the way in which you use them? Are you locked into a routine of read assignment, recite in class, listen to lecture, take test? Do you tend to start and finish classes in the same way day after day?" If the answers to these questions indicate lack of variety, the solutions should be obvious. Sameness, routine, and uniformity in teaching should be avoided.

Enthusiasm. The term *enthusiasm* can mean different things to different persons, and it is difficult to be specific about how to measure it. In part, it can be observed through analysis of audio or video tapes and in terms of gestures, movements, and oral expressions. The use of varying inflection, tone, and pace can impart a sense of enthusiasm. Observers can provide information about such factors, although it is best to brief them on what specific attributes of enthusiasm to watch for. Using the same recorder over a period of time might also be important here.

Another factor, questions calling for interpretations of facts and ideas, has already been pointed out as being part of enthusiasm. In asking this kind of question, the teacher projects the unstated feeling that: "These facts or ideas are especially important or relevant. I think that you students can analyze them or put them together so as to go beyond them, and that will be interesting!" This is a different kind of feeling than the more pedestrian attitude that might be transmitted in the absence of interpretation questions: "We're going to remember these facts and ideas for the test, whether or not we'll ever use them in any other way."

Interpretation questions can be isolated and counted. Especially in class sessions characterized by a fairly high proportion of thinking on the memory and recall level, the presence of these questions might be the difference between enthusiastic and unenthusiastic teaching. If they are absent or very rare, you can start to insert them, examining the difference in reception on the part of your students.

Businesslike behavior. Teachers can generate several useful indicators of businesslike behavior which can help aim efforts at producing more on-task learning behavior. The first indicator is the result of simply recording the amount of time in class in which the teacher and students are on task—what it is that they are saying that has to do with the objectives set out for that session. It is good to keep separate records for the teacher and students, since there may be a difference in on- and off-task behavior for the two sources. If the teacher is mostly on task and if the students deviate greatly, this may indicate lack of interest or confusion. If both sources are considerably off task, this may signal lack of clarity, ill-defined goals and objectives, poor planning, or other similar problems. You may be surprised at the amount and length of irrelevant and digressive behavior, both student and teacher originated.

Another pair of indicators, which are rather easy to generate, are how quickly the class session came to on-task behavior and whether the class ended on or off task. Using several class sessions of the same general type—lecture, discussion, recitation, reports—record the time from the start of class to the beginning of steady on-task performance. Similarly, determine whether the end of the class was marked by on-task performance and, if not, what was happening. Was there a long digression on a different topic, were students trying to obtain clarification on unrelated points such as administrative details, and so on? If the lessons seem to take more than a couple of minutes to start, or if they end consistently off task, these factors need attention. More careful planning, more powerful attention getters to catch and sustain interest, and perhaps more stimulating instructional modes, techniques, or materials may need your attention. Finally, you may be avoiding on-task behavior yourself, perhaps for unconscious or unanalyzed reasons. If the evidence indicates that this is a possible explanation, you may need to rethink your goals.

Statements that structure information. Because these statements lend organization and coherence to teaching and because they are positively linked to student outcomes, they deserve careful scrutiny. As with the behavioral indicators associated with clarity, these statements can be observed, and teachers can practice their use while using a recorded version of class sessions. If few structuring statements are found and if the lessons seem to jump from topic to topic with a lack of "verbal connecting tissue," try to find logical points in the lesson where structuring statements might better explain to the student the "connectedness" of what is going on. Then try to insert these connectors in actual classroom teaching. Their use can mean the difference between understanding and not understanding for your students.

Probing. Teacher reactions that try to elicit clarification and elaboration of student ideas are also important in social studies teaching, especially in the discussion technique. You can listen to a record of a discussion and mark your reactions to students' ideas for one of two categories: (1) The reaction probed the student to clarify or elaborate his idea; (2) The reaction caused him either to accept or reject the idea but did not cause him to work on it further. By categorizing teacher reactions in this way, you can determine the extent of your probing behavior. Although it probably does not make sense to probe all student ideas, it is worthwhile, according to research evidence, to probe at a fairly high level. This may be especially true if the thinking level is divergent or evaluative, where explaining and clarifying are especially important to the achievement of goals at those cognitive levels.

Use of students' ideas and criticism: The need for classifying verbal interaction. In dealing with the last two teacher behaviors known to be linked to student outcomes—use of students' ideas and criticisms—it will be helpful to describe a system for classifying all verbal interaction in the classroom into a set of ten mutually exclusive categories: the Flanders' Interaction Analysis Categories system.[4] This simple system, or others like it containing different categories, can prove to be a valuable tool for self-assessment and professional growth of teachers.

To use the system, an observer sits in the classroom or listens to a video- or audio-tape record of the classroom. At regular three-second intervals he codes the present state of verbal behavior into one of the ten categories. At the end of a lesson, the totals for each category are figured, and other, more sophisticated sequential analyses can be made. By using this systematic procedure, an accurate record of several important indicators can be generated—including those of criticism and use of students' ideas, both of which represent categories of the system. Table 11.1 shows the categories of the system with brief descriptions of each category.

Use of this category system generates a frequency measure of the use of students' ideas. If there is very little teacher behavior evident in category 3, then attention should be paid to generating more such behavior. The creative use of students' ideas can take many forms. Probing for clarification and elaboration is one. Forming a new question from a student's idea is another. Asking another student to reflect on the idea is still another. With some practice this act of focusing attention on a student's idea by using it in some way becomes easier and more natural.

To obtain useful information about the incidence of criticism, go a step beyond the Flanders category 7, *criticizing or justifying authority.* In the earlier section where the relationship of criticism and student learning was

TABLE 11.1.
*Flanders' Interaction
Analysis Categories*[a]
(FIAC).

TEACHER TALK	*Response*	1. *Accepts feeling.* Accepts and clarifies an attitude or the feeling tone of a pupil in a nonthreatening manner. Feelings may be positive or negative. Predicting and recalling feelings are included.
		2. *Praises or encourages.* Praises or encourages pupil action or behavior. Jokes that release tension, but not at the expense of another individual; nodding head, or saying "Um hm?" or "go on" are included.
		3. *Accepts or uses ideas of pupils.* Clarifying, building, or developing ideas suggested by a pupil. Teacher extensions of pupil ideas are included but as the teacher brings more of his own ideas into play, shift to category five.
		4. *Asks questions.* Asking a question about content or procedure, based on teacher ideas, with the intent that a pupil will answer.
	Initiation	5. *Lecturing.* Giving facts or opinions about content or procedures; expressing *his own* ideas, giving *his own* explanation, or citing an authority other than a pupil.
		6. *Giving directions.* Directions, commands, or orders to which a pupil is expected to comply.
		7. *Criticizing or justifying authority.* Statements intended to change pupil behavior from nonacceptable to acceptable pattern; bawling someone out; stating why the teacher is doing what he is doing; extreme self-reference.
PUPIL TALK	*Response*	8. *Pupil-talk–response.* Talk by pupils in response to teacher. Teacher initiates the contact or solicits pupil statement or structures the situation. Freedom to express own ideas is limited.
	Initiation	9. *Pupil-talk–initiation.* Talk by pupils which they initiate. Expressing own ideas; initiating a new topic; freedom to develop opinions and a line of thought, like asking thoughtful questions; going beyond the existing structure.
SILENCE		10. *Silence or confusion.* Pauses, short periods of silence and periods of confusion in which communication cannot be understood by the observer.

SOURCE: Ned A. Flanders, *Analyzing Teaching Behavior*, Addison-Wesley Publishing Company, 1970.

[a]There is *no* scale implied by these numbers. Each number is classifactory: it designates a particular kind of communication event. To write these numbers down during observation is to enumerate not to judge a position on a scale.

discussed, the distinction between mild and harsh criticism was made. Harsh criticism is negatively related to student learning, while mild criticism is not. The present category 7, therefore, needs to be broken down into *subscripts:* mild criticism (7A) and harsh criticism (7B). The former includes teacher feedback that is negative but helpful—designed to help the student discriminate, for example, between two related concepts. The latter, harsh criticism, contains an element of hurtfulness; it is intended to make the student feel bad. This often includes sarcasm. If you find that harsh criticism is a regular part of your teaching, this requires rethinking and perhaps restraint on your part, as it may be leading to unintended negative outcomes.

This subscripting of categories of the Flanders system is an important way to get extra information from its use. The teacher questions, category 4, and the two student categories, 8 and 9, are often subscripted to reflect different cognitive levels of discourse.

Another bit of information that can be generated from a coded lesson record is the proportion of teacher talk. The totals for categories 1 through 7, teacher talk, are summed, and a proportion is computed by dividing by the grand total of tallies. (Extensive research has shown that between 60 and 70 percent of class talk is teacher talk.) Your particular objectives might dictate a large teacher talk proportion, but if the emphasis is on student verbalization of ideas, then the more teacher talk there is, the more interference with that objective. Many teachers are surprised at the high proportion of talking they do in their own classes. This coding scheme allows a quick and objective check on this characteristic. As teachers become aware that they are talking excessively, they can control and reduce systematically the teacher talk proportion.

Similarly, the coding system allows the teacher to examine how much of his talk is devoted to lecturing. If he has chosen a discussion or discovery mode for a lesson but finds that instead of using student ideas, questioning, and encouraging, most teacher talk is lecturing, then this incongruence must be removed. Otherwise, it will interfere with the achievement of objectives. A similar analysis can uncover excessive direction giving.

An earlier section explained the concept indirectness as a teacher's verbalization quality that places emphasis on students', rather than on teachers', ideas and direction. The Flanders system makes it possible to compute a ratio by combining several category totals according to the following formula:

$$\text{Indirectness ratio} = \frac{\text{Total tallies in categories } 1 + 2 + 3}{\text{Total tallies in categories } 1 + 2 + 3 + 6 + 7}$$

If this ratio is very low, then the denominator, containing the totals of categories 6 (directions) and 7 (criticism), must be large relative to the numerator, which contains the student-oriented categories (accepts feeling, praises or encourages, and accepts or uses students' ideas). Conversely, if the ratio is large, the numerator is larger compared with the denominator, and the ratio, coming closer in value to 1.0, indicates more indirectness. As was explained before, this quality is linked to student learning when the cognitive level is relatively abstract. The Flanders coding system gives an indicator of this important factor and points the direction for changing a very low ratio—more emphasis on categories 1, 2, and 3 and less emphasis on categories 6 and 7.

In the student talk categories the Flanders system generates an important indicator of the kinds of student thinking being exhibited in class through verbal statements. By forming a ratio of $9/8 + 9$, it can be determined what proportion of student talk was self-initiated as compared with student talk in response to teacher initiation. Thus, if an objective includes the creative use by students of a set of historical evidence to solve a particular problem, you have to expect a higher student-initiated idea ratio than if the objective centered around recitation from a reading assignment. A high ratio does not insure that students are using the evidence in a thoughtful, creative way. But if the ratio is low, you can be reasonably sure they are not, and this may point to possible problems and their solutions. Again, teacher awareness of a problem that has been previously undetected is a necessary first step in solving the problem.

Many other category systems for coding verbal interaction in the classroom exist, and descriptions of nearly all can be found in an anthology called *Mirrors for Behavior*, edited by Anita Simon and E. Gil Boyer.

Theodore Parsons has developed a very comprehensive system that he calls Guided Self-analysis.[5] Designed to aid teachers employing a method of inquiry, this set of materials guides and supports both pre- and in-service teachers in recording and analyzing their teaching behavior in a systematic fashion, much as has been suggested in this chapter. The system is broken into several task areas: (1) teacher questioning strategies, (2) teacher response patterns, (3) teacher talk patterns, (4) teacher-pupil talk patterns, and (5) student experience referents in concept teaching. This very comprehensive self-analysis system is particularly well suited for use by secondary social studies teachers, and its use in school systems is increasing.

Summary

Eight teaching characteristics have been linked through educational research to student learning outcomes. They are: clarity, variety, enthusiasm, businesslike behavior, use of students' ideas and indirectness, use of criticism, structuring statements, and probing. All except criticism are positively related to learning by students.

Using these characteristics as standards, teachers can use information from both students and peers to evaluate their own instruction. More important, these standards can be used in a process of self-evaluation. Flanders' Interaction Analysis Categories and other coding systems can be used to gather information in this process.

APPLICATION 11.3: EVALUATION OF AN ACTUAL CLASS ON THE BASIS OF THE TEACHING CRITERIA

To demonstrate the application of several teaching evaluation concepts presented in this chapter, here is a 4 1/2-minute discussion with ninth graders. This discussion, although short, contains several interesting elements, some of which you will want to discover. Additional information is needed before presenting the discussion as it actually happened. This teaching was done in a small group, numbering five ninth graders, of average to somewhat above average intelligence. The teacher's principal objective was to elicit student hypotheses and to discuss these hypotheses with respect to the problems that he posed. The content of the discussion has not been changed in the transcript. A video-tape record was employed to create the transcript as well as the verbal interaction coding used later. Directions follow the dialogue.

---

1.   TEACHER: *The Vietnam War has been going on for many years with losses of thousands of lives. Why do you think our country originally got involved over there?*

2.   LINDA: *Because they asked for help.*

3.   (Pause)

4.   SARA: *Which one of us did you want to have answer?*

5.   TEACHER: *Well, you.*

6.   SARA: *Well, there's one thing, that supposedly, uh, we had a treaty, or something like that, supposedly, uh, hoping with that involvement that we would help them, I think it was . . .*

7.   TIM: *SEATO.*

8.	SARA:	*Yes . . .*

9.	EMILY:	*South East Asia Treaty Organization.*

10.	SARA:	*Yes, but well, it said that—I don't really think it says it, but that's what they claim it says, that we were committed to help them in time of war, that if they get attacked, or something, but I don't think SEATO says that.*

11.	TEACHER:	*Okay, uh, what consequences could have come out if we wouldn't have gone there?* (To student) *Okay.*

12.	TIM:	*South Vietnam would have gone communist, and they would have had one more country in their power, and they would, uh, maybe have more people in control that would have wiped out more people.*

13.	EMILY:	*Also, if we hadn't gone there, there wouldn't be so many American soldiers dead.*

14.	SARA:	*The draft would be lower, if there wasn't . . . something like that.*

15.	TEACHER:	*Okay, what do you think of the domino theory in Vietnam?*

16.	TIM:	*I've heard of that.*

17.	EMILY:	*What's that?*

18.	SARA:	*That's like when you have them all like dominoes, where if you push down Vietnam, they all go. Something to that effect.*

19.	TIM:	*Oh, yeah.*

20.	EMILY:	*Vietnam's so small . . .*

21.	SARA:	*Well, I don't think so. I don't think the rest of the world would go, because I think the rest of the world is too powerful, or something like that. I mean, I admit somewhere in that area there might be takeovers, but you've also got Communist China. If Russia was backing North Vietnam, you might have, you know, Communist China backing other countries, so . . . because I don't think Communist China wants other people in that area, where they're situated.*

22.	TEACHER:	*Uh, okay. What would be some of the consequences of our pulling out of there?* (Pause) *Like now, or like earlier?*

23.		(Pause)
24.	SARA:	*They said at one point that Communist China might come in and try to take over. I don't know about the likelihood of something like that.*
25.	TEACHER:	*What things do you think would happen in our country if we pulled out?*
26.	EMILY:	*There would probably be a lot less unrest . . . in youth.*
27.	SARA:	*We could put all the money that's in the war into better uses.*
28.	ALL STUDENTS:	*Yeh.*
29.	TEACHER:	*Don't you think there would be more unrest in our country with all these people coming back? People might concentrate on different things that are wrong with the country.*
30.	EMILY:	*Um, I don't know . . .*
31.	TIM:	*I think war is good—it keeps down the population* (Nervous laughter)
32.	TIM:	*Well, that's one of the biggest problems now—overpopulation.*
33.	SARA:	*You . . . there's better ways of curbing it . . .*
34.	TIM:	*I know . . .*
35.	SARA:	*You know, than putting people in a war.*
36.		(Pause)
37.	TEACHER:	*Okay. How do you think the economy would be affected?*
38.	EMILY:	*It would go down.* (Teacher nods in agreement)
39.	EMILY:	*Because in wartime the economy flourishes.*
40.	TEACHER:	*Okay . . . What else do you think might happen with the economy, like with all these people coming in . . .*
41.	SARA:	*High unemployment. Or higher . . .*

42.   EMILY: *But with all the money we'll save they'll reduce it.*

43.   SARA: *Yeh, well no, because it has . . . let's say you've got a lot of people coming back in, and they've been trained for certain things. Maybe, they say, supposedly, you're supposed to be able to put them into civilian-life jobs, then there are only so many you can put in.*

44.   TEACHER: *How do you think the rest of the world would feel about us pulling out . . . like our allies . . .?*

45.   EMILY: *Well, they would probably . . .*

Note: The discussion continues in this vein for a few more moments, and then stops when the teacher has no more questions. They begin a new activity after that.

How well do you think the teacher performed? Using the eight main assessment criteria outlined in this chapter, plus any additional ones you believe are important, support your evaluation of the teaching in this example.

_____

_____

_____

_____

_____

_____

_____

_____

_____

_____

_____

_____

Here is our evaluation of the teaching and the grounds for that assessment. We hope you have made similar points in your evaluation.

The teaching was very weak. *Clarity* of the teacher's individual questions was good; they were crisp and short, and not repeated. But the *organizational clarity* of the discussion as a whole was almost nonexistent. The teacher jumped from question to question with no apparent coherence or structure; the topics seemed unrelated. If you have not done so, read just the teacher questions in sequence in the following order: numbers 1, 11, 15, 22, 25, 29, 37, 40, and 44. Related to this criticism is the complete lack of *structural statements*. The first sentence is an introduction but does not prepare the students with a cognitive organization for what is to follow. Closely related are the lack of any *probing* and the nearly total absence of the *use of students' ideas*.

At no point does the teacher probe the students—and some of the students' ideas are interesting and often unexplained—for clarification, elaboration, further explanation, and so on. At only one point, number 29, does the teacher use a student's idea. Here the teacher challenges the student's "less domestic unrest" hypothesis with the counter hypothesis in number 29. But this is not carried beyond the student's tentative "I don't know . . . ," which sounds on the tape as if the student *could have* and *wanted to* reason further, if she had been invited to do so. Although it is difficult to infer from the transcript alone, *enthusiasm*, as evidenced on the video-tape record, was almost zero.

To examine the discussion in a different way, we coded it with the Flanders' Interaction Analysis Categories system, with the following distribution of tallies in each category of the system:

Number of Tallies	Percent of Tallies	Category Number	Category Description
3	3	2	Teacher praise or encouragement
2	2	3	Teacher acceptance or use of students' ideas
17	18	4	Teacher question
3	3	5	Teacher lecture
23	25	8	Teacher-initiated student response
40	43	9	Student-initiated student response
6	6	10	Silence or confusion
94	100		

An inspection of the results of the interaction analysis shows the almost total lack of category 3 entries. The level of category 5 is also very low;

this is not necessarily a bad indicator, except that it signifies, among other things, the lack of structuring statements. On the good side there is an admirably low teacher talk proportion (about 0.26) and an equally admirable high student-initiated talk proportion (about 0.63). But a close examination of the *sequence* of verbal interaction codes in this discussion reveals that the teacher almost never reacted to students' ideas but went right on with the next question, from either a written or memorized list. Because of this behavior pattern, the "discussion" turns into a "recitation," with a teacher question–student response–teacher question–student response sequence. In this case the low teacher talk and high student initiation means much less than if it had occurred in a coherent, organized discussion in which students got the teacher's reactions. The few category 2's that are coded are only "okay" (numbers 11, 15, 22, 37, and 40) and seem to represent a verbal habit of the teacher rather than praise or encouragement. The lack of teacher reaction to and use of student responses, we believe, is the single most important feature of this discussion. It, as much as lack of organizational clarity, is responsible for the overall lack of coherence in the lesson and is the reason that it appears to lead nowhere.

APPLICATION 11.4: CORRECTION AND IMPROVEMENT OF TEACHING FOLLOWING EVALUATION

To build on the basis of this evaluation, practice correcting some of the faults noted in the critique. Invest ways you could *use students' ideas, probe,* or both after numbers 10, 12–14, 21, 24, 28, 36, 39, 42, and 43 of the transcript. Invent actual statements or questions you might use in the class as if you were the teacher. Also, invent a *structuring statement* for the opening and at other points that you believe warrant such statements.

_____

_____

_____

_____

_____

_____

_____

_____

_____

_____

_____

_____

_____

_____

_____

_____

_____

_____

_____

_____

_____

Notes

1. This and the next section draw heavily on the work of Barak Rosenshine and Norma Furst, "Research on Teacher Performance Criteria," in *Research in Teacher Education: A Symposium,* ed. by B. Othanel Smith, Englewood Cliffs, N.J.: Prentice-Hall, 1971, pp. 37–72. For an expanded analysis of this subject, see Barak Rosenshine, *Teaching Behaviors and Student Achievement,* London: National Foundation for Educational Research in England and Wales, 1971.

2. Ned A. Flanders, *Analyzing Teaching Behavior,* Reading, Mass.: Addison-Wesley, 1970, pp. 403–409. Robert S. Soar and Ruth M. Soar, "An Empirical Analysis of Selected Follow Through Programs: An Example of a Process Approach to Evaluation," in *Early Childhood Education,* National Society for the Study of Education Seventy-first Yearbook Pt. 2., Chicago: N.S.S.E., 1972, pp. 229–260.

3. Arno A. Bellack et al., *The Language of the Classroom,* New York: Teachers College Press, 1966, pp. 185–189.

4. A more complete description of the categories can be found in several sources. They include: Ned A. Flanders, op. cit., and Edmond J. Aimdon and Ned A. Flanders, *The Role of the Teacher in the Classroom*, rev. ed., Minneapolis: Association for Productive Teaching, Inc., 1967.

5. Theodore W. Parsons, *Guided Self-analysis: System for Profession Development Education Series, Teaching for Inquiry*, Berkeley, Calif.: University of California, 1971.

Suggested Reading

Simon, Anita, and E. Gil Boyer (eds.). *Mirrors for Behavior*. Philadelphia: Research for Better Schools, 1970.

12

Survival
and
Growth

AMERICAN HIGH SCHOOLS are similar in some ways but quite different in others. They have similar purposes; they hire people trained in similar ways; they serve identical age cohorts, provide similar courses using identical instructional materials, and offer the same extracurricular activities.

But the differences among schools are as important as the similarities. Not only do schools differ in size (ranging from 5,000 or more students to 50 or less) and location (rural and urban scattered over all regions of the nation), but they vary also in their attitudes toward and their capacities for adapting to change. Some schools are stiff, formal, authoritarian places which have many rules for governing all aspects of schooling. Often such schools seem committed above all else to maintaining past ways of doing things, regardless of social changes that are breaking around them.

Some schools are engulfed in conflict. Conflict may be raging between the faculty and administration, leading to strikes and other forms of confrontation; conflict may exist between students and faculty, leading to student boycotts of school. It may be a battle between groups of students, taking the form of racial strife, or conflict may be underway between the community and the professional staff over who will control and set policy for the school. In each of these cases, the traditional ways of making decisions and old patterns for distributing resources are being challenged by those who want more influence over policy making and a greater share of the school's resources.

Some schools are in a state of innovation and program change. New programs have begun, based on experimentation and trial. These programs involve not only new courses and new extracurricular activities, but they may also include new forms of governance in the school. In an effort to capture the loyalty and interest of those students who have given up on high schools, some communities have even taken the step of creating "alternative" schools that differ significantly from the more typical American high school. In Philadelphia the "Parkway school" operates under a program based on community action that finds students spending many hours outside of the school building and acquiring instruction through participation in various community service and civic action programs in the city. Storefront schools have been established in some large cities to provide schooling for students who "drop in from the street."

We hope that those who read this book and seek to implement its suggestions find positions in schools where there is a high commitment to education on the part of all—students, faculty, administration, and community—where there are interesting instructional experiments under way, where the faculty is encouraged to test new ideas. In schools where conflict is the order of the day, little but survival may be possible. And schools where preserving the traditional ways of behaving is uppermost in everyone's mind can be boring places to work.

While the categories described above are useful for classifying schools, only a small proportion of schools are likely to satisfy any single ideal type. Typical schools, like most complex social institutions, combine many of the features just mentioned. For example, in one school tensions may be rising from conflict between faculty and administration over salary issues; the teaching strategy of the mathematics department may be identical with that of the past, while the social studies department is developing new programs.

The pages that follow suggest ways by which a teacher can contribute to the social system in which he is working that make it a more interesting and rewarding place to teach. Two questions are considered: "What can a new social studies teacher do to ensure a good start that will lead to his own survival and success?" "What can a social studies teacher do that will help his colleagues teach better, thereby making the entire school setting more enjoyable and productive?" Answers to the first question precede the second, because a teacher is unlikely to influence others effectively if he is unable to demonstrate success in his own work and maintain his own position.

Achieving Good Relationships

Two feelings fight for control of a new teacher on his first day in class. One is the excitement and delight he feels for having the opportunity to put into practice four years of training; the second is the sense of being an outsider in an ongoing social system. Together with other newcomers—new students and other new faculty—the beginning teacher must quickly learn the rules, customs, and procedures of his new environment. He must learn who people are, what they do, and how their duties affect him. As in other social situations, some people will make a special effort to help a new teacher adjust to his surroundings; others will expect him to make his own adjustments. Following are some guidelines to help a new teacher make a satisfactory beginning.

THE PRINCIPAL

Unless a teacher has a good working relationship with the building principal, it is unlikely that he will be very happy in his job. It is surprisingly easy to establish a good relationship with the principal. Most principals are eager to foster good relations with their staff, for they are concerned about their own survival and success, and little is accomplished by a staff riddled with dissension and conflict.

A high school's success is often judged according to three criteria: successful academic programs, successful extracurricular programs, and an orderly instructional setting. If a teacher contributes positively toward maintaining these standards, he will be a winner in the principal's eyes, whether or not he is the principal's personal friend.

Contributing to the school's academic success does not mean that all students must become National Merit scholars or attend college. Indeed, a new teacher may find that his lack of seniority has earned him the right to teach those students who are the least prepared for and least interested in becoming successful social studies students. Nevertheless, the principal—and others—expect that the beginning teacher will accomplish the best possible for whatever students he has. If the teacher has clear educational goals and objectives and is pursuing them with skill and tenacity, he is likely to earn respect.

A common error of new teachers is to equate a commitment to teaching with establishing high—even unrealistic—academic standards. New teachers frequently wish to teach their high school courses as they were taught in favorite college courses, regardless of the obvious differences in experience, ability, and interests of their students. Such teachers sometimes grade students very harshly when they fail to meet the unrealistic demands the teachers have placed on them. The teacher may insist that the students have failed, but the principal will know that the major weakness lies in the inability of the teacher to design instruction appropriate to his students.

Unless the teacher is a coach or a sponsor of extracurricular activities, his influence on the school's success in this domain is likely to be only marginal. However, he can stumble into having a negative influence if he is not alert. Eligibility rules make it possible for teachers to have some influence in deciding which students will have the opportunity to participate in extracurricular activities, especially athletics, and which will not. Some teachers take the position that their classes are more important than the football team, for example, and that they will hold to their standards regardless of the consequences. The fact is that the football team may be more important to far more people than the world history class, and the teacher who ignores this fact is flirting with trouble. This does not mean that teachers are under severe pressure to alter grades or to offer special favors to athletes. It does mean that wise teachers will not treat the extracurricular programs of the school in a cavalier way. If a student is encountering difficulty in class and is bordering on failure, the teacher should bring this to the attention of the coaches and others who are depending on the student, and seek their help.

Finally, the teacher who maintains order in his own classroom is more apt to get along well with the principal. Most principals assume that a new teacher will require some help with discipline from time to time, but no administrator respects a teacher who dumps all of his disciplinary problems in the principal's office. When a student is sent to the office, someone has to deal with him. Thus, the principal or vice principal must put aside other tasks to attend to the problem. (Incidentally, it is important to remember that sending a student to the principal's office is not the same as banishing him forever. Ordinarily, after a brief time in the office, he will return to take his place in the class.)

Fortunately, the size and strength of a teacher are not related to good learning environments. The smallest female teacher may be the ablest person in a school in handling students. What the new teacher needs most is a clear sense of purpose, tact, patience, a sense of humor, and an even temperament that prevent his venting a momentary frustration on a hapless student. It is not necessary to run a class like a military camp—indeed, that solution is sure to lead to trouble. It is important to convey to students a set of teacher expectations about the value of education and the need to make the classroom a suitable setting for learning. If such an atmosphere is created, the teacher may never have the occasion to "send a pupil to the office" and will therefore be ahead in winning the respect and loyalty of the principal.

THE SUPPORTING STAFF

A number of people who make contributions to schooling are not students or members of the teaching faculty. Some of these are the principal's secretary, the counselors, the librarian, the social studies supervisor, and the janitor. All of these occupy positions in which they can help or hinder a teacher's performance. It is important to win their support from the beginning.

The *principal's secretary* has the responsibility for making certain that the routine business of the school is conducted efficiently. Financial accounts, enrollment records, and grade reports are but a few of the routine responsibilities that must be carried out in an efficient and businesslike manner. A teacher who is slovenly about record keeping may expect to face the secretary's wrath. The clerical work may seem trivial to the teacher, but it is vital to her performance. Frequently the secretary must make decisions about the use of the telephone, copying equipment, and clerical assistance. The teacher who makes an effort to lighten the secretary's workload may find certain resources available to him that would have been unavailable without her support.

Counselors are asked to play their role differently in various schools. Often they serve as guidance counselors, helping students to plan their course schedules and to choose among a variety of school programs. Occasionally they serve as ombudsmen, acting as advocates for students when situations that students have difficulty meeting arise in school. On other occasions they serve as agents of the administration and faculty in carrying out school policies. It is important for a new teacher to know the counselors well and to learn how they conceive their roles. It is possible for teachers to work closely with them without interfering with the counselor-student relationship. For example, if a teacher wants feedback on what students in general think of his instruction, the counselor may be in the best position to report student opinion. Teachers may alert counselors to students who seem to be having unusual difficulties in class. By working together they may be able to ease the difficulty. A teacher may also ask the counselor to guide certain types of students into a particular course because of the special instruction the teacher is planning for it. In these and other ways the counselor can be an important ally of the instructional team.

It is surprising how little effort some social studies teachers make to cultivate a good relationship with the school *librarian,* who can help the teacher in many ways. For example, the librarian usually has control over the budget for books and periodicals. If a teacher prepares a list of books he and his students need, it is likely that the librarian can order at least part of them. The librarian is usually pleased to help assemble materials needed for students' oral and written reports and to place them on reserve, if he has advance notice that reports will be assigned. If he is asked, the librarian is often willing to provide for new students orientation sessions on the use of the library. If the teacher consults with the librarian about future topics he expects to handle in his classes, the librarian can bring instructional materials to his attention that he might otherwise have overlooked.

Many large school systems employ a *social studies supervisor* who is usually based in the central administration office. His duties typically include planning system-wide social studies programs and helping new teachers. Ordinarily the supervisor does not teach, although he may formerly have been a social studies teacher. Usually he spends much of his time going from one building to another, observing classes, consulting with teachers, and planning curriculum committee meetings with faculty and staff.

In some systems the supervisor is expected to observe all nontenure teachers and rate their performances. It can be a stressful situation when a supervisor visits a teacher's classroom. Usually, however, the supervisor is eager for the teacher to succeed in order that he can file a favorable report. In general, a new teacher should treat the supervisor as an ally, one who has relevant experience that he can depend on and who has access to curriculum resources that he needs. Typically, the supervisor is eager to find teachers who wish to establish good working relationships with him, and is likely to respond positively to indications that the teachers want to do so.

The new teacher should be alert to one possible complication. The role of supervisor sometimes conflicts with the principal's role and with the department chairman's role. For example, the supervisor may be urging a type of instruction that is not favored by the principal or department chairman, or there may be a clash over who has ultimate authority over what should be taught in social studies. Therefore, the wise teacher attempts to identify any apparent conflicts and reacts to such in sensible ways.

The *janitor* is probably more likely to be passed over as an ally than is any other member of the supporting staff. The janitor has an overall responsibility for the appearance of the building. A teacher can either help him and make his load lighter, or frustrate his efforts to keep the classrooms clean and bright. Teachers acquire reputations in part on the basis of how janitors react to the appearance of their classrooms. Moreover, by helping make the janitor's work easier, teachers can expect certain support from the janitor in, for example, rearranging furniture, hanging objects from the walls, installing bookcases, and receiving special equipment.

COLLEAGUES

A new teacher is especially eager to be accepted by other social studies teachers. Following are a few guidelines that can help pave the way to satisfactory relationships with colleagues.

Maintain a businesslike approach to instruction. Social studies teachers begin to make judgments about a new teacher from the first time they meet him. Soon word spreads throughout the school regarding the kind of teacher he is. In general, teachers have little respect for a slovenly instructor. If they find the new teacher wandering the halls, bothering them when they are trying to teach, arriving late to class, holding students beyond the dismissal bell, and being lax about school rules, they will form a bad impression of his ability and intentions. Students will quickly tell others if nothing important is occurring in class and if the beginning teacher seems ill prepared or lacks knowledge of his subject. No matter how friendly he is, if the faculty lacks respect for him as a teacher, he is unlikely to be held in high esteem.

Related to this is the matter of classroom discipline. In much the same way that winning a first fight is a test of a young boy's manhood, the ability to maintain a good learning climate for all students is a basis for teachers' judging other teachers. Those who depend on the principal's office or on other teachers for classroom control win no respect from colleagues.

Recognize the faculty's customs. Certain customs and procedures characterize most faculties. Teachers should be sensitive to these norms and conduct themselves with some consideration for them. Some norms may be disfunctional and should be ignored or changed. Nevertheless, teachers should be alert to the consequences of their actions.

One typical norm in a school is that teachers do not visit other teachers' classes. This probably has developed out of teachers' insecurities, fear that they are teaching poorly, and concern for reprisals. Thus, for a beginning teacher to ask if, during his free period, he may visit a colleague's class may be threatening to the experienced teacher, however noble the purpose. The norm against visiting classes probably has negative consequences for instruction and should be changed. Nevertheless, it can be changed only through subtle and careful strategy. For example, a beginning teacher might invite an experienced teacher to visit his class in order to advise the new teacher on ways in which he can improve his instruction. Later, after the confidence of the more experienced faculty member is won, the two may agree to visit each other's classes periodically as a way of helping both of them. Hopefully, the idea of exchanging visits will spread to other teachers.

In general, faculty members do not borrow ideas and materials from other teachers or recommend to other teachers that they try what another teacher is doing. Teachers do not borrow probably because they do not wish to admit that another teacher has something to teach them. They do not share what they are doing because they do not want "to toot their own horn." Again, this norm is an obstacle in the path of better professional relations and instruction. But the teacher who wishes to overturn and change the norm must do so cautiously.

Another norm is that teachers do not typically discuss their instructional problems. At lunch, over coffee, at faculty meetings, and at other times they discuss *other* problems: conditions for teaching, disciplinary problems, and so on. But seldom, if ever, will a teacher confess that he is having trouble capturing the interest of his students or that they are failing to learn from his instruction. He will admit that students do not always do as well as they should, but the blame is usually placed on others: instructional materials are too difficult, students are not trying, counselors did a poor job in structuring the class. One way to modify this norm is for a teacher to admit to others that he is having difficulty and to seek advice on specific issues. It is not necessary to admit to a general failure to begin a dialogue directed toward improving instruction in the department as a whole.

Find out who the leaders are. In nearly every group setting, some are decision-makers, a few are innovators, others are opinion leaders, and still others are resisters.[1] In some cases roles overlap; in other cases they are quite distinct and are embodied in different individuals. It is necessary to interact with the various roles in different ways.

The department chairman may be an important *decision-maker*. If he has the authority to make department-wide decisions about social studies instruction, it is necessary to work through him. It would be a mistake to approach the principal directly, thereby undercutting the department chairman, unless the chairman proves intractable. In those schools where the department chairman has little or no authority, the principal may make all key decisions relating to instruction. In such cases it is appropriate to provide the chairman with information but not to depend upon him to make and implement policy decisions.

An *innovator* is someone who frequently offers and tests new ideas. Depending on the quality of his ideas as judged by other members of the faculty, he may be seen as an important, talented person or judged an eccentric. A new teacher can profit by seeking close ties with able innovators. Not only can the teacher acquire fresh ideas that he can test in his own classes, but through a trustful relationship he can have opportunities to try out some of his own instructional opinions on a talented person without fear of sanction.

An *opinion leader* is a person whose advice is respected within the group. He may or may not hold a ranking position such as department chairman; he may or may not be particularly innovative. When he lends support to an idea, it is more likely to win the approval of others than when he is neutral or opposes it.[2] The wise teacher works hard to win the trust and confidence of an opinion leader because the ideas of someone liked and trusted are given greater credence than the ideas of those who lack such status.

The *resister* is well known in every group. He is the last to change; he can talk endlessly about the times an idea was tried in the past and failed, and why it is certain to fail again. Resisters are poor allies, if you are seeking to work change. On the other hand, his fears must be listened to and at least partially resolved, if possible, in order to win the support of others.

While these categories do not exhaust the kinds of people you might discover within the formal and informal structures of a social studies department, they should alert you to the need to attend to them and to take advantage of them rather than to be tripped by them.

STUDENTS

Perhaps the greatest emotional need of a new teacher is to be liked and respected by his students. This need sometimes prompts strange behavior on the part of the teacher who reaches desperately for friendly and respectful relation-

institutions that provide a service to clients in the community that supports them. The possibilities for conflict between what the professionals think schools should be and what the clients are willing to pay for is always present, especially in the social studies. Another relevant characteristic of schools is that they are sheltered institutions. Seldom affluent, neither do they starve.[4] While professional associations, universities and colleges, and accreditation associations set standards for schools to meet which bring certain pressures on the schools, the money to operate schools is based primarily on customer satisfaction. Schools that have found a balance between these two sources of pressure are unlikely to undertake willingly programs that may be unsettling. In addition, there is no particular incentive for school employees to threaten the balance by launching reform. Their pay is based on a salary schedule that rewards service and training but has no formal way to compensate them for becoming leaders in their profession.

In general, schools tend to adopt programs that are favored locally, and then find professional justification for them. They avoid programs opposed by the community. This may be especially pernicious in the social studies, as many school administrations engage in prior consorship of programs they believe will lead to local disapproval. A typical illustration is community opposition to instructional materials containing lessons on the theory of evolution.

In general, if a teacher wishes to make a change that does not threaten colleagues, does not cost money, and is likely to attract favorable, little, or no community attention, he will have little opposition. When any of these factors becomes an issue, however, he should expect to face obstacles.

Ordinarily, if the school board wants a new program, it will get its way, whether teachers endorse it, whether there is money for it, and—for a time at least—whether the community overwhelmingly approves it. In general, teachers have opposed electing school board members with strong opinions about instruction because they are unable to resist boards that have decided to take the initiative.

WITH TEACHERS

The school's vulnerability to outside pressures contributes to a conservative bias on the part of teachers.[5] They tend to avoid undertaking programs that are likely to provoke controversy among colleagues, school administrators, and the community. This fear is not without substance. Each year a few teachers come under attack. Although only a very small number of them actually lose their jobs because of opposition to their performances, a large number calculate the pressures operating on them and tailor their instruction in ways to avoid attracting attention. Mediocre, dull, and uninspiring instruction is less likely to cause a teacher trouble than brilliant but exciting and controversial instruction.

Teachers also fear failure. If a teacher has enjoyed some, however limited, success with a particular approach to instruction, he is unlikely to change unless he is certain that the innovation is better than what he has been doing. There is no particular, tangible reward for changing; teachers share identical positions, unless they become administrators, and their pay is not tied to change. On the other hand, failure is likely to bring loss of face with students, colleagues, and administrators.

Obviously, merely asking teachers to change or scolding them for not changing is insufficient motivation. A strategy that may remove or circumvent barriers to innovation is required. The agent of change must be prepared to minimize the risk of failure by setting models of innovative behavior and by providing material and psychological support.

BUILDING ACCEPTANCE OF CHANGE AS A PROCESS

There are some specific things a change agent can do to help establish teacher commitment to change. These techniques are designed to contribute to building a new norm for teachers: every teacher should be involved in program development. In schools where this norm is not accepted, teachers find it difficult to be fully professional. They find themselves limited to carrying out the instructional decisions made by others.

Try to find rewards for those who change. Teachers, like other people, crave recognition and appreciation for their work. They should be encouraged to share their ideas. A change agent must respond to their ideas by demonstrating interest, by offering constructive criticism, and by helping to muster support. If an idea requires funds in order to become operational, the agent can offer to write a proposal for the principal to learn if some funds can be provided. (Nearly every principal has some discretionary money to spend as he likes. A well-written, two-page proposal justifying the need for $100 or $200 can often win approval.)

If the teacher should wish to visit another school to observe a similar program, the change agent can offer to teach his classes in order that he might go. He can suggest to the teacher that he report his idea to the social studies department or to the faculty as a whole; he can propose that the teacher write an article on his idea and submit it for publication, or agree to help publicize the idea in other ways. Finally, the agent can stress "adventure" as an important element of innovation. It is possible to take advantage of the "fear of failure" problem by his suggesting that there is excitement in taking risks and by offering to support the colleague in his risk taking. In these and other ways, the agent of change can build rewards for innovative behavior.

Win the trust and confidence of the faculty. Regardless of the knowledge and skill of the change agent, he will be ineffective if he is disliked or distrusted. There are a number of ways in which an agent can deliberately build trust and confidence.

First of all, the person who stands apart from the rest of the faculty, who is unfriendly, or who is contemptuous of his colleagues will not be accepted as an agent of change. Being "one of the fellows" is very important—at least to a point. Therefore, the change agent should not exaggerate the role of intellectual leader. At the luncheon table the men may want to talk about the football team; the change agent should be ready to participate in these discussions as well as in conversations on the need for better instructional objectives. The teacher who is the change agent should meet faculty members socially outside of school hours in order to build friendly ties; he should volunteer to help a coach or a sponsor with one of the extracurricular activities as a way of building a mutually helpful relationship. Offering to do small favors for colleagues as opportunities arise, without using them to attract publicity, will also contribute to strong, dependable personal relationships.

The teacher who expects to lead others should be a model for the desired behavior. Thus, the change agent must be exemplary: a teacher knowledgeable in his subject, a skilled instructor, and an artist in working with youth. It is not necessary to boast about one's capacity as a teacher. Teachers learn who are the good teachers and respect them both for their skill and their modesty.

Communicate innovation in a positive way. Much can be gained by the way in which an innovation is described. It is probably best not to describe a new program as a "critical examination of the beliefs and values of our society." Rather, the same program can be described as a *"serious study* of the beliefs and values of our society." It is a small point, but the term *critical* may be seen by some as an effort to debunk American beliefs.* Few,

---

*Incidentally, we believe the word *critical* to be a perfectly respectable term to refer to one kind of scholarly activity and have used it at various points in this book. Nevertheless, some laymen understand *critical* to be synonymous with faultfinding and debunking. Thus, a teacher should be careful in the use of such terms with particular audiences in order that his purposes are accurately represented.

if any, will object to a *serious study*. Nor, in explaining a program to colleagues, administrators, or parents is it useful to describe it as an accomplished fact. The innovation should rather be described as an "experiment" aimed at resolving some of the problems present in the current program. Moreover, it is useful to report that the experiment will be "evaluated" before any decision is made regarding its full-scale adoption. Few people oppose experiments, especially those that are evaluated; they become upset when they think that untested programs are being installed without sufficient consultation and supporting evidence.*

Acquire support from significant individuals and groups. Successful innovations require the support of a number of people, including school administrators, department chairmen, students, and parents. The principal plays a key role in supporting an innovation. He may be needed for resources, in the form of teacher time and money; he must also protect the innovation. When a problem occurs in a teacher's class, the concerned parent is more likely to call the principal than the responsible teacher. Thus, principals are often asked to explain and justify their schools' programs to parents and other adults in the community. It is important for the principal to be fully informed about the innovation, especially in regard to the reasons for it and what outcomes are intended.

If treated fairly and properly, the chairman of the social studies department is more likely to be an ally than an obstacle. His reputation is enhanced by a strong, active department. On the other hand, clumsy moves on the part of an inexperienced change agent can poison relations with a department chairman when simple tact might avoid unpleasantness.

Whenever possible, the change agent should work through the department chairman in seeking changes. He should participate fully in department activities, attend department meetings, and undertake tasks assigned by the chairman. While responding to the chairman's agenda for work, however, the agent should offer suggestions from time to time on what he believes the department's priorities should be. If he volunteers to do some of the unpleasant tasks, for example, serving on committees and writing reports, he will soon find himself in positions where he can influence department priorities to a significant degree.

Student advice and support for social studies innovations should be sought

---

*While the purpose of the paragraph has been to indicate how one can build support for innovations, we do not wish this to be construed as a mere "public relations" technique. The fact is that programs *should* be viewed as experimental and fully evaluated prior to a decision for or against adoption.

also. Student opinion is valuable at three stages. First, students may have ideas for innovations or have concerns that make certain changes necessary. Second, student advice and participation are needed for the development of the innovation. Third, while the experimental program is under way and after it has been completed, student evaluation of the experiment is useful in order to decide whether to continue, to drop, or to modify the innovation.

The support of parents and other adults in the community is necessary. It is often useful to involve some members of the community in all stages of the innovation in ways similar to those involving students. At a minimum the adults need information about the new practice. If the innovation is a significant one, it is certain to be discussed in the community in any case. It is important to the change agent that the information available be complete and free of negative bias.

Often community support can be encouraged by linking the innovation to such as national trends in education and well-publicized national projects. In short, community anxiety may be allayed in part if it can be shown that the innovation has been carried out successfully in other communities and has contributed positively to their instructional programs.

If possible, the agent of change should identify certain influential people in the community and win their support. Support by the media and opinion leaders can contribute significantly to a program's acceptance by the community as a whole.

PLAN FOR CHANGE

Everett M. Rogers has described five stages in the adoption of innovations.[6] Knowledge of these stages can serve teachers who wish to devise strategies aimed at affecting change in a social studies department. The five stages are *awareness, interest, evaluation, trial,* and *adoption.*

Even though the effort to reform social studies nationally has been under way for more than a decade, it is surprising how little the "new social studies" has touched some schools. The first step in encouraging change in a department is to make people *aware* of the possibilities that exist. Perhaps, the most useful function that a change-oriented teacher can perform is to become a self-appointed disseminator of new ideas. The more information department members have about new programs, the more likely they are to adopt them.

Appendix A (following this chapter) is an annotated list of organizations that provide publications and services useful to social studies teachers. A change agent should have his name placed on the mailing lists of organizations that distribute newsletters and free materials. Above all, he should become a member of the National Council for the Social Studies and of his state and local social studies councils. Membership in these organizations, attendance at their meetings, and subscriptions to their publications will provide access to up-to-date, relevant information for encouraging innovation.

After the change agent is linked to information networks and can bring new ideas to the attention of his colleagues, he must find some way to *interest* them in one or more ideas. There are several factors to keep in mind. First of all, the teacher is more likely to be interested in an idea if it can be incorporated without altering his entire program. For example, a teacher is more likely to be interested in a game or simulation that will help him teach better a topic he already includes in his course than he is in an entirely new program. However, by starting with small changes and helping the teacher to experience success, the change agent may later succeed in helping him overhaul his entire program.

Second, the teacher is more likely to accept a new idea if it seems compatible with his goals.[7] Third, the more complex the innovation is, the less likely it is to be adopted. Fourth, if the innovation can be observed in practice before being used by the teacher and if it can be tried on a limited basis before being adopted totally, the teacher is more likely to be willing to test the new idea.[8] For example, he may decide to use a game or simulation to treat a topic because it will be more interesting to students than the former technique and because it makes it no longer necessary for him to prepare a lecture or lead a discussion on the topic. Thus, the students like the new approach better than the old one, and it demands less energy from the teacher.

After a teacher has shown an interest in new ideas, new instructional materials, or new pedagogical techniques, he will wish to *evaluate* them. The change agent can help by providing information about their use in other schools. Perhaps he can locate published evidence relating to the success of the ideas. Maybe a teacher in a nearby school is using the new materials or techniques; the change agent can arrange for the teacher to visit the school, to observe them in practice, and to talk with the teacher and students.

Certainly the change agent must provide the instructional materials themselves in order that a teacher can read through them and make judgments about them. Often the agent's job will include ordering examination copies of materials from publishers.

If the teacher evaluates the materials positively, he may be ready to *try* them. Again, the agent of change can play an important role. He can help secure money to purchase a trial set of materials. If special permission is required of local or state educational authorities, he can agree to write letters seeking this permission. He can offer suggestions for ways to evaluate the results of the trial. And he can offer moral, intellectual, and psychological support for the teacher as problems develop. In short, he can take steps to ease the frustration that arises from launching an experiment and to create supports toward ensuring its success.

Finally, if the trial succeeds, the teacher—and perhaps the entire school—will wish to *adopt* the new materials, procedures, or practices. This means that others must become fully informed about the innovation and give support to it. The trial teacher should be one who commands the respect of the entire faculty. Thus, his testimony of success can be used to build support with others.

While these suggestions do not exhaust the range of activities that the teacher who is the change agent can undertake to promote improvements in instruction, they do indicate the need for a carefully planned strategy. The agent need not announce his long-range goals, but they should be clear in his mind. While he is unlikely to be able to take giant strides toward the accomplishment of any single set of goals, he should make certain that the small steps taken are on the right path.

CHANGES THAT COULD BE ACCOMPLISHED IN ONE YEAR

Significant changes in education are not achieved in a day. They require careful planning, diligent effort, and patience. Most important, someone has to do something, to begin. Following are ten ideas that could be implemented during the course of one year. By themselves they will not achieve miracles, but they could be the basis for more profound change. And, while a teacher might be able to accomplish only one or two such ideas each year, he would know that he was acting on the system purposefully, rather than merely responding to it.

1. *Gain approval from the board of education for a statement on teaching with controversial issues.* Many school systems have adopted official statements of policy which support freedom of inquiry in the classroom while providing protection for students. The adoption of such a statement by a school board can provide psychological support to both teachers and administrators. A teacher might write a statement for his school, secure the support of the faculty and administration, and ask the board of education to adopt it. Appendix B (following this chapter) is such a statement.

2. *Secure authority to recruit, interview, and counsel during the employment of new members of the social studies department.* Typically, only the building principal and central office staff recruit and employ new teachers for the school system. Because the success of any instructional program

depends primarily on the quality of the faculty, a teacher might convince his colleagues and later the principal that the social studies department should have veto power over the employment of new faculty. Not only will this give the social studies faculty a stake in who will be hired, but it will also lead to a dialogue within the faculty about criteria for good teaching and about what kinds of people are needed to fulfill program goals.

3. *Establish a social studies council.* A teacher might persuade members of his department and teachers in nearby elementary and secondary schools to establish a social studies council. When ten or more people agree to form such a council, they should write to the Executive Secretary, National Council for the Social Studies (1201 Sixteenth Street, N.W., Washington, D.C. 20036), and ask what procedures are required to secure affiliation with the National Council for the Social Studies and with the relevant state council. A local social studies council will provide a reference group for people who wish to make changes in social studies, and will provide an outlet for professional activity, affording status and rewards.

4. *Create an extracurricular activity in social studies.* All schools have at least a few students with a special interest in social studies. In many there is no formal outlet for this interest. Athletics and social clubs predominate. An organization could be launched for those concerned with politics, history, the stock market, or public issues. The existence of the club will attract the loyalty of students seeking ways to advance their interests in social studies, will give visibility and legitimacy to the social studies program, and may draw the support of some faculty members.

5. *Devise a plan for more effective training and utilization of student teachers.* Most schools take little advantage of the increase in instructional resources made possible through student teachers, and these teachers usually profit less than they should from their internship experience. A systematic training program would provide them with opportunities to gain practice in all aspects of the teacher role, under supervision and without serious risk of failure. At the same time, the wise use of teachers-in-training would increase the number of teachers available for remedial instruction, individualized instruction, and planning.

6. *Develop a social studies resource center.* A teacher might locate an underused room in the school and seek the principal's permission to have it set aside as a resource center for social studies. This would be a room

where teachers can work during their free periods and meet as a group before or after school. The resource center should contain a collection of professional literature that informs teachers about new developments in social studies. It should also have all the instructional materials to be shared by the department. One way to increase the total resources of the department is to convince individual faculty members to pool their requests for such as equipment, filmstrips, and maps in order to avoid duplication and thereby to increase the scope of materials available to all.

7. *Gain control of the in-service day.* Nearly every school system sets aside one or more days each year for in-service training. Often the program is planned by the central administration; frequently the faculty believes it has not been fully satisfying. Rather than complaining about the in-service day, the social studies teachers could devise their own workshop, indicating the goals they wish to accomplish, specifying how the program they are planning will contribute to their instructional efforts, and noting any outside consultants whom they wish to use. After they have developed a good plan, they should be able to convince the administration to give them the responsibility for taking charge of in-service training for the social studies.

8. *Organize a teaching team.* It may be possible for a teacher to find at least one colleague who would like to join a teaching team. The colleague would likely be a social studies teacher, but he could be a business education teacher, an English teacher, or a foreign language teacher, for example. The team would agree to offer a new course, a new method of instruction, or both for at least one class. The principal is likely to support the plan if the team agrees to assume responsibility for the same number of students as under the regular plan, if they use existing school facilities, and if the class schedule does not have to be altered drastically.

   For purposes of promoting system change, the content of the program is less important than having two or more members of the faculty meeting regularly to plan instruction, observing each other teach, and sharing ideas. The idea of team teaching could contribute to new norms regarding sharing which could spread to other members of the faculty.

9. *Seek approval to purchase at least one classroom set of "new social studies" materials.* If the high school is one that has used only traditional kinds of textbooks and if the school board has been unwilling to buy other materials because the textbooks are purchased by the state, a teacher could write a proposal seeking the principal's support for the purchase

of a class set of materials produced by one or more of the special projects. The teacher may wish to argue that the primary purpose of the purchase is to support in-service training for teachers. Having available models of instruction different from those represented by typical textbooks may lead teachers to use their textbooks in new and imaginative ways.

10. *Encourage the practice of visiting innovative teachers in other schools.* Surprising as it may seem, it is easier to convince a teacher to visit a class in another school than to observe one of his own colleagues teaching. Apparently, it is less threatening to both parties for an outsider to do the observing.

   The practice of visits to other schools is not difficult to begin if someone can identify clearly what is worth seeing in another school and how it relates to the sending school's program and if arrangements can be made for the teacher to be away from his class without having his absence cost the school a great deal of money. All teachers in the department might agree to cover the absent teacher's class during their free periods. In return, the visitor must agree to report on his experience on his return.

Summary

Good situations in which to teach do not occur accidentally. They are created by people who are willing to invest the time necessary to secure a proper climate for instruction. The fortunate teacher is one who finds employment in a school in which all parties are committed to the best social studies program possible, have plans for further instructional improvements under way, and are eager to use his talents. When a teacher is in a school not so blessed, he must make an effort to create conditions that will make his instruction more effective and that will help his colleagues to grow as professionals. This is a proper commitment for all social studies teachers.

APPLICATION 12.1: THE INITIATION OF A PLAN FOR CHANGE

Imagine that you have accepted a position as an American history teacher in an urban high school where the social studies program has changed very little during the past fifteen years. The school system provides the textbook for the students but has supplied few additional instructional materials. The texts for each social studies course are selected by the social studies supervisor; all teachers of the same course use identical textbooks.

   Teacher morale is low in your high school. Many of the faculty seem cynical about teaching. They complain bitterly about low salaries, poor pupil attitudes, and an indifferent administration. The department chairman rarely calls a meeting of the social studies teachers. When he does, it is usually to handle typical administrative details such as requests for supplies and film schedules.

Although the social studies teachers rarely discuss what they are doing in their courses, you have learned that one of the other American history teachers has a reputation for being an outstanding teacher. Apparently some parents apply pressure on counselors to have their children assigned to his classes, and you have noticed students excitedly discussing the work they are doing for him. While other members of the department acknowledge that he is an outstanding teacher, a few seem to resent his achievements rather than to admire them. They imply that he has been given special favors by the administration and has only superior students. Others treat him as if he were somehow disloyal to the profession because he devotes far more hours to lesson preparation than do other members of the faculty.

These factors are disturbing to you. On the one hand, you like your job, are challenged by the students, and have established a cordial relationship with most of the members of the social studies department. However, you are annoyed by the lazy, just-get-by attitude that many display toward their work. While it is tempting merely to get by also, as other teachers suggest you should, you know that you will not be proud of the results, will lose the respect of your students, and may even tire of teaching. On the other hand, you are uncertain whether there is anything you can do to improve the situation. It is tempting to devote full attention to your classes and to ignore the other department members. Yet, you wonder whether you should take initial actions that would make the school an even better place for students and faculty. You decide to try.

1. Drawing on ideas presented in earlier chapters of this book—for example, using instructional objectives, teaching concepts, evaluating instruction—decide how one might begin a dialogue among members of the social studies department for the purpose of contributing to professional growth and enhancing instruction. Write a plan containing your strategy for involving one or more members of the department. Refer, if helpful, to the Rogers five-stage adoption sequence (pages 422–424) in the development of your plan.

_____

_____

_____

_____

2. Choose one of the ideas from the list of "ten changes" described on pages 424 to 427. Prepare a memo for other members of the department in which you explain and justify why they should join you in accomplishing one of the ten changes. In a separate paragraph indicate the kinds of arguments you expect them to use in opposition to your proposal and how you would answer them.

PART FOUR / PROFESSIONAL TEACHER

Notes

1. Ronald G. Havelock, *A Guide to Innovation in Education*, Ann Arbor, Mich.: Center for Research on Utilization of Scientific Knowledge, Institute for Social Research, University of Michigan, 1970, pp. 130–133. Havelock describes three important groups: the innovators, the resisters, and the leaders. We have included a fourth group, the decision-makers, those who may be needed to legitimate an innovation.
2. Thomas E. Woods, *The Administration of Educational Innovation*, Eugene, Oreg.: Bureau of Educational Research, School of Education, University of Oregon, 1967, p. 56.
3. Sam D. Sieber, "Organizational Resistances to Innovative Roles in Educational Organizations," New York: Bureau of Applied Social Research, Columbia University, Sept., 1967.
4. Richard O. Carlson, "Barriers to Change in Public Schools," in *Change Processes in the Public Schools*, Richard O. Carlson et al., Eugene, Oreg.: Center for the Advanced Study of Educational Administration, 1965, pp. 6–7.
5. Harmon Ziegler, *The Political Life of American Teachers*, Englewood Cliffs, N.J.: Prentice-Hall, 1967, pp. 121–122.
6. Everett M. Rogers, *Diffusion of Innovations*, New York: Free Press, 1962, pp. 81–86.
7. Everett M. Rogers and F. Floyd Shoemaker, *Communications of Innovations: A Cross-Cultural Approach*, New York: Free Press, 1971, p. 351.
8. Ibid., p. 352.

Suggested Reading

Bryant, Bunyan, Janet C. Huber, and Debra K. Stowe. *Resources for School Change, III: A Manual on Issues and Strategies in Resource Utilization.* Ann Arbor, Mich.: Educational Change Team, School of Education, University of Michigan, 1972. This volume suggests how one may use outside resources to effect changes in schools. A substantial part consists of an annotated list of organizations a change agent might use with suggestions for how these resources can be tapped.

Havelock, Ronald G. *A Guide to Innovation in Education.* Ann Arbor, Mich.: Center for Research on Utilization of Scientific Knowledge, Institute for Social Research, University of Michigan, 1970. This is a comprehensive guide that provides a detailed outline of stages in the educational change process. The various stages are illustrated by specific case studies and are supported by references to research on innovation and change.

Jwaideh, Alice, and Gerald Marker. *Bringing about Change in Social Studies Education*. Boulder, Colo.: ERIC Clearinghouse for Social Studies/Social Science Education, 1973. The authors summarize research on the diffusion of innovation and apply the results to problems of promoting change in the social studies. Chapter 6 contains a detailed description of a "field agent" program directed by Marker. This description could be helpful to a teacher wishing to fulfill the role of change agent in his school.

Kenworthy, Leonard. *Guide to Social Studies Teaching*, 3d ed. Belmont, Calif.: Wadsworth, 1970. This book is a helpful guide for social studies teachers. It provides lists of sources and practical suggestions for ways to manage resources efficiently.

Appendix

Appendix

A. An Annotated List of Organizations Providing Publications and Services for Social Studies Teachers in Secondary Schools

Social studies instruction need not be bound by the textbooks available to students and by the prior training of teachers. A large number and a wide variety of organizations exist to provide publications and services to extend social studies instruction beyond the textbook. Most teachers tap some of the resources available through these organizations; surely no one has used them all.

The material that follows provides a representative sample of the range of resources available to social studies teachers. The list is not exhaustive. Rather, it should be viewed as a starter list, a basic core of useful organizations to be supplemented by the teachers themselves. For the most part the organizations selected not only provide publications and services but are also sources of information about other resources. In this way, when a teacher taps into one of these organizations, he will often be directed to other sources as well.

A common problem in preparing annotated lists of organizations providing publications and services is that the information is quickly out of date. Organizations die or change their characteristics; new organizations appear. In general, we have selected organizations that have existed for many years and seem likely to continue. Nevertheless, even stable organizations change over time; a teacher may learn that the publications and services referred to have been replaced by new efforts.

Finally, we have chosen not to provide complete addresses and annotations of publications and services available from such groups as textbook publishers, governmental organizations, and foreign embassies. It is easy to find their addresses and to send for free materials. In the section below are some notes on how to make good use of the organizations and what you may expect from them.

GENERAL INFORMATION

1. *National Council for the Social Studies* is the primary professional organization for social studies teachers and is an affiliate of the National Education Association. Its members include educators from all levels—elementary, secondary, college, and university.

A "regular membership" (dues $15 per year) pays for a subscription to: *Social Education,* the Council's official journal published monthly except in June, July, August, and September; *The Professional,* a quarterly newsletter;

and the *Yearbook.* In addition to these items, the Council publishes bulletins, curriculum studies, pamphlets, and other materials of practical use to teachers. A recent publication was *Guide to Reading for Social Studies Teachers* (1973). A "comprehensive membership" (dues $25 per year) entitles a member to all publications of the Council without further cost.

Applications for membership should be sent to the Executive Secretary, National Council for the Social Studies, 1201 Sixteenth Street, N.W., Washington, D.C. 20036.

2. *The Educational Resources Information Center Clearinghouse for Social Studies/Social Science Education* is one of several ERIC centers established by the U.S. Office of Education and presently administered by the National Institute of Education. The main purpose of the ERIC Clearinghouse on Social Studies/Social Science Education is to monitor the wide range of publications and nonpublished materials relating to social studies and make the ideas these documents contain available to social studies educators. One task is to acquire speeches, papers, curriculum materials, project reports, curriculum guides, newsletters, bulletins, etc.; select the most significant of these items; prepare annotations of the materials; and submit the annotations for inclusion in *Research in Education,* a monthly publication that contains annotations submitted by all of the various ERIC centers. Another task is to monitor, select, and annotate major articles on social studies that have appeared in journals. The annotations are published in *Current Index to Journals in Education,* along with the contributions of other ERIC centers.

But ERIC/ChESS does more than monitor, evaluate, and annotate the work of others. It also initiates publications. It has published a number of "state-of-the-art" papers that summarize trends in teaching various fields in social studies, useful booklets that provide tips for teaching various aspects of social studies, and "Profiles of Promise," leaflets that describe innovative school-based social studies programs that can be adapted easily by teachers in other schools. Finally, a free newsletter entitled "Keeping Up" provides information about current ERIC/ChESS activities as well as up-to-date information regarding other activities in social studies. "Keeping Up" can be obtained by writing: Director, ERIC/ChESS, 855 Broadway, Boulder, Colorado, 80302.

3. *Social Science Education Consortium* is a nonprofit, educational organization consisting of social scientists and educators who are actively engaged in promoting improvements in social studies instruction. The Consortium's guidelines restrict membership to no more than 150; most new members are recruited through invitation.

The Consortium provides a number of services and publications for both members and nonmembers. It conducts special clinics for teachers. It maintains a large resource library of materials available for the use of teachers and markets bibliographies, occasional papers, and analysis reports on curriculum materials.

The *SSEC Newsletter* is available free upon request. The *Data Book*, an especially valuable resource for teachers, contains detailed analyses of social studies products; it is kept up-to-date with periodic supplements. Write the Consortium, 855 Broadway, Boulder, Colorado 80302, for current costs of the *Data Book*.

4. *University-based social studies centers* plan for instructional changes. While most colleges and universities employ faculty who work with social studies teachers, a few universities have established multipurpose centers or institutes designed to effect changes in social studies instruction nationally. Each institute or center employs professionals who develop and test new instructional materials, who conduct in-service training programs for teachers, and who disseminate information about innovative social studies programs.

Following are the addresses of four centers that have been active in recent years. Write to the director of each center and ask to be placed on the center's mailing list.

   a. Director, Social Studies Development Center, Indiana University, 1129 Atwater, Bloomington, Indiana 47401
   b. Director, Lincoln-Filene Center for Citizenship and World Affairs, Tufts University, Medford, Massachusetts 02155
   c. Director, Social Studies Curriculum Center, Carnegie-Mellon University, Pittsburgh, Pennsylvania 15213
   d. Director, Center for Education in the Social Sciences, University of Colorado, 970 Aurora, Boulder, Colorado 80302

5. *Commercial publishers* produce instructional materials for school use. A large proportion of these publish textbooks; others publish materials such as films, filmstrips, games, maps and globes, and current events newspapers. Their business is to produce items that schools will purchase. While they are interested in improving instruction, they must also be interested in making a profit if they are to survive.

Publishers are eager to provide teachers with catalogues and promotional materials. These are easy to obtain by writing and asking to have your name added to their mailing list. In some cases publishers will provide free samples of products for teacher examination. Obviously, the teacher must be sensible in his requests. It is reasonable for an American government teacher to ask for a free sample of a textbook when considering an adoption for his class; it is not reasonable to ask for free samples of classroom maps, films, and other expensive items that are not likely to be followed with bulk orders.

When possible, cultivate a close relationship with the textbook salesmen who live in your area and sometimes visit your school. They will often lend materials for classroom use or provide samples of some of their products. Most salesmen are eager to develop close contacts with teachers and will accept the teacher's obligation to maintain impartiality among publishers. It is not ethical, on the other hand, to accept unusual gifts from publishers' representatives when you are in a position to influence the decision to make a large textbook adoption for a school system.

6. *Government agencies* produce materials that are useful in social studies classes. Many of these publications are free; the rest are quite inexpensive. The Government Printing Office publishes a bi-weekly newsletter entitled "Selected U.S. Government Publications" containing information about inexpensive government publications. You can receive this newsletter by writing to the Superintendent of Documents, U.S. Government Printing Office, Washington, D.C. 20402, and asking to be added to the mailing list. Often, you can avoid paying anything for the publication listed in the newsletter by writing directly to the agency that initiated the publication and asking for a free copy.

It is impossible here to list all the many agencies and the kinds of materials they provide. However, some examples will suggest the range of materials available. The Department of Labor has produced an instructional unit on the topic of unemployment insurance. The kit of materials can be obtained through local unemployment insurance offices. The Internal Revenue Service provides kits for teachers and students about the federal income tax. The Bureau of Indian Affairs, U.S. Department of the Interior, 1961 Constitution Avenue, N.W., Washington, D.C. 20242, provides materials on the history and current status of American Indians. The U.S. Department of State publishes a variety of materials relating to American foreign policy.

You may find instructional use for the *Congressional Record*, the daily record of the proceedings and debates within the House of Representatives and the Senate. Each Senator and Representative may add a limited number of his constituents to the list of those who receive the *Congressional Record* free of charge. If you are certain you can use it, write to your Representative. It is also possible to receive publications of various Congressional committees, for example, the Senate Foreign Relations Committee. Write to the relevant committee chairman and ask to be added to the committee mailing list.

7. *Foreign embassies and consulates* are maintained in Washington, D.C., by nearly every nation. Many also support consulates in large American cities. Most also have a mission at the United Nations. Each embassy, consulate, or mission has promotional material about the nation it represents. Some provide reprints of speeches by their political leaders and translations of important national documents, as well as the more typical kind of descriptive information about the history and culture of the nation.

Two publications are helpful in locating names and addresses of representatives of other nations residing in the United States. *Permanent Missions to the United Nations* lists the names and titles of all members of U.N. missions as well as the addresses of the missions. This publication is available through the United Nations. The U.S. Government Printing Office publishes *Diplomatic List*. This pamphlet lists the names and addresses of all embassy officials in Washington, D.C. Write the "public affairs" officer of each of the various embassies or missions that interest you and ask for any free material they distribute. You may be surprised by the quantity of publications you will receive.

8. *Commercial sources* can provide general sources of information for teachers. A few of the important ones are the following:

    a. Social Studies School Service (10,000 Culver Boulevard, Department F, Culver City, California 90230) prepares an annual catalog containing a comprehensive list with descriptions of materials for teaching social studies. The catalog provides teachers a single source for the selection and ordering of a large variety of materials. The catalog is free upon request.

    b. CCM Information Corporation (909 Third Avenue, New York, New York 10022) publishes *Directory of Educational Information Resources*. This directory identifies and describes services available from state, local, and national educational information centers. The cost is $4.

    c. Fearon Publishers/Lear Siegler, Inc. (Education Division, 6 Davis Drive, Belmont, California 94002) markets a publication entitled *Selected Free Materials for Classroom Teachers*. The cost is $2. It provides names, addresses, and descriptions of services and materials available to teachers, including a wide variety of free instructional media.

    d. Educators Progress Service, Inc. (Department SE-2, Randolph, Wisconsin 53956) publishes *Educator's Guide to Free Social Studies Ma-*

terials. The price is $9.50 plus $.70 for handling and postage. This multimedia guide to free materials may be ordered on a thirty-day approval.

e. Croft Educational Services, Inc. (100 Garfield Avenue, New London, Connecticut 06320) publishes "Professional Growth for Teachers." Subscription rates are available on request.

f. Scholastic Teacher (50 West 44th Street, New York, New York 10036) publishes a *Guide to Teacher Centers* for $1. The Guide lists dozens of centers and gives information about their services, workshops, and publications.

SPECIAL AREAS

1. *Teaching History*

   a. The American Historical Association (400 A Street, S.E., Washington, D.C. 20003) is the principal scholarly association for historians in the United States. Most members are college and university historians, but elementary and secondary school teachers are welcome. The association's principal publication is *The American Historical Review*. More useful to teachers are AHA pamphlets which are narrative and critical essays on historical topics. Write for a current list of these pamphlets. The association has a Committee on Teaching that includes precollegiate education as one of its interests. A recent project of the association is the AHA History Education Project, directed by Mr. Eugene Asher. Write to Mr. Asher, California State University, 6101 East Seventh Street, Long Beach, California 90840, for up-to-date information about the project's work.

   b. *The History Teacher* is a journal aimed at improving the teaching of history at all levels of schooling. It is published quarterly by the Society for History Education at the Department of History, California State University, Long Beach (6101 E. Seventh Street, Long Beach, California). The annual subscription rate is $6 for individuals.

2. *Teaching Political Science*

   a. The American Political Science Association (1527 New Hampshire Avenue, N.W., Washington, D.C. 20036) is the principal professional association for individuals specializing in research and instruction in political science. The majority of members are college and university political scientists, but elementary and secondary school teachers may join. The principal journals are *The American Political Science Review*, a quarterly journal containing scholarly articles and book reviews, and *PS*, a quarterly publication providing news of the profession. Membership dues vary according to income and status. Write to the association to learn what dues are required.

The association sponsors the Committee on Precollegiate Education, under the chairmanship of Richard Snyder (Mershon Center, 199 West 10th Avenue, Ohio State University, Columbus, Ohio 43201). One of the activities has been the Political Science Education Project which has been focused on building interest among political scientists in pre-collegiate political science instruction. A second activity is the Political Science Course Content Improvement Project for Elementary and Secondary Schools, a curriculum development project supported by the National Science Foundation. This project has two components: an elementary school project based at the Mershon Center (see above) and a high school project based at the Social Studies Development Center, Indiana University, Bloomington, Indiana 47401. For information about these projects, write to "director" of each project at the appropriate addresses.

b. Citizenship Education Clearinghouse (411 N. Elizabeth Avenue, St. Louis, Missouri 63135) is a service agency for high school teachers, stressing the use of the community as a laboratory for civic education. For information, write the director, Mrs. Joseph C. Bastian.

c. Lincoln-Filene Center for Citizenship and Public Affairs (Tufts University, Medford, Massachusetts 02155) sponsors a variety of activities aimed at improving citizenship education. The Center produces instructional materials and provides consultants and workshops. Write the director, John S. Gibson, for information.

d. League of Women Voters (1730 M Street, N.W., Washington, D.C. 20036) produces a wide variety of materials on current political topics that can be used in schools. The League can be particularly helpful to teachers through its 1300 local leagues.

e. *Teaching Political Science*, a journal published by SAGE Publications (P.O. Box 776, Beverly Hills, California 90210), aims to promote an interest in the teaching of political science at all levels of schooling. The journal appears twice each year and costs $8 for an individual subscription.

f. Some teachers may wish to subscribe to a British journal, *Teaching Politics*, published by The Politics Association. Members of the association receive the journal free. Write Assistant Secretary, Politics Association (Birkbeck College, Gresse Street, London WIP IPA, England) for information about membership.

3. *Teaching Law-related Education*

A recent interest in the study of law as it affects the social education of youth has prompted the growth of a number of organizations that provide publications, programs, and services relating to education about law.

   a. Special Committee on Youth Education for Citizenship, American Bar Association (1155 E. 60th Street, Chicago, Illinois 60637) serves as a clearing house for information about law-related educational activities. Write for the free *Directory of Law-related Educational Activities.*

   b. The National Center for Law-focused Education (33 North LaSalle Street, Room 1629, Chicago, Illinois 60602) conducts in-service programs and publishes a journal for teachers entitled, *Law in American Society.* This journal, as well as other occasional papers, may be obtained free of charge by writing the director.

   c. The Constitutional Rights Foundation (609 South Grand Avenue, Suite 1012, Los Angeles, California 90017) conducts workshops and programs to promote instruction on the Bill of Rights. It also publishes a bi-annual newsletter for teachers, for a cost of $2 per year.

   d. Law in a Free Society Project (606 Wilshire Boulevard, Suite 600, Santa Monica, California 90401) in cooperation with the State Bar of California, is designing a comprehensive K-12 curriculum in legal and political education for the California public schools. The Project also provides consultant service to schools on a limited basis.

4. *Teaching World Affairs*

   a. Center for War/Peace Studies (218 East 18th Street, New York, New York 10003) is a research, development, and consulting, non-profit agency concerned about global education. Although the Center's programs span kindergarten through university levels, major attention is directed toward secondary education. Among the Center's publications are *Intercom* and *War/Peace Report.*

   b. Foreign Policy Association (345 East 46th Street, New York, New York 10017) is a non-profit organization interested in promoting understanding of world affairs. *Great Decisions*, packets of material on major world problems and published annually, are used widely by secondary schools. The *Headlines Series* are brief easy-to-read pamphlets on major topics in international affairs. Write to the Foreign Policy Association for information about current prices.

   c. Institute for World Order (11 West 42nd Street, New York, New York 10036) is a nonprofit organization directed at promoting public education on world-order issues. The Institute sponsors a School Program that publishes an informative newsletter and a tip-sheet for teachers called

"Ways and Means of Teaching about World Order." Write Betty Reardon, Director of School Programs, to receive these and other materials.

d. The Center for Teaching International Relations (Graduate School of International Studies, University of Denver, Denver, Colorado 80210) publishes a newsletter and other materials on teaching about international relations. The Center consults with schools, conducts programs, and sponsors workshops. Write the director, Charles Rivera, for up-to-date information.

e. Intercultural Social Studies Project (3 Lebanon Street, Hanover, New Hampshire 03755) develops ideas and materials for teaching international and human dimensions of cultural values in secondary schools. The project is directed by James Oswald and sponsored by the American Universities Field Staff.

f. A number of organizations encourage study of specific world regions. Many of these organizations produce free or inexpensive materials. Among the most prominent are:

(1) The Asia Society, 112 East 64th Street, New York, New York 10021

(2) African-American Institute, 866 United Nations Plaza, New York, New York 10017

(3) Service Center for Teachers of Asian Studies, Ohio State University, 29 West Woodruf Avenue, Columbus, Ohio 43210

(4) Pan American Union, Washington, D.C. 20006

5. *Teaching Geography*

a. The principal professional association for geography teachers is the National Council for Geographic Education (Room 1226, 111 West Washington Street, Chicago, Illinois 60602). The Council publishes a variety of materials focused on improving geography instruction, including the *Journal of Geography*. Membership dues are based upon amount of income.

b. The Association of American Geographers (1710 16th Street, N.W., Washington, D.C. 20009) is the principal scholarly association for professional geographers. While the majority of members are college and university geographers, elementary and secondary school teachers are welcome. The membership dues are $25 annually for which members receive the association journals, *Annals of the Association of American Geographers* and *The Professional Geographer,* both published quarterly. One of the school-related activities of the Association is a curriculum development project that produced *Geography in an Urban Age,* a year-long course of study designed for secondary schools and published by the Macmillan Company.

6. *Teaching Sociology*

    a. The American Sociological Association (1722 "N" Street, N.W., Washington, D.C. 20036) is the principal scholarly association for professional sociologists. A majority of its members are college and university faculty; elementary and secondary teachers may participate as associate members upon payment of $20 annual dues. The principal journal is the *American Sociological Review,* published bi-monthly.

    One school-related activity of the Association was a curriculum development project, entitled "Sociological Resources for the Social Studies." The project produced three major sets of materials: *Inquiries in Sociology,* an introductory, one-semester sociology course; *Episodes in Social Inquiry,* a series of twenty-three paperback units on current topics; and *Readings in Sociology,* seven paperbound books of readings that describe interesting research on important sociological topics. These materials may be purchased from the publisher, Allyn & Bacon.

    b. *Teaching Sociology,* a journal published by SAGE Publications (P.O. Box 776, Beverly Hills, California 90210), seeks to promote dialogue among teachers of sociology at all levels of schooling. The journal appears twice each year; the subscription rate is $8 annually.

7. *Teaching Psychology*

    a. The American Psychological Association (1200 17th Street, N.W., Washington, D.C. 20036) is the principal scholarly and professional association for psychologists. High school teachers may become "affiliates" by paying $7.50 dues annually. One activity of the association is the Clearinghouse on Precollege Psychology and Behavioral Science which publishes a newsletter called *Periodically.* It is published once each month, September through May, and is available free upon request. In 1973 the Association was about to launch a major curriculum development project aimed at improving high school instruction in psychology.

    b. *People Watching,* a journal published by Behavioral Publications, Inc. (2852 Broadway-Morningside Heights, New York, New York 10023) appears twice each year. An annual subscription costs $5. The journal provides information on behavioral science curricula in elementary and secondary schools.

    c. Association for Humanistic Psychology (416 Hoffman Street, San Francisco, California 94114) is the principal association for those interested in humanistic psychology. It publishes a journal, a monthly newsletter, and other publications. Membership dues are $29 annually.

8. *Teaching Economics*

   a. The Joint Council on Economic Education (1212 Avenue of the Americas, New York, New York 10036) was established to promote and support efforts to improve economic education in the schools. The Council sends two publications free of charge to those on its mailing list: *Progress in Economic Education*, a newsletter describing national and state council activities in economic education, and *School Services Curriculum Newsletter*, an occasional paper describing resources for teaching economics. The Council's *Journal of Economic Education* is sent twice annually in return for a $4 subscription.

   b. American Economic Association (1313 21st Avenue, South, Nashville, Tennessee 37212) is the principal scholarly association for professional economists. Annual membership is $21.00 which entitles one to a subscription to the *American Economic Review* and *Journal of Economic Literature*. In addition to being one of the sponsors of the Joint Council for Economic Education, it has encouraged the teaching of economics through some of its own committees and publications.

   c. A large number of business organizations, trade associations, and labor unions provide free or inexpensive material that could be used for school instruction. Some examples of these groups are the following:

      (1) New York Stock Exchange (School and College Relations, 11 Wall Street, New York, New York 10005) provides free materials on stock market operations and investments.

      (2) National Consumer Finance Association (Educational Services Division, 1000 16th Street, N.W., Washington, D.C. 20036) provides free materials on consumer finance, including bibliographies, wall charts, and a teacher's kit on consumer finance.

      (3) National Industrial Conference Board (845 Third Avenue, New York, New York 10022) publishes semi-monthly "Road Maps of Industry," a series of charts and tables on current economic topics.

      (4) Changing Times Education Service (1729 H Street, N.W., Washington, D.C. 20006) publishes resource kits for teaching budgeting, spending, borrowing, etc. Special school rates are available for the journal *Changing Times*.

      (5) American Federation of Labor and Congress of Industrial Organizations (Pamphlet Division, 815 Sixteenth Street, N.W., Washington, D.C. 20036) provides free materials relating to social and economic issues. Teachers may also obtain free subscriptions to the *American Federationist*.

9. *Teaching Anthropology*

The major professional organization for anthropologists is the American Anthropological Association (1703 New Hampshire Avenue, N.W., Washington, D.C. 20009). Annual dues are $21 for which one receives the journal, *The American Anthropologist*. The association sponsored the Anthropology Curriculum Study Project which produced *Patterns in Human History* for secondary students, available for purchase from the publisher, the Macmillan Company.

The Council on Anthropology and Education, an association of anthropologists and educational researchers concerned with the application of anthropology to research and development in education was organized in 1968. The purpose of the Council is to advance the coordination of anthropological data, theories, methods and insights with educational problems, practices, and institutions. The CAE membership fee of $5.50 yearly includes subscription to the *CAE Newsletter*.

10. *Teaching Environmental Education*

Public interest in issues such as population growth, pollution control, energy crisis, and environmental decay has prompted an interest in instruction concerning the relationship between man and his physical environment. While no single agency exists to represent all of the interests embraced by this concern, a great many organizations provide free or inexpensive materials that relate to one or more aspects of the topic. Following is a small sample of these organizations.

   a. The Population Council (245 Park Avenue, New York 10019) publishes pamphlets, articles, and books on population issues. Many of these items are useful for reference purposes and as background reading for teachers. The Assistant Director for the Demographic Division is particularly interested in promoting school programs on population education. Write the Assistant Director for details on current activities.

   b. Population Reference Bureau (1755 Massachusetts Avenue, N.W., Washington, D.C. 20036) provides reprints, essays, annual data sheets, and an occasional newsletter—all free upon request. The Bureau takes a scholarly, non-crisis oriented approach to population issues.

   c. National Wildlife Federation (1412 16th Street, N.W., Washington, D.C. 20036) publishes a bi-weekly newsletter "Conservation News and Conservation Report," free upon request. The newsletter treats a wide range of topics dealing with environmental issues and proposed legislation affecting these issues.

   d. Environmental Action, Inc. (Room 731, 1346 Connecticut Avenue, Washington, D.C. 20036) publishes "Environmental Action," a bi-weekly publication on environmental subjects. Subscription cost is $7.50 per year.

e. Earth Science Education Program (Box 1559, Boulder, Colorado 80302) is a curriculum development project established to produce instructional materials for use in secondary schools. It publishes a newsletter, called "Sensorsheet," that is free upon request.

f. ERIC Clearinghouse for Science, Mathematics, and Environmental Education (1460 West Lane Avenue, Columbus, Ohio 43210) publishes "Environmental Education Newsletter" available free of charge. SMEAC is also a source of information regarding a variety of speeches, articles, and reports on environmental topics.

11. *Teaching Multi-ethnic Studies*

Many organizations have been established to promote understanding of various ethnic and racial groups in the United States and to foster better understanding among all people. A majority of these organizations provide free and inexpensive publications. A "starter set" of organizations you might wish to contact are the following:

a. *American Jewish Committee,* Institute for Human Relations, 165 East 56th Street, New York, New York 10022.

b. *Anti-Defamation League of B'nai B'rith,* 315 Lexington Avenue, New York 10016.

c. *Association on American Indian Affairs,* 432 Park Avenue, New York, New York 10016.

d. *Foundation for Change, Inc.,* 1619 Broadway, New York, New York 11119.

e. *UW System Ethnic and Minority Studies Center,* University of Wisconsin, Stevens Point, Wisconsin 54481.

f. *Afro-American Studies Resource Center,* Circle Associates, 126 Warren Street, Roxbury, Massachusetts 02119.

12. *Teaching with Simulations and Games*

Social studies teachers have found simulations and games to be interesting and powerful aids to social studies instruction. The rapid growth in the number and availability of simulations and games has led to efforts to review and monitor their development and use. Teachers who are interested in simulations and games may wish to subscribe to *Simulation/Gaming/News* (Box 3030, University Station, Moscow, Idaho 83843). This is an informative newsletter/ journal about games and simulations. It is published every other month throughout the school year and costs $4 annually for five issues.

B. Policy Statement on Controversial Issues

SCHOOL DISTRICT NO. _____, POLICY ON TEACHING
ABOUT CONTROVERSIAL ISSUES

1. Consideration of issues on which there is public disagreement is a primary responsibility of education for effective citizenship. Therefore, the treatment of controversial subjects deserves a central place in our educational process, since the ability to cope with differences of opinion is fundamental to living effectively in a free society.

2. A significant part of typical classroom instruction involves the examination of controversial issues. All classroom teachers are expected to respond appropriately to these issues when they arise spontaneously in class and to plan consciously for their inclusion in the curriculum when appropriate.

3. In all instruction teachers should nurture the spirit of inquiry and develop in students skills of critical thinking. Teachers must ensure the right of students to express unpopular views without fear of sanction.

4. All teachers are free to explore factually, thoroughly, and objectively controversial issues without fear of penalties by the administration and members of the Board of Education. At the same time teachers do not have license to indoctrinate their students to one point of view.

5. Administrators, together with classroom teachers, will be responsible for making systematic evaluations and for reporting to the Board of Education regarding progress in preparing students to cope effectively with controversial issues.

Adopted at the regular meeting of the Board of Education on _____, 197_, with the recommendation that the Superintendent of Schools distribute this policy statement among faculty members and interested citizens.

President, School Board

Index

and mastery learning, 336
from students, 385–388
from testing, 327–329
Fenton, Edwin, 72–81
Flanders' Interaction Analysis Categories (FIAC), 396–400, 404–405
formative evaluation, 326–327

Gagné, Robert M., 113, 120
Gallup organization, 203–205
games, educational, 303–307
general education program, 53–54
Girl Watchers experiment, 220–229
Glaser, Edward G., 362
goals, educational, 75–83
    categories of, 77–79
    sources of, 79–82
government agencies, and goals, 80
grades and grading. *See also* evaluation
    as control device, 40
    criterion-referenced, 331, 335–340
    of essay questions, 347–349
    norm-referenced, 330–334
    philosophies of, 330–340
    scores on standardized tests, 361–362
    and teacher bias, 361
guidance counselors, 411–412
Guided Self-analysis, 399
Guskin, Alan, 141
Guskin, Samuel, 141

Hanvey, Robert, 72, 131
Hastings, J. Thomas, 356
High School Geography Project, 307
high schools
    course offerings in, 20–28
    criteria of success, 410
    differences among, 408
    effecting changes in, 417–427
    new teacher's survival in, 409–417
    schedules for, 28, 34–36
    teacher's relationships within, 409–417
    as undemocratic, 42

higher-level learning, 125
Holmes, Sherlock, 59–60
Hullfish, H. Gordon, 59, 210
Hunt, Maurice P., 18
hypotheses, 196–255
    data collection for testing of, 202–207
    and deduction vs. induction, 211–212
    formulation of, 197–200, 232–252
    and social science inquiry method, 210–213, 246
    teaching the skills of, 214–255
    testing of, 200–255

Images of People (SRSS unit), 220–224
improvement, of instruction, 55–56
inculcation, core values, 261–262
Indiana. *See also* Bloomington, Indiana
    social studies courses in, 27–28
    state's influence on instruction, 26–28
indirect teaching, 378–380, 398
induction, in social sciences, 211–212
influences on teachers, 29–44
    college professors, 29–32
    institutional demands, 32–38
    student culture, 38–44
information derived from testing, 327–329
inquiry
    method of teaching, 64–68, 384
    as term, 72–73
in-service training, 426, 427
institutional demands, 32–38
instruction
    assessment of, 373–407
    competency-based, 111–155
    definition of, 113
    described, 111–114
    devices for, 62
    modes of, 125–149
    objectives of, 75–76, 83–105
    strategy for, 295–319
instructional objectives, 75–76, 83–105
    advantages of, 90–91
    arguments against, 94–96
    characteristics of, 86–88
    classification of, 97–105

relevance
    in education, 122–125
    and value analysis, 280–281
remediation, 116
Remy, Richard C., 49–50
research, on teaching, 374–384
resource center, for social studies, 425–426
Rickover, Hyman, 81
Roanoke, colonists of, 233–245
Rogers, Everett M., 422, 428
role
    reversal, 283–285
    and status, lesson on, 182–188
rule-example instruction, 176–177
rural vs. urban characteristics, 251–252

sample surveys, 204–205, 213, 216–220. *See also* polls
Sanders, Norris M., 356
Schaar, John, 167
schedules
    for social studies classes, 28
    teachers' daily, 34–36
school boards
    and change, 418
    and controversial issues, 424
schools
    change in, 417–427
    course offerings in, 20–28
    differences among, 408
    influence on educational goals, 81
    relationships within, 409–417
    as undemocratic, 42
scientific culture, 56–58
scores, test, 361–362
secondary schools. *See* high schools
secretary, principal's, 411
self-assessment, by teacher, 389–399
sequencing lessons, 295. *See also* instructional
    strategy
services to teachers, organizations providing, 435
Shaver, James P., 18
Sherif, Muzafer, 209
Simon, Anita, 399

"Site Map Lesson, The," 129–139
Smith, Lee, 13–17
Smith, Philip G., 59, 210
social action, and value analysis, 262–263
social education, 125
socialization, 54–55
social sciences. *See also* "new" social studies; teaching social studies
    conceptual frameworks of, 173–175
    method of inquiry, 210–213, 246
    social studies as distinct from, 18–20
social studies
    content of, 3–26
    courses, 20–26
    council, establishment of a, 425
    described, 3–49
    as distinct from social sciences, 18–20
    employment of new teachers for, 424–425
    extracurricular activity in, 425
    image of, 3–26
    plan for changes in, 424–427
    reform movement in, 44–46, 59, 175, 422–427
    resource center, 425–426
    specialists' opinions on, 17–20
    student opinion on, 4–13
    teacher opinion on, 13–17
societal relationships, and values, 260–261
society and educational goals, 79–80
Sociological Resources for the Social Studies, 220, 307
specialists, opinions of, on social studies, 17–20
SRSS. *See Sociological Resources for the Social Studies*
staff, supporting, 411–413
standardized tests. *See* tests
state, influences on courses, 20–28
statements
    on controversial issues, 424, 448
    that structure learning, 381–383, 395
    value, as compared to factual, 259
status
    and role, lesson on, 182–188
    of teacher, 33–34
stimulation, of thought, 271–273

strategy for teaching. *See* instructional strategy

Street Corner Society (White), 206

structure, and concept learning, 173–175

structuring statements, 381–382, 395

students

and change, 421–422

concerns and value judgements, 257n–258n

discipline of, 37–43

evaluation of teacher by, 385–388

ideas of, for use in teaching, 378–380, 396–399

instructional objectives for, 91

influence on teachers, 38–44

new teacher's relationship with, 415–416

opinions of courses by, 4–13

participation in class discussion, 384

research on learning by, 374–384

value analysis as challenge to, 283–285

student teachers, 425

Studying Societies (Anthropology Curriculum Study Project), 182–183, 225

From Subject to Citizen (Education Development Center), 233–238

subject offerings, national, 21–23

summative evaluation, 326–327

supervisors, 412–413

supporting staff, 411–413

Survey Research Center, 203

surveys, sample, 204–205, 213, 216–220. *See also* polls

synthesis, and cognitive domain, 101

Taba, Hilda, 126

task similarity, and variety, 214

taxonomy

of affective domain, 103–104

of cognitive domain, 99

teachers

approaches to instruction by, 111–113

assessment of, 373–407

and authority vs. inquiry method, 384

beginning, 408–432

"best" way to teach, 58–62

as change agents, 417–427

characteristics to strive for, 374–384

and colleagues, 388–389, 413–415

college professors' influence on, 29–32

educational goals for, 81–82

effectiveness of, 374–384

employment of new, 424–425

evaluation of, 373–407

as evaluators of colleagues' teaching, 388–389

influences on, 26, 29–44

in-service day for, 426–427

institutional demands on, 32–38

opinions on social science instruction, 13–17

organizations aiding, list of, 433

and parents, 416–417

plan for effecting changes by, 422–427

and principal, 409–411

relationships within school, 409–411

research on effectiveness of, 374–383

review of tests by other teacher, 348, 354–355

schedules for, 34–36

self-assessment by, 389–399

status of, 33–34

student evaluation of, 385–388

student influence on, 38–44, 415–416

and student learning, 374–384

and supporting staff, 411–413

survival plan for, 409–417

and team teaching, 426

training of, 29–32, 45–46, 425–427

visiting innovators in other schools, 427

Teachers' Guide for American Political Behavior (Mehlinger and Patrick), 143, 177

teaching characteristics, 374–384

authority method, 384

businesslike behavior, 378, 395

clarity, 375–377, 392–393

criticism, 381, 396–399

enthusiasm, 377–378, 394

indirectness, 378–380, 398

inquiry method, 384

praise, 383–384

probing, 382–383, 395–396

structuring statements, 381–382, 395
and student learning, 374–383
student participation in discussion, 384
unrelated to student learning, 383–384
use of student ideas, 378–380, 396–399
variety, 377, 393–394
teaching model. *See* model
Teaching Plan, Studying Societies (Anthropology
Curriculum Study Project), 182–183
teaching social studies, 52–74. *See also* social studies
assumptions on, 52–58
criteria for, 58–62
method of, 64–68
mode of, 63
strategy for, 63–64
technique for, 62–63
team teaching, 426
techniques, instructional
discussions, 301–303
games, 303–307
innovative materials, 426–427
lectures, 300–301
textbooks, 307–310
variety of, 62–63
teen-age culture, 38. *See also* students
terminology, instructional, 62–68
tests, 343–369. *See also* evaluation
construction decisions, 359–361
and convergent vs. divergent thinking, 343–345
of critical thinking, 362–365
diagnostic, 361–367
essay, 345–349
function of, 323–330
and instructional objectives, 90–91
objective, 349–359
reading, 365–366
scores on, 361–362
standardized, 361–367
time involved in invention and grading, 360
types of, 343–345
writing questions for, 345–359
textbooks, innovative, 307–310, 426–427
thinking

convergent vs. divergent, 343–345, 393
critical, 362–365
stimulation of, 271–273
by students, 59–60
Thomas, Elizabeth Marshall, 230
Thorndike, Lynn, 356
thought stimulation, 271–273
training, teachers', 29–32, 45–46, 425–427
transfer of learning, teaching for, 214–216
transparencies, 182–185

University School, Bloomington, Indiana, 28
urban vs. rural characteristics, 251–252

value analysis, 256–294
and affective domain, 104
classroom problems in teaching, 283–290
discussion control, 283–290
and emotional development, 262
goals or elements of, 269–282
and inculcation of core values, 261–262
and instructional strategy, 298, 314–315
objections to, 266–269
and social action, 262–263
in social studies classes, 261–269
values
core, 261–262
compared with facts, 259
compared with hypotheses, 197
described, 258–261
importance of, 260–261
procedural, 103
relationships as influenced by, 260–261
substantive, 103
variety in teaching
analyzed by classroom recordings, 393–394
on cognitive level, 377
use of differing techniques, described, 62–63
use of differing techniques, examples of, 299–310
verbal interaction, coding of, 396–399
video-tape equipment, 390
visits to other schools, 427
voting behavior, 142–148, 160–162, 204, 216–220

Credits

PAGES 184–185

Reproduced by permission from the American Anthropological Association. Adapted from STUDYING SOCIETIES AND TEACHING PLAN STUDYING SOCIETIES (ACSP), 1971

PAGE 218

From TEACHER'S GUIDE FOR AMERICAN POLITICAL BEHAVIOR by Howard Mehlinger and John H. Patrick, © Copyright 1972 by Indiana University. Published by Ginn and Company. Used with permission.

PAGES 223, 226

Adapted from IMAGES OF PEOPLE and the Instructor's Guide for IMAGES OF PEOPLE by Sociological Resources for the Social Studies, an agency of the American Sociological Association (Boston: Allyn and Bacon, Inc., 1969). Reprinted by permission. Upper center photograph by Debbe McMorris.

PAGES 240–245

By permission of the Folger Shakespeare Library, Washington, D.C.